AF775317

IS IT OURS?

Furthermore:
a program of the J. M. Kaplan Fund

THE PUBLISHER AND THE UNIVERSITY OF CALIFORNIA PRESS FOUNDATION GRATEFULLY ACKNOWLEDGE THE GENEROUS SUPPORT OF FURTHERMORE, A PROGRAM OF THE J. M. KAPLAN FUND, IN MAKING THIS BOOK POSSIBLE.

IS IT OURS?

Art, Copyright, and Public Interest

Martha Buskirk

UNIVERSITY OF CALIFORNIA PRESS

THE PUBLISHER AND THE UNIVERSITY OF CALIFORNIA PRESS FOUNDATION GRATEFULLY ACKNOWLEDGE THE GENEROUS SUPPORT OF THE BEN AND A. JESS SHENSON ENDOWMENT FUND IN VISUAL AND PERFORMING ARTS, ESTABLISHED BY A MAJOR GIFT FROM FRED M. LEVIN AND NANCY LIVINGSTON, THE SHENSON FOUNDATION.

University of California Press
Oakland, California

© 2021 by Martha Buskirk

Cataloging-in-Publication Data is on file at the Library of Congress.

ISBN 978-0-520-34459-4 (cloth : alk. paper)

Printed in Malaysia

29 28 27 26 25 24 23 22 21 20
10 9 8 7 6 5 4 3 2 1

CONTENTS

ACKNOWLEDGMENTS

FEW THINGS ARE MORE VALUABLE to a writing project than time, and I was lucky enough to be accorded that luxury by fellowships from the Guggenheim Foundation and the Clark Art Institute. Therefore my first thanks go to those programs and to the people whose advice and assistance helped me down that path: Peter Chametzky, Caroline Jones, Virginia Rutledge, and Jeffrey Weiss. I am also grateful for a sabbatical leave from Montserrat College of Art, supported by Brian Pellinen, Stephen Immerman, and Kurt Steinberg.

When I initially began to focus on these issues many years ago, Rosalind Krauss offered a model for considering the forces surrounding art's production and reception, and she prompted my first major foray into the topic of fair use. Since then I have had the pleasure of deliberating the strange intricacies of intellectual property, as well as intersections of art and law, with many who have been active in these areas. Virginia Rutledge has been a regular interlocutor, and I have enjoyed lively discussions with Amy Adler, Mario Biagioli, Boatema Boateng, Joy Garnett, Peter Karol, Joan Kee, Jill Magid, Daniel McClean, Gala Porras-Kim, Sergio Muñoz Sarmiento, Winnie Wong, and Carey Young (though

I should be quick to say that any errors or misrepresentations are solely my own responsibility).

A sense of community and access to research resources are each essential in their own right, and both were combined at the Clark Art Institute as well as during a number of years when I was able to return to the Radcliffe Institute for Advanced Study as a summer fellow. Members of the vital and engaged community at the Clark included Mieke Bal, Rachel Burke, Emmelyn Butterfield-Rosen, Lauren Cannady, Laure de Margerie, Ashton Fancy, Deborah Fehr, Marc Gotlieb, Brynn Hatton, Christopher Heuer, Michael Ann Holly, Gillian McKenzie, Olivier Meslay, Marden Nichols, Stephanie Porras, Susan Roeper, Avinoam Shalem, Robert Slifkin, and Ernst van Alphen. From summers at Radcliffe, I would like to express my particular appreciation to Sharon Bromberg-Lim, Lewis Hyde, Priyamvada Natarajan, Judith Vichniac, and Patricia Williams. The opportunity to teach a graduate seminar on art/law at MIT also helped bring some of these matters into focus, so my thanks to Nisa Ari, Jordan Karney Chaim, Ravi Charan, Jackson Davidow, Jesse Feiman, Grace Kim, and Floor van de Velde for their enthusiastic participation.

I am indebted to all the artists who have been kind enough to discuss aspects of their practice with me and to provide images of their work—with particular thanks to Nora Al-Badri, Greg Allen, Tania Bruguera, Lauren Clay, Eric Doeringer, Maria Eichhorn, Hans Haacke, Robert J. Lang, Louise Lawler, Annette Lemieux, Ibrahim Mahama, Allan McCollum, Jan Nikolai Nelles, Richard Serra, Arne Svenson, Liselot van der Heijden, and Angela Washko. My gratitude as well to the galleries, museums, artists' assistants, and others who helped me in my image quest. My thinking has greatly benefitted from numerous lecture, symposium, and essay invitations over the years, which have allowed me to hone these ideas. In the end, I was very pleased to find a home for the book at University of California Press, where Nadine Little, Archna Patel, Catherine Osborne, Steve Jenkins, Jessica Moll, Teresa Iafolla, and Peter Perez have guided its passage through various steps in the publication process.

It would have been difficult to stay the course without many friends and colleagues who have provided dialogue, assistance, and inspiration of all kinds during the years of research and writing, including Anthony Allen, Gordon Arnold, Caroline Bagenal, Peter Ballantine, Tiffany Bell, Catherine Belloy, Ethan Berry, Fred Bohrer, Charles Boyer, Cheri Coe, Lynne Cooke, Paula Cooper, Dieter Daniels, Eric de Bruyn, Dina Deitsch, Erin Dionne, Ron DiRito, Arindam Dutta, Susan Edwards, Francesca Esmay, Rachel Esner, Jane Farver, Susan Felleman, Briony Fer, Ann Goldstein, Susan Hapgood, Nate Harrison, Henriette Huldisch, IJsbrand Hummelen, Colleen Kiely, Elka Krajewska, Katja Kwastek, Cornelia Lauf, Pip Laurenson, Tom Learner, Michael Lobel, Joanne Lukitsh, Sven Lütticken, Carol Mancusi-Ungaro, Ted Mann, Mary Bucci McCoy, Trina McKeever, Jen Mergel, James Meyer, Terry and Sam Moriber, Liz Munsell, Mignon Nixon, Kathy O'Dell, Marcia Pointon, Kristine Roan, Judith Rodenbeck, Angelica

Rudenstine, Matt Saunders, Christian Scheidemann, Jill Sterrett, Marianne Stockebrand, Lena Stringari, Gloria Sutton, Laura Tonelli, Rebecca Uchill, Beatrice von Bismarck, and Greg Williams.

I am equally grateful for family support from Fred Buskirk, Janet Buskirk, Jim Koudelka, Jasper Buskirk, and Katherine Hartford. Most of all, I could not have completed the book without Robert Moeller's unflagging encouragement and feedback at every stage of this multi-year endeavor.

INTRODUCTION

The Convenient Fiction of Authorship

THE VITRINE AT THE END of the gallery presented a dramatically lit but otherwise conventional looking diamond ring (figure 1). Before reaching the 2.02-carat gem, however, visitors encountered a series of documents revealing its striking origins, including a certificate from the laboratory that created the stone from carbon extracted from the ashes of architect Luis Barragán, a contract between Barragán family members and artist Jill Magid, and a video of the 2015 exhumation that allowed Magid access to Barragán's cremated remains (figure 2).

The 2016 exhibition, entitled *The Proposal*, at the Kunst Halle Sankt Gallen in Switzerland is only one aspect of Magid's fascination with the intricate rights and restrictions surrounding Barragán's life and work, which have arguably stood in the way of full recognition of his austere yet sumptuous version of modernism, realized in residential and institutional buildings across Mexico. Following Barragán's death in 1988, his personal archives and library were left in the care of Ignacio Díaz Morales, who established a foundation that also oversees the Casa Luis Barragán in

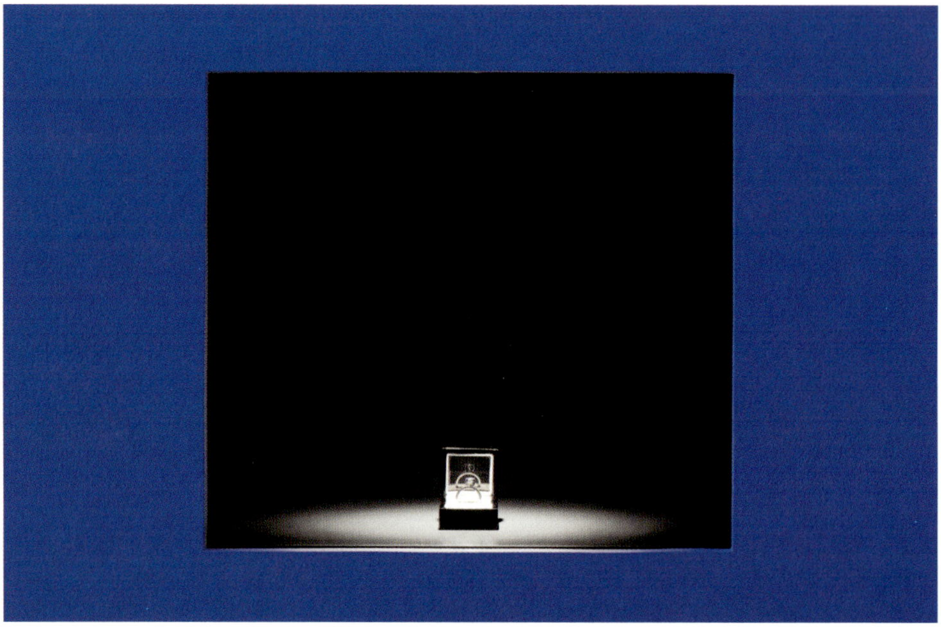

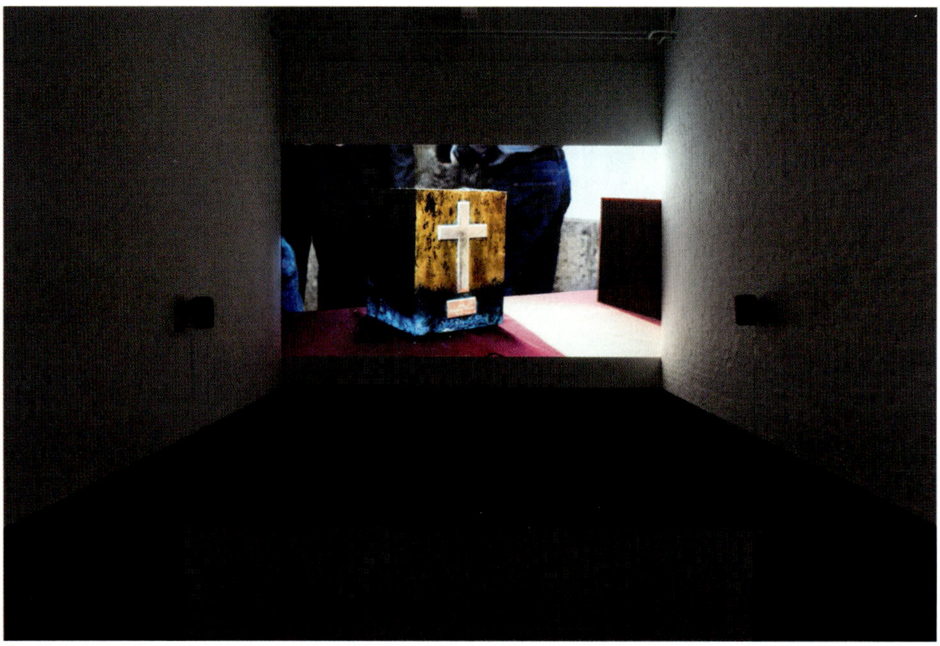

FIGURE 1 ▲

Jill Magid, *The Proposal* (detail, ring), 2016. 2.02 carat, blue, uncut, diamond, ring box, documents. Photo: Stefan Jaeggi, Kunst Halle Sankt Gallen. Courtesy the artist and LABOR, Mexico City.

FIGURE 2 ▼

Jill Magid, *The Exhumation,* 2016. HD Video, 6:07 minutes. Photo: Stefan Jaeggi, Kunst Halle Sankt Gallen. Courtesy the artist and LABOR, Mexico City.

Mexico City. His professional archive, however, was willed to his partner and subsequently acquired (from his partner's widow) in 1994 by Rolf Fehlbaum, head of the Vitra furniture company in Switzerland. In 1996, Fehlbaum established an alternate Barragan Foundation (spelled, as many have pointed out, without an accent on the architect's name), housed in Vitra headquarters, which now holds both the documents and associated copyrights. The longtime rumor was that he purchased the archive as an engagement present for his wife, Federica Zanco, an Italian architectural historian who has announced a planned catalogue raisonné based on the material while sharply limiting access by others.

Characterizing this history as "surreal," art-law expert Daniel McClean has stressed the paradox that Barragán's private legacy has remained accessible even as the professional archive has been sequestered.[1] Magid's response to this arbitrary division has been playfully provocative. Weaving a narrative of her intrusion into an imagined romantic relationship between Zanco and Barragán, she used *The Proposal* and a 2013 exhibition entitled *Woman with Sombrero* to present objects and images that push up against the edges of the Swiss foundation's copyright claims. The increasingly involved series of gestures culminated in her offer to give Zanco the diamond ring made from Barragán's ashes in exchange for the return of the professional archive to Mexico.

There is a double issue at play here. Blocked access to archival research is no small matter, but the intellectual property (IP) is potentially more significant, since the Swiss foundation claims ownership of "complete rights to the name and oeuvre of Luis Barragán."[2] Control is further ensured by their acquisition of the photographs and associated rights for the work of Armando Salas Portugal, Barragán's official photographer. But their copyright claim is actually far more encompassing—extending to all of Barragán's architecture, including his iconic house in Mexico City, which has been open to the public as a museum since 1994 and designated a UNESCO World Heritage Site since 2004. The Mexican foundation, headquartered at the Casa Barragán, has found the rights asserted by the Swiss oppressive, complaining to the *New York Times,* "From time to time, they claim that we cannot publish books, photographs or have films made in our own house—or for that matter in any other of Barragán [sic] works, without 'proper' permission from their lawyers, and, of course, a fee."[3]

This example provides a fascinating indication of some of the issues at stake when creative expressions become property. At what point does protecting an artistic vision or legacy shift to denying access, controlling interpretation, or even censorship? And what role does the back-and-forth between authorship and ownership play in this dynamic? It is not difficult to support the proposition that creators should profit from the popularity of their work and have the ability to protect its integrity. Yet it is equally imperative to make sure that these protections are consistent with broader public interest. Particularly for phenomena that achieve popular success or are distinguished as culturally significant, the rights of audience members are equally essential, including situations where production and reception become increasingly intertwined.

Given the ever-expanding scope of intellectual property in general, and copyright specifically, it is impossible to explore questions of artistic authorship without considering how it is defined in legal terms, its potential monetization, and the constant interplay between individual expressions and corporate interests.

Despite widespread recognition of copyright's broad reach, however, it is striking how little understanding there is of exactly what it does and does not cover. Some artists have made legal concerns the express subject of their work. But many more have wound up demonstrating their extent unintentionally, when hit with lawsuits for acts of quotation or appropriation. Nor should copyright constraints, and particularly their relentless expansion, be accepted as inevitable. Issues that were already pressing in the context of analog reproduction have become far more urgent in relation to digital circulation—and not just for artists, since anyone with a computer or smartphone is likely to be part of a cycle of incessant recirculation.

The discussions that follow address the intersections of art and law that emanate from articulating creative expressions as property. Copyright is an essential part of this inquiry, but not the only thread. Within the art world, there are less evidently codified conventions that also protect and constrain artistic authorship. Lawsuits prompted by perceived violations of norms or conventions often turn on other areas of law, including contracts and fraud. In the process, such conflicts help reveal assumptions about artistic authorship that only become fully evident when brought to the surface by divergent expectations. The issues extend beyond the art world as well. Just as many contemporary artists use their work to point outward to wider social and economic concerns, this analysis does the same. Challenges associated with ownership over creativity open onto an array of questions about how individuals interact with their surroundings, ranging from remix cultures to right-to-repair advocacy and privacy expectations. The fulcrum for this book is the intersection of art and copyright, but from that starting point I address both specialized conventions within the art world and the profound implications for everyone when daily lives are permeated by intellectual property interests.

"IS SHE OURS?"

The question asked by the title and wall text for Louise Lawler's *Is She Ours?* relates directly to the topics under discussion (figure 3). The photograph is part of Lawler's extended consideration of the impossibility of separating works of art from the contexts in which they are encountered. Pointing out that Edgar Degas's *Little Dancer Aged Fourteen* in the foreground is owned by the Boston Museum of Fine Arts could raise the role of museums in preserving and providing access to our shared cultural heritage. Or there is the specific history of a sculpture whose disconcerting realism confounded early Parisian viewers when Degas exhibited the original wax version in the 1881 impressionist exhibition. The bronze figure at the MFA reflects shifting circumstances surrounding Degas's work by the early 1920s, when his heirs authorized posthumous

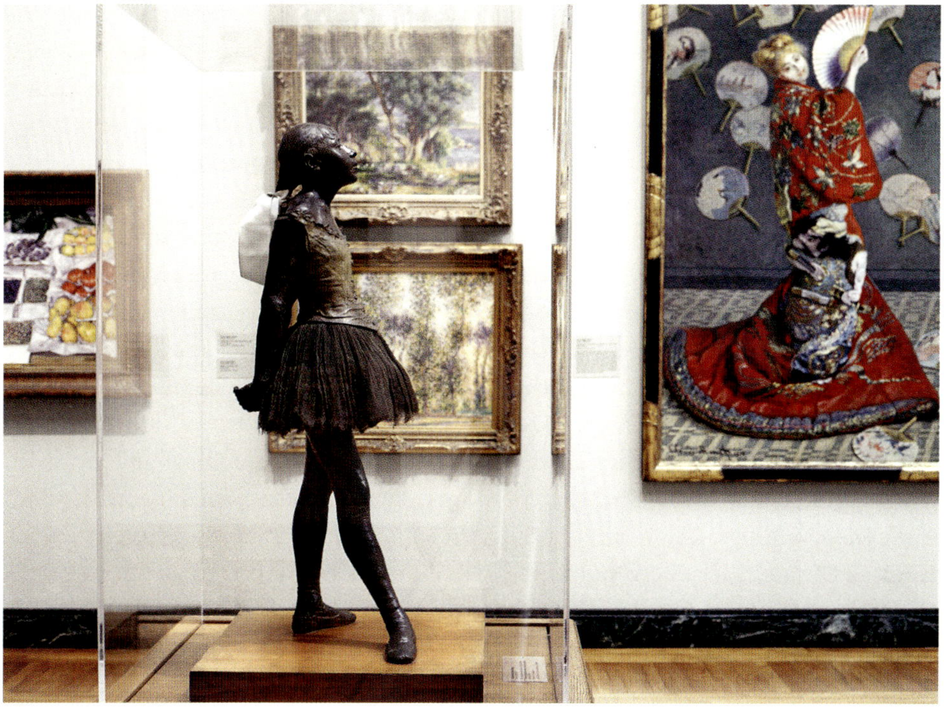

FIGURE 3
Louise Lawler, *Is She Ours?*, 1990. Silver dye bleach print with text on wall; image: 40 × 53 in.; wall text: same as title. Courtesy the artist and Metro Pictures, New York.

casts of the dancer along with many other sculptural objects that Degas never exhibited publicly. Growing enthusiasm for an artist's work (and financial motivations) can inspire posthumous editions that potentially facilitate wider access even as they alter the scope of an artist's oeuvre. From a contemporary perspective, however, there are equally urgent questions regarding an individual's ability to respond to the vast range of cultural material encountered on a daily basis. Degas's sculpture and the impressionist paintings visible behind it were no longer under copyright at the time of Lawler's encounter. Yet even if they had been, there should be no question that her visual interrogation of their impact would constitute fair use. In the context of increasingly pervasive intellectual property claims that are remarkable for their extent and duration, Lawler's question suggests the need to understand our ongoing right to respond to the surrounding cultural landscape.

In fact, it would be difficult to overstate the role of intellectual property as both a central economic engine of our time and a vastly misunderstood force interwoven into the daily lives of anyone who participates in a media-saturated environment. What happens, for example, when an object on public display is captured within a still or moving image of its larger context? If you take a photograph of someone's house with works of art on the walls, to what extent are you supposed to ask permission from the makers or rightsholders before circulating that image? Some television shows play it safe by blurring any art that appears as part of interior views. And what constitutes "publication" in the era of social media? What if you have no plans to share your image with anyone, but you accidentally select the wrong privacy setting for your cloud-based file? Is there a meaningful distinction between commercial and noncommercial when every click is potentially monetized? Even under analog regimes the issues were already complex, and they have become infinitely more so in relationship to the weightlessness of digital transmission. Potential answers to these questions will also vary dramatically depending on which country's laws you are consulting, even though many forms of dissemination are technically unhindered by such boundaries.

Copyright and related trademark claims concerning architecture are particularly striking for their potential impact on the interplay between physical and virtual in one's experience of daily life. There are, for example, tremendous inconsistencies from one country to the next regarding "freedom of panorama"—generally understood as the right to record publicly situated art and architecture. Some countries allow people to take and circulate images of copyrighted works as long as they are recorded from the vantage point of public rather than private property; others allow photographs of potentially copyrighted architecture but not related public art. A 2016 ruling by the Supreme Court of Sweden against Wikimedia Sverige, ordering it to stop hosting crowdsourced photographs of Swedish public art uploaded to a site where they were paired with maps and descriptions, provided dismaying evidence of how IP complaints can disrupt the interplay between digital and physical commons.

So far Egypt hasn't followed through on proposed legislation to copyright the pyramids, but many building owners have turned to trademark law to establish iconic edifices as brands. Certain assertions of rights are highly specific: the Eiffel Tower website, for instance, indicates that images of the monument taken by day fall under the public domain but asserts that professional photographers are supposed to get permission to capture its nighttime illumination (expressly including, but presumably not limited to, "golden illumination, twinkling, beacon and events lighting").[4] Nor are accessible physical zones necessarily as public as they may appear, given the large role played by privately owned public spaces (POPS) in contemporary urban development schemes.

Another artist who has often turned her attention to contexts of display, Liselot van der Heijden, has focused on audience interactions, including looking at art and, just as often, the acts of photography that are increasingly integral to such encounters. Whereas the silhouetted individuals she captured in front of Piet Mondrian's work at the Stedelijk (figure 4) hearken back to tropes of contemplative engagement familiar from romanticism, *Untitled, Vermeer I* (figure 5) speaks to crucial aspects of contemporary life. In contrast to earlier film cameras, where the viewfinder functioned as an extension of sight when capturing images only discernable after the film was

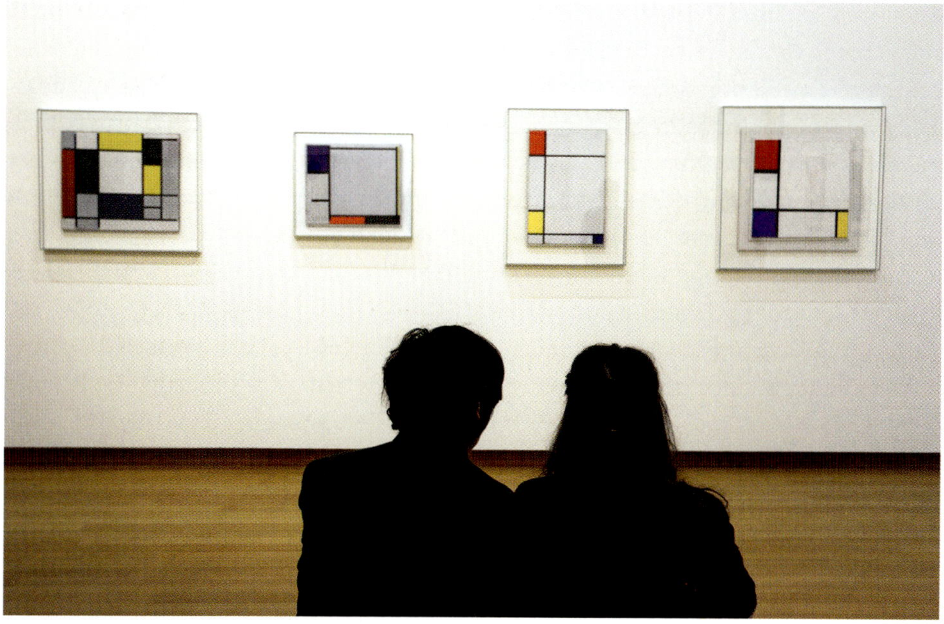

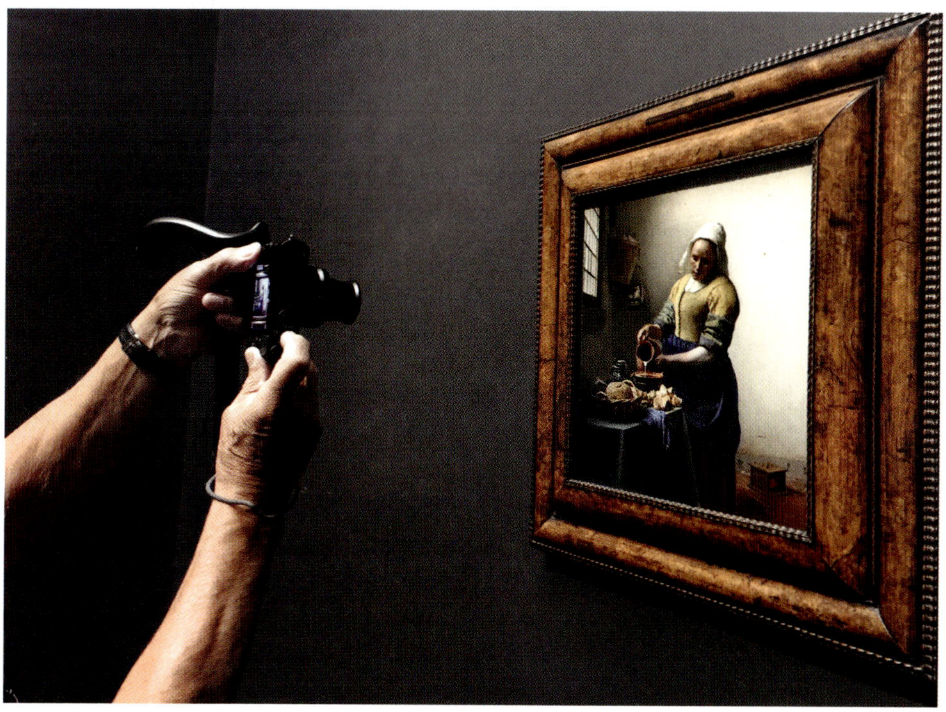

FIGURE 4 ▲
Liselot van der Heijden, *Untitled, Stedelijk I,* 2011. C-print, 16 × 19 in. © Liselot van der Heijden. Courtesy the artist.

FIGURE 5 ▼
Liselot van der Heijden, *Untitled, Vermeer I,* 2018, 16 × 20 in. © Liselot van der Heijden. Courtesy the artist.

developed, digital devices present the mediated image of the world in real time, encouraging viewers to perceive via their screens even in the presence of an object. As continuous mediation becomes part of every occasion, including wearable technologies that promise integrated experiences once limited to the realm of science fiction, then looking and recording will only continue to merge. In such a future, the very act of looking might be articulated as a form of copyright violation. Van der Heijden's intentional distortion of her image from the Stedelijk for the cover of this book, in a manner that evokes the incessant blurring that characterized Google's Art Project, suggests some of the issues at stake.[5]

Everyone is recording still and moving images; and everyone is constantly sharing material that includes fragments and traces of many acts of authorship. Yet despite copyright's central role in both modern economic developments and daily life, there is limited understanding (and a great deal of misinformation) about this ubiquitous form of intangible asset—"property" that is, at its root, simply the right to copy. The already complex interplay of authorship and ownership developed in response to analog modes of reproduction has become infinitely extended by the financial stakes, pitfalls, and possibilities for loss of control introduced by evolving modes of digital transmission. Within the art world, there is the added complexity of increasingly rarified conceptions of authorship as well as a range of moral rights statutes that potentially extend an artist's long-term control over the disposition of work quite apart from the economic emphasis of copyright.

AUTHORSHIP AND OWNERSHIP

Authorship is a central organizing principle, both for copyright and for art, but there are many reasons to describe it as a fiction. Although copyright's earliest formulation, in the 1710 British Statute of Anne, articulated the prohibition against reprinting as protecting authors, it was primarily printers who benefited.[6] Once the right to exploit creative work is defined as property that can be bought and sold, the originator whose name is attached may receive little economic benefit and potentially have limited control over its final form. The music recording business that developed over the course of the twentieth century provides numerous examples of well-known musicians who lost ownership of their output, and in some cases of the name under which it was presented. In the art world, a romantic attachment to the artist as singular source persists, regardless of practices that rely on huge studios filled with assistants as well as extensive utilization of outside fabricators in the realization of work that is often generated in response to specific institutional invitations and requirements. The degree to which both authentication and even production can continue after an artist's death provides further evidence of how the framework of authorship depends on a shared consensus about the nature of an author's work, rather than on the isolated decisions of a single individual.

Any discussion of authorship is bound to include two key essays from the late 1960s—Roland Barthes's "Death of the Author" and Michel Foucault's "What Is an

Author?"—which underscore the fundamentally arbitrary boundaries between claims of individual expression and the larger set of textual possibilities upon which they depend. Their profound poststructuralist critique of any attempt to base the interpretation of a text on assertions about the inner life of the author—in which they were joined by Jacques Derrida—dramatically reoriented critical assumptions about the status of the work as part of a relay that includes both creator and audience. Yet their sustained theoretical assault hardly resulted in the overturning of associated conventions: according to a much-quoted summation by Seán Burke, from the prologue to *The Death and Return of the Author*, "the concept of the author is never more alive than when pronounced dead."[7]

Via such pithy statements as "It is the language which speaks, not the author," Barthes attacked the idea that interpretation of a literary text should look for illumination in a writer's biography or statements of intent.[8] Not surprisingly, his argument that literary works need to be understood as a mix of already existing expressions quickly found a sympathetic audience among artists and critics engaged with strategies of image reuse in pop and appropriation art. Famously, too, Barthes paired the death of the author with the birth of the reader, based on how divergent traditions brought together in any given text achieve a form of unity in the act of reception.

Without directly naming Barthes, Foucault clearly wrote his essay in response. Rather than projecting the end of authorship, however, he underscored its role as a legalistic category. Referring to the author as a "figure," and taking as a given that the critic should focus on examining the structure of the work itself, rather than searching for connections between a text and the writer's interior life, he addressed more basic questions about how the "work" is defined. Only certain types of writing are presented with a proper name, and that classification is one way that the work is distinguished from many other examples. Yet there is still the intriguing question of why some pieces of writing produced by an established author are considered "works," while others are not, and then there is the interplay between proper names as a form of literary classification versus their association with specific individuals. Significantly, Foucault also posited a link between what he termed the "author-function" and the historical development of copyright.

Foucault both introduced and concluded his essay with a quote from Samuel Beckett: "'What does it matter who is speaking,' someone said, 'what does it matter who is speaking.'"[9] In many respects, the relationship Beckett established to his own work was very much in line with arguments by both Foucault and Barthes, given his refusal to elaborate on the meaning of his plays—a clear rejection of the position of "Author-God" portrayed by Barthes when he ruled out looking to that source for interpretive statements.[10] Yet Beckett was notoriously inflexible about the staging of his plays, objecting to novel settings, added musical elements, and various attempts to change the casting of roles initially performed by white men. His estate has continued to demand close adherence to Beckett's directives, enforcing these strictures by refusing to license noncompliant productions. Responding to threats to shut down a version of *Waiting for Godot* over the inclusion of a musical accompaniment, one aggrieved director decried the estate's "dead, controlling hand," and denounced Beckett's nephew as an "enemy of art" for his refusal of new interpretations that would potentially sustain the vitality of the work for contemporary audiences.[11] Creative decisions made in the process of staging a play are just one example of a complex relay where production and consumption cannot be disentangled. So there is an obvious irony in Beckett's commitment to leaving certain aspects of interpretation in the hands of his audience while obstructing other forms of engagement by those responsible for presenting his plays—a refusal now adamantly pursued by his estate.

Regarding Foucault's emphasis on the author as a "figure," the ongoing power of Beckett's estate is just one instance of how this role can indeed be understood as an administrative function that is potentially taken up by others acting, quite literally, in the author's name. This example also presents evidence of how two major strands of intellectual property are potentially conflated. Copyright is primarily framed as an economic right, and it applies to a wide range of expressions without regard for artistic quality. Another series of laws, known generally as moral rights, apply to creative work. Also described as personality rights, they potentially grant authors or their heirs the power to prevent distortion or other threats to the work's integrity. In practice, however, granting or withholding copyright permission is frequently used by both authors and estates to prevent forms of interpretation with which they disagree.

One also wonders what Barthes might have said about today's dizzying recirculation of digital material (in contrast to the one-directional or centralized distribution largely typical of earlier media). With easy-to-use software tools, just about anyone can produce and upload their own creative gesture, even as corporate copyright holders have become ever more aggressive in response to the web's continually expanding corpus. Caught in the flurry of takedown notices are multitudes of YouTube videos set to popular songs or remixing found footage. There is also the tremendous popularity of fan fiction emanating from communities of readers who express their responses by writing sequels or variants. It seems worth noting that E.L. James's bestselling *Fifty Shades of Grey* trilogy actually began its life as vampire-themed fan fiction written in response to the *Twilight* series and, in its defanged manifestation, inspired its own legions of enthusiasts—with one reviewer suggesting that some of those offshoots were substantially better realized than James's own sequel.[12]

Social media has mixed things up as well, with authors often interacting fairly directly with their readers as part of a dialogue that has the potential to shift the boundaries of what might be defined as the work. J.K. Rowling's extensive fan base has typically paid obsessive attention to tweets and other pronouncements about all things Harry Potter, particularly new information about characters (for example, her 2007 clarification that Dumbledore is gay—specifying something that was not clear in the novels themselves). A *New York Times* article on the phenomenon outlined a tension strikingly in line with theoretical debates. According to the proprietor of a major fan site devoted to Rowling, "Some people say the canon is within the actual covers of the seven books and that anything she says afterward you should take as opinion," in contrast to others who hold that "anything she says is true, no matter if it's on Pottermore or on Twitter or wherever—no matter what she says, it's canonical."[13] Yet even if, according to the same article, fan fiction generally treats "ex parte remarks by an author . . . as the Word of God," that stance has been put to the test in recent years by Rowling's increasingly strident transphobia.[14]

Most authors and publishers have found it in their interest to embrace these communities of avid fans, but Rowling sued successfully to prevent a print version of *The Harry Potter Lexicon,* an exhaustive web-based compendium of information about characters, plot lines, and other details that she and her publisher tolerated in its online version. One commentator, arguing for the book's fair use status, complained that "Giving Rowling what she wants would be like giving Egypt the power to control guides to the pyramids"—presumably not realizing that Egypt has considered that very proposition.[15]

The poststructuralist framing of the author as a function of writing was summed up succinctly by Emily Apter: "For Derrida, language maintains copyright on all originals, rendering words fundamentally untenable by any author."[16] In contemporary practice, however, it is remarkable how a commercially successful work can become the basis for expansive attempts to claim rights over just about anything that might be understood as derivative. In the process, the vision of a public domain based on a shared vocabulary runs up against a vast web of ownership assertions. In one key example, representatives of Margaret Mitchell's estate sued to block publication of Alice Randall's 2001 *The Wind Done Gone,* an alternate telling of Mitchell's 1936 novel *Gone with the Wind* from a slave's viewpoint—with an out-of-court settlement that allowed publication to move forward coming as a relief to those who feared the potential precedent.

Limited tolerance for fan fiction presents a strategic exception to vigilant efforts to counter all forms of trespass on the universe of goods potentially produced under licensing and spin-off agreements. The fan fiction realm has also yielded an example of corporate copyright claims that encompass language itself. When Paramount and CBS sued to shut down a crowdfunded fan film project called *Axanar,* based on the *Star Trek* franchise, one of the many contentions regarding potential infringement focused on use of the Klingon language. Paramount claimed that the language was "wholly fictitious, original and copyrightable." But an amicus brief filed by the Language Creation Society pointed to a widely sold Klingon dictionary and multiple other appearances of Klingon outside the context of the television series and films as evidence that the language had escaped the bounds of copyrightable expression.[17]

There's also the matter of "naming rights" for both cultural institutions and some of the collections they house, including wealthy former owners who sometimes even manage to impose their eccentric arrangements on public museums. Artist Gala Porras-Kim's

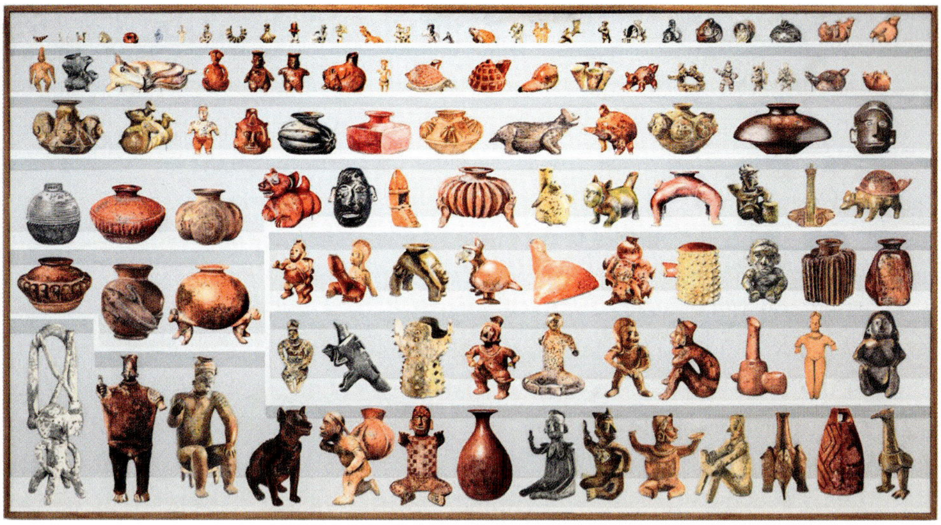

FIGURE 6
Gala Porras-Kim, *109 West Mexico Ceramics from the LACMA Collection: Colima Index*, 2017. Graphite, colored pencil and acrylic ink on paper, 73½ × 133½ in. Collection of the Los Angeles County Museum of Art. Courtesy the artist.

interrogation of the so-called Proctor Stafford collection of West Mexico ceramics at the Los Angeles County Museum of Art has addressed this elite form of pseudo-authorship through a series of responses that includes an annotated letter to LACMA pointedly questioning the role of the collector, drawings of collection objects arrayed according to size, and various sculptures created in response.[18] As Porras-Kim pointedly underscores, these objects, whose makers are unknown, acquired another name in conjunction with their removal from their original context—including the likelihood that they were available to be collected (and stripped of important information about find spots) because they were looted. Paradoxically, the value of the assembly was enhanced by this decontextualization, since the objects were imported to the United States before both a key 1970 UNESCO Convention and strengthened laws in Mexico to protect cultural patrimony.[19] Her elegantly precise scale drawings, including *109 West Mexico Ceramics from the LACMA Collection: Colima Index* (figure 6), reflect another modern overlay, with the general subcategories of Nayarit, Jalisco, and Colima based on contemporary state lines in Mexico. In a further twist, this example of Porras-Kim's critical response to museum practices was acquired by the same institution, and thus incorporated into the already contradictory narrative whereby cultural institutions described as serving the public are shaped by the agenda of powerful elites.

FROM ANALOG TO DIGITAL

The continued proliferation of forms of reproduction, first analog and now digital, has been accompanied by similarly dramatic growth in the basic vocabulary for cultural expression, evident in widespread practices of appropriation and sampling. But incessant replication and dissemination has been met with an equally extensive network of ownership claims over this expanding universe of potential intellectual property. Fan fiction is just one example of the complex back and forth between consumption and production within an economy driven by technology dynasties built on liking and sharing user-generated or modified content. Rather than being confined to esoteric theoretical debate, the interplay between authorship and ownership is therefore an inescapable dynamic across all areas of contemporary culture and commerce.

Current copyright scope has much more to do with corporate interests than with protecting the rights of individual creators: the trend toward increasingly long duration has sometimes been referred to as the Mickey Mouse rule, based on Disney's advocacy for copyright extension legislation whenever their famous cartoon rodent has been in danger of falling into the public domain. Even before shifts from analog to digital, it was therefore abundantly clear that efforts to engage with modern culture would necessarily include the landscape of commercial imagery, populated by a tangle of copyrighted expressions and trademarked products. Although key theoretical statements (as well as copyright itself) emerged in the context of literary culture, crucial recent challenges have come from the visual arts and music. Pop art in the 1960s, strategies of appropriation from the 1980s, as well as closely related developments in musical sampling, remix, and mashups have all explicitly emphasized the reorientation of preexisting cultural material. These practices also quickly came to embody the potential disparity between critical or cultural acceptance and legal understandings of authorship, as exemplified by varied results in US courts when the fair use exception to copyright has been invoked as a defense.

Art therefore provides a frame of reference to explore larger concerns, including what it means to engage with a shared cultural vocabulary during an era marked by pervasive assertions of ownership. Through their sheer range, encompassing image and text, unique and replica, physical and virtual, aesthetic and political, as well as myriad forms of performance, sound, and moving image, contemporary artistic practices have challenged medium-specific understandings of both art and copyright. Similarly, complications associated with collecting and conserving newer media (often requiring various forms of replication or emulation) help highlight the impact of IP regulations on cultural preservation and dissemination in general.

The relatively small number of cases regarding appropriation of copyright-protected imagery that have actually gone to trial demonstrate both the frequent divergence between art-world rhetoric and legal acceptance and also the potential for dramatically varied outcomes when invoking fair use. Jeff Koons faced an alarming series of losses in the early 1990s, in cases where he defended his use of various forms of appropriated imagery from his 1988 *Banality Show* as fair, but he later managed an important win on the same principle. Richard Prince experienced an equally noteworthy shift of fortunes in the two stages of a lawsuit concerning his 2007–8 *Canal Zone* works, losing his district court case only to have that decision reversed on appeal. Apparently undaunted, Prince continued to test the limits of artistic appropriation through a series of works based on screenshots of Instagram feeds.

In the interval since these debates began to play out, however, digital transmission has changed the playing field. Although emanating from related impulses, a key difference between a mixtape cassette, passed from one friend to another, versus the relatively frictionless exchange of music uploaded to a sharing site like the now defunct Napster, is the potential to reach an unquantifiable number of interested users with minimal effort or expenditure by the person doing the uploading. Appropriation is now everywhere, widely practiced not only by artists, but by anyone inclined to use readily available software and social media platforms to manipulate or simply repost existing material. Potential infringement is both impossible to suppress and much easier to discover via automated search functions.

Shifts from analog to digital have therefore changed how copyright infringement is pursued. Corporate investments in programs that will automatically scour the web for possible infringement have resulted in millions of takedown requests per day, and there are constant refinements to software that can examine material in the split-second delay between a user's click and the appearance of a post on their social media feeds. One might extrapolate, science-fiction style, to a moment when digital devices interwoven into our daily existence could be programed to automatically blur or silence anything in our physical surroundings potentially subject to a copyright claim—which could prevent the material from being recorded in the first place, rather than worrying about subsequent circulation. Yet news that Apple has a patent on technology that could employ infrared signals to block recording in performance situations indicates that this is already more than mere fantasy.

The use of networked devices and the acquisition of digital content is potentially far more contingent than owning a traditional physical copy, as Amazon Kindle users discovered in 2009 when certain books began to disappear from their tablets, including, in a remarkable bit of irony, an edition of George Orwell's *1984*. The doctrine of first sale, which allows users a large degree of freedom to manipulate or dispose of physical copies of books, music, and video, has been extensively curtailed in relation to digital media, including sharp limits on reselling electronic downloads. Library patrons have probably noticed the geographic constraints on e-books, which are generally tethered to specific institutions by complex licensing agreements, in contrast to print copies, which can travel great distances, in all their cumbersome glory, via interlibrary loan networks. Users are likewise forbidden, under threat of prosecution, from circumventing digital locks and thereby exploring the inner workings of many of the objects that they own. As Eduardo Peñalver and Sonia Katyal presciently observed in their 2010 book *Property Outlaws*, one key component of the shift to digital transmission is a tremendous expansion in both control and surveillance—with this erosion of privacy only increasing in momentum.[20]

In the United States, evidence of the chilling effect of the 1998 Digital Millennium Copyright Act can be seen in ongoing advocacy for exceptions, ranging from audio versions of books for the visually impaired to allowing researchers access to computer code integrated into a host of goods, from the cars we drive to medical devices implanted in our bodies. For similar reasons, the seemingly mundane area of archival preservation and retrieval has become a hot IP topic, since copying is central to basic preservation for many types of cultural material recorded in fragile analog formats, with even higher stakes for quickly obsolete digital files where access is tied to proprietary software.

Still other tensions arise when IP codes based on modern Western conceptions of authorship or ownership are applied to traditional cultural practices—particularly because the weight on individual authorship under established copyright regimes creates a strong bias toward treating communally developed forms as part of the public domain. And despite the central role of IP in today's cultural and economic landscape, there is still extensive confusion about what can potentially be copyrighted, including core distinctions between idea and expression. Legal conflicts highlight yet another crucial dynamic: one of the significant problems with this form of property is the uneven playing field when it comes to protecting one's rights in the face of individuals or entities with deep pockets for lawyer's fees.

Artistic appropriation continues to offer an important framework for contemplating the widespread urge to respond to preexisting forms. But conceptual practices are likewise relevant, given that versions of authorship based on collecting and archiving bear a striking resemblance to many popular web-based activities. "Everyone is an artist" was the often-quoted dictum of Joseph Beuys, well-known for his inclusive conception of art-making. "Everyone is an author" would be an obvious extension for our own era, given that in fact everyone *is* an author, according to copyright principles that articulate originality criteria separate from judgments of quality, while also doing away with both registration and notice requirements. But "everyone is a curator" might be even more appropriate as the new mantra for an era characterized not only by the blurring of job descriptions within the art world, but the current popularization of the term to describe just about any activity of assembly, arrangement, or presentation. What's equally typical, unfortunately, is the attitude of the estate associated with Beuys's expansive sentiment: Eva Beuys, Joseph's widow, is notorious among curators and historians for her use of inherited copyright and moral rights prerogatives to shut down interpretations that do not conform to her vision of the work. In situations where explicit permission is required—including academic publications such as this one—material that can be readily discovered through standard internet search functions is potentially unavailable for the very forms of criticism and commentary that fair use promotes. Equally worrisome is the threat to fair use when take-down notices as well as filters that prevent uploading in the first place operate at the sole discretion of algorithm-driven software.

DECLARING ART

Certain conflicts about art are important for what they can reveal about the wider world. But there are also fundamental questions about the category itself. Whether a particular phenomenon is defined as "art" is often highly significant, even though the basis for classification can be far from self-evident. A mural on the side of a building will generally qualify for very different legal protections than an advertisement (notwithstanding a great many examples, both contemporary and historical, that embody elements of both functions). A 1927–28 case involving the refusal by US customs officials to accept Constantin Brancusi's highly abstract *Bird in Space* as sculpture, and thereby as exempt from import taxes, is an early example of problems of misrecognition when nontraditional work intersects with bureaucratic officialdom. Or there is the mobile clinic that Atelier van Lieshout designed within a transportation container for the abortion rights group Women on Waves: in 2001, when the Dutch transport ministry demanded that the clinic be removed from the group's ship because its presence violated the vessel's inspection certificate, the group was able to address the problem by providing documentation from Joep van Lieshout asserting the container's status as a work of art called *A-Portable*.[21]

Some of the more contentious disputes have arisen when an artist asserts a definition contrary to a collector's interests or expectations. Cady Noland and Sotheby's were sued by the owner of a work that Noland renounced due to damages—essentially an attempt by the owner to recoup the monetary loss associated with the artist's refutation and the auction house's consequent decision to remove the work from sale. It is striking that Noland, who is notorious for her retreat from the art world, made her statement through the intermediary of her lawyer, speaking on her behalf and articulating her authorial renunciation in legal terms. Even more surprisingly, Peter Doig was forced to go to court in 2016 to avow that he had not painted a canvas—defending his right not to authenticate after the work's owner became convinced, on the basis of rather improbable evidence, that he had somehow acquired a youthful effort by the now-famous artist.

So who gets to proclaim the status of a work? To what extent are the players in agreement about the rules of the game? What can or cannot be framed or codified in legal terms? In his reading of the disruptive power of Marcel Duchamp's readymades, Thierry de Duve stressed the importance of the declarative act, "this is a work of art" (whether explicit or implied) as the basis for its creation. And over the course of the twentieth century, Duchamp's once provocative gambit was transformed into a widely practiced artistic strategy. But there is obviously much more to the story, given that anyone can stand in their garage and declare their snow shovel a work of art—just as anyone can declare themselves an art expert. The impact of a given declaration quite obviously depends on the relationship between the person making the statement and a whole series of values, assessments, and judgments understood and shared within the relevant field. Building on Foucault's conception of the author-function, it is important to consider who or what entity has the authority to define a work, or to take away that status, with the role of both experts and heirs over authenticity (or inauthenticity) determinations as a fascinating extension of authorship. Given the vast expansion in the art market, particularly for contemporary works, during the last half-century, matters of authorship are big business.

In his exploration of performative statements—speech acts such as "I thee wed" or "I bequeath"—J.L. Austin highlighted utterances where "to *say* something is to *do* something."[22] To the extent that a claim of authorship or judgment of authenticity is believed, it functions as a performative statement with the potential to change the status of an object dramatically, including its monetary value and perceptions of it, without altering its physical presence. Legal decisions are also performative, since rendering a judgment presumably does make it so (unless a conclusion is overturned on appeal to a higher court). The legal association is equally important in relation to Judith Butler's exploration of agency, including state authority, in the exercise of the performative.[23] But Austin also underscored the role of context in the function of such statements, with a wedding ceremony taking place within a play as one example where the operation of the performative is suspended, and it is certainly the case that not all authorship denunciations have the same impact. When Robert Morris issued a notarized withdrawal of authorship from a 1963 construction entitled *Litanies,* it was received as an ironic and playful gesture, despite Morris's recourse to legal authority. More recently, commentators have suggested that Prince's renunciation of a 2014 Instagram-based portrait of Ivanka Trump that she had commissioned (a gesture of protest by Prince in response to Donald Trump's inauguration as US president) is likely to increase rather than decrease its value.[24] While the power of the artist to declare or disown work is in some circumstances legally established by moral rights statutes, procedures for how the work is defined as such in the first place, and subsequent judgments of authenticity, are much more commonly rooted in field-specific expectations and conventions that rely on largely uncodified or tacit criteria.

These targeted and specialized strategies correlate with Pierre Bourdieu's conception of fields of practice, all with their own rules and forms of knowledge—which are to some degree autonomous, despite the many situations where they overlap with one another. Within the field of law, Bourdieu has observed, conflicts need to be reframed according to legal norms, and in the process they are transformed into debates between professional proxies. Thus one aspect of filing a lawsuit is the requirement to completely restate the facts of the case so that they conform to legal conventions and terminology.[25] Because of this need for translation, however, disputes that wind up in the court system often help bring to the surface otherwise unexamined assumptions—not only distinctions between art-related and legal expectations, but also specialized customs associated with different spheres within the art world. Not surprisingly, given the scale of the present art market, many conflicts in the art-law arena involve matters of authenticity, and therefore encompass authorship issues that extend beyond the scope of copyright.

While it might not be terribly dangerous to declare, rhetorically, that something isn't art, it can be quite risky to say that it is not the work of a particular artist, especially if that statement is made by an individual or entity with any form of presumed authority. Indeed, a number of estates and foundations have stopped authenticating work specifically in order to avoid the threat of legal action, and the once-staid project of assembling a scholarly catalogue raisonné has become equally fraught territory. Dissatisfied owners have taken to the courts at various points, hoping to compel a declaration of authenticity not available elsewhere. An individual or organization does not even need to have an explicitly defined legal role in order to be hit with a lawsuit; their authority can arise from only a perceived consensus regarding the status of their opinion.

Given the delegated production behind much contemporary art, as well as the many proxies involved in the life of art over time, it is equally striking how tenaciously the system of individual authorship has been maintained as an organizing principle within art institutions, scholarship, and quite obviously the marketplace. Copyright is an important part of this story, with its evolving set of artificial limits on multiplication and proliferation in response to challenges posed by analog and digital reproduction. But the narrowly focused body of law known as moral or personality rights is also important. The latter generally includes integrity protections as well as provisions covering an artist's prerogative to claim and disclaim authorship—conditions that remain in force even after a work changes ownership. In addition, the art world has developed its own procedures, often determined more by convention than actual law, for articulating the boundaries of the work. In the absence of laws specifically codifying many art-world assumptions, disputes often center on contract law or accusations of fraud. The right to engage in the formalities of authorship is still tenaciously articulated as the prerogative of the individual artist, but conflicts over how artists exercise these powers, as well as the extent to which certain aspects of the author-function can be assumed by an artist's heirs or representatives, indicate tensions and contradictions underlying this consensus-built edifice. For work of any significant stature, the death of the artist gives rise to the birth of the committee, as authorship considerations shift into the hands of estates and associated professionals.

BY RIGHTS

It is easy to be sympathetic to the idea that artists should have the final say when it comes to determining the integrity of their creations. Yet to the extent that protections for works of art that supersede absolute property rights are based on a presumption of art's shared cultural significance, it is important to interrogate the degree to which authorial control coincides with public interest in cultural objects. On the one hand, there is an understandable desire by artists to shape how their work can be employed, including resistance to its assimilation into commercial agendas or other potentially cynical uses. But granting artists, and particularly their heirs, the ability to control the contexts in which their work is exhibited or reproduced can result in the suppression of critical discourse. Therefore these twin foundations—cultural significance and personality rights—do not necessarily function in tandem.

The larger IP environment encompassing copyright as well as patent protection is similarly riven by contradiction: granting limited monopoly rights to creators is supposed to encourage invention, but overly long or expansive IP regimes accomplish the opposite. It is important to remember that this highly artificial form of intangible property was created not just for the purpose of putting money into certain people's pockets, but for the greater cultural good derived from incentives for innovative work. Likewise, even though moral rights are often described as personality rights, a key rationale for limiting absolute property rights is the protection of shared cultural heritage, over and above individual whims. It is not difficult to find moments of bad faith, where authors or owners (artists included) demand absolute control over forms that rely on creative activity by others. It is equally important to recognize the degree to which esteemed examples derive their value from a sense of investment by the culture at large.

A number of scholars have characterized the twentieth- and early-twenty-first-century expansion of IP claims and limitations as a new enclosure movement, likening the transition from public domain to private property in cultural realms to the fencing off of physical commons.[26] When authors or other intellectual property proprietors use legally conferred interests to shut down subsequent creative work or discourse, not only is the idea of a shared commons undermined, but the public is denied potential benefits from a form of property that would not exist without constant reiteration as part of the larger social contract. Arguments for the rights of creators, including advocacy for an expansive understanding of fair use, therefore need to be linked to support for the rights of all participants in a broader cultural dialogue. It is equally important to explore alternate models, including the Creative Commons initiative, that potentially articulate a more flexible understanding of layered or shared authorship.

Clearly we are in the midst of profound transformations—in our economic structures and our daily lives—linked to the development of networked information technologies. Artists need to understand how legal definitions of intellectual property shape dynamics surrounding both production and consumption. Just as significantly, issues relating to art can provide a crucial framework for looking outward to quickly evolving intellectual property developments. Both copyright and moral rights legislation are evidently here to stay, but it is still possible to campaign for curtailing excessive duration, reducing inequalities based on access to legal support, and an expansive definition of fair use. Building from an examination of the current landscape, it is essential to advocate for the importance of a vital cultural commons.

SCOPE AND CHAPTERS

One challenge posed by this material is a potentially infinite series of interconnected topics. A fully international approach would require engaging with the intricacies of a multitude of related but also distinct legal systems across the world. Yet limiting the scope to a single country would come at the expense of comparing alternative models and also acknowledging the international movement of both cultural goods and their creators. The majority of legal cases and conflicts explored in this book unfolded in the United States. But examples from other regions highlight parallel concerns as well as contrasts, including how crucial historic differences between Anglo-American and continental European copyright laws have continued to play out.

Ultimately the examples in this book are case studies, with the facts of an interesting conflict driving the selection of which artists and other creators are examined. The discussions therefore skew toward individuals or entities with the resources to pursue a court action, or whose prominence drew attention to gestures that were perceived by others as copyright violations. In shifting from wider cultural spheres to art-world activities, the book also draws out connections between copyright ownership and protocols around authorship that are less explicitly codified. There is a general movement from legal articulations of copyright to forms of authorship specific to the art world, including highly nuanced attitudes toward quotation and copying.

Chapter 1, "From Privilege to IP," begins with copyright's prehistory in earlier privilege systems and then examines different copyright trajectories in Anglo-American and European contexts, as well as global pressures to adopt these models. The early debates still resonate for questions about the nature of literary property, including whether it should be perpetual, what aspects of a work merit protection, and the significance of different contributions to a book publication. It also references the work of key historians and theorists whose insights into changing conceptions of authorship, audience, and ownership rights are crucial for understanding the implications of this highly artificial form of property. The chapter sets the stage for copyright's ever-broader reach by considering how laws initially developed in response to text were extended to images.

Chapter 2, "The Appropriation Game," considers artistic appropriation against a cultural landscape where it is impossible to avoid interacting with various forms of protected imagery. A series of high-profile cases have indicated the crucial importance of fair use for attempts to engage with copyrighted material—while also highlighting challenges associated with this defense. Yet copyright principles are hardly sufficient to account for subtle articulations of authorship as they play out in the contemporary art world, and courtrooms are an extremely constrained, as well as expensive, forum within which to mount such discussions.

Starting with litigation over rights to the song "Happy Birthday," chapter 3, "Art, Life, and Infringement," considers, on the one hand, the role of copies in relation to museum conventions and, on the other, significant copyright issues beyond the realm of visual art. Music sampling cases are crucial, due to parallels with artistic appropriation, even as they also highlight key differences in distribution, audience, and business models. Shifts from analog to digital technologies have resulted in an exponential increase in both creative forms of sampling and the danger of being subject to an infringement accusation. Issues raised by social media circulation and copyright conflicts around tattoos help to underscore the broad reach of copyright concerns, and the chapter continues the discussion of fair use principles.

Chapter 4, "Moral Rights and Beyond," opens with artists' rights advocacy, including the model provided by the Siegelaub-Projansky contract and the eventual enactment of limited moral right protections in the United States. It also considers other types of behind-the-scenes agreements that often pertain more to market concerns, and typically come to light only when they become embroiled in conflict. Building on Hans Haacke's use of a version of the Siegelaub-Projansky contract, the chapter examines how a number of contemporary artists, including Tania Bruguera, Maria Eichhorn, and Carey Young, combine strategies of institutional critique and tactical legal intervention.

Ranging across a series of interrelated topics, chapter 5, "Public Matters," explores the interplay between public interest and private ownership in shared spaces, both physical and virtual. The bundle of rights and restrictions referred to as "freedom of panorama" articulates various ways that IP may constrain how one is able to interact with publicly visible phenomena, and private property opens onto broader questions about privacy rights in a data-driven world. Other crucial considerations include distinctions between commercial and noncommercial expressions as they pertain to different types of public art, ranging from commissioned projects to unsanctioned graffiti.

Examining issues of authorship specific to the visual arts, chapter 6, "Authorship and the Undead," traces various forces involved in defining works that continue to be presented under a single name. Activities connected to the estates of three artists—Alberto Giacometti, Piet Mondrian, and Constantin Brancusi—draw attention to struggles for control over legacy, the potential for ongoing production of the work, and contrasts between extensively codified patrimonial and moral rights under French law, on the one hand, and practices largely based on art-world consensus and market forces in the United States, on the other. The chapter ends with recent cases, including Ibrahim Mahama's conflicts with early promoters, where living artists have fought to control the making of their own work.

Chapter 7, "Status Shifts," surveys tensions associated with the process of defining a work, including the artist's declarative act, monetary interests, and bureaucratic operations. Artists' rights are one crucial thread, particularly the prerogative to renounce work compromised by damages or other problems. Another topic concerns conflicts that arise when artistic production does not conform to a collector's expectations. Especially striking, however, are the borderline cases, where an object's status as art can shift for both dramatic and unexpected reasons.

Continuing the examination of art-world practices, including consensus-based codes among industry players, chapter 8, "From Authentic to Fake," explores the demand for, and administration of, authenticity. Market pressures can have a chilling effect on authorship issues that extend well beyond copyright, with artists' estates and foundations increasingly reluctant to authenticate. Cases that do wind up in court, including forgery claims, help to highlight the potential incompatibility between legal determinations of authenticity, art-world expertise, and sometimes even the word of the artist. Beyond the art world, there are larger implications for a culture driven by branded goods and content.

Pivoting back to broader social repercussions, the coda, "Life in the Virtual Commons," considers some of IP's present-day consequences, as individuals become enmeshed in a tangle of ownership claims and disadvantageous terms of use. Questions raised by artistic appropriation have renewed relevance for a freewheeling internet culture where consumption and production are increasingly indistinguishable. Seemingly everything is shared, but possible infringement is readily searchable in the context of proprietary platforms that depend on user-generated content while blurring distinctions regarding commercial speech. As we all move, both willingly and unwillingly, into a future where physical space and data become ever more intertwined, it is essential to remain vigilant about how IP shapes our world.

1

FROM PRIVILEGE TO IP

AN AUTHOR WRITES A TEXT. The words used by the author are part of a common vocabulary and belong to no one. But through a specific arrangement of that shared language, the author creates something that is identifiable as individual expression. In earlier eras, that composition of words was likely to be first recorded in a handwritten manuscript; more recently it is generally typed into some sort of electronic device. To sell a manuscript or other tangible object is not the same thing as selling the right to reproduce that array of words in another format. It is also important to distinguish between a specific articulation and the thoughts that are conveyed by it—since copyright protection generally covers expressions, not ideas. What has just been outlined is, therefore, a system where language that belongs to everyone is potentially used to express abstract concepts that are equally open to all, but a particular arrangement of words does become the property of an individual author, who then has the right to exploit its value or transfer ownership.

This description conveys a basic definition of copyright as it was formulated in response to the market for printed books. Today's vast network of intellectual property (IP) therefore emanates from protection for literature initially codified into law during the eighteenth century. There are two important points to take from this thumbnail sketch. The first is the fact that the origins of copyright reflect a response to a specific category of work and associated distribution mechanism: literary expression and the printing press. Each time these protections are extended to additional media and technologies, the criteria for determining what is covered have to be articulated anew. The second point is that the exact scope of what copyright does and does not encompass—and by extrapolation, what remains in the public domain—has always been a highly artificial, perhaps even arbitrary construct.

Looking at the origins of how and why copyright protections were formulated is important for a number of reasons. In the context of today's disruptive technologies, along with evolving IP laws that provide the underpinning for much of their economic power, it is helpful to view recent developments in relation to a far longer history of innovation that is necessarily linked (as both motivator and beneficiary) to changes in legal definitions. It is equally essential, with respect to copyright's ever-expanding purview, to test claims regarding purpose against actual impact. Although the third major component of IP, trademark law, is primarily significant in the context of recent commercial markets, the genesis of copyright and patent protections can be traced back to traditions of aristocratic privilege originating in fifteenth-century Europe. Initial debates about copyright are striking for the questions they raise about the nature and purview of this highly specific form of property. The dialogue quickly extended from text to image rights, and comparisons that articulated key differences in their reproducibility foreshadowed some of the tensions when copyright protections are granted to a multitude of forms. Key distinctions in the Anglo-American and European prioritization of economic considerations versus other types of authorial rights remain important, even during an era characterized by pressure to conform to major international accords.

LITERARY PROPERTY

Just what type of property is a work of literature? This question was asked repeatedly during the early history of what has, over the course of recent centuries, become a pervasive field of intellectual property rights and restraints. But even though copyright legislation was first formulated in response to the dissemination of text, images were not far behind, due to the market for prints. At the same time, protections for texts were sometimes similar to those provided for inventions, reflecting certain shared origins for both copyrights and patents.

The major precursor to modern copyright was the privilege system, which involved temporary monopolies over both printed works and inventions, granted by sovereigns. But this type of aristocratic patronage (often linked to requirements for prepublication approval, and therefore control over content) was gradually displaced by market-based systems. The transformation of literature into a form of property was also driven in no small part by the increasing readership for books by the late eighteenth century. Therefore the push for copyright followed the convergence of a number of factors. One, obviously, was the advance that facilitated copying by mechanical or technical means—moveable type front and center, but likewise image production via printed copies. Audience was equally crucial, however, with an expanded reading public as a major impetus for market developments.

Bound up with definitions of literary property are questions about the role of the author and the rights of the public. Theoretically, copyright protections should allow authors to reap economic benefits from the fruits of their labor, as opposed to depending on patronage (the dominant standard prior to the middle of the eighteenth century). According to this model, the author has been described by Mark Rose as the proprietor over a specific type of commodity known as "the work."[1] But starting with the 1710 Statute of Anne in England, the emphasis on authors in early articulations of copyright was more in name than practice, since printers largely retained control over literary property. Providing benefits to creators was a sympathetic reason to argue for expanding copyright protection, but then, like now, the returns from treating culture as property frequently wound up in other hands.

This history varies dramatically from region to region, based on multiple factors ranging from industrial or economic development to distinctions between systems rooted in common law and civil code. The two major copyright models that eventually developed—Anglo-American and continental—articulated the relationship between work and author differently. Under the common-law framework in England and the United States, the emphasis was economic and utilitarian. Allowing authors as well as inventors a limited monopoly over works shared with the public would motivate them to pursue their creative activity, with the results of this incentive benefitting society at large. Therefore contributions to the public sphere are somewhat counterintuitively linked to the monetization of cultural property. The dialogue in France and Germany, however, was grounded in a romantic understanding of the relationship between author and work, and this led to greater priority for authorial rights (now often articulated as personality or moral rights). If a literary work was a form of personal expression, it was an open question whether something so closely connected to the individual could be fully bought or sold. To the extent that the literary work was not entirely alienable, it was not strictly properly. The continental articulation of authorship was potentially achieved at the expense of the public, however, given that protections were not framed in terms of cultural accessibility.[2]

PRIVILEGE

Options for producing multiple printed copies facilitated by the invention of moveable type in the 1440s were followed in fairly short order by efforts to constrain this potential through the granting of monopoly rights. Early evidence of the technology's rapid dissemination can be found in privileges issued in fifteenth-century Venice—with precursors to copyright intermixed with inventions that would now be covered by patents, including a five-year monopoly on printing technology granted to John of Speyer in 1469. The first recorded privilege for a printed work, issued in Venice to Marcus Sabellicus in 1486 for his history of the city, was a direct outgrowth of protections granted to mechanical inventions.[3] By the 1550s, an increasingly vital market for engraved prints led to similar measures. In her discussion of privileges issued for texts and images, Lisa Pon has traced how this form of governmental favor, bestowing permanent or fixed-term monopolies, was granted to a variety of innovations including experiments with poison gas, mining techniques, and windmill improvements.[4] While granting privileges was common across Europe, however, enforcement was limited to the boundaries of the government issuing them. This localized authority was particularly problematic in regions where power was distributed across many small principalities—and a few enterprising individuals attempted to secure privileges in more than one place.

Early text privileges were generally granted to printers, but some did go to authors. And it did not take long for conflicts between them to wind up in court. In 1504, André de la Vigne succeeded with his petition to prevent a French printer from publishing an alternate edition of *Vergier d'honneur,* a poetic anthology that included several of his works. The ruling by the French parliament, which determined that the publication was protected for approximately ten months, was, according to Cynthia Brown, "the first known lawsuit initiated by a vernacular writer," with the author assuming "the duties of a publisher by challenging a printer's unsanctioned use of his texts."[5] Brown presents this early recognition of the text as potentially profitable on the open market, rather than being the means to a court appointment, as a counterpoint to accounts that date authorial ownership developments to the eighteenth and nineteenth centuries, and she also highlights the pivotal function of printed books, rather than manuscripts, in establishing authorship.[6]

Given the central role that conceptions of originality eventually came to play as the basis for copyright (even if only gradually, and in sometimes remarkably attenuated circumstances), it is interesting to consider earlier conventions regarding what were acceptable practices, and what went over the line. A dispute between Marcantonio Raimondi and Albrecht Dürer involving Marcantonio's copies of Dürer's *Life of the Virgin* print cycle is particularly noteworthy. Dürer's 1511 edition appeared with a stern warning as part of the colophon: "Envious thieves of the work and invention of others, keep your thoughtless hands from these works of ours." And, based on the authority of a privilege issued by Maximilian, Emperor of Rome, the colophon also enjoined their printing or sale "in spurious forms" within the boundaries of the Empire.[7]

The dispute regarding Marcantonio's copies is well known because of Vasari's account of Dürer's trip to Italy to complain to the Venetian senate. Although Vasari

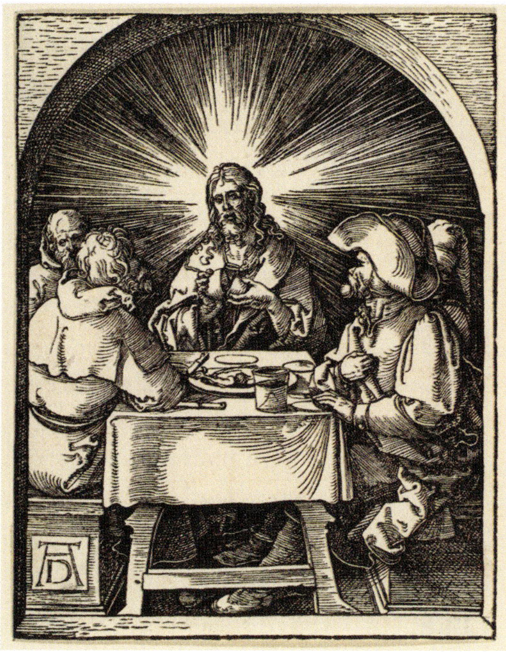

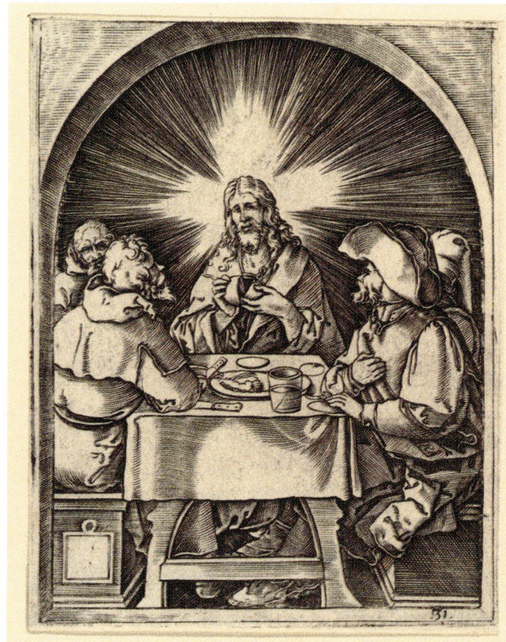

FIGURE 7 ◀
Albrecht Dürer, *Christ at Emmaus, from The Small Passion,* ca. 1510. Woodcut; sheet: 5 × 3⅞ in. Metropolitan Museum of Art, CC0 1.0, Public Domain Dedication.

FIGURE 8 ▶
Marcantonio Raimondi, *Christ at Emmaus, after Dürer,* ca. 1500–34. Engraving, second state of three; sheet: 5⅛ × 3⅞ in. Metropolitan Museum of Art, CC0 1.0, Public Domain Dedication.

was wrong in many of the details, Dürer's grievance apparently did prompt Marcantonio to remove Dürer's monogram from future pressings, and in fact the resulting blank plaquette eventually became his own signature (figures 7 and 8).[8] This type of emblem, which could be understood as a precursor to today's trademarks and logos, was used consistently in prints of the time, even by artists who did not similarly sign their paintings—though Joseph Leo Koerner points out that Dürer did both.[9] According to Evelyn Lincoln, the artist's "invention," in this context, referred to the central arrangement of figures, which was freely reproduced in prints. Marcantonio exceeded norms by not only creating prints closely based on Dürer's, but including the monogram that was a marker of quality and value through its association with a famous artist.[10] In another case lodged by Dürer in Nuremberg, the 1512 decision by the Nuremberg council likewise stressed both the copying of the print overall and the inclusion of Dürer's monogram on the pirated copy, with the latter constituting a form of deception or fraud with parallels to counterfeit coins, forged signatures, untrue weights, and adulterated goods.[11]

A crucial aspect of the process was the skill required to create the plate or matrix from which multiple prints could be generated. Lincoln has described prints as a form of currency where their value, as objects of trade, was linked to quality, and creating works for the print market was an early way for artists to free themselves from working directly for a patron.[12] A crucial issue was possession of the matrix, which was typically signed within the plate itself (the all-important monogram). In contrast to today's ethos of the print edition, with artificial limits on the total number of copies attested by hand numbering as well as the artist's signature on each imprint (sometimes accompanied by a separate certificate of authenticity), the priority for many centuries was to use the matrix to its full capacity. Present-day copyright conventions generally draw a sharp distinction between possession of a physical object and acquiring associated reproduction rights. During the sixteenth and seventeenth centuries, however, buying a plate was synonymous with acquiring the prerogative to strike prints. The urgent area of theft was not appropriated images, but purloined plates. "Possession of a plate was like money in the bank," according to Lincoln, who observes that "much of what we know about Renaissance printing comes from legal suits about stolen plates."[13]

It is equally important to distinguish two major categories: reproductive prints were created to convey information about works of art in another medium, while for prints of invention, the print was itself the work of art.[14] Although reproductive prints fulfilled many functions that were later supplanted by photography, this version of documentation was handmade, and therefore involved significant interpretation, over and above the inherent shifts associated with the translation from one medium to another. Attitudes regarding the relationship between originality and imitation have likewise evolved. In the introduction to the third part of his *Lives,* Giorgio Vasari characterized Raphael's greatness as his ability to synthesize. But certain limits are suggested by an early seventeenth-century controversy about a work by Domenichino, which erupted when a rival accused him of having stolen from his teacher, Agostino Carracci, for his version of *The Last Communion of Saint Jerome.*

There was no question that the Domenichino and Carracci works resembled one another in key ways, but imitation was standard practice, so the issue was the artist's ability to use what was taken. In her study of the dispute, Elizabeth Cropper stresses the role of memory, such that a later response to a work would not be a copy, but instead, the imitation of an idea.[15] Tellingly, Cropper opens her book with a reference to her opportunity to see the two *Last Communion of Saint Jerome* paintings exhibited side by side in Rome, in a 1996 presentation that could be read as a restaging of another moment they were shown together, two centuries earlier in Paris, while both were lodged in the Louvre as Napoleonic loot. Present-day viewers take the ability to see comparisons via high-resolution color photographs for granted. But during the time of the initial controversy, and for some centuries after, prints constituted the primary means, other than memory, for closing the distance in both time and space separating the two works. This is important in relation to what information is communicated by a print (always an interpretation) versus what is conveyed by a photograph's mechanical translation.[16]

Controversies about the potential copying of prints do have many parallels to initial threats posed by the reprinting of text. But there are key distinctions based on the techniques required for each. Even if early typesetting was labor-intensive by today's standards, an accurately reprinted book was treated as an exact copy of the text itself, regardless of the degree of elegance or luxury associated with the binding.[17] By contrast, the identity of an engraving or other type of print resides in the interplay between motif and how it is rendered. Yet copyright protections for text were soon extended to printed images, giving an early indication of the potential challenges when adapting such regulations to an ever-expanding range of forms.

EARLY COPYRIGHT IN ENGLAND

A number of factors converged in the eighteenth century, with technologies that allowed printed texts and images to be widely circulated intersecting with economic and social shifts crucial to an expanded audience. A gradual move away from reliance on aristocratic support in favor of income from a market system was accompanied by the loosening of the guild system's grip on training and professional activity. In addition to the precedent for copyright in aristocratic privilege, the stage was also set by trade practices. Printers in various cities established registers where they listed titles they planned to publish, and these two systems (state prerogatives and trade conventions) often worked in tandem.[18]

In England, imperial authority and trade were linked via the royal charter granted to the Stationers' Company in 1557.[19] A crucial motivation was controlling the content of printed books through requirements for prior approval, but the record kept by the Stationers' Company of licensed books eventually came to indicate not only what had been approved by royal censors, but also a printer's exclusive right over the book in question. When the British parliament allowed the Printing Act to lapse in 1695, however, the Stationers' Company lost its monopoly, and its members were unable to prevent independent printers from producing competing copies. The eventual response to their complaints was the bill known as the Statute of Anne, introduced in Parliament in 1709 and enacted in April 1710, which became the first copyright legislation. The full title was "An Act for the Encouragement of Learning, by Vesting the Copies of Printed Books in the Authors or Purchasers of Such Copies, During the Times Therein Mentioned," and it established a fourteen-year period of protection (with the option of a second fourteen-year renewal), as well as a single twenty-one-year term for books already in print. Despite this ostensible emphasis on authors, however, it was still largely the publishers who benefitted—and they had already been motivated to feature the author's name on the title page in order to avoid being held solely responsible for libel or blasphemy.[20] In subsequent maneuvers to expand copyright protections, benefits to authors continued to be frequently invoked, but typically more in form than substance.[21]

The Statute of Anne was only the beginning of a longer series of steps in the establishment of British copyright during the eighteenth century, with one key point of contention being why literary property should be subject to a term limit if other forms of property were perpetual. Once copyrights granted under the Statute of Anne began to expire, English publishers pushed for new legislation that would extend their duration, and they attempted to achieve the same goal through the courts. They scored a victory in 1769 when *Millar v. Taylor* concluded that copyrights, like other property, had a perpetual existence. But that decision was overturned in 1774 by *Becket v. Donaldson,* which found definitively against the concept of perpetual copyright, holding that these rights could be fixed by statute.[22] At least some members of the early reading public understood the implications of this decision, since there were newspaper accounts of people celebrating in the streets.[23] The ruling's impact was felt particularly by who had invested in certain classics assuming that they were acquiring perpetual rights—with income from exclusive control over Shakespeare, Bacon, Milton, or Bunyan resembling the money generated by landed estates.[24] Given that few authors were in a position to retain control over their literary property, they benefitted from relatively short copyright terms because their finite duration gave publishers an incentive to seek out and promote new works.

In 1735, similar protections were extended to engravings, via an act largely modeled on the Statute of Anne. The Engraver's Act, also known as the Hogarth Act, followed closely upon a public petition signed by William Hogarth and others, so in that respect it was directly promoted by authors. Highlighting the role of skill versus mechanical copying, the petition framed the issue as a conflict between engravers and the print sellers who would often commission their own versions of popular prints. Ronan Deazley has outlined key differences from the Statute of Anne reflecting the specific nature of the medium, including a prohibition on partial taking and provisions that the acquisition of a plate included the right to run further prints.[25] In addition, authors of the petition were careful to draw a distinction between direct copies and other interpretations of the same subject, foreshadowing, according to Deazley, the idea-versus-expression dichotomy that has become a core copyright principle.[26]

Many of the tensions that continue to be part of the copyright landscape are evident in this early history. There is the potential divergence between authors wanting compensation for their work, and readers looking for inexpensive cultural goods. At the same time, authors needed an audience, while readers had an interest in authors continuing to produce. Over the course of the nineteenth century, both the centrality of the author and the duration of copyright were extended under English law, with copyright terms of twenty-eight years or the author's lifetime, whichever was longer, established in 1814, and forty-two years or the author's lifetime plus seven years, in 1842. But even though authors' rights were repeatedly invoked when campaigning for longer terms, the early history of copyright indicates that limited terms of protection gave publishers a strong incentive for developing new material. Affirming the principle that this form of ownership was restricted by statute provided another important benefit: the establishment of a public domain inhabited by works clearly free from copyright restrictions.

DECENTRALIZATION, PIRACY, AND REPRINTING

During the eighteenth and nineteenth centuries, as in the present, unauthorized reprints of popular works were widely blamed for diminished authorial income, and they also hurt publishers who were attempting to support a range of titles while losing profits from their bestsellers. However, early copyright protections, like the privileges that preceded them, tended to be relatively localized in their coverage. England's pioneering legislation could not, for example, prevent the development of printing industries in Ireland and Scotland during the eighteenth century that specialized in reprinting books originally released in London. Even though the London publishers treated these as piracies, their attempts to bring action against such reprints in Scottish courts were unsuccessful.

In the United States, the basis for both federal copyright and patent legislation was established in Article 1 of the Constitution, which held that "Congress shall have Power . . . To promote the Progress of Science and useful Arts, by securing for limited Times to Authors and Inventors the exclusive Right to their respective Writings and Discoveries," and this authority was realized in 1790 when the first Congress enacted a copyright statute closely modeled after the Statute of Anne. Yet despite the fact that the United States thus established copyright law in advance of most European countries, it only protected American books published by domestic publishers—meaning that for a full century, until the United States passed an international copyright law in 1891, American publishers were free to reprint British and other foreign books. And the establishment of federal copyright notwithstanding, according to Meredith McGill, early literary culture in nineteenth-century America was highly decentralized, with each major city functioning as a regional publishing center, and trade in reprinted British literature as one of the few unifying features. McGill insists on using the term reprint rather than piracy for this widespread appropriation, since it was entirely legal under US law.[27]

The reading public was hardly averse to reprints, given that they kept costs low. When Charles Dickens came to the United States in 1842, he was enthusiastically welcomed by a mass readership facilitated by such editions. Rather than viewing this popularity as its own reward, however, he spoke out in favor of international copyrights. Compounding the perceived infractions, even his account of the trip, *American Notes,* appeared in an unauthorized US edition to which the publisher appended an "Appeal to the Reading Public" that defended reprints based on affordability and therefore broader access.[28] Obviously recognizing the futility of his complaints, Dickens changed course with a subsequent visit in 1868, where he made a substantial amount of money from public readings.[29] From the contemporary perspective, it is

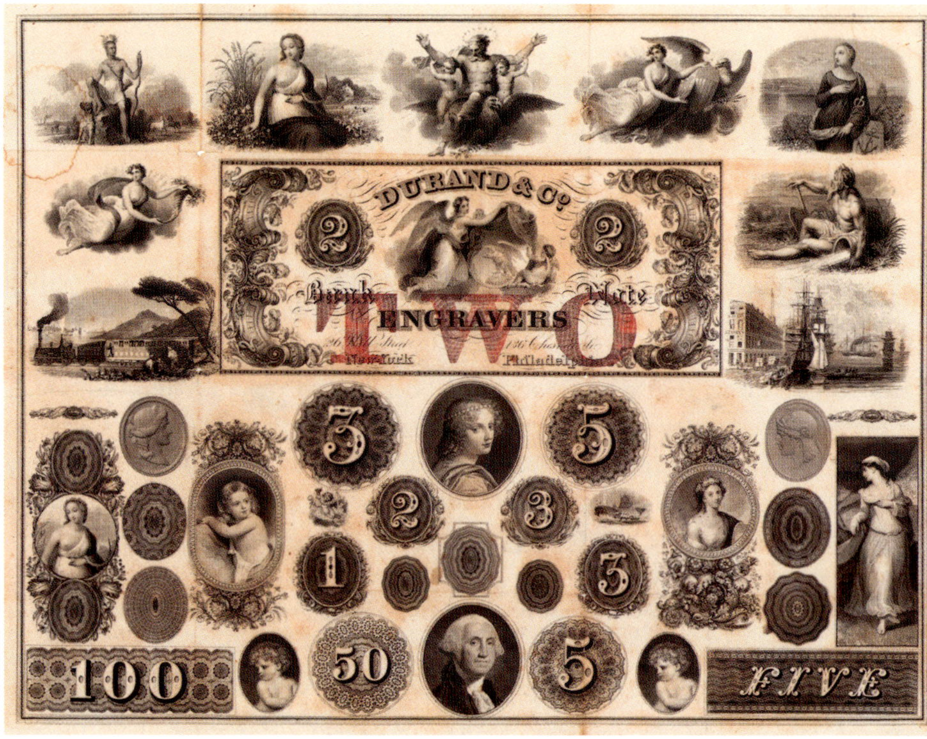

FIGURE 9
Durand & Co. bank note engravers, print showing a sample bank note surrounded by vignettes of allegorical scenes, portraits, including George Washington, numbers, and various designs, possibly engraved by Cyrus Durand or Asher B. Durand between 1824 and 1840. Library of Congress.

interesting to note how this maneuver foreshadowed the focus on concert-tour revenue necessitated during recent years by rampant recirculation of recorded music.

Different timelines for developments in the reproducibility of printed text and imagery draw attention not only to initial distinctions in how copyright protections might apply to each form, but also their shifting roles in relation to one another. "While type could easily be reset," McGill points out, "engravings were more difficult and expensive to reproduce, enabling publishers to secure property in their texts by investing heavily in ornamental plates."[30] Closely related to this form of "proprietary illustration" was a new category of gift books, with little connection between word and image.

Engraved banknotes produced by nineteenth-century American painter Asher Durand provide further evidence of efforts to harness print technology to create inherent limits on reproducibility. According to Jennifer Roberts, the combination of his designs and his brother's innovations in machine engraving helped counteract counterfeiting through elaborate, difficult-to-reproduce designs known as "security printing" (figure 9).[31] In keeping with the localized economies of the era, however, such notes were closely tied to their place of origin: their value was backed by silver or gold held by the issuing bank, and since they could only be redeemed at that venue, their authority diminished as they became removed geographically.[32] In turn, this absence of a shared national currency hampered early attempts to distribute magazines through the mail, adding one more challenge to those already posed by widespread copying of content by other publications.

Such decentralization meant that early nineteenth-century authors often had little control over how or where their work appeared. According to McGill, "The regional and ephemeral nature of most of the periodicals in which Poe and Hawthorne published in the 1830s and '40s, and the availability of their texts for unauthorized reprinting, meant that complete or even coherent bodies of their work were unavailable to readers. Authors themselves had difficulty determining exactly where, in what formats, and how extensively their poems and tales circulated."[33] Given that these practices arose in the context of regionalized print distribution, there are surprising echoes of today's internet circulation of memes and other material, where even with modern search functions it is often difficult to identify a definitive source or point of origin.

Many of the debates prompted by the nineteenth-century culture of reprinting remain relevant. One was the idea that free circulation of texts plays a critical role promoting democracy. An equally important aspect of US copyright history is the shifting balance of cultural production, with the United States initially supporting relatively short terms and not offering protection for foreign works. Only in 1891, at a point when domestic producers had more to lose from foreign reprints, did the United States recognize international copyright. That same opportunistic relationship to copyright protection persisted within specific industries, with US motion picture companies treating literary sources, particularly nonfiction, as stockpiles to be freely mined, but taking a far more protectionist attitude toward the films that resulted.[34] There were also compelling questions about the significance of publication: should it be understood as the point when authorship is declared, and therefore secured, or should the emphasis be on publication as an act of sharing that transforms the work into public property?

CREATION OF LITERARY PROPERTY

Debates about the nature of literary property went hand-in-hand with copyright's establishment as a legal principle. Where did literature come from? If it was simply a rearrangement of language that already exists (an argument foreshadowing Jacques Derrida's "always already"), how could that be reconciled with a conception of the author as a creative originator? Mark Rose has traced a series of tensions in these discussions. One line of reasoning was based on occupancy—claiming that which was previously unclaimed—but this argument ran counter to a romantic notion of the author as the creator of something new, and therefore as its first possessor. Equally important was the conception of where the work stands in the interface between author and the world: was the work simply a mirror of nature (with the author as conduit), or did it embody the personality of the creator?[35]

Land ownership was an obvious point of comparison, both for the model of perpetual property, and the ability to derive income from its exploitation, including frequent references to John Locke's labor theory of property acquisition. According to this framework, there is initially no private ownership, but the labor needed to move land out of a state of nature is the basis for its transformation into property. The creation of literary works through intellectual labor applied to a shared vocabulary would therefore support proprietary claims. However, Locke himself drew distinctions between different forms of property in a 1694 commentary where he argued in favor of limited ownership periods for literature.[36] Conventions developed in relation to patents likewise presented a crucial counterpoint to perpetual property models, with exclusive rights to an invention limited specifically so that others could subsequently build or improve upon the initial concept and, in so doing, provide an important societal benefit.[37]

What is now known as the idea/expression dichotomy also has its roots in a lively eighteenth-century discourse about how to draw distinctions between the physical book, the words printed on its pages, and the ideas thus conveyed. Martha Woodmansee quotes from a 1753 definition that elaborates numerous contributors to a book: "The scholar and the writer, the papermaker, the type founder, the typesetter and printer, the proofreader, the publisher, the book binder, sometimes even the gilder and the brass-worker, etc."[38] Thus the focus on the author as the primary generator of this mode of property was not necessarily a given. The moment of publication was also crucial, since it made something public that would otherwise be private, and in the process, enabled those who acquired the book to appropriate the ideas it contained through the act of reading.

The significance of creative genius emerged with particular strength in German debates, even though copyright law as such developed relatively slowly, in large part due to a division of power among many separate principalities. Edward Young's 1759 "Conjectures on Original Composition," which posited literary compositions as unique, original works, reflecting the brilliance of their creators (in contrast to imitation), found fertile ground, with two separate German translations within two years of its initial publication.[39] But one of the most sustained analyses was articulated by Johann Gottlieb Fichte, a follower of Kant, whose 1793 essay "Proof of the Illegality of Reprinting: A Rationale and a Parable" built its argument against unauthorized copying via an investigation of the nature of literary property.

The issue Fichte set out to address was the question of ownership over something that cannot be physically appropriated. As outlined by Fichte, a book combines elements that are alienable, shareable, and inalienable. The buyer of a book acquires a tangible thing. The ideas are not, however, simply attained via purchase; rather, the owner of the book has to read and engage with a book's content in order to take possession of them, and to the extent that multiple readers participate in this fashion, the ideas become "the common property of many."[40] Thus Fichte made an early case for the distinction between idea and expression central to modern copyright regimes. The author and the reader are both rightful owners of the thoughts thus conveyed, yet this does not change the author's claim over the form through which those concepts were articulated, with readers necessarily retransmitting the ideas they acquire in an altered form.

Although a key rationale for copyright presented in the Statute of Anne was the larger cultural good associated with support for authors, Mario Biagioli has stressed how Fichte rejected a justification based on utility and instead framed his argument around natural law.[41] Building on a romantic conception of unique, individual expression, Fichte asserted perpetual ownership over the aspects or elements of a book that are inalienable. The physical book is alienable—with purchasers having the right to manipulate or dispose of it as they please. But, Fichte argued, the form of the ideas can never be appropriated, since understanding the ideas means making them one's own and inevitably altering their form (in contrast to verbatim copying, or mere plagiarism). Within this nexus, the printer acquired neither the author's rightful property (the work's form) nor the ideas, but merely the work's usufruct—referring to a prerogative to enjoy the use of another's property, without actually changing its character. The usufruct was also what was stolen when a text was reprinted without authorization.[42]

In somewhat of an aside, Fichte considered how his arguments, centered on text, would translate into the visual realm when applied to reproductive prints. For Fichte, the interpretation required to copy a work of visual art qualified it as a new form: "They end up as engravings and not paintings."[43] And he even extended the argument to include an engraving after another engraving, asserting that a unique form would be unavoidable in a handmade copy. In the visual realm, he concluded, the term "reprint" would apply only to multiple prints pulled from the same plate.

This brief point of comparison indicates one of the major challenges associated with the expansion of copyright beyond its origins as a response to the marketplace for printed books. For literary works, the author's expression was identified with an arrangement of words, largely disconnected from how those words were presented through the dynamics of type set on a page. Books might be illegally reprinted, and the expression of the author plagiarized, but the term "forgery" generally does not apply, in contrast to its use to denounce unauthorized replicas of visual works.

Even within the textual realm, however, there was still the challenge posed by translation. As late as 1853, Harriet Beecher Stowe was unsuccessful in a copyright infringement claim concerning a German translation of *Uncle Tom's Cabin* sold in the United States. According to Judge Robert Grier of the Third Circuit Court of Appeals, "the same conceptions clothed in another language cannot constitute the same composition; nor can it be called a transcript or 'copy' of the same 'book.'"[44] In the United States, this specific point of ambiguity regarding derivative material was addressed in 1870, when Congress enacted revisions to the Copyright Act covering translation and dramatization rights. Yet each expansion of copyright to cover additional media—

starting with the 1735 Engraver's Act in England and continuing with the ever-widening scope of present-day coverage—requires a new set of definitions regarding both the identity of the work and what constitutes its reproduction. Given the degree of difficulty of establishing these principles in response to printed text, copyright's foundational example, it is hardly surprising that every move to broaden those protections brings fresh challenges.

RIGHTS OF THE AUTHOR

The natural law argument evident in the German dialogue eventually became the basis for an important point of contrast with respect to how Anglo-American and continental European copyright systems address the relationship between work and author. In England and the United States, both largely governed by common law, there was a strong emphasis on utility: providing authors and inventors with compensation for their work is good not only for individual creators, but for the society that will benefit from encouraging their pursuits. Areas of continental Europe with civil codes based on Roman or Napoleonic law, by contrast, have given much greater priority to a natural law justification that stresses the innate connection between work and creator. The current French legal code is particularly notable for its detailed elaboration of forms of authorial prerogative now widely known as personality or moral rights.

The French version of the privilege system, which dated to the fifteenth century, came to an abrupt end in 1789, with freedom of the press established as an early revolutionary principle, followed by the abolition of the book guild in 1791. Similar to the British Stationers' Company, the Paris book guild had enjoyed a monopoly over book trade based on royal patronage, printing works "avec permission et privilege du Roi." A postrevolutionary act of 1793 established literary and artistic property—and also, by extension, the public domain, once works lost protection ten years after the author's death. But certain aspects of moral rights (integrity, paternity, disclosure) were articulated incrementally over the course of the nineteenth century. Similar to elsewhere, the scope of protection gradually expanded, with sculptors and designers added in 1902, and a major consolidation in 1957.

Even though the privilege system was decisively upended by the revolution, certain aspects of postrevolutionary legislation can be traced to prerevolutionary customs, particularly traditions developed around the Comédie-Française during the seventeenth and eighteenth centuries, which allowed playwrights to be involved in decisions about how their work was recast for later versions even when they were not receiving additional income from a revival production. In this respect, according to Susan Liemer, the "eighteenth century playwright was essentially exercising the right of integrity separately from any ownership claim to income derived from the work."[45] Immediately following the French Revolution, some of these playwrights successfully proposed legislation, passed into law in 1791, requiring written consent from the author when a play was performed, and giving heirs ownership over the work for five years following a playwright's death—after which it would become "public property," or public domain.[46] Two years later, a 1793 law provided similar rights to a far wider range of authors and their heirs, and these rights were in turn incorporated into the Napoleonic code of 1804.

As eventually consolidated into law in 1957, the French code recognizes a series of rights, some of which are economic in nature and limited in their duration, and some, under the category of moral rights, that are both inalienable and perpetual (lasting the lifetime of the author and passed down to heirs or even certain third parties). The four basic moral rights are the rights of integrity, attribution, disclosure, and withdrawal. Of these, integrity tends to get the most attention, in the context of cases involving attempts by artists and other authors to prevent the alteration or destruction of their work. However, the others are interrelated, since they encompass the rights of authors to decide or declare whether something is their work, and to assert that something is not a work, including disowning an example that has been altered or damaged. The United States, by contrast, adopted moral rights legislation far later, and with a relatively limited scope. Moral rights were only incorporated into US federal law with the 1990 Visual Artists Rights Act (VARA)—legislation that is limited, as the name indicates, to works of visual art and, more specifically, to unique objects and certain limited editions. VARA also includes provisions allowing artists to waive its protections, and the rights end upon the death of the artist.

Copyright and moral rights are intertwined yet distinct. Copyright's ostensible focus is economic (though that is not always how it is deployed), whereas moral rights prioritize the ability of creators to exert control over the ongoing life of their work. Moral rights protections generally emanate from two key assumptions. One is that creative works embody cultural values that extend above and beyond their property status. The second is a romantic conception of authorial privilege that stresses the creator's expression of personality through the work. There is an understandable desire by authors to shape how their work can be employed, including resistance to assimilation into commercial agendas or other potentially cynical uses. But giving authors or their heirs too much control over how others respond to their work can profoundly curtail vital forms of creative and critical discourse. In jurisdictions where moral rights are perpetual, their duration after the death of the original creator provides the legal foundation for heirs having authority over the work, including matters of reinterpretation and determinations of authenticity. The unfortunate corollary to perpetual moral rights is also a more limited public domain.[47]

In a counterpoint to the tendency to blame romantic ideals of authorship for overly expansive copyright restrictions, however, Lionel Bently has argued the opposite—that if authorial interests, rather than those of publishers, had been consistently favored, copyright history would have had a very different trajectory.[48] From copyright's early articulation in the Statute of Anne to the present day, the rhetoric associated with promoting its protections as a benefit for authors has often functioned as a cover for commercial interests. This divergence is particularly evident in the push for ever-longer copyright duration, now set at the lifetime of the author plus seventy years in many jurisdictions, with the impact of these extended terms often little different than perpetual copyright. The international copyright protocol known as the Berne Convention, first established in 1886, has been instrumental in promoting minimum copyright terms of the life of the author plus fifty years, default copyright that is automatic upon publication (rather than requiring affirmative registration), and a crucial articulation of moral rights in article 6*bis*. Although the United States did not join the Berne Convention until 1989 (and even then with severe limitations on its adherence to moral rights), default copyright was instituted with the 1976 revisions to the copyright code, and terms have been repeatedly lengthened. Many of these shifts, including the removal of registration requirements, or even publication with notice, have greatly extended the scope of this form of property, making it the default assumption that a work is born into copyright, rather than entering the world as part of the public domain unless actively protected. Thus potential copyright claims are everywhere, even as relatively few are positioned to reap substantial gains from exploiting these intangible resources.

GLOBAL IP

Intellectual property's initial trajectory—from aristocratic privilege to national law in England and various European countries, and a founding constitutional principle in the United States—might appear to indicate an inevitable path, with protections driven by both technological and marketplace developments. Globally, however, the story is very different. For many countries outside of Europe, intellectual property laws were instituted as part of colonial rule, rather than emanating from regional traditions. This dynamic has been reinforced by international pressure to adhere to major treaties, starting with the Berne Convention and continuing with World Trade Organization (WTO) insistence that developing nations draft intellectual property laws in conformity with the 1994 Agreement on Trade Related Aspects of Intellectual Property (TRIPS). In contrast to Anglo-American and European contexts, where the legal framework gradually evolved in response to internal economic and technological developments, international agreements required developing nations to adopt comprehensive IP laws by 2005 or face potential sanctions. Even though a major stated goal was, once again, supporting the rights of creators and inventors, additional emphasis on preventing digital piracy reveals a focus on protecting IP emanating from developed nations. Tellingly, the United States has been a particularly strong advocate for TRIPS protection to prevent duplication of entertainment media, computer programs, and pharmaceuticals.

The most striking counterpoint to the Anglo-European trajectory is presented by China, with its long history of technological innovations and relatively recent embrace of intellectual property protocols. Early Chinese developments could arguably have established the need for intellectual property regulation, independent of Western interactions. However, pioneering inventions with respect to paper, moveable type, and ink were not matched by equivalent legislation. There has also been a substantial history of IP intervention, as Western pressure to institute trademark, patent, and copyright legislation followed upon the forced opening of trade during the Opium Wars of the nineteenth century. According to William Alford's classic account of Chinese IP, the 1883 Paris Convention agreements on patent and trademark, along with the 1886 Berne Convention regarding copyright, led foreign merchants to expect trademark integrity in their dealings with China, even though China was not part of the accords.[49]

Although various laws were enacted over the course of the twentieth century, China's current copyright regime dates only to the 1980s.[50] Treaties that China made with Britain and the United States in 1902 and 1903 called for trademark protection based on a system of registration that would need to be established, but negotiations dragged out, with China rejecting a British regulation draft filled with details that put British interests first, and other European countries pushing against a subsequent proposal from China's Ministry of Commerce that was seen as too closely tied to Anglo-American models. Therefore it was not only disagreements between China and Western nations about how to proceed, but also between competing common law and civil law regimes, that helped to delay implementation of Chinese trademark law until 1923. Even then, Alford suggests, it was "more in name than fact," due to the mismatch between Western expectations and the existing legal system.[51] Countering suggestions that delayed implementation can be attributed to cultural incompatibility, however, Peter Yu has stressed both the long history of foreign exploitation and, in the modern context, isolationist tendencies after the 1949 establishment of the People's Republic of China.[52]

China became increasingly identified with the production of unauthorized goods following the reopening of trade relations in the 1970s. As in the United States during the nineteenth century, however, there was limited enthusiasm for paying royalties to foreign interests.[53] Dickens undoubtedly would have been amused at American outrage over Chinese IP violations, once the United States was no longer a developing nation.[54] Given the notoriety of Chinese copies and fakes, as well as substantial international pressure on China around IP issues, it is equally important to recognize the very short history of modern Chinese IP law, which began with trademark protection established in 1982, followed by patent law in 1984 and copyright in 1990. These still-recent laws were extensively rewritten in 2000–01, in advance of China joining the WTO in 2001, in part to conform with associated obligations under TRIPS.[55] Pushing back on the narrative of China as an IP outlaw, Yu points out that, by the second decade of the twenty-first century, China had signed a higher number of World Intellectual Property Organization (WIPO) treaties than the United States.[56] In addition, there have been substantial efforts to alter Chinese consumer attitudes toward fakes and counterfeits.[57]

China's increasing focus on shaping both internal law and external agreements to align with its agenda and needs is evident in the decision to join a group of developing countries in 2006 to cosponsor a proposed amendment to TRIPS, Article 29*bis,* that would require patent applications to disclose where biological material was obtained. The requirement was clearly framed in response to Western patent claims based on traditional medicines and seed stocks (frequently described as biopiracy), which are only the latest manifestation of a long history of European and North American creators and inventors incorporating material borrowed from other cultural contexts. China then went ahead with a 2008 patent law revision that created a similar requirement for disclosure of traditional knowledge and genetic material upon which an application is based.[58] With these moves, China took a leadership role in addressing a major area of tension when IP codes based on modern Western conceptions of authorship are applied to traditional practices, where there has long been a bias toward treating communally developed forms as part of the public domain.

Given that all creative work builds upon past developments, the task of separating out specific elements to be protected from the substrata of shared conventions is never straightforward. But for traditional forms, there is often a double agenda of how to recognize individual creative contributions to a living set of practices and the need to protect entire genres from exploitation by outside interests. Unwritten or unfixed genres, including songs, myths, dances, and various types of design present a challenge to copyright's typical fixation requirement. And it can be equally problematic when a nation-state asserts ownership over traditional forms understood to be communal in nature. Pioneering studies of IP issues in Indonesia and Ghana point to a series of interlinked challenges associated with attempts to align current IP standards and traditional cultural expressions.

Some of these tensions are evident in Indonesia's 2002 copyright law, prompted by the need to conform to TRIPS, which included atypical provisions granting perpetual state-controlled copyright for folklore, along with state guardianship over copyright interests for a period of fifty years when individual creators are not identified. One of the cross-cultural problems, according to Lorraine Aragon, was the frequent absence of a Western version of "authorship consciousness," with Indonesian communities generally not seeking the "erasure of the multiple sources contributing to any creative work," and therefore not conforming to "the required legal fiction of authorship."[59] Another basic mismatch, encountered in research pursued by Aragon and James Leach, was the refusal of artists "to define themselves as the 'creators' of their works," with both Hindu and Muslim artists claiming to be merely "followers" of ancestral traditions while "the term creator . . . is applicable only to God."[60] In addition to the emphasis on individual invention, Western IP requirements for originality or novelty are potentially at odds with cultural forms based on carrying forward ancestral traditions.

The Indonesian solution granted the state "copyright over *folklore* and products of people's culture that are owned in common," including "stories, epics, myths, legends,

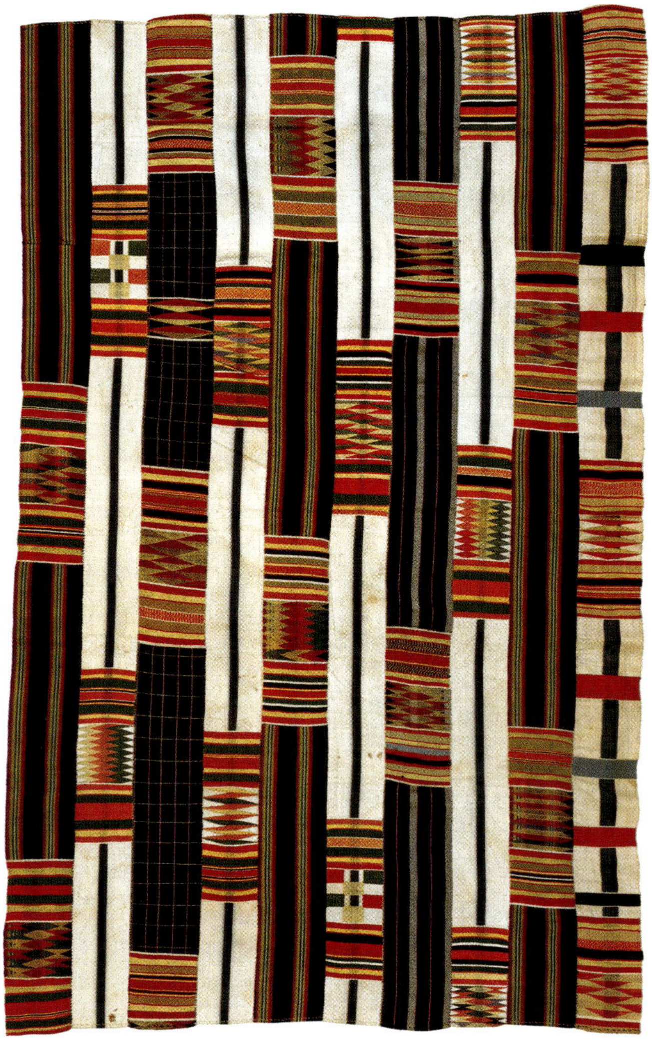

FIGURE 10
Wrapper, Asante artist, Ghana, early twentieth century. Cotton, silk, indigo dye, natural dye, synthetic dye, $51\frac{15}{16} \times 34\frac{3}{4}$ in. National Museum of African Art. Photo: Franko Khoury, National Museum of African Art, Smithsonian Institution.

chronicles, songs, handicrafts, choreography, dances, calligraphy, and other art works."[61] One motivation for this protectionism was fear of foreign cultural appropriation, including IP claims. Yet the state assertion of ownership rights raised other concerns regarding control over local cultural traditions, including a Balinese dancer who asked, "Imagine if our troupe wanted to perform an old work and had to ask permission of the state?"[62] The various interests at play include state-sponsored promotion of traditional cultural forms as part of an appeal to global tourism.[63] As Aragon and Leach point out, these tensions are central to participation in international protocols: "When international institutions such as WIPO speak of using IP legal solutions to protect 'local' knowledge and cultural expressions, they, in fact, mean 'national' ones."[64]

In Ghana, a similar pull between recognizing individual contributions and the wish to protect an entire genre comes into play around textile designs. Both adinkra and kente cloth reflect a long tradition of creative input, which Boatema Boateng has described as a conscious sense of collaboration with past creators, including both recent and early pioneers (figure 10).[65] Even so, the designation of certain designs for the Asante ruler could be understood as something akin to copyright, or at the very least its precursor in aristocratic privilege. Although the Asante ethnic group is dominant in Ghana, which distinguishes it from countries where the protection of traditional cultural expressions is part of wider efforts to respond to the needs of a minority group, Boateng argues that this advantage does not necessarily prevent marginalization in relation to the interests of the nation state.[66]

One enduring tension is the problem of understanding the nuances of individual contributions to communal traditions. Adinkra and kente cloth production, as described by Boateng, is "neither solely communal nor solely individual," and the creative processes "also transcend time as measured in individual lives," meaning that "they cannot be adequately captured by an exclusive focus on living cloth producers."[67] There is a significant irony, she suggests, in the willingness of industrialized nations to extend the enlightenment emphasis on the individual so that corporations can be granted the status of "legal person," even as the same system is unable to adapt its categories to more diffuse communities.[68] To the extent that indigenous cultural production is understood as communal in nature, belonging to no individual, it is also, if protected according to custodianship principles, inalienable.[69] The question of who can claim ownership over work that inevitably draws from cultural precedents—already a major challenge in the Anglo-American and European traditions where copyright arose—takes another turn when protection of a genre potentially results in a refusal to acknowledge individual contributions, along with payment streams that are claimed for state coffers. In a transaction involving music, Paul Simon paid a $16,000 royalty to the Ghana Copyright Administration for permission to use the song "Yaa Amponsah" on his 1990 album *The Rhythm of the Saints.* But even though Simon identified the work as the composition of a specific individual, Kwame Asare, also known as Jacob Sam, the National Commission on Culture declared it "anonymous folklore" based on characteristics shared with similar melodies.[70]

Frictions between traditional cultural expressions and legal structures imposed by modern nation-states are potentially even more complex in countries such as the United States, Australia, and New Zealand, where dominant power is in the hands of colonial settlers. Attempts to make amends for past abuse include Australia's 1984 Aboriginal and Torres Strait Islander Heritage Protection Act, intended to assist "in the preservation and protection of places, areas and objects of particular significance to Indigenous Australians," and, in the United States, the 1990 Native American Graves Protection and Repatriation Act, which allows tribes to seek the return of both human remains and sacred objects.[71]

In the context of Australian Aboriginal paintings, an interest in the art itself has been accompanied by frequent acts of appropriation. A series of late-twentieth-century court cases demonstrated not only the challenges associated with addressing these abuses via a legal system based on British conventions, but also links between intellectual property and land rights. Two crucial cases concerned the work of Johnny Bulunbulun, in response to reproductions of his paintings used on t-shirts and to create textile designs. Defending Bulunbulun's copyright required countering long-held assumptions that Aboriginal paintings were too embedded in folkloric tradition to meet copyright's originality requirement. At the same time, however, the need to frame the work in terms of individual creativity ran counter to its very nature. As explained by Colin Golvan, who represented Bulunbulun in both copyright cases, artistic traditions are owned collectively, and tribal members decide who is permitted to depict specific designs. But those individuals do not, in turn, have the authority to grant permission for reproductions of their work; such licensing rights are reserved for tribal owners collectively.[72]

The first of the two Bulunbulun lawsuits, from 1989, was settled shortly before going to trial in exchange for a substantial payment from the t-shirt company.[73] The initial case established the basic principle that Aboriginal art was protected by copyright, but the second, *Bulun Bulun and Milpurrurru v. R & T Textiles,* argued in 1997 and decided in 1998, provided a more significant precedent with respect to how it navigated the two systems. In the second lawsuit, concerning a textile design based on Bulunbulun's *Magpie geese and waterlilies at the waterhole* (figure 11), both the arguments presented to the court and the decision by judge John von Doussa looked for ways to reconcile Western copyright's emphasis on individual creativity with Aboriginal collective ownership. Under the Australian Copyright Act, the copyright holder is generally an individual author, unless the example conforms to the act's definition of a joint work. Because the painting was not a joint work as specified by law, the Ganalbingu people could not hold the copyright communally. However, the court created a Western work-around, finding that there was a fiduciary relationship whereby Bulunbulun was allowed to use traditional Ganalbingu knowledge to create his work, and that generated obligations for Bulunbulun in turn. If Bulunbulun, or any other artist from the community, did not take action to protect their work against unauthorized reproduction, then the Ganalbingu would be able to step in and pursue a copyright infringement case. Thus the decision established a second order of rights claims, even as it still gave priority to individual creators.[74]

The most provocative aspect of *Bulun Bulun and Milpurrurru v. R & T Textiles,* however, was the reference to "native title" in arguments initially presented to the court. This explicit association between painting and land rights was fully consistent with their interconnected nature in Aboriginal customs and beliefs, but more immediately, it potentially linked the IP issues to a then-recent case that significantly transformed the status of Aboriginal land claims. Prior to 1992, Aboriginal land was treated as unoccupied, or *terra nullius* ("nobody's land"), and therefore property of the Crown unless

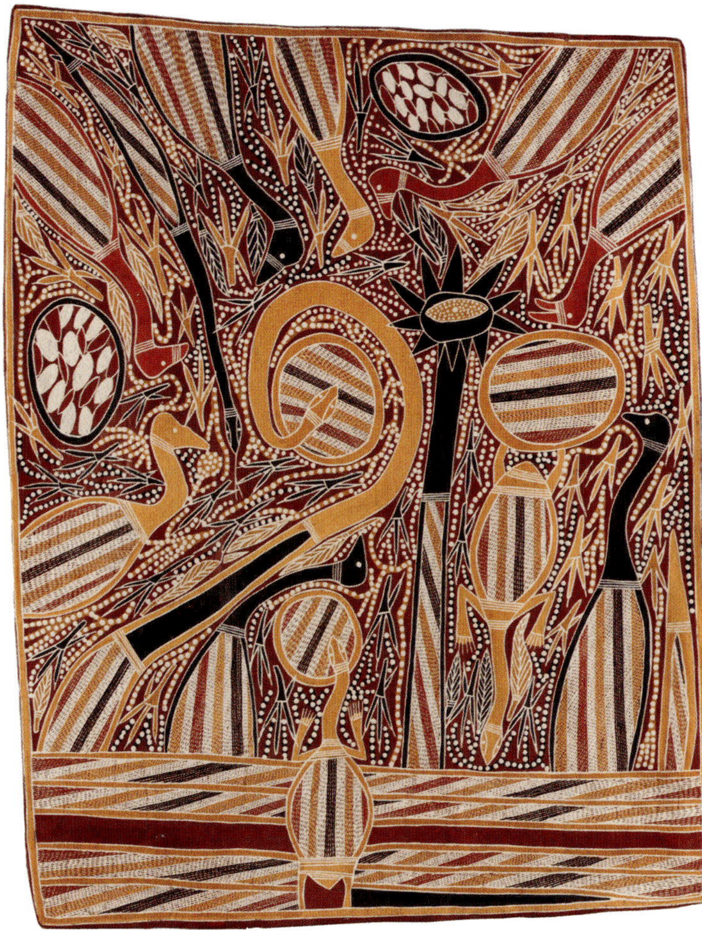

FIGURE 11
Johnny Bulunbulun, *Magpie geese and waterlilies at the waterhole*, 1980. Ochres on bark, 39⅝ × 31⅜ in. Museum and Art Gallery of the Northern Territory. © Johnny Bulunbulun/Copyright Agency. Licensed by Artists Rights Society (ARS), New York, 2019.

subject to conventional ownership documentation. But the High Court ruling in *Mabo and Others v. Queensland* recognized indigenous peoples' common-law claims to land they had traditionally inhabited, and the government was therefore required to demonstrate absence of occupation or voluntary abandonment as a condition for asserting ownership.[75] The common-law doctrine of native title was then codified with the 1993 Native Title Act, which established procedures for recognizing and protecting indigenous lands through the court systems, including a National Native Title Tribunal to assess new registration claims.

Since an ongoing connection to the land was crucial for establishing native title, then Aboriginal paintings could potentially serve as one form of evidence due to their references to specific places and associated traditions. But the ruling in *Bulun Bulun and Milpurrurru v. R & T Textiles* insistently separated the two issues, based on the fact that copyright and land claims were administered by different courts. Though he was prepared to find a creative way to address communal IP ownership, von Doussa explicitly distinguished IP and land claims. "The principle that ownership of land and ownership of artistic works are separate statutory and common law institutions," he found, "is a fundamental principle of the Australian legal system."[76]

From early applications of Locke's labor theory of property to the present, there have been many highly opportunistic constructions of what is unowned and, by extension, who can claim ownership. Exploitation of traditional cultural innovations has often been justified by treating collectively shared knowledge and artistic conventions as part of the public domain. But problems with this type of virtual land grab are particularly evident when the assertions operate on a cross-cultural basis, made from the vantage point of countries with long-established IP laws. Claims by nation states, instituted with the goal of protecting traditional cultural expressions, have been one response. But Golvan has also posited an alternate understanding of the public domain in relation to Aboriginal community property. Both cultural expressions and land could be described as a form of public domain *within* a specific community, but not available to outsiders, and with communal ownership as perpetual in nature.[77] This alternate framework, more in keeping with the principle of the commons, could support collective control over traditions, but it does not fully mesh with role of the public domain as a crucial counterpoint to increasingly restrictive ownership regimes promoted by Western IP interests. Nonetheless, defining either cultural expressions or land as nobody's property in order to justify later ownership is diametrically opposed to the goals associated with an expansive public domain.

EXTENSION AND DIFFUSION

Molly Nesbit opened her 1987 essay on French authorship and copyright by pronouncing that the French definition of the author had "gone vague," becoming "too diffuse to be useful" as it was stretched to apply to multiple activities besides writing.[78] Since then, the challenges have become even more dramatic, with copyright laws continuing to be recast in response to evolving digital transmission. The expansion of copyright and all types of IP protection has to be viewed from a number of perspectives. One is the export of Anglo-American and European copyright conventions to other regions (even as key differences between the two traditions have remained in play). The other series of vicissitudes referenced by Nesbit is the trajectory whereby national laws originating in protections for printed texts have been repeatedly extended to cover an ever-greater range of forms.

Even though the widening purview of copyright protection has a distinct history from country to country, changes to US code indicate some of the shared challenges. It is worth remembering that the first US copyright legislation enacted in 1790—based closely on the Statute of Anne—was limited to books, maps, and charts, which were protected for fourteen years, with a potential fourteen-year renewal period. Over the nineteenth century its scope was repeatedly augmented, covering prints (1802), musical compositions (1831), dramatic works, including public performance rights (1856), photographs (1865), visual art (1870), rights over derivative works, particularly translations and dramatizations (1870), copyright relations with foreign countries (1891), and public performance rights for musical compositions (1897). Initial copyright terms were also lengthened to twenty-eight years in 1831. As this list suggests, expanding coverage was motivated not only by new inventions (such as photography) but also the increasing importance of commercial markets for a range of cultural goods.

During the twentieth and twenty-first centuries, US copyright updates were typically prompted by new technologies. Although congress attempted to craft a comprehensive approach with a major new copyright act in 1909, it already had to be amended by 1912 to cover motion pictures. Compulsory licensing provisions of the 1909 act focused on player piano scrolls helped shape subsequent music industry norms, in part because, rather remarkably, it was not until 1972 that protection was extended to sound recordings (as opposed to the underlying musical composition thus immortalized). Increasingly long terms included an extension of the renewal period to twenty-eight years under the 1909 act (for a potential total of fifty-six) and a major copyright revision in 1976 that shifted the standard to the lifetime of the author plus fifty years thereafter. As an important corrective to this overall escalation, the 1976 act also incorporated a section codifying fair use exceptions that had previously been established on a piecemeal basis through the courts.

Although the 1976 act (which took effect in 1978) still provides the framework for current US copyright law, it has been repeatedly augmented, both in response to new technologies and to bring US law into conformity with international treaty obligations. Protection for computer programs in 1980 was followed by aspects of semiconductor chip design (mask works) in 1984 and rights associated with the digital transmission of sound recordings in 1995. A 1992 amendment attempted to address home recording technologies through a combination of indemnification for the companies selling the devices and an early version of anti-circumvention regulation. Coming from a rather different direction, the 1990 Visual Artists Rights Act instituted the first federal moral rights protection for certain types of visual work, and it was accompanied by newly established copyright for architecture. On the eve of the twenty-first century, the 1998 Copyright Term Extension Act prolonged copyright protection to the lifetime of the author plus seventy years, with ninety-five-year terms for many works published before 1978, and even longer for certain works for hire.[79] With equally far-reaching consequences for how individuals are allowed to interact with goods and services, the 1998 Digital Millennium Copyright Act—in conjunction with the 1996 WIPO copyright treaty it implemented—established greatly expanded anti-circumvention provisions along with the framework for now-ubiquitous takedown demands.

In an ultimately unsuccessful challenge to the Copyright Term Extension Act, Lawrence Lessig argued against the threat to the public domain posed by terms that were little different, in their impact, from perpetual copyright.[80] Perhaps there is some slight comfort to be had in the fact that terms were not extended anew before 2018, meaning that certain works first published in the United States in 1923 did finally enter the public domain in 2019 rather than having that status pulled away once again.[81] Yet that is no guarantee, since copyright extensions have typically applied to past as well as future works, meaning that material once in the public domain in the United States has frequently had copyright protection restored on a retroactive basis. Nor is the United States an outlier regarding duration, with many other countries extending the Berne Convention's minimum standard of life plus fifty years to seventy, and sometimes longer.

It is important to take a step back and consider the goals associated with copyright specifically, and IP in general. If the purpose of such laws is to enrich the many powerful interests surrounding creators, including corporations that succeed in gaining ownership rights over valuable properties, or various heirs who continue to speak for, and potentially distort, cultural legacies long after an author's death, then they are doing an admirable job. Yet there is no reason that the expansive reach of this highly artificial form of property should be treated as inevitable. The specific legal cases and conflicts explored in the following chapters indicate some of the ways that these dynamics are unfolding, including the multitude of IP strictures that individuals encounter, and potentially violate, on a daily basis.

In *Copyrights and Copywrongs,* Siva Vaidhyanathan's analysis of the scope of US copyright through the twentieth century led him to argue for "thin" copyright protection (just enough to give incentives to creators, without impeding creative exchange).[82] One of Lessig's responses, in addition to ongoing legal advocacy, has been his leadership of the Creative Commons initiative, which provides creators with model license agreements that enable them to set conditions for sharing and attribution of their work while clearly allowing various downstream uses. Overall, however, both IP in general and copyright in particular inescapably shape all facets of cultural production and consumption. In an era characterized by an excess of property relations, it is essential to interrogate exactly what interests are being served by expanding protections that were initially framed as providing compensation to individual creators or inventors in order to promote shared public interest. Legal standards that fail to acknowledge and support the many ways that existing works provide the foundation for future innovations fall woefully short of that goal.

2

THE APPROPRIATION GAME

THE POSSIBILITY THAT AN ARTIST'S vision might encompass a range of sources and voices, while their disparate origins (and perhaps destinations) remain evident, received a telling demonstration in a 1984 exhibition by Annette Lemieux (figure 12). A row of small relief constructions turned the colorful geometric pattern designed by Leo Lionni from the cover of MoMA's 1955 *Family of Man* catalogue into a physical frame, not for the Eugene Harris image of a piper from Peru on the original, but for photos taken by her father as a marine in Vietnam. An actual World War II military helmet carried a printed overlay of a verse from an anonymous German waltz. A grid of photos of hands conducting with the poetic yet descriptive title *Transmitting Sound* appeared next to an illuminated emergency beacon with the more unexpected name *Mother*. Lemieux described her decision as the result of a realization "that I could represent my voice in many different forms," but her wide-ranging series of associations and materials caused some viewers to mistake it for a group show, according to Lemieux's amused recollection.[1]

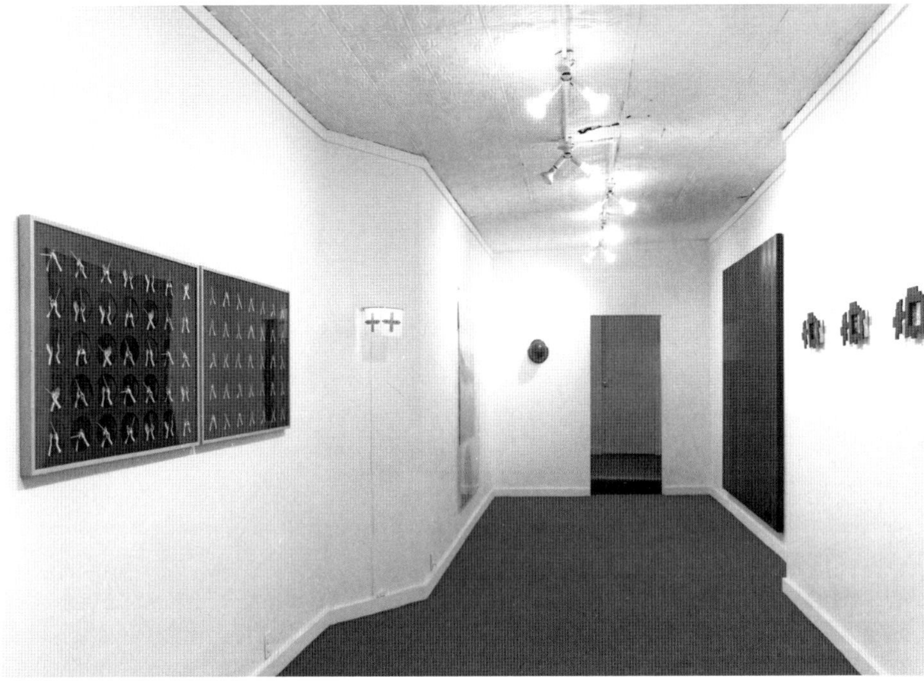

FIGURE 12
Annette Lemieux, installation view of solo exhibition, Cash/Newhouse Gallery, New York, 1984. Courtesy the artist.

The backdrop against which Lemieux developed her multivalent approach was a series of responses to an image-saturated media environment that Douglas Crimp immortalized in a 1977 exhibition called simply *Pictures*. Artists from the "pictures generation" were steeped in representation, both drawing upon and subverting an all-encompassing image culture. For a number of artists, that meant creating works that evoke familiar prototypes or situations. Others, including Lemieux, have engaged with sources that are extensively transformed and recontextualized, including disconcerting juxtapositions of divergent modes of address. And for some, the critique of originality has involved wholesale acts of appropriation.

Early cases brought against artists who insistently foregrounded strategies of appropriation quickly highlighted potential disparities between art-world interpretations of these practices and legal support for other authorship claims. They also drew attention to operations of authorship that far exceed copyright's purview. It is essential to consider how attempts to respond to the world of the already-encoded can run up against a range of intellectual property interests. But it is equally necessary to explore some of the more esoteric mechanisms whereby certain artists transform found material into high-value works of art, regardless of their own direct involvement in production or the inherent uniqueness of the expressions that result.

FAIR USE

In a landmark 1903 US case involving circus posters, Supreme Court Justice Oliver Wendell Holmes drew a distinction between different types of copying, stating that "Others are free to copy the original. They are not free to copy the copy. . . . The copy is the personal reaction of an individual upon nature."[2] But over the course of the twentieth century, the panorama to which artists were responding became inescapably filled with cultural markers ranging from trademarked goods to ubiquitous forms of copyright-protected media—with Andy Warhol's photo silkscreens from the early 1960s standing as an emblematic example of this shift. Although Warhol did face several claims from photographers whose imagery he incorporated into his silkscreen paintings, he quietly settled, thereby avoiding the uncertainty of a precedent-setting legal judgement. Since the late 1980s, however, a number of artists have chosen to defend themselves in court, asserting the principle that any response to the contemporary cultural landscape will necessarily incorporate various forms of protected imagery, but also demonstrating, in the process, the potential mismatch between critical approbation and legal judgments. In particular, lawsuits involving appropriation have tested the scope of the fair use exception to the US copyright code for criticism and commentary.

Fair use provisions in the United States (and related "fair dealing" elsewhere) provide an important corrective to copyright claims that would otherwise restrict many vital forms of response or interaction. As established first in common law, then codified in the 1976 Copyright Act, US law specifies that "the fair use of a copyrighted work . . . for purposes such as criticism, comment, news reporting, teaching . . . scholarship, or research, is not an infringement of copyright," and it lists four factors to be taken into consideration: "(1) the purpose and character of the use, including whether such use is of a commercial nature or is for nonprofit educational purposes; (2) the nature of the copyrighted work; (3) the amount and substantiality of the portion used in relation to the copyrighted work as a whole; and (4) the effect of the use upon the potential market for or value of the copyrighted work." The open-ended nature of these criteria, however, including questions about the relative significance of each, leaves substantial room for both interpretation and litigation.[3] With their varied outcomes, relatively infrequent fair use cases highlight not only potential ambiguities in the application of this essential principle, but also the fact that mounting a defense against even an obviously unfounded cease-and-desist letter generally requires hiring a lawyer.

Some of the evident limitations will be apparent not only via the descriptions that follow, but also from what's missing. In academic publishing—one area where criticism, comment, scholarship, and research clearly pertain—a general reluctance to put fair use principles to the test has reinforced a "permissions culture."[4] As a consequence, many works from key court cases could not be illustrated in this book, due to the impossibility of obtaining explicit authorization from artists or their representatives. But readers will hopefully appreciate the irony that most of those examples can be readily viewed by means of a simple Google search, since restrictions that have curtailed their publication here have not reduced their wider circulation.

All creative work necessarily builds upon earlier expressions, with explicit forms of quotation and reference as part of a larger continuum. But theoretical speculation regarding originality and authorship provoked by wholesale acts of appropriation does not necessarily establish the foundation for successful legal arguments—as Jeff Koons found when he took to the courts to defend his use of a photograph by Art Rogers that had been reproduced on a greeting card as the basis for his 1988 *String of Puppies* sculpture, losing at both the district court level and later on appeal.[5] The work in question, from Koons's 1988 *Banality* show, was one of a series of wood and ceramic sculptures fabricated for him by skilled artisans. Despite dramatic alterations in scale and medium associated with the shift from a small black-and-white photo to a large, polychrome sculpture, the courts found the two works "substantially similar." Moreover, Koons's lawyers failed to persuade either the district court or the court of appeals to give him precedence based on his participation in the rarified fine art world, finding that the gallery sales of Koons's work meant that it, too, like Rogers's card, could be described as commercial in nature. Another challenge was the fact that the large sculptural work (over five feet wide) was presented to the court via a photograph, therefore appearing more closely equivalent to the small greeting-card image than if viewed in person. Nor did Koons help his cause with rather glib responses when asked to explain the significance of the work.

Not long after Koons's 1992 appeals court loss, however, the US Supreme Court's 1994 decision in *Campbell v. Acuff-Rose Music, Inc.*, gave some reason for hope, even in situations involving direct copying or sampling. Finding in favor of 2 Live Crew's fair use defense regarding their hip-hop parody of Roy Orbison's "Oh, Pretty Woman," the Court stressed the transformation of the source material as the most important consideration.[6] And Koons subsequently fared much better in response to a copyright lawsuit brought by Andrea Blanch, who objected to Koons's incorporation of a portion of one of her photographs in his 2000 painting *Niagara*. Blanch's photograph depicting a woman's legs, crossed at the ankle, wearing Gucci sandals, and resting in a man's lap within what appears to be an airline interior, was published in the August 2000 issue of *Allure* magazine as part of a feature about metallic makeup. In Koons's painting, the ankles and sandals appeared as part of a row of legs dangling over glistening pastries, with Niagara Falls in the background. Koons's successful fair use defense in *Blanch v. Koons*, both at the district court level in 2005 and in the Second Circuit Court of Appeals in 2006, was clearly due not only to the transformative standard established by *Campbell v. Acuff-Rose Music, Inc.*, but also to Koons's willingness to be a more strategic witness in his own defense, offering statements of intent carefully crafted in relation to legal precedent. The district court judge referred to the transformative nature of Koons's use "as described" in his June 10, 2005, affidavit, and the appeals court decision clearly relied on this same source for its finding that "Koons's appropriation of

Blanch's photograph in 'Niagara' was intended to be—and appears to be—'transformative.'"[7] The appeals court ascribed its transformative nature to its different purpose, emphasizing how Koons had used Blanch's photo as part of "commentary on the social and aesthetic consequences of mass media." This finding—that Koons could use material drawn from Blanch's image to make a generalized comment about contemporary society—stood in sharp contrast to *Rogers v. Koons,* where Koons's claim to be using the photograph as the basis for a parody of modern society was roundly rejected, with the appeals court ruling that "the copied work must be, at least in part, an object of the parody, otherwise there would be no need to conjure up the original work."[8]

It is equally important to note that Koons's shifting legal fortunes, and any precedents set by the 2006 appeals court victory, were strictly a US phenomenon. When a 2014 retrospective that began at the Whitney Museum in New York reached its second venue at the Centre Pompidou in Paris, works from Koons's 1988 *Banality Show* suddenly became the focus of a whole new round of infringement accusations. Although Alain Seban, president of the Centre Pompidou, was quoted in press accounts defending the work on the basis that "similar questions" about the *Banality* works had already been dealt with in America, the litigants were apparently undeterred.[9]

One suit, filed on behalf of the heirs of Jean-François Bauret, concerned a 1975 photograph, *Deux enfants,* which Koons had drawn upon for his 1988 porcelain sculpture *Naked,* depicting two nude children standing side by side. For that case, decided against Koons in 2017 and affirmed on appeal in 2019, both the Pompidou and Koons's limited liability company (Jeff Koons LLC) were ordered to pay €20,000 to the photographer's heirs, with Koons's LLC also on the hook for another €4,000 due to a reproduction of the sculpture posted to Koons's own website.[10] *Naked* was not even on display at the Pompidou, since minor damage to the sculpture was discovered when it was unpacked in Paris, but its representation in the catalogue and associated publicity was sufficient for the copyright action.

A second case, involving Koons's 1988 *Fait d'Hiver,* a sculpted depiction of the upper body of a reclining woman clad in a fishnet top, was filed by Franck Davidovici, who cited the close resemblance to his "Fait d'Hiver" ad created for Naf Naf in 1985 (though Koons had changed out the clothing and added a couple of penguins alongside a curious pig that was already part of the ad image).[11] Under the threat of a lawsuit demanding both monetary damages and the work itself, *Fait d'Hiver* was quickly pulled from the show and whisked out of France (with the work's owner identified in some accounts as the Prada Foundation, which bought one example from the edition at auction in 2007). In his complaint, Davidovici sought €300,000 in damages as well as the seizure of the sculpture. Although the court did not award him the full amount, or direct the work to be confiscated, it did order Koons to pay €135,000 for the appropriation, with an additional €11,000 fine against Koons for reproducing the sculpture on his website, and €2,000 against the publisher of the Pompidou's catalogue.[12]

Notwithstanding the Pompidou president's observations, the French courts were clearly not bound by precedent with respect to Koons's 2006 win in the US, even as the different legal systems intersect with a highly interconnected art world characterized by collaborative exhibition projects and the international movement of art—and of course websites that can be accessed from many locales. Attempts to draw distinctions among different types of creators, which have proven challenging enough in the US context, would be even more difficult under French law, which largely precludes the typical commercial stratagem of asking authors to sign away their rights via work-for-hire agreements. In this instance, two types of movement converged—the shipment of art objects to venues around the world, and the associated publicity, amplified by digital transmission, which drew renewed attention to some of Koons's early sculptures. As the works in question indicate, images were in constant motion even during earlier analog eras, with Koons having ready access to French print sources during the 1980s, despite the fact that then, as now, regulations regarding their use remain tied to national legal codes. Although a defense mounted by Koons's LLC hardly fits the model of an idealist underdog battling commercial forces, the sizeable damage awards, not only in response to the work, but also for its appearance in secondary sources, clearly set a chilling example.

The scope of US fair use protection has also continued to be in the news, due in part to the roller-coaster fortunes of Richard Prince following an infringement accusation by photographer Patrick Cariou. The work that prompted Cariou's lawsuit was Prince's *Canal Zone* series, in which he incorporated extensive photographic material using a combination of inkjet printing, collage, and acrylic paint on canvas to create a series of large-scale works exhibited and sold by art-world power broker Larry Gagosian. Much, though certainly not all, of the recombined photographic source material consisted of images of Rastafarians drawn from Cariou's 2000 book *Yes, Rasta,* including certain motifs that reappeared across multiple canvases, some more dramatically altered than others.

Despite an eventual victory on appeal, the dangers associated with a fair use defense were readily apparent in Prince's initial 2011 loss, when a US district court found his *Canal Zone* works to have infringed on Cariou's copyright. The ruling's draconian provisions included directives that all unsold examples be turned over to Cariou for potential destruction and that nothing from the series could be displayed or published. But the big guns came out for the appeal, with arguments by Prince's own lawyers supported by amicus briefs from various quarters, including the Warhol and Rauschenberg Foundations. Evidently the pleadings were persuasive, since in 2013 the Second Circuit Court of Appeals overturned the district court decision and found in Prince's favor, judging twenty-five of the thirty works to be sufficiently transformative to merit fair use protection as a matter of law, and sending the decision on the other five back to the district court on remand, for reconsideration according to a transformative standard.

Although this affirmation of the transformative standard—meaning that a direct critique of the source material was not essential—was widely hailed as a victory for fair use, Amy Adler has raised important questions about associated risks, including how it forces judges to make aesthetic assessments, and she cites the lack of obvious logic for some of the distinctions in the appeals court ruling as evidence of that danger.[13] One of the works sent back to the lower court on remand was Prince's *Graduation.* There he employed almost the entirety of Cariou's photo of a standing Rastafarian in a forest setting, though rendered in softer focus, together with the addition of a blue guitar that the man seemed to be playing and blue ovals blocking his eyes and mouth. That same figure, with a guitar and oval additions, but lacking much of the background, appeared in another composition, *Untitled (Rasta)*, along with two female nudes whose facial features were also obscured. *Graduation* was one of the five returned to the lower court for further consideration, whereas the appeals court found *Untitled (Rasta)* to constitute transformative use. Going by this comparison, one can speculate about why the court might have perceived one to be more dramatically transformed than the other, due to differences in the amount of the original photo incorporated in each and the inclusion of additional figures in one. For other works, however, the logic was far less apparent. Sections from a Cariou photo of a Rastafarian seated on a donkey appeared twice in *Back to the Garden,* flanked by two female nudes: one rendering encompassed most of the Rastafarian figure and animal, but with painted marks that broke it into three segments; next to it was the same figure in a more fragmentary version, with a guitar (as if playing) superimposed, and ovals covering the eyes, nose, and mouth. *Back to the Garden* was ruled transformative. The same Rastafarian appeared in *Charlie Company,* as part of a vertical composition where nearly identical top and bottom registers each included the figure twice, along with a female nude on the right side, all with their facial features blocked by ovals. But in that instance, the court did not find decisive evidence of transformative use in a very similar compositional strategy.

Another crucial aspect of the decision was its de-emphasis of statements of intent—and it is indeed striking how reluctant Prince was to play along with the process, refusing to provide accessible explanations (in contrast to Koons's clear willingness to learn how to testify effectively). Regarding the "message" of *Graduation*, Prince testified: "He's playing the guitar now, it looks like he's playing the guitar, it looks as if he's always played the guitar, that's what my message was."[14] However, others attempted to fill this breach, including the relatively unusual submission of amicus briefs in conjunction with the district court reconsideration. A joint brief by the Warhol and Rauschenberg Foundations argued for an expansive understanding of transformative use that would go beyond questions of visible differences to take into account changes in context. This position was aggressively contested by a second amicus brief filed by a consortium of photographers' associations. But the five works remanded to the lower court for reconsideration, along with the expansive reading of transformative use argued by the Warhol and Rauschenberg foundations, were left as dangling threads, since their final fate was decided by a confidential out-of-court settlement. Clearly that agreement included Prince's right to show and sell the work, however, since the resolution was followed by a new 2014 *Canal Zone* exhibition at Gagosian that included a number of examples from the remand.

Rather than retreating to safety after his appeals court victory, however, Prince turned right around and created a series of works made from direct printouts of Instagram posts. For the Instagram works, Prince (or, some have speculated, youthful assistants) added one line of text, then created large-size canvases out of what appear to be simply a series of screen captures. Some of the Instagram images were circulated by their original authors, but others taken up by Prince were already reposts, disseminated via an internet culture based on incessant circulation of pre-existing material.

Prince has described his sudden discovery of Tumblr while looking over his daughter's shoulder at her feed: asking her a series of questions including whether they were her photos, could they be manipulated, and did she need permission to post them, he concluded, "What's yours is mine."[15] He also came relatively late to the iPhone universe, recounting his first purchase of one three years before the *New Portraits* series, and being amazed by the ease of taking pictures with minimal equipment. A year or so later, his niece showed him how to do a screen save. After joining Instagram as RichardPrince4, he claimed to have figured out himself how to make most comments disappear from his view of someone's feed by labeling them as spam. That allowed him to capture screenshots where his own recent comments—which he characterized as "Non sequitur. Gobbledygook. Jokes. Oxymorons. 'Psychic Jiu-Jitsu.'"—would appear in close proximity to the initial posts.[16] The resulting works, with the screenshots blown up and printed out on canvas, were quickly presented in a series of high-profile exhibitions at Gagosian's uptown New York gallery in 2014, Gagosian's London gallery and Frieze Art Fair booth, 2015, and Blum & Poe, Tokyo, in 2015. They also appeared in catalogues produced by both the Gagosian and Blum & Poe galleries, and an installation view of the initial Gagosian show was reproduced on a New York billboard.

A number of the images were appropriated from a group of women who use the collective identity of SuicideGirls for their conscious play with alluring self-presentation. They responded with publicity-generating humor by making their own nearly identical large-scale canvas printouts, which they sold for $90 rather than $90,000 (as they pointed out, a discount of 99.9 percent), with profits designated for the Electronic Frontier Foundation (figure 13). But a new round of lawsuits by creators who were clearly less amused quickly put to the test the proposition that transformation is a matter of context. Three of the four lawsuits came from photographers: Donald Graham, for his photo *Rastafarian Smoking a Joint;* Dennis Morris, for an image of the Sex Pistols' Sid Vicious; and Eric McNatt, for a portrait of Sonic Youth's Kim Gordon. The fourth plaintiff was Ashley Salazar, a makeup artist also known as Mynxxi White, who had posted a selfie holding her phone and layered with a row of cat emojis up the right side.

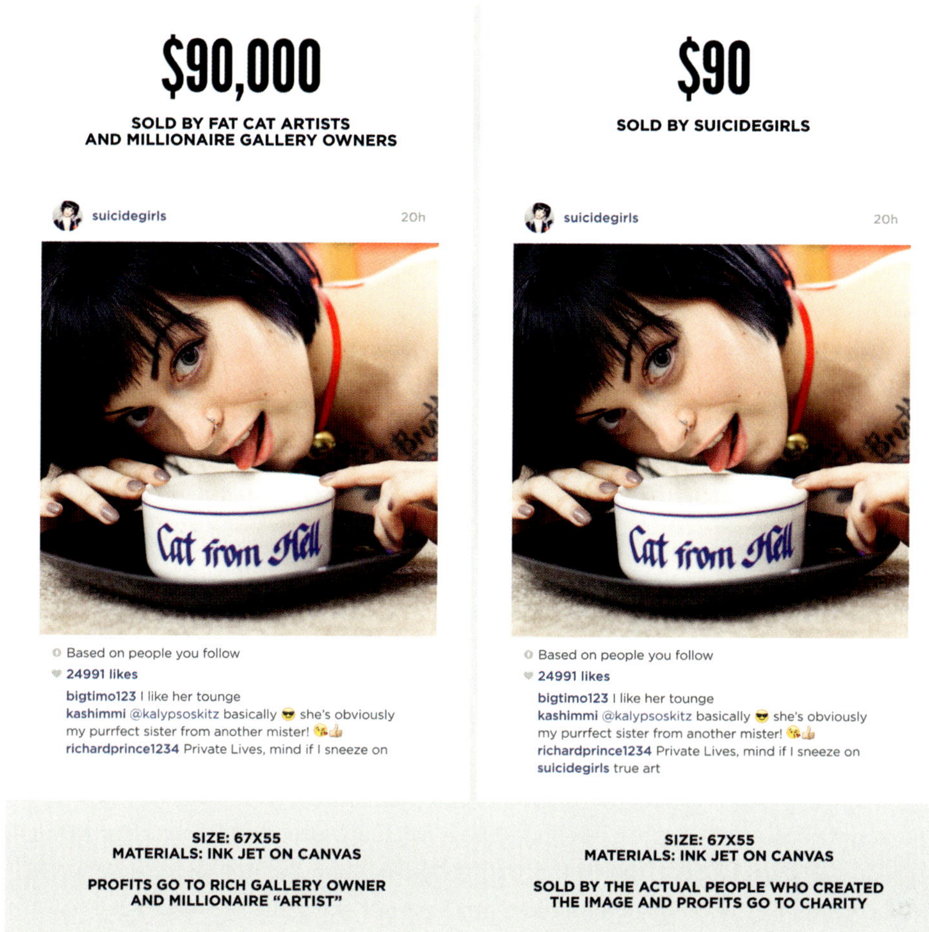

FIGURE 13

Comparison between a Richard Prince work based on a SuicideGirls Instagram post and their work made in response, as shown on the SuicideGirls website, May 2015. Courtesy the SuicideGirls.

In rejecting Prince's motion to dismiss the suit brought by Graham, the district court rather ominously indicated that "the Court cannot conclude that any of the four use factors favors defendants." The judge did not see "substantial aesthetic alterations," and appeared to give credence to Graham's argument "that Prince's presentation of Graham's photograph in a social media frame, with the addition of a single line of what Prince himself calls 'gobblygook' ('Canal Zinian da lam jam [emoji of a raised fist]') cannot be transformative."[17] The judge's ruling on the motion to dismiss characterized both Prince's work and the catalogue as commercial, based on the fact that they were for sale. And on the question of market usurpation central to the fourth fair use factor, the judge seemed receptive to Graham's contention that they were both aimed at the same audience, including "fine art collectors" and "fine art galleries," though he did allow that Prince could potentially show that his work "appeals to an entirely different sort of collector."[18]

But Prince's lawyers responded forcefully, stressing Graham's willing participation in the circulation of images. Graham, they argued, had posted his photo on various social media sites without privacy settings or any indication of restrictions; he had not objected to the Instagram reposts by Rastajay92 and Idigoochild (one reposting from the other) that led to Prince's Rastajay92 screenshot; he had reposted work by other photographers on his own Instagram, including installation views of Prince's show taken by the professional photographer employed by Gagosian; and Graham had, in turn, not obtained a written release from his image subject. Graham's decision to post the image himself, on multiple occasions over a ten-year period, they argued, amounted to an implied license for Prince's use.[19]

Prince's bid for summary judgment pursued the line of argument posited in the *Cariou* case endgame, that transformative use should not be judged in purely visual terms. And his lawyers attempted to turn the tables regarding questions about the amount taken by emphasizing a message only made possible by the presentation of the entire screenshot. Prince, they argued, "has imbued what was once an austere depiction of a Rastafarian smoking marijuana into part of Prince's ode to social media." Only by blowing up the image in its entirety was this commentary evident, so therefore, the fact that "Prince did not cut, mark, paint over, scratch or otherwise obscure the image of the Photograph (as he did in the *Cariou* case) is critical, *not detrimental,* to his fair use of the Photograph."[20] Given the general problem of similarities between works of art and source material being heightened when both are presented to courts through reproduction, it is likewise telling that Prince's lawyers filed a motion to present a full-sized replica of Prince's Instagram blow-up as part of the court proceedings.[21]

HIERARCHIES OF AUTHORSHIP

Even if contemporary codes tend to be quite egalitarian in their sweeping recognition of copyright, there can be no doubt that certain forms of authorship are typically accorded more prestige than others. It is likewise significant what material is identified as authored in the first place. As the tradition developed, particularly during the second half of the twentieth century, of artists responding to mass media imagery, the general tendency was to treat it as an anonymously produced resource, even in circumstances where initial creators could potentially be identified. One notable case in point was the Museum of Modern Art's 1990 exhibition *High and Low: Modern Art and Popular Culture,* where the stories being told focused on a narrative of artistic developments mounted in response to surrounding cultural material, with little attention to histories of the forms to which they were reacting (advertising, illustrated magazines, comic books, etc.), and even less to individuals active in those spheres. In this respect, the exhibition was of a piece with MoMA's far more notorious 1984 *"Primitivism" in 20th Century Art: Affinity of the Tribal and the Modern,* where examples of tribal work were stripped of their specific significance, and presented primarily in relation to claims about "affinities" with European and North American avant-garde achievements.[22] These examples provide ongoing evidence of the trajectory described in Michel Foucault's groundbreaking authorship essay, where he emphasized that divisions regarding what is circulated with an author's name attached are not historically fixed (giving as examples both literature and scientific claims).[23] It is therefore important to go beyond points of law, to consider the larger dynamics at play regarding who gets the credit—and the money—as barriers between commercial and fine art realms are simultaneously broken down and reestablished.

Koons, following in Warhol's footsteps, can readily be described as a type of brand, offering a cachet evidently recognized by consumers of luxury goods that circulate in the same ecosystem. In stark contrast to the vast majority of exhibiting artists, who are lucky if they are able to support themselves with their creative practice alone, Koons has established himself as an art-world power broker. With activities that have included overseeing an extensive studio operation with round-the-clock shifts of painters executing his works, design projects for luxury good firms, a personal collection of old masters installed in a residence carved out of interconnected New York City townhouses, and attendance at the Davos World Economic Forum, he is firmly entrenched as part of the proverbial 1%.[24] The names of the artists who actually make his works (undoubtedly on the basis of work-for-hire contracts) are fully effaced, as are those associated with producing the media imagery upon which he draws.

Witness the promotional copy for the November 2007 Christie's sale where the artist's proof of *Fait d'Hiver* sold for $4,297,000. Simultaneously highlighting and glossing over Koons's reliance on source material, the catalogue described the work as "a surreal and witty disruption of the conventions of sculpture, using an almost photographic composition in order to emphasise the collage-like nature of the content," which, it indicated, was "in part based on a picture that had appeared in Stern magazine."[25] Yet this description is in keeping with the fact that specific credit for who creates an ad—both copy and artwork—is generally known only among industry insiders, since it is, after all, the client who is being promoted. The Guggenheim's website description of *Niagara* is even more generalized, referring to Koons's composition of the *Easyfun-Ethereal* series by culling imagery "from a wide spectrum of popular culture, focusing especially on advertising for fashion, cosmetics, and food," in order to create a collage-like effect even as the imagery "is repainted with photorealist perfection."[26] Given Blanch's lawsuit, there can be no question about at least one of his sources, but any detailing of the specifics is likely to be found only in specialized art historical literature, if at all. One set of authorship attributions not lost in the Koons shuffle, however, was the series of canonical artists he drew upon for his 2017 "Masters" collection of handbags designed for Louis Vuitton, where familiar fragments of painting's greatest hits (Gauguin, Manet, Monet, Turner, Fragonard, Rubens, etc.) were reinforced by lettering with the artists' names superimposed over the reproduced details. And all were conveniently out of copyright, meaning there was no IP impediment to the three-way conflation of Koons, Louis Vuitton, and old-master paintings.

In the case of Prince, it is striking that an artist who, by his own account, began his career with limited technical knowledge of photography, has indeed, through gestures that could be read as conceptual in nature, propelled a range of photographic images into the rarified reaches of the art world. There is, in this respect, a sharp contrast between Prince and artists like Cindy Sherman, Jeff Wall, Gregory Crewdson, or Laurie Simmons, who have employed strategies associated with commercial-style photo shoots in order to produce works that evoke this type of imagery. But even if it is not clear whether Prince's cowboy images, begun in the early 1980s, would be covered by the transformative principle articulated in the 2013 *Cariou* appeals court ruling, this earlier series is striking for how well it succeeds in interrogating the imagery thus reframed and re-presented. The power of the work is inseparable from the skills employed by those who composed the scenes of the mythic American west for their client. Yet Prince's versions accomplish something that the original commercial images do not, and that is to prompt viewers to critique the mythologies—rugged masculine individualism, conquest of nature, etc.—that commercial photographers employed by Philip Morris so skillfully marshalled specifically *in service* of the Marlboro brand.

Within the larger art-historical context, Prince's cowboy imagery is therefore a relatively deadpan entry in a history of critique that Hans Haacke notably pursued with his 1990 *Helmsboro Country* (figure 14), where a massively enlarged pack of Marlboro cigarettes, each individually wrapped in the United States Bill of Rights, responded to Philip Morris on a number of levels. The general context was Philip Morris's sponsorship of art institutions as part of their brand image, together with their support of Jesse Helms, who was simultaneously one of the loudest critics of National Endowment for the Arts funding and a major backer of the tobacco industry. The more specific inspiration was Philip Morris's 1989 acquisition of the right to "sponsor" the Bill of Rights for an entire year in exchange for a payment of $600,000 to the National Archives.[27] Although Haacke's stance is far more explicitly critical, it is part of a larger dialogue encouraging viewers to interrogate cynical messaging, which Prince tapped into through a fairly straight-forward act of recontextualization.

As should be obvious, however, there are authorship interests preceding Prince. Jim Krantz, a photographer who contributed to the Marlboro ad campaigns he appropriated, spoke of the arresting experience of finding his image outside the Guggenheim's 2007 Prince retrospective, as an advertising poster for the show, saying "When I left, I didn't know if I should be proud, or if I looked like an idiot."[28] (And there is no small irony in the fact that a "commercial" work, brought into the gallery and museum world, was redeployed to function as publicity for the exhibition.) Sam Abell, another photographer who worked on the ad campaign, spoke about his relationship to Prince's work in an interview circulated on YouTube. According to Abell, "Photographs have lives," and he described the "curious experience" first of seeing Prince's appropriation of his

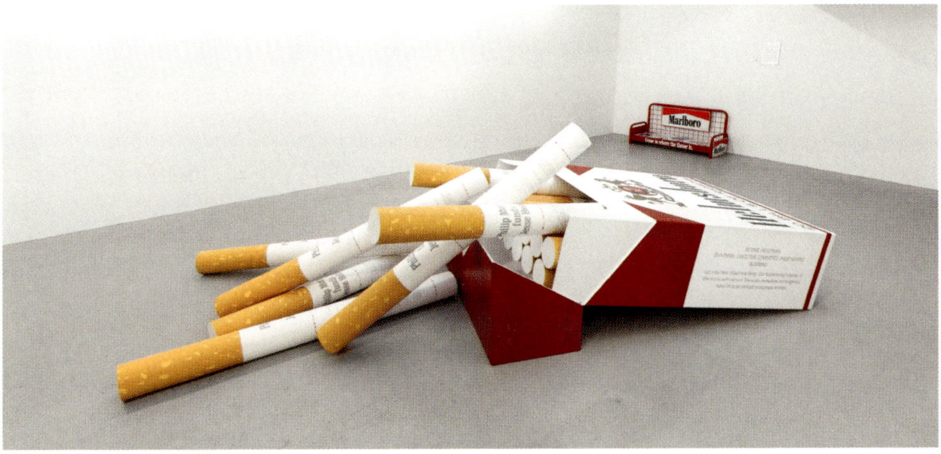

FIGURE 14
Hans Haacke, *Helmsboro Country,* 1990. Silkscreen prints and photographs on wood, cardboard and paper; box: 30½ × 80 × 47½ in.; 20 cigarettes, each: 6½ × 6½ × 69½ in. Photo: Steven Probert. © Hans Haacke/Artists Rights Society (ARS), New York. Courtesy the artist and Paula Cooper Gallery, New York.

work, then discovering its value in the eyes of the art community. Abell elaborated: "A photograph of mine could never be in the Guggenheim museum, could never be on the cover of their guide, couldn't be on the cover of the D.A.P. catalogue, and that is because editorial photography, for the most part, is considered by those entities, by the Guggenheim and by the art establishment, to be not worthy. But copied by someone else, it is worthy. So the art world has something to answer for. . . ." [29] Prince's only response to a *New York Times* request for comment about his use of such source material was an email statement: "I never associated advertisements with having an author."[30]

There is also nothing to prevent someone else from doing exactly the same thing—as Eric Doeringer has handily demonstrated as part of a larger practice that has frequently engaged with playful appropriations of work already based on that maneuver.[31] Prince's hold on his appropriated imagery was, however, paradoxically confirmed by Doeringer's gesture of photographing the identical Marlboro ads Prince had already used for the cowboy series (figure 15). As should be evident, Doeringer was deliberately attempting to provoke questions about authorship by responding to the same source from the world of already-encoded imagery, rather than directly from nature. Moreover, Doeringer extended this strategy via his July 2012 Cowboy Photography Workshop, held at Printed Matter in New York, where he invited members of the public to come and take their own photographs from his collection of Marlboro ads.

It is not clear whether Prince had any response to Doeringer's provocation. But he has gone on record regarding a couple of other appropriations. One was a series of copies of Prince's work produced at another artist's behest by Chinese copy painters and exhibited in February 2014 under the title *Banal Zone.* Prince indicated his

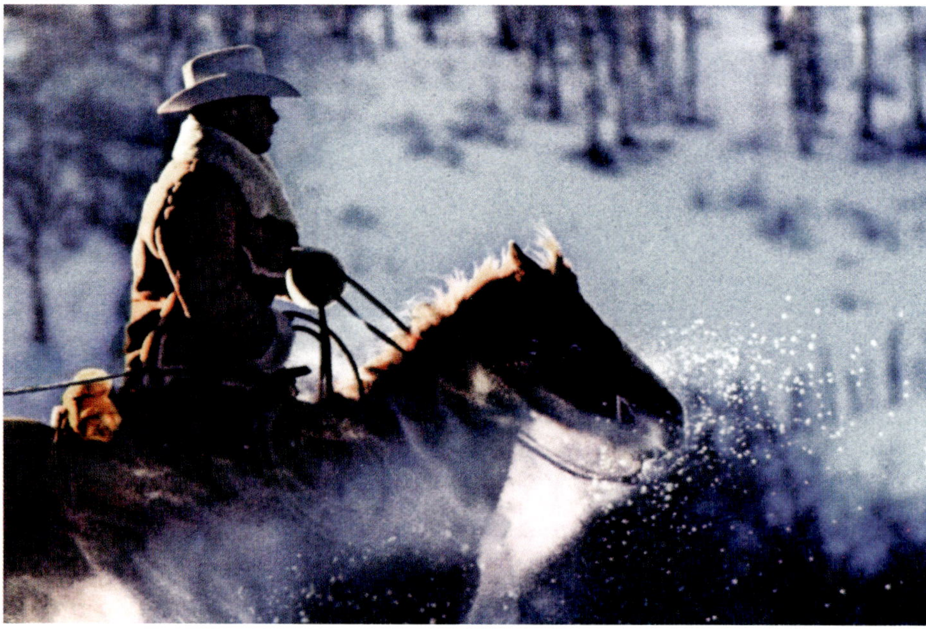

FIGURE 15
Eric Doeringer, *Untitled (Cowboys)*, 2011. Archival inkjet print, 20 × 24 in. Courtesy the artist.

"couldn't care less" position in the "Birdtalk" section of his web site. Referring to the *Cariou* case (at a point when the works sent back to the district court for review were still in limbo), he asked, "why would anyone in China, or for that matter, anyone in any other country, take the time to make 'another copy' of works that according to the courts . . . don't belong to me in the first place?" When plays on Prince's work were incorporated into the décor of a New York restaurant called the Lobster Club, he was quick to emphasize that they had nothing to do with him. "I've been sampled," he wrote. But even though they had not asked permission, he went on, "I will not lawyer up. I will not sue," saying "I'm not interested in that little 'c' in a circle."[32] Nowhere in the entry, however, did he mention that the works in question were based on a 2011–13 series he created by riffing on Picasso's work.

Prince's relatively open attitude toward references to his work in the visual realm does not, however, appear to extend to criticism and commentary (even though this is a key goal of fair use), since Prince and his representatives have maintained tight control over how his art is contextualized. A particularly notable example is a 2007 catalogue, published in conjunction with an exhibition of Prince's pre-1978 work, which Michael Lobel organized specifically in order to reexamine early work that Prince has attempted to disown. Despite the fact that some of these pieces are part of museum collections, Prince's efforts to efface them from the historical record meant that the catalogue wound up being published with empty rectangles in the place of the unrepresented works (figure 16).[33]

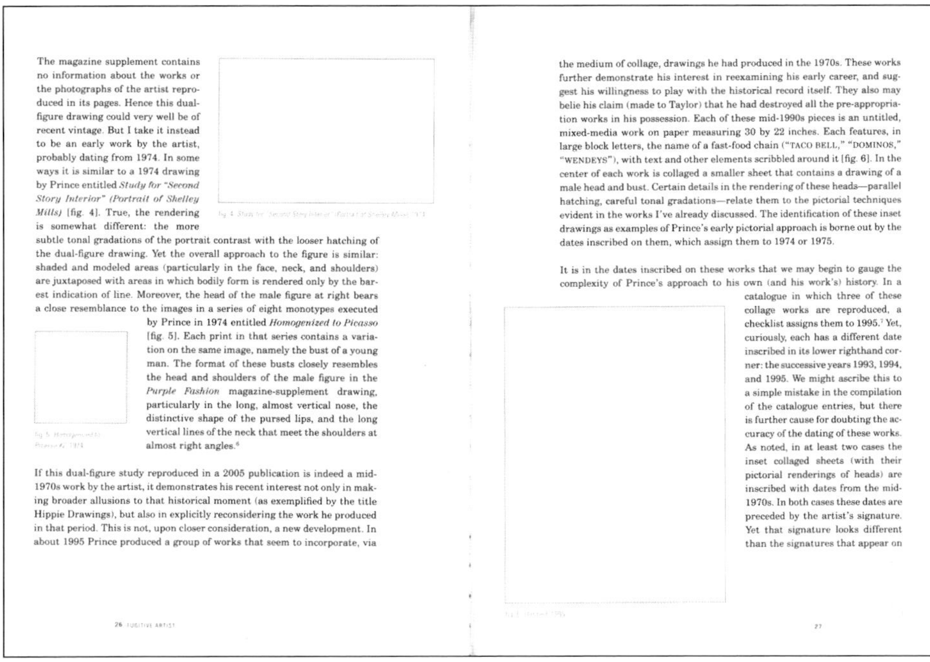
The magazine supplement contains no information about the works or the photographs of the artist reproduced in its pages. Hence this dual-figure drawing could very well be of recent vintage. But I take it instead to be an early work by the artist, probably dating from 1974. In some ways it is similar to a 1974 drawing by Prince entitled *Study for "Second Story Interior" (Portrait of Shelley Mills)* [fig. 4]. True, the rendering is somewhat different: the more subtle tonal gradations of the portrait contrast with the looser hatching of the dual-figure drawing. Yet the overall approach to the figure is similar: shaded and modeled areas (particularly in the face, neck, and shoulders) are juxtaposed with areas in which bodily form is rendered only by the barest indication of line. Moreover, the head of the male figure at right bears a close resemblance to the images in a series of eight monotypes executed by Prince in 1974 entitled *Homogenized to Picasso* [fig. 5]. Each print in that series contains a variation on the same image, namely the bust of a young man. The format of these busts closely resembles the head and shoulders of the male figure in the *Purple Fashion* magazine-supplement drawing, particularly in the long, almost vertical nose, the distinctive shape of the pursed lips, and the long vertical lines of the neck that meet the shoulders at almost right angles.[6]

If this dual-figure study reproduced in a 2005 publication is indeed a mid-1970s work by the artist, it demonstrates his recent interest not only in making broader allusions to that historical moment (as exemplified by the title Hippie Drawings), but also in explicitly reconsidering the work he produced in that period. This is not, upon closer consideration, a new development. In about 1995 Prince produced a group of works that seem to incorporate, via

26 FUGITIVE ARTIST

the medium of collage, drawings he had produced in the 1970s. These works further demonstrate his interest in reexamining his early career, and suggest his willingness to play with the historical record itself. They also may belie his claim (made to Taylor) that he had destroyed all the pre-appropriation works in his possession. Each of these mid-1990s pieces is an untitled, mixed-media work on paper measuring 30 by 22 inches. Each features, in large block letters, the name of a fast-food chain ("TACO BELL," "DOMINOS," "WENDEYS"), with text and other elements scribbled around it [fig. 6]. In the center of each work is collaged a smaller sheet that contains a drawing of a male head and bust. Certain details in the rendering of these heads—parallel hatching, careful tonal gradations—relate them to the pictorial techniques evident in the works I've already discussed. The identification of these inset drawings as examples of Prince's early pictorial approach is borne out by the dates inscribed on them, which assign them to 1974 or 1975.

It is in the dates inscribed on these works that we may begin to gauge the complexity of Prince's approach to his own (and his work's) history. In a catalogue in which three of these collage works are reproduced, a checklist assigns them to 1995.[7] Yet, curiously, each has a different date inscribed in its lower righthand corner: the successive years 1993, 1994, and 1995. We might ascribe this to a simple mistake in the compilation of the catalogue entries, but there is further cause for doubting the accuracy of the dating of these works. As noted, in at least two cases the inset collaged sheets (with their pictorial renderings of heads) are inscribed with dates from the mid-1970s. In both cases these dates are preceded by the artist's signature. Yet that signature looks different than the signatures that appear on

27

FIGURE 16

Michael Lobel, *Fugitive Artist: The Early Work of Richard Prince, 1974–77* (Purchase, NY: Neuberger Museum of Art, 2007), pages 26–27. Courtesy the author.

A less extensive refusal came to light mainly because of Greg Allen's reaction to the situation. When *Slate* was not allowed to reproduce one of Prince's cowboy works in a photo essay by Sarah Boxer about MoMA's *Into the Sunset* exhibition (a 2009 show exploring photographic imaging of the American West), Allen created his own alternative artwork based on a screengrab that he resized at a much lower resolution and retitled *300 × 404, After Untitled (Cowboy) 2003 by Richard Prince* (with the title indicating its pixel dimensions) (figure 17). He then offered to let *Slate* publish his distorted example in place of Prince's, and posted it on his own site when *Slate* did not take him up on the possibility.[34] In offering his strategically pixelated image as an alternate work, Allen was playing off of fair use decisions and guidelines that have made allowances for the online circulation of lower-resolution images, or thumbnails, by tacitly questioning how much the resolution might need to shift in order to be considered a different image. And he was, of course, also responding to the irony of Prince's authorship hold over a photo actually created by Abell.

It is problematic under any circumstances when artists or their representatives attempt to control discourse about the work by limiting reproduction and associated analysis, but it seems like an act of particularly bad faith act when the artistic practice in question is based on appropriated imagery or forms. The complex dynamics when artists shift from irreverent outsiders to members of the art world establishment are

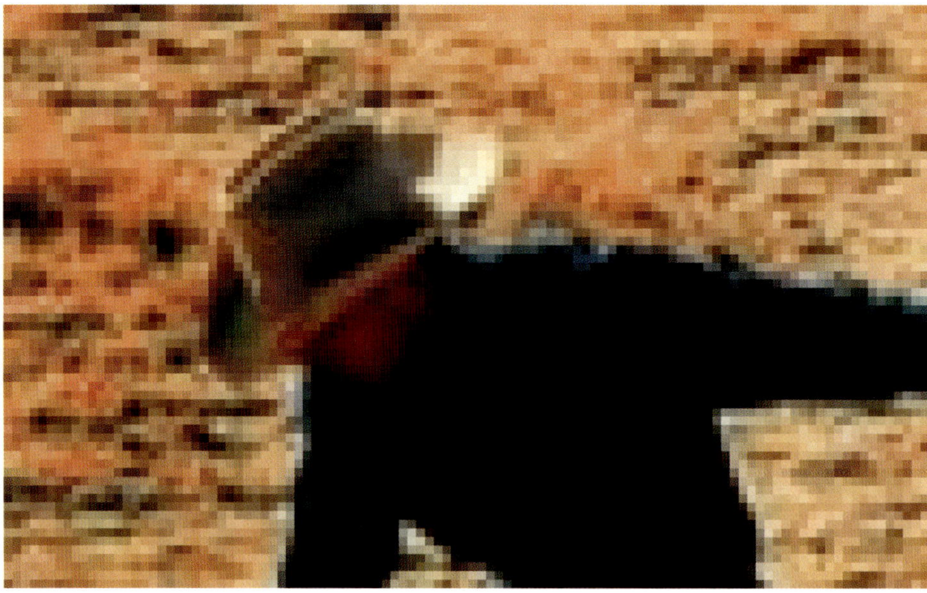

FIGURE 17
Greg Allen/greg.org, detail from *300x404, After Untitled (Cowboy)*, 2003, 2009. 300 × 404 pixel JPEG. Courtesy the artist.

suggested by Nate Harrison's assessment that court affirmation of postmodernism in *Cariou* extinguished "any embers of criticality" still associated with the pictures generation.[35] It is important not to turn away from supporting fair use, even when an artist's stance toward use by others is highly problematic. Yet the same fair use principles that artists rely upon when they respond to the surrounding image world should necessarily extend to others who respond to their work—thereby linking a broad and robust support for fair use within artistic production to an equally expansive understanding of its significance for interpretive realms.

Even if many of the issues were initially rooted in analog practices, it is equally important to recognized how dramatically matters have been intensified by shifts in image circulation. With respect to Prince's Instagram series, the circuit he interrupted is very different than the one in operation when he began photographing magazine ads with the copy cropped out in the late 1970s. As opposed to relatively centralized points of origin associated with earlier channels of mass-media communication, social media business models depend on an ever-increasing flow of multidirectional recirculation. The real provocation of Prince's Instagram series was not the impulse to share—since that is a core principle—or even presenting images by others without proper attribution. Rather, it was the move from one platform to another (from online space to gallery), along with the paradox that his artistic use was far more lucrative than most who are operating in designated commercial arenas could ever hope to reach.

The SuicideGirls foregrounded this disparity when they decided to respond to his appropriation of their Instagram photos, not through the court system, but by producing their own identical series of five of the images, and using social media to emphasize the price differential of $90 versus $90,000. According to Selena Mooney, known as Missy Suicide, "Richard Prince is an artist and he found the images we and our girls publish on Instagram as representative of something worth commenting on, part of the zeitgeist, I guess? Thanks Richard!" For her, the transformation into the artistic realm was significant: "If I had a nickel for every time someone used our images without our permission in a commercial endeavour I'd be able to spend $90,000 on art. I was once really annoyed by Forever 21 selling shirts with our slightly altered images on them, but an artist?"[36] Stratospheric valuations are inseparable from the artist-brand established by Prince, since otherwise there would be little reason for a 99.9 percent price differential between highly comparable works made to the same scale and via a similarly hands-off production process.

The strange alchemy associated with artistic name value was highlighted in a different way by the Graham case. As outlined in court documents, Graham has distinguished between two aspects of his work, commercial and fine arts, with the latter generally not subject to licensing agreements. But even if some of his photographs circulate as art, Graham and Prince move in distinct spheres: Prince's lawyers stressed not only their different markets, but also that publicity associated with the appropriation had contributed to increased sales of the underlying work.[37] According to arguments they presented to the court, "it would make no sense for someone to pay for a Richard Prince if they wanted the Graham Photograph, which they could easily purchase for a fraction of the price of a New Portrait."[38] Even though the legal briefs were circumspect about identifying the purchaser of the work featuring Graham's photo, press accounts were more explicit. Laura Gilbert, writing for *Art Newspaper*, highlighted the somewhat paradoxical hierarchy when she identified Prince's dealer as its owner: "Larry Gagosian, who bought the Graham-based work and exhibited it in his gallery, says he would neither show nor buy a Graham photograph."[39] One day after the denial of Prince's motion to dismiss the case brought by Graham, Prince tweeted his attitude toward the claims against him: "Phony fraud photographers keep mooching me. Why? I changed the game. &their wizardry professorial boredom keeps coughing up a vick'sVAPOrub."[40] The arrogance of this reversal—people whose work he appropriated were "mooching" on Prince—is perhaps why the tweet was later deleted. But it is only a small step further than the suggestion, already present in the legal arguments on Prince's behalf, that Prince's acts of appropriation provided a benefit to the photographers in question due to publicity and increased sales following their forced entry into the orb of Prince's authorship.

As Prince's lawyers pointed out, the images that Prince appropriated were in wide circulation via a rampant culture of reposting. But Prince's shift to a different platform—the physical space of the art gallery—and his ability to command substantial sums for the results of that maneuver were perhaps the real offence. Professional photographers do indeed derive income from licensing their images. Yet an interview-based study of how contemporary photographers exercise copyright by Jessica Silbey, Eva Subotnick, and Peter DiCola found that it was primarily useful in the context of initial negotiations with clients, rather than in protecting against downstream circulation of copies, even though it did provide leverage to prevent unapproved uses. Thus, a key conclusion was that "the traditional economic account of copyright fails to explain photographers' behavior."[41] Amy Adler has gone much further, arguing against the useful role of copyright for the visual arts in general, based on the conclusion that it does not fulfill its traditional justification of providing a utilitarian incentive, in relation to a creative arena where income (to the extent that it is significant at all) is derived primarily from the first sale of unique or limited edition objects whose value is not hampered by acts of copying. According to her, the "off-label," non-economic deployment of copyright has transformed it into a stealth version of moral rights.[42]

SYMPATHY FACTORS

There are the legal judgments—generally few and far between—and then there is the question of where one's sympathies might fall, which can potentially be a very different matter. Even holding onto the importance of fair use, along with related protections outside the United States, it is not difficult to understand the annoyance or distress associated with discovering that significant elements of one's work have been taken up by another artist. It is therefore not surprising that a key request, sometimes even more important than financial compensation, is credit for the underlying work.

In a 2013 dispute between Bridget Riley and Tobias Rehberger, Riley demanded the removal of *Uhrenobjekt,* a large-scale black-and-white painting by Rehberger that had been installed in the Staatsbibliothek zu Berlin, Haus Unter den Linden, as the result of a federally funded commission. She cited its close (and undeniable) resemblance to her 1961 painting *Movement of Squares,* whereas Rehberger asserted his belief that the geometric pattern was part of the public domain.[43] While the dispute was being adjudicated, the Berlin court hearing the case ordered Rehberger's painting, which had only briefly been on view, covered up. The resolution was that the work could stay in place, but that it would carry a new label, "*Uhrenobjekt* nach *Movement in Squares* von Bridget Riley" (figure 18).

The painting at issue was a well-known example of Riley's linked exploration of form and perception, where subtle shifts in pattern and scale establish a complex visual experience. For Riley, this was just one of a long string of appropriations, stretching as far back as 1965, when op art collector Larry Aldrich celebrated her work's appearance in MoMA's exhibition *The Responsive Eye* by commissioning fabric patterns based on the paintings. A 1965 *Life* magazine feature on the phenomenon, "Fashion Op from Toe to Top," summed up her discontent: "The artist protests her work was sold to hang on a wall, not a girl."[44] One wonders which was more annoying to Riley—to see her paintings quickly transformed into a pop culture product line by an apparent

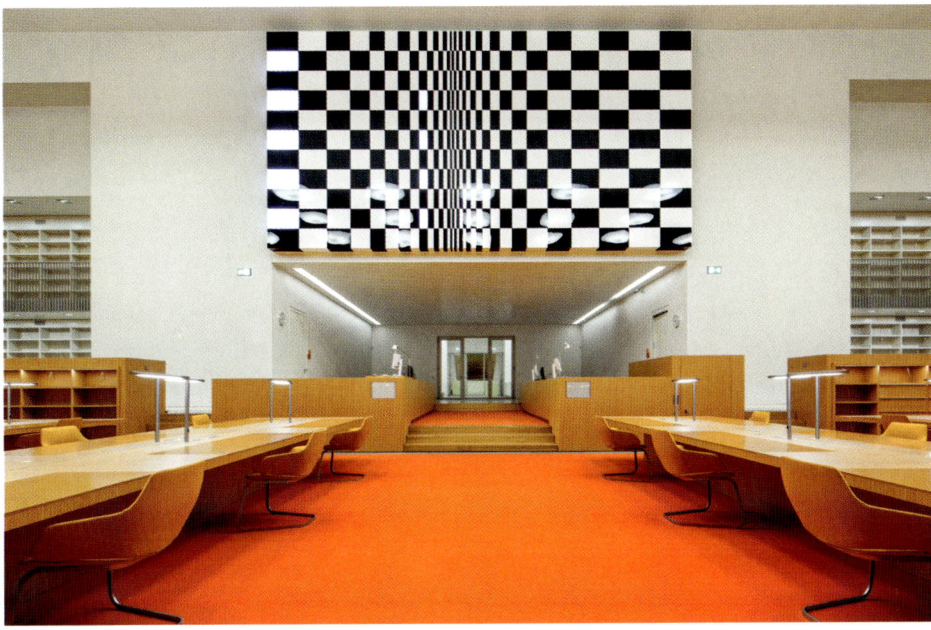

FIGURE 18
Staatsbibliothek zu Berlin, Haus Unter den Linden: Rara reading room, after completion, before the opening, December 1, 2012, Berlin. Above the entrance: Tobias Rehberger's *Watch Object after Movement in Squares by Bridget Riley*. Photo: bpk Bildagentur/Jörg F. Müller/Art Resource, NY.

supporter, or to have one of her paintings transformed into another painting. There are inescapable gender dynamics at play as well, with a woman artist who had to struggle for visibility in a male-dominated art world witnessing yet another act of erasure by a male artist from a later generation. But even so, it is important to acknowledge a potential counterargument, based on the question of how much ownership to grant to any artist over a design constituted by a pattern of alternating black and white rectangles whose width diminishes and then expands across a surface.

Then there is the series of abstract paintings by Sarah Morris, based on origami crease diagrams which she treated as found patterns. For Morris, the work was a continuation of her exploration of formal arrangements derived from different types of built structures, which she used to generate paintings that were both evocative of the architectural and urban dynamics of specific locales and strikingly transformed through the play of color and line crucial to their abstract power. Morris also explored many of these places in films—the other side of her practice—and she has clearly been adept at navigating the legal and bureaucratic hurdles necessary to secure access, including remarkable footage in Washington, DC, near the end of the Clinton presidency and Beijing at the time of the 2008 Olympic Games. But when she expanded her engagement with painted pattern to include compositions based on knots, paper clips,

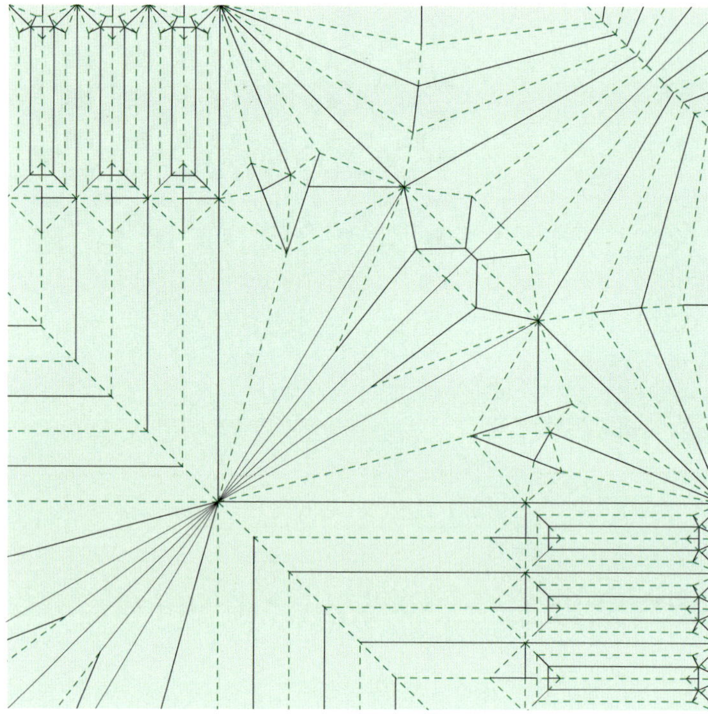

FIGURE 19
Robert J. Lang, *Cooper's Hawk, Opus 464*, 2005. Courtesy the artist.

and origami crease diagrams, she apparently did not anticipate any obstacles associated with her interpretations of these sources.

During the spring of 2009, Robert J. Lang, a former physicist who had become a central figure in the origami world, was contacted by a fellow origami artist who alerted him to paintings by Morris that were derived from crease patterns by Lang and others (figures 19 and 20). Lang initially described "mixed feelings" in response to this news. "On the one hand," he wrote, "she is clearly creating new works of art that can stand on their own merits (as opposed to merely copying something and passing it off as her own). On the other hand, I'm not so crazy about having my own work described as being merely 'found diagrams' as she's done here."[45] Soon after, Lang contacted galleries that represented Morris, asking them to forward his request to discuss her "colorized" versions of his crease patterns. In a June 23, 2009 reply to Lang, Morris confirmed her use of his diagrams as inspiration, but with qualifications that sound like the groundwork for a legal defense: "I think that any fair observer would acknowledge that I have radically transformed them in the course of my work." She emphasized the "different purpose and meaning" of the original patterns and her paintings, due to the fact that the "diagrams are created and distributed to serve a purely practical purpose, instructional folding (i.e. to be folded into three dimensional origami objects, thereby 'erasing' the original diagram)." And she expressed confidence that, if Lang saw the paintings, he "would understand and appreciate this difference."[46]

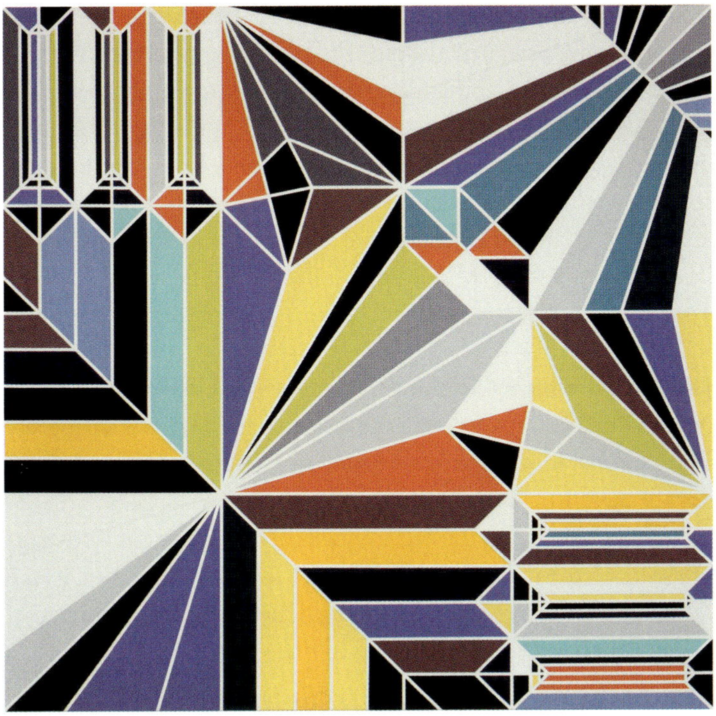

FIGURE 20
Sarah Morris, *Falcon* [*Origami*], 2008. Based on the crease pattern *Cooper's Hawk, Opus 464* by Robert J. Lang. Household gloss paint on canvas, 84¼ × 84¼ in. Courtesy the artist and Petzel, New York.

Whether Lang had the opportunity to see the works in person is not clear; what is certain is that he and other origami artists whose patterns had been taken up by Morris filed suit in California in March 2011. That suit was dismissed in October 2011, for lack of personal jurisdiction, since Lang (a California resident), had failed to prove any direct California connection for this body of work by Morris (though the paintings had been exhibited, as the court noted, in New York, Miami, London, Berlin, Tokyo, Frankfurt, and Abu Dhabi). But that was hardly an end to the matter, since Lang quickly refiled the lawsuit in New York, in December 2011.

Working in conjunction with the Stanford Center for Internet and Society's Fair Use Project, Morris's lawyers made a strong case for the fair use status of the paintings, citing her "dramatic transformation of her source material," as she used often tiny printed diagrams as "a launching pad" for "large, wall-sized paintings of dramatic color and shape" painstakingly crafted by Morris and her studio assistants. They pointed to origami's thematic significance for Morris, as a form of harbinger (referencing her interest in the appearance of origami cranes in Ridley Scott's film *Blade Runner*), together with a sense of impossibility related to the complexity of these patterns in the context of paintings where the folds will never be realized. Of equal significance, they asserted, was a largely nonexistent market for the crease patterns themselves, stressing their typical presentation in conjunction with the folded paper sculptural forms to which they relate.[47]

Lang and his fellow origami artists were obviously disturbed that Morris referred to the crease patterns as "traditional designs," despite the fact, they asserted, that she clearly knew they were modern, including the identity of the origami artists who had created them, given that she made reference to specific sources in the titles for many of the works.[48] Moreover, the crease patterns did not constitute folding instructions, but rather, a summation that stands apart from the step-by-step practical guides necessary to realize each example. As such, they constitute a statement in themselves that Lang claimed as "the creative expression of an artist with an aesthetic vision," and he argued that they were therefore "entitled to the respect and protection that are afforded to other visual arts."[49]

Despite a strong fair use case to be made, two circumstances provided an incentive for Morris to settle. One was the fact that the lawsuit was moving forward during the period after Prince's district court loss in *Cariou v. Prince* in March 2011, but before its reversal on appeal in April 2013. Moreover, in February 2013, the presiding judge ordered a jury trial—which would have increased the legal expenses and uncertainty of outcome. Although most details of the March 2013 settlement were confidential, it evidently included new attributions to be incorporated into the titles for a number of Morris's origami series paintings.[50] In this instance, as in many others, it is possible to understand both sides of the dispute. There is a compelling argument that Morris should have prevailed on fair use grounds, since she did indeed utilize the diagrams as inspiration for strikingly different forms of expression that were highly transformative with respect to both appearance and purpose. Yet one can also see why the origami artists found it disturbing to witness their designs treated as nothing but found pattern.

When the work of a less well-known creator becomes source material for someone more powerful or successful, it is frequently tempting to root for the underdog, despite the legal principles at stake. But what of the reverse, when a younger artist creates a work that is clearly a form of homage, and is faced with legal action? Given the degree to which all artists learn via a process of imitation and reference, it is highly problematic when an established artist, or the artist's estate, attempts to suppress an emerging artist's response to already historical material. This was certainly true of a conflict involving small-scale, tabletop reinterpretations of stainless-steel works from David Smith's *Cubi* series that Lauren Clay produced using basic DIY materials and patterned paper (figure 21). Clay made news in fall 2013 when a show of her work slated for the Grounds for Sculpture exhibition space in Hamilton, NY, was put on indefinite hold after VAGA (the licensing and rights organization representing the copyright interests of Smith's estate) lodged a complaint.

Although Clay was initially described by *ArtInfo* as scornful of VAGA's statement that she should have requested permission for her reinterpretation, she apparently capitulated, since *Art in America* soon thereafter reported that she had reached an agreement allowing her to show and sell the seven works as long as she acknowledged their source in Smith's work, did not make any more in the series without consent, did

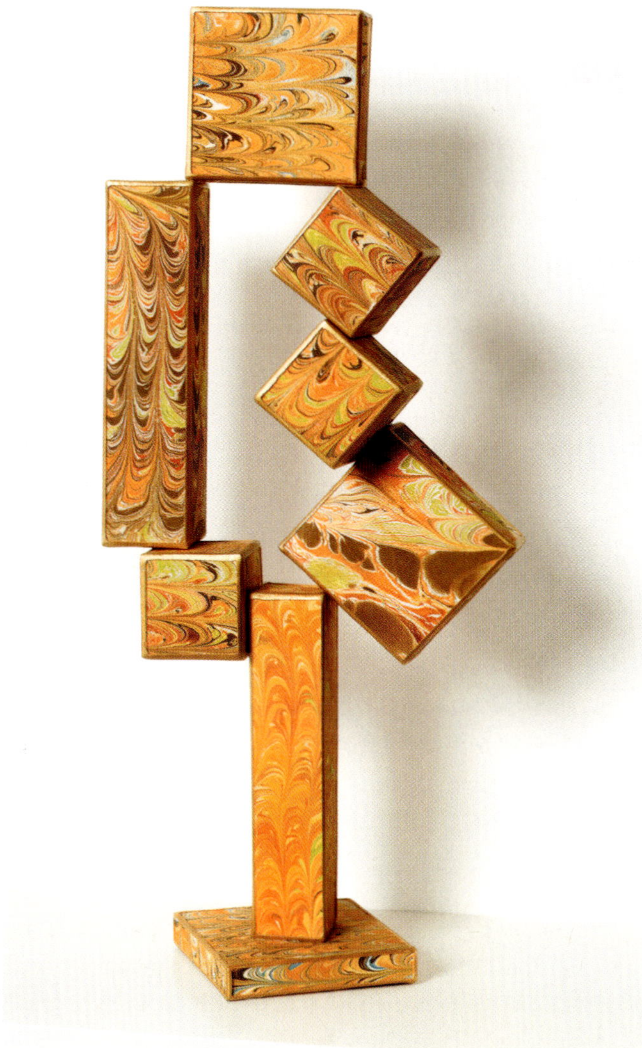

FIGURE 21
Lauren Clay, *No side to fall in (Cubi XII)*, 2012. Paper, acrylic, wooden armature, 18½ × 7 × 3 in. Courtesy the artist.

not make multiples based on the works, and exhibited an agreed-upon artist's statement alongside the sculptures.[51] There is every reason to think that the appeals court ruling in the *Prince* case would have provided a strong precedent for a fair use defense based on their transformative nature, including the craft associations evoked by a young female artist responding to the work of a canonical male modernist. But she was under pressure from a major rights organization, and she also failed to get much support from her exhibition venue, which refused even to take delivery of the work while the dispute was ongoing.

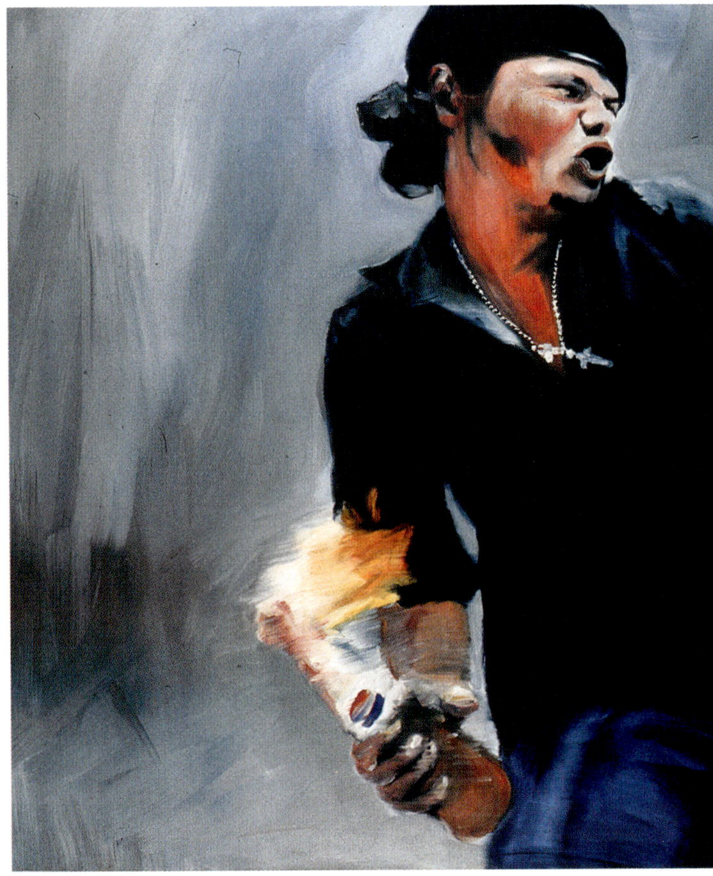

FIGURE 22
Joy Garnett, *Molotov,* 2003. Oil on canvas, 70 × 60 in. Private collection. Courtesy the artist.

Still more striking was the evidence of a rather remarkable misunderstanding of the impact of Smith's sculpture by its purported defender, Robert Panzer, executive director of VAGA. Panzer was quoted by *ArtInfo* to the effect that she "should get permission for that kind of thing . . . because they look just like the original works."[52] It is difficult to imagine how Clay's small-scale versions, covered in marbleized and faux woodgrain paper, could be understood as directly equivalent to Smith's substantial, stainless-steel forms. Furthermore, VAGA's history of charging high fees even for scholarly reproductions of works by the artists and estates they have represented (a form of criticism and commentary that ought to covered by fair use) renders Panzer's suggestion that she should have asked permission patently absurd.

When conflicts of this type reach the point where the issues have been translated into opposing legal briefs, it is easy to lose sight of deeper issues related to shared cultural reference points. Even in situations where money is not the motivating factor (which it often is), the adversarial structure of court cases, the need to frame the issues to fit legal criteria, and the strategic importance of each potential legal prece-

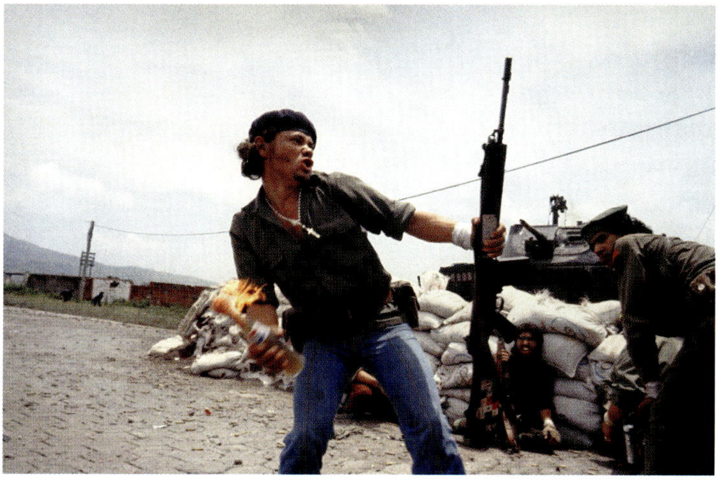

FIGURE 23
Susan Meiselas, *Sandinistas at the Walls of the Esteli National Guard Headquarters,* 1979. © Susan Meiselas/Magnum Photos.

dent add up to a major incentive to choose sides. But the potential for a more nuanced dialogue between the creators themselves, rather than their legal representatives, is indicated by the debate around Joy Garnett's 2003 painting *Molotov* (figure 22), based on a photograph from Susan Meiselas's book *Nicaragua, June 1978–July 1979* that became known as *Molotov Man* (figure 23).

The conflict began in typical fashion, with a cease-and-desist letter sent by Meiselas's lawyer demanding that Garnett sign a retroactive licensing agreement that would require a credit line citing Meiselas's work as a source, along with permission from Meiselas before the painting could be reproduced. When Garnett responded that she would be willing to provide a credit line, but no more, she was hit with further threats as well as a demand for $2,000 for the licensing fee.[53] However, Garnett had been a long-time participant in the pioneering online community Rhizome.org, focused on new media culture, and once she shared information about her travails, fellow members responded with their own reinterpretations of the painting, in a collective online copyright action that was dubbed "Joywar" (a play on an earlier Toywar campaign prompted by a domain name action by toy retailer eToys.com against the digital art group etoy.com). If she had gone to court, Garnett would have defended her work on the basis of fair use. But ultimately Meiselas did not pursue a lawsuit, and after the initial dust had settled, both were invited to present their perspectives at a 2006 symposium and in a 2007 *Harper's* feature based on their talks.

When painting from photographs found in mass media sources, Garnett was specifically interested in the circulation of images, and what happens when they enter into new contexts. By the time Garnett took up *Molotov Man* it had already escaped into the world in multiple versions, including a cropped copy of the photo that Garnett found on an anarchist web site where it was presented without credit. The frame of reference she established was a series of paintings from photographs of figures in physical or emotional extremes, presented in a 2004 exhibition entitled *Riot* at the Debs & Co. gallery. For Meiselas, the act of decontextualization was counter to her wish to provide specific historical reference points for her work—in this case, July 16, 1979, one day before the Sandinista rebels succeeded in taking control of Nicaragua's capital and President Somoza fled the country. Yet Meiselas seemed to welcome its unauthorized dissemination within Nicaragua, thus recognizing its circulation, and the potential range of meanings attached to it, even as she protested against Garnett's use.[54] The publication of their side-by-side statements emphasized this inherent tension, between the desire of the original creator of the image to articulate the significance attached to the moment of its production, and the response by a member of its subsequent audience to its shifting social and historical value as it became part of an extended cultural discourse.

The symposium and associated publication provided a forum where it was possible to appreciate both authorial perspectives, but the impulse to curtail creative engagement was still problematic. Despite the fact that Garnett had a strong fair use case, her perceived need to consult a lawyer for her initial rejoinders meant, in her words, that "it was costing me money merely to hold my ground."[55] Therefore even though Garnett and Meiselas eventually debated their work in a forum where their respective positions did not have to be translated into legally actionable points, Garnett got to that place only because she was able to employ a spokesperson to push back against the initial demands made by Meiselas's representative. As long as hiring a lawyer remains the only effective way to assert one's fair use rights, the vast majority of cease-and-desist letters, even when founded on legally indefensible claims, will remain unanswered, thereby closing down avenues of exploration that should remain free and open.

3

ART, LIFE, AND INFRINGEMENT

THE YEAR 2015 WAS MOMENTOUS for putting children across the world onto the right side of the law. In response to a lawsuit brought by a group of filmmakers who were required by Warner-Chappell to pay licensing fees to use the song "Happy Birthday" in their work (including Jennifer Nelson, the maker of a documentary questioning its copyright status), US District Court Judge George H. King concluded that the music publishing behemoth did not actually own the rights they were vigorously enforcing.

Most people reading this text are probably familiar with the song in question and, truth be told, private singing in the context of a typical birthday celebration was never a copyright issue. But public performance of the twentieth century's most popular song has been another story, involving a long history of payments collected by the music rights association known as ASCAP (the American Society of Composers, Authors and Publishers), with an already substantial revenue stream eventually joined by licensing of film, television, and other recording rights worth millions.

The history reaches back to 1893, when "Good Morning," a song by Mildred and Patty Hill with the same melody but different lyrics, was published by Clayton F. Summy as part of a songbook called *Song Stories*. Somebody (maybe Patty Hill, maybe not) composed alternate "Happy Birthday" lyrics, and that version enjoyed the pre-internet equivalent of viral popularity, entering into general usage in the first decade of the twentieth century, and appearing in plays and films by the early 1930s. A fairly convoluted chain of events included various updated editions of the song book, a 1934 lawsuit by the Hill sisters over the use of the song in a play, a second agreement between the sisters and the publisher in 1934 or 1935, and a 1942 lawsuit brought by the sisters against their publisher over the licensing of movie rights (an issue not covered by their original agreement, since the industry did not yet exist). The crucial matter, however, was Summy Company's 1935 copyright registration for a piano arrangement of "Happy Birthday." By the time that the filmmakers filed suit in 2013, there was no disagreement that the melody had long been in the public domain; the question concerned the associated lyrics, which Warner-Chappell (having acquired the rights from the successor to Summy) argued were protected for ninety-five years after the 1935 registration—therefore until 2030.[1]

When Warner acquired the rights in 1988, they were projected to expire in 2010, but Warner stood to reap annual film and television royalty revenues of $1–2 million per year until that time. Even at that point the song's copyright was notorious as an example of excessive duration, no matter how viewed, and the rights became only more expansive, as well as valuable, following the 1998 US Copyright Term Extension Act. Based on a close analysis of the provenance history on which the claim was based, however, the court concluded that Summy, and therefore Warner, had never actually acquired rights to the lyrics. Warner's proposed settlement not only clarified the public domain status of the words, but also included money to repay past royalty fees—though the clearest winners, based on total percentages, were undoubtedly the plaintiff's lawyers.

There are many issues raised by this example. One is the duration of copyright, with terms that have been repeatedly lengthened over the last two centuries, such that they verge on perpetual. Another is the web of ownership claims associated with images, texts, and sounds that pervade many forms of everyday usage, with challenges exacerbated by problems determining copyright status in the absence of registration requirements. A third is the potential layering of rights in any cultural form that incorporates a response to previous material. Finally, there is the difficulty of defending those rights to which one is clearly entitled, if the only recourse against an infringement accusation is to hire a lawyer.

At the root of copyright is a simple premise: authors should be able to benefit from their work by preventing unauthorized copies. But little is so straightforward. No creative activity takes place in a vacuum, absent of influence, so original and derivative are never all that far apart. It is equally apparent that many changes to copyright law, including ever-longer terms and anti-circumvention regulations, are designed to protect corporate interests rather than individual authors. And copyright is just one segment of an immensely complex economy driven by equally dense networks of trademark and patent claims. It also quickly becomes clear that intellectual property's basic utilitarian justification—that it provides an economic incentive to innovate—is not necessarily supported by analysis of current dynamics. In her study of the role of IP for a range of creators and inventors, Jessica Silbey found that it functioned this way only sporadically, sometimes helping, but often hindering creativity and invention, and in that respect undermining the standard incentive theory of IP.[2] This breakdown in copyright's basic rationale is potentially even more dramatic in the post-internet world: Mark Lemley points out, for example, that even though the music industry as such has experienced declining revenues during recent decades, more songs than ever are now being released.[3]

One frequently referenced example of copyright's negative consequences is *Eyes on the Prize,* Henry Hampton's fourteen-part PBS series tracing the civil rights struggle in the United States. The documentary debuted to tremendous acclaim in 1987, but could no longer be rebroadcast by the mid-1990s because of difficulties renewing rights for archival footage, images, and music incorporated into the narrative. Responding to a 2005 initiative to promote unauthorized screenings of *Eyes on the Prize* that was designed to dramatize, through an act of transgression, the vital importance of access to information, Sonia Katyal and Eduardo Peñalver drew crucial parallels (as well as contrasts) to the lunch-counter sit-ins of the early 1960s.[4] Although new licensing agreements and the removal of some material did eventually enable the rerelease of the first six episodes, along with a version of the other eight for educational institutions, the larger message concerns increasingly high fees for source material crucial to understanding recent historical events.[5] Ironically enough, music requiring copyright clearance included the anthem "We Shall Overcome" and "Happy Birthday," the latter captured in footage of Martin Luther King Jr.'s staff singing to him on his thirty-ninth birthday.

A wave of derision did cause ASCAP to back down from a 1996 demand that the Girl Scouts pay royalties for singing songs like "Edelweiss," "This Land Is Your Land," or "God Bless America" around the fire during summer camp, though only because their dunning letters were publicized by a *Wall Street Journal* article.[6] But seemingly no amount of persuasion will convince the family of Martin Luther King Jr. to forego hefty licensing fees for his 1963 "I Have a Dream" speech, which is not due to enter the public domain until 2038. In the meantime, his heirs aggressively police unauthorized uses in the name of protecting his legacy while selling the rights to employ it in commercial pitches ranging from cell phones to luxury cars.[7]

But it is not always just about the money, as a lawyer for the three surviving Beatles asserted when filing suit to halt a 1987 Nike commercial that incorporated their 1968 song "Revolution," in a fruitless attempt to head off what would become an onslaught of iconic musical statements appropriated for commercial purposes. The quest was doomed by the degree to which the Beatles had lost ownership of their musical achievements, with licensing rights to the original recordings then held by EMI-Capitol, while publishing rights had been acquired by Michael Jackson.[8] As this example indicates, monetization of culture is often linked to loss of creative control.

On the one hand, widespread digitalization has created a climate where there is at least the illusion of access to cultural material on demand. But the flip side to this abundance is an ever-expanding network of copyright claims, joined by increasingly pervasive mechanisms to discover and suppress potential infringement. These tensions were already present, in response to analog modes for recording and distribution that developed over the course of the twentieth century. But the current speed by which groundbreaking technologies are rolled out, only to be replaced by others in short order, is the basis for an ongoing dance between new ways that individuals can interact with their digitalized surroundings, and renewed attempts to control or restrict those exchanges.

While the efficient commercialization of culture does benefit creators to some degree, it is important to look closely at what is potentially lost. In particular, the value of any creative work is directly dependent on its significance for a wider audience. An overly restrictive understanding of authorship, and associated ownership, fails to acknowledge how works derive their fame from a dialogue in which the audience plays an active role. "Happy Birthday" presents a striking example. The status of the intellectual property that Warner-Chappell claimed to own was directly tied to its cultural ubiquity—with each and every performance at a child's birthday party or other unofficial event therefore contributing to the monetary value of the copyright the media company so aggressively pursued. "Happy Birthday" is now freed from such restraints, but many other aspects of our shared cultural heritage are accompanied by surprising restrictions. For much of the twentieth century, such property claims had little direct impact on the private lives of most individuals. But as daily existence is digitalized and shared, almost anyone can find themselves accused of trespass.

Building on the previous discussion of artistic appropriation, this chapter traces some of the ways that proprietary claims over culture are continuing to play out, ranging from how museums manage intellectual property rights in relation to collection objects, to the continuum between shared building blocks and direct quotation in popular music, and certain issues raised by tattoos. These varied examples help demonstrate the palimpsest of ownership assertions often attached to cultural phenomena. They also suggest the many dangers posed by intellectual property land grabs, as both individuals and institutions attempt to navigate terrain filled with unclear boundaries that foster a climate of caution, even fear, rather than incentive.

MUSEUM OWNERSHIP

For art museums, traditionally focused on the display and preservation of objects, an evolving relationship to copyright reflects a series of forces, including changes in law, greater attention by artists to their authorial rights, transformations in the nature of the art that enters the collection, and the increasing deployment of public-facing digital resources. For the majority of modern and contemporary works in their collections, museums have to consider the distinction between owning an object and controlling reproduction rights—including sometimes exorbitant demands from heirs, operating through rights organizations, when reproducing exhibited works in their own publications. Museums are also facing challenges associated with preserving a range of newer media. Such conservation efforts often require migration or other forms of replication, and in this respect, art museums are grappling with the same fast-moving cycles of obsolescence and decay that threaten many facets of contemporary archival preservation. At the same time, however, scholars have railed against image fees some museums demand for art clearly in the public domain, made possible by controlling access to the object.

Reproductions have long been part of the picture, including nineteenth-century copy collections and the resplendent gift shops woven into modern museums. During the nineteenth century, museum galleries were typically filled with both copies and copyists, and institutional participation in the production of the objects on exhibit included traffic in plaster casts. The Boston Museum of Fine Arts actually sold an initial bequest of paintings in order to acquire the plaster casts on display when the museum opened in 1876 (figure 24).[9] It is striking how intensively casts were collected during the nineteenth century, and how decisively they went out of fashion during the early decades of the twentieth century, in favor of unique originals. That pivot was obviously part of the backdrop for Walter Benjamin's classic 1936 essay describing the impact of mechanical reproduction on the character of authenticity he encompassed under the term aura, even as he also implicated exhibition value as another factor in extracting works of art from the fabric of tradition. Under the auspices of postmodern strategies of appropriation, however, copies have reentered museum galleries as works of authorship, and museums have become increasingly attuned to the copyright challenges associated with their collections as they continue to redefine their role in a culture permeated by image replication and circulation.

Although there is a troubling history of museums asserting copyright over reproductions of works in their collections—often in combination with prohibitions against visitor photography—many have begun shifting away from both restrictions. In 2009, London's National Portrait Gallery sent notice to Derrick Coetzee threatening legal action regarding over three thousand high-resolution images he had uploaded to Wikimedia Commons. He initially downloaded the images using a script that allowed him to capture the entirety of high-resolution files presented on the museum's website via software that was supposed to limit viewers to zooming in on details. Coetzee, who lived in the United States, responded by also sharing the cease-and-desist letter, and enlisting the support of the Electronic Frontier Foundation. The EFF argued forcefully against the implication that material would have to be in the public domain in every part of the world in order to be posted to the internet, while also citing US precedents

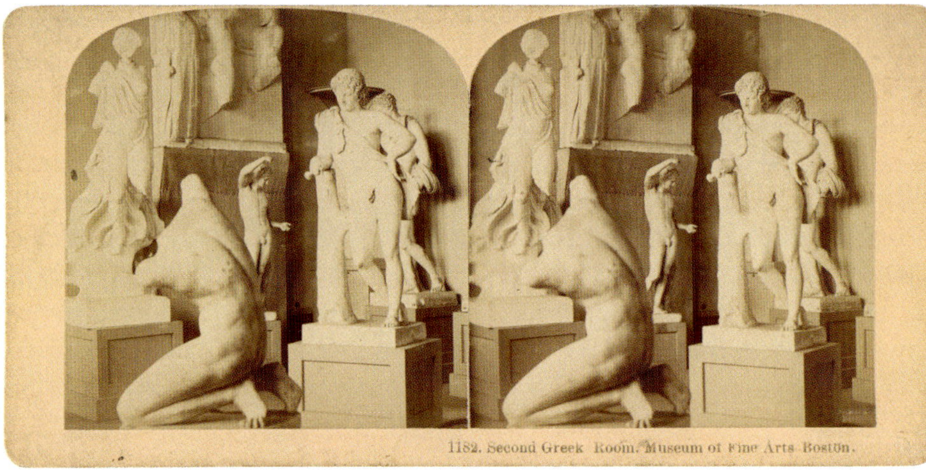

FIGURE 24
Littleton View Co., *Second Greek Room, Museum of Fine Arts, Boston,* ca. 1870–1900. Stereograph, Library of Congress.

that would not accord copyright protection to such two-dimensional images regardless.[10] Interestingly enough, the upshot of this dispute was not a lawsuit, but rather an apparent shift in policy at the National Portrait Gallery, which in 2012 announced the release of 53,000 low-resolution images for use under a Creative Commons license, together with an additional 87,000 high-res images free for academic use.[11]

The museum's change of heart is paralleled by decisions at an increasing number of institutions to begin making high-resolution images of public domain works from their collection freely available for scholars, and sometimes even more widely—with the Victoria and Albert Museum, Metropolitan Museum of Art, British Museum, Rijksmuseum, J. Paul Getty Trust, and Yale Museums taking some of the first steps in this direction. A related choice by many museums to ease restrictions on visitor photography reflects both acknowledgment of a losing battle and potential advantages from social media sharing. Fulfillment of their public mission is proffered as one reason for the shifts, though there is also the practical matter of how little revenue was actually generated in proportion to the logistics of image fulfillment. But even fairly recently, there is the counterexample of Mannheim's Reiss-Engelhorn-Museen, which mounted a 2016 lawsuit against a visitor for uploading photographs of collection objects to Wikimedia—with the images in question including both his own photos and some scanned from museum reproductions.[12]

In the United States, the 1998 decision in *Bridgeman Art Library v. Corel Corp.* determined that a photographic reproduction of a two-dimensional object is not, in itself, sufficiently original to merit copyright protection. Although officially limited in scope to the specific jurisdiction covered by the lower court where it was issued (New York's southern district), the ruling has not been challenged, and it has become an assumed standard in the US context. Wikimedia has likewise followed this model, promoting the principle that faithful reproductions of 2D public domain works of art remain in the public domain.

Despite the growing consensus that reproductions of 2D objects do not merit copyright protection, the same is not necessarily true in relation to photographs of sculpture or other three-dimensional works, given the much greater range of choices that have to be made, including vantage point and lighting. But what about a faithful 3D scan of a 3D object? Might the *Bridgeman* principle apply? Given the increasing accessibility of 3D scanning technology, these questions are quickly becoming urgent. Still other issues come into play in circumstances where the copy has proven more stable than the original, with historical examples including now-eroded sculptures that have lost many of the details recorded in plaster casts, and various recent campaigns to use 3D scanning to preserve a semblance of cultural material threatened with acts of destruction.

Under what circumstances does a 3D copy have the potential to become a new work of authorship? One answer can be found in a series of responses by Allan McCollum to material more likely to be found in a natural history museum—where he created direct copies of preexisting, often ancient examples, under circumstances that required institutional participation. McCollum's 1991 *Lost Objects*, first shown at the 1991 Carnegie International, presented a dramatic array of 750 reproduction bones (made from fifteen different molds), each complete with the type of inventory number typically found on natural history specimens (figure 25). Dinosaur bones are certainly not covered by copyright, but gaining access to such material requires a different form of permission. In order to create the work, McCollum had to enter into a contractual agreement with the Carnegie Museum of Natural History authorizing the use of the replicas "as art objects" and specifying that they would not be "sold as natural history objects (e.g., to natural history museums, private collectors of fossils, natural history casting labs)."[13] McCollum has attributed this limitation to the fact that natural history museums do sell various forms of replica to other institutions, but there is an obvious irony in requiring an artist to agree only to make art as a condition for access.

As consumers acquire increasingly powerful and portable scanning tools, however, museums are facing the possibility that 3D scanning may become as ubiquitous as 2D photography and video—and artists have been quick to highlight this transition. In something of a demonstration case, Nora Al-Badri and Jan Nikolai Nelles made headlines in 2015–16 with their claim to have created an illicit 3D scan of the bust of Nefertiti that is a star attraction at Berlin's Neues Museum (figure 26). The virtual heist was dramatized through two videos, one showing Al-Badri circling the bust in the act of surreptitious recording, and a second that appears to capture the 3D rendering being unearthed from shifting sands. Equally noteworthy was their gesture of releasing their data file to the general public under a Creative Commons license. But questions were quickly raised about their story of achieving the scan with a hacked Kinect Sensor, both because of its

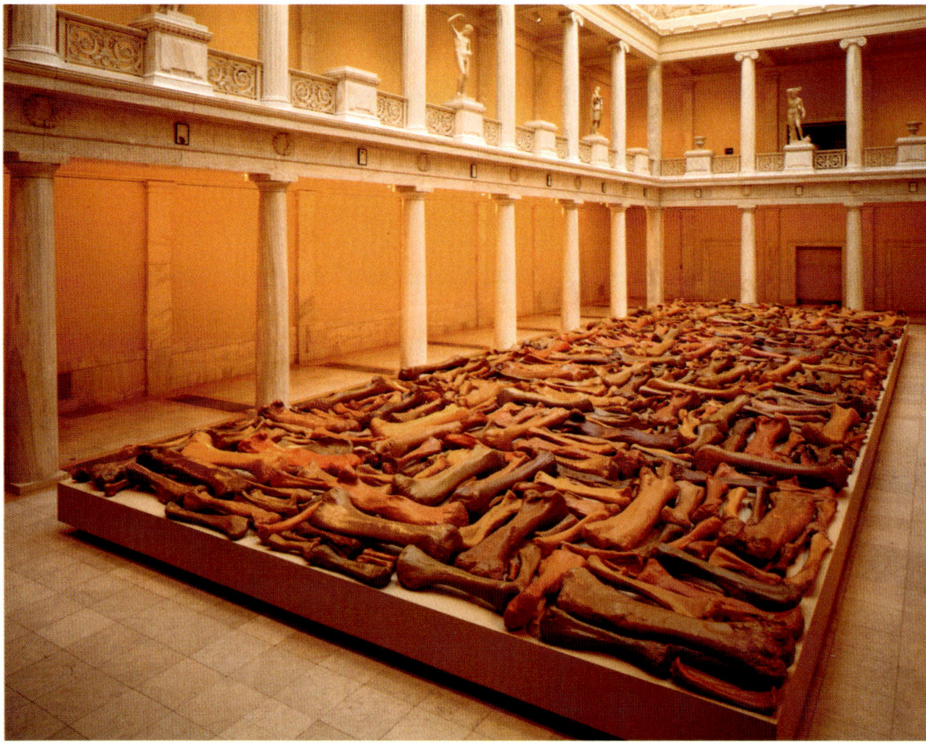

FIGURE 25
Allan McCollum, *Collection of Seven Hundred and Fifty Lost Objects,* 1991. Enamel on glass-fiber-reinforced cast concrete. Installation: 1991 Carnegie International, curated by Lynne Cooke and Mark Francis, Carnegie Museum of Art, Pittsburgh, Pennsylvania, 1991–92. Courtesy the artist.

high resolution and details from the top of the sculpture that were inconsistent with the story of walking around it with a scanning device hidden beneath a scarf. Some speculated that they had obtained a scan produced by the museum itself.[14]

By displaying a physical realization of their 3D scan in Cairo, not far from its original find spot, Al-Badri and Nelles also inserted themselves into a broader dialogue about rights over cultural patrimony. The bust was originally discovered in Egypt in 1912, where it was excavated from the site of the sculptor Thutmose's studio as part of a dig led by Ludwig Borchardt of the German Archeological Institute in Cairo. Under the partage system then in effect, the results of the dig were divided between Egypt and the holder of the excavation permit. Various requests have since been made for the work's return to Egypt. Nefertiti, along with the Parthenon marbles in the British Museum, and many holdings of Benin objects dating to the British Punitive Expedition of 1897 (to mention just two prominent examples), has thus been the focus of repatriation demands that far exceed provisions of the 1970 UNESCO convention for the protection of cultural property—which guards against illicit traffic in cultural property

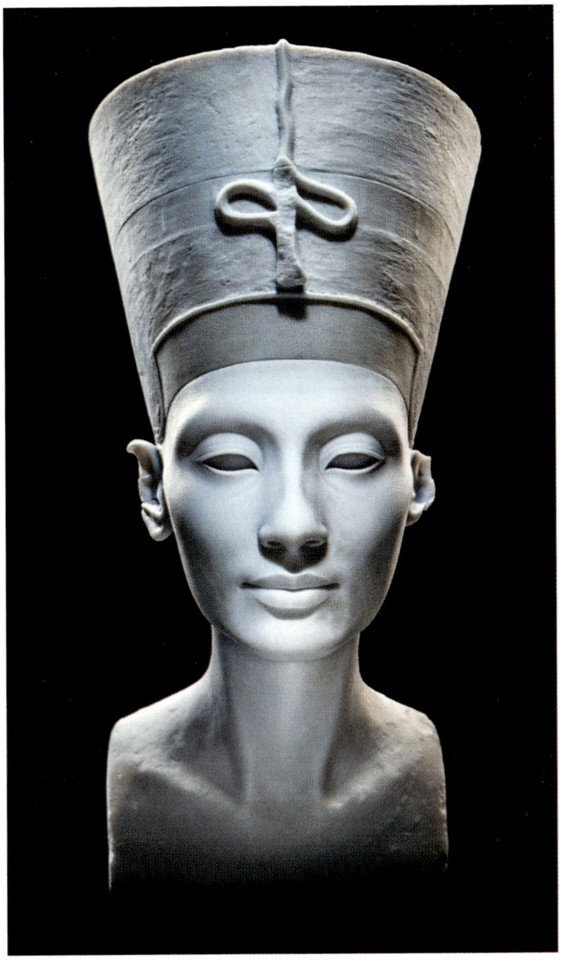

FIGURE 26
Nora Al-Badri and Jan Nikolai Nelles, *The Other Nefertiti,* 2015. 3D print. Courtesy the artists.

starting in 1972, but not retroactively. The timeliness of the issues raised by the Nefertiti intervention was confirmed by a new series of repatriation initiatives, starting with the 2018 release of a report, commissioned by French President Emmanuel Macron, calling for the return of looted African works, with the French announcement quickly followed by promised action in other countries.[15]

The Nefertit case also took a new turn in 2019. Intrigued by the story of the digital heist, Cosmo Wenman filed a freedom of information request for the Neues Museum's scan, based on the fact that it is a state-owned institution. After a three-year quest, the museum eventually handed over the file, and he in turn posted the digital information to Thingiverse (figure 27).[16] But he and others quickly noticed an oddity, in the form of a Creative Commons license issued by the Staatliche Museen zu Berlin that appears (virtually) incised on the base of the sculpture. If valid, the primary effect would be to limit commercial exploitation of the file. Yet only a rightsholder has the authority to

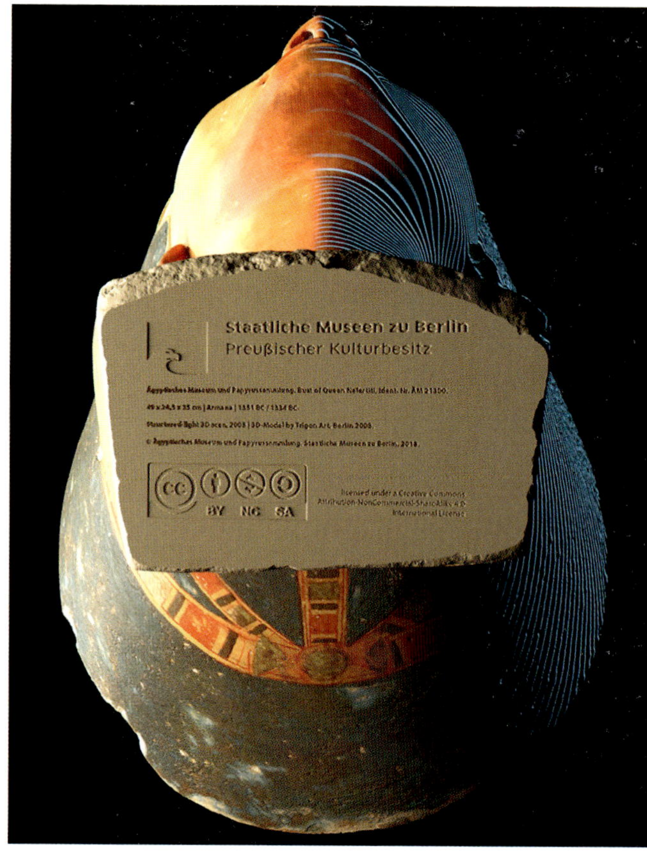

FIGURE 27
Cosmo Wenman, Bust of Nefertiti, FOIA results, posted to Thingiverse, November 13, 2019, under Creative Commons license CC BY-NC-SA 4.0.

issue a Creative Commons license, and there is general agreement that the work itself was made circa 1351–1334 BCE. Moreover, the principle that exact digital copies of public domain works do not qualify for copyright was affirmed by Article 14 of the otherwise problematic copyright directive passed by the European Union in 2019.

Despite various ownership claims, one maneuver museums have generally not tried is asserting copyright based on changes to the object. Works that have been extensively reconstructed are, in a sense, partially authored by the institutions that house them. There are numerous examples of supposedly original works subject to invasive reworking over the centuries (including the exceedingly heavy-handed interventions undertaken by Joseph Van der Veken that were featured in a 2004 exhibition *Fake or not Fake*), with some of those restorations taking place within the timeframe covered by typical copyright codes.[17] As a work moves through time, the additions by others tend to increase. However, claiming copyright over purportedly historical works because of changes to the objects themselves is hardly an argument most museums are apt to make. One can only hope that it will likewise be increasingly insupportable for museums to restrict the circulation of reproductions of public domain objects that they hold in trust.

It is equally important to recognize the leadership role that museums have been taking in relation to new media preservation. Art museums, along with libraries and archives of all kinds, have been racing to address threats to cultural heritage posed by perilous cycles of decay and obsolescence for the media within which texts, sounds, images, and other related forms have been recorded. For analog forms, the challenges include both inherent vice (materials prone to disintegration regardless of how well they are cared for) and the disappearance of playback equipment. In the wake of widespread digitalization, problems with physical decay have been exacerbated by quickly evolving software. Under these circumstances, a conservation paradigm that emphasizes maintaining physical material in its original form (the traditional museum standard) is a potential death warrant for works dependent on compatibility with available technologies. Yet many of the obvious strategies for maintaining viability, including copying material to different formats and rewriting software code to address playback functionality, run up against copyright and anticircumvention restrictions. Because of the multiple ways that contemporary artists have incorporated different technologies, and the lessons learned from early collecting activities in this area, art museums already have a significant track record of grappling with challenges facing all modes of cultural preservation.[18]

MUSIC SAMPLING AND THE TYRANNY OF LICENSING FEES

Comparisons to music sampling abound in early discussions of artistic appropriation—with good reason. Both forms aggressively borrow from preexisting expressions, incorporating quoted elements into new works even as the source is likely to remain recognizable. In a world saturated with images and sounds, both practices treat the landscape of the already recorded as fair game. Their legal fortunes are intertwined as well, with key court decisions serving as precedents in both spheres. Yet there are significant differences with respect to the logistics of authorship, inseparable from distinctions in form, audience, and business models—with music industry revenue based on licensing fees, in contrast to the sale of unique or limited-edition art objects.

In the visual arts, it is typical to find quite elaborate productions presented under singular authorship, and demands for credit or acknowledgement are potentially more a matter of honor. In the music industry, as with other evidently collaborative forms, including film and theater, the tradition of recognizing particular contributions is often enforced by union agreements. Nor is this simply a matter of principle, given the degree to which credit is linked to shared financial gain from royalty-based revenue streams—in contrast to the one-time sale of a work of art. For music there are generally at least two sets of rights at issue, with ownership of musical compositions distinct from control over a specific recording. The broad audience reach associated with musical fame and fortune is linked to pervasive industry forces that can strip musicians of ownership rights as well as control over their careers. In one widely publicized act of resistance, the creator of *Purple Rain* (1984) and other milestones became "the artist formerly known as Prince" when he changed his name to an unpronounceable symbol in order to protest Warner Brothers' contractual control over how and when his music was released.[19]

During a brief window in the 1970s and 1980s, as recording artists built on DJ strategies for looped or layered sound, remix culture was sufficiently removed from the mainstream that it had a chance to develop without major hurdles. But once hip-hop and rap began to reach wider audiences, with attendant publicity and financial success, sampling practices prompted legal action on behalf of rightsholders—often not the musicians in question, but rather companies that have managed to acquire musical properties. Adding to the complexity has been the layering of rights, with owners of the musical composition often not the same as those holding rights to a specific recording.

The first US music sampling case to be pursued to a decisive conclusion in the courts (rather than being settled) was *Grand Upright Music, Ltd v. Warner Bros. Records Inc.* At issue was Biz Markie's 1991 "Alone Again," which incorporated elements from Gilbert O'Sullivan's 1972 "Alone Again (Naturally)"—both a few bars sampled from the original piano riff and Markie singing part of the hook.[20] Markie's legal case was not helped by the fact that his label had tried to get permission for the use, then released the song anyway despite O'Sullivan's refusal. But the judge was also profoundly unsympathetic. In addition to forbidding continued sale of both the song and the album, and ordering Markie to pay $250,000 in damages, the judge assailed the sampling as outright theft that would merit criminal charges.

The second major case, however, gave somewhat more room for hope. The Supreme Court's 1994 decision in *Campbell v. Acuff-Rose Music, Inc.* established an important precedent when it articulated a transformative standard in determining that 2 Live Crew's parody of Roy Orbison's "Oh, Pretty Woman" was an example of fair use. 2 Live Crew did indeed sample extensively from the Orbison original, including guitar, bass, and drums, but the twisted version of the lyrics also fit the framework of parody. As subsequent visual arts cases involving appropriation by Jeff Koons and Richard Prince attest, the transformative principle established by *Campbell* was a crucial turning point for fair use claims. But in the music world, when samples are treated as a form of raw material to be incorporated into a new, potentially unrelated whole, there has been surprisingly little reliance on fair use.

One of Markie's responses to his legal troubles was his 1993 album *All Samples Cleared.* Even if this was meant as a jab, however, the title points to an actual music industry shift, with record companies insisting on preapproval for samples. The associated fees, assessed on a case-by-case basis, mean that any attempt to incorporate large numbers of musical quotations is likely to become prohibitively expensive. Not only is clearing samples a major hurdle under any circumstance, but each can require more than one set of negotiations, if composition and recording rights are held by different entities. Sometimes a partial workaround is to replay the sample in question, thus cutting out recording rights from the permissions equation, but transforming a sample into a cover is a potentially a dramatic shift in practice as well as ethos.

A company called Bridgeport has been at the center of many key infringement cases due to its aggressive monetization of samples drawn from the extensive back catalogue of rights it has managed to acquire. The volume of litigation has caused it to be described as a "sample troll," akin to "patent trolls" that base their business model on taking legal action against businesses or individuals over claims of similarity to patents they own, rather than attempting to develop anything themselves.[21] In particular, Bridgeport's control over George Clinton's widely sampled work, including albums by his Parliament and Funkadelic ensembles, has resulted in an insistently pursued revenue stream, and Kembrew McLeod has pointed out how Bridgeport's maneuvers have included action against Clinton himself.[22] Clinton did win a partial legal victory in 2005, regaining ownership through court order of the master recordings for four Funkadelic albums from the 1970s, which opened up the possibility that he might derive some of the benefit from licensing fees. But he was less successful in his attempts to win back rights over his musical compositions, losing cases against Bridgeport in both 2001 and 2013.[23]

With ownership rights affirmed by their initial victory against Clinton, Bridgeport filed no fewer than 476 copyright infringement actions in 2001. Although most were presumably resolved privately, a 2005 Sixth Circuit ruling in *Bridgeport Music v. Dimension Films* further narrowed the field of possibility for sampling by explicitly negating the *de minimis* exception, which refers to something too small or trivial to merit court consideration. The case concerned a two-second sample of a three-note arpeggio from Clinton's "Get Off Your Ass and Jam," which was lowered in pitch and looped to form sixteen beats for its incorporated into N.W.A.'s "100 Miles and Running." No sample size is too small to escape clearance requirements, according to Sixth Circuit Judge Ralph Guy, whose analysis included a draconian instruction to musicians: "Get a license or do not sample."[24] More recently, however, the Ninth Circuit took a divergent view in their 2016 decision in *VMG Salsoul, LLC v. Madonna Ciccone,* affirming a 2013 lower court ruling that a 0.23-second horn blast, borrowed from a 1976 song called "Love Break" and incorporated by Madonna into her 1990 song "Vogue," would not be recognizable to the average listener, and therefore, as a *de minimis* exception, did not constitute infringement.

The judge in *Bridgeport Music v. Dimension Films* insisted that requiring all samples to be licensed would not constitute "stifling creativity in any significant way," since, "if an artist wants to incorporate a 'riff' from another work in his or her recording, he is free to duplicate the sound of that 'riff' in the studio."[25] But sampling cases involving Kraftwerk give striking evidence that even remaking a sound effect might not be enough. For Afrika Bambaataa's 1982 "Planet Rock," Bambaataa and producer Arthur Baker responded to two Kraftwerk songs, but without actually sampling. Rather, they relied on the same type of synthesizer to create similar drum machine and other sounds. As Bambaataa recounted, "John Robie was a bad-ass synthesizer player, so he was just so good in playing stuff, that it sounded like they sampled off the record."[26] But this did not stop Kraftwerk from coming after them, and they apparently wound up settling out of court for a significant sum of money.[27]

Courts outside the United States are wrestling with similar issues. In 2012 Kraftwerk won an initial ruling in a German lawsuit involving a two-second drum sample from their 1977 "Metall auf Metall"—incorporated by hip-hop producer Moses Pelham into Sabrina Setlur's 1997 song "Nur Mir." That initial decision indicated that an independent simulation of Kraftwerk's sounds might have been permissible, but that direct sampling was not. However, the decision in the case was reversed by a 2016 ruling by Germany's highest court, which found that the impact on Kraftwerk was not sufficient to outweigh the importance of artistic freedom. According to Supreme Court Vice President Ferdinand Kirchhof, by using the sample, Pelham and Setlur had created "a completely new and independent work of art" without "lessening the potential of the original (Kraftwerk) recording."[28] It is unfortunate that this logic—emphasizing the question of whether the quotation has an appreciable impact on the viability of the original—does not prevail more often.

It is equally important to recognize the complex interplay between composition and recording rights. For many sampling cases, the quoted material relies on widely shared chords or rhythms. In such instances, it is only the use of fragments of a composition, as performed on a particular recording, that provides the basis for copyright claims. The associated digital signatures are also increasingly subject to software-driven search functions, even in instances where the sample is not readily discernable through listening alone. The reliance on technology to discover brief samples that might otherwise pass unnoticed is just one marker of the excesses that result when the act of authorship is viewed almost exclusively through the lens of property creation. Courts, and particularly jury trials, are unfortunately a highly unpredictable forum for addressing what is and is not protectable in the context of creative works that draw heavily on a tapestry of intersecting traditions and formal devices.

BLURRED LOGIC

Explicit sampling is part of a larger story of contested authorship of popular music, including a substantial history of white rock musicians borrowing heavily from blues or Motown conventions. When vast disparities in popularity and financial reward are involved, it can be difficult to disentangle participation in a shared tradition from simple exploitation—with the separation between influence and direct borrowing often dependent on who has the resources to assert a claim. As important recent cases have demonstrated, the court system is a crude instrument for sorting out such questions, both because of the inherently adversarial structure, and the likelihood that those making the decisions will have little musical expertise.

A particularly troubling lawsuit involving the work of Marvin Gaye highlighted the difficulty of asking judges and juries to sort out distinctions between common traditions and direct appropriation. The decision went in favor of Gaye's estate, in their conflict with Robin Thicke over similarities between "Blurred Lines" (2013) and Gaye's "Got to Give It Up" (1977), despite strong evidence that the later work was written independently by Thicke and Pharrell Williams, not copied. Lawyers for Thicke and Williams were sufficiently confident that they responded to the initial infringement accusation by preemptively suing the accusers to get a declaration of non-infringement. It is worth noting, too, that the shorthand for the initial suit was *Pharrell Williams et al v. Bridgeport Music Inc et al*, since Bridgeport was asserting that "Blurred Lines" also infringed on Funkadelic's "Sexy Ways." By early 2014, however, the opposing field had been narrowed down to Gaye's descendants.[29]

Thicke and Williams scored what appeared to be an early victory when their lawyers succeeded with arguments that sound recordings of the two songs should be inadmissible, based on provisions of the 1909 copyright act, still in effect in 1977, which defined publication, for the purpose of registering copyright, in terms of the sheet music deposited with the Copyright Office. Significantly, Gaye did not read music, so the sheet music was an after-the-fact translation that served to reduce the totality of Gaye's performance-based authorship to a series of notations (with an amicus brief filed in support of the estate emphasizing the disadvantage for aural musicians in the face of this type of intellectual property requirement). However, Thicke didn't do himself any favors with testimony where he described being wasted on alcohol and Vicodin when composing the song, or statements made beforehand where he recounted telling Williams how much he liked "Got to Give It Up," and that they should make something "like that, something with that groove."[30]

In a March 2014 interview, Williams expressed faith in their position, voicing "utmost respect for Marvin Gaye and his music," but insisting, at the same time, that "you can't trademark a groove." According to Williams, "If I play a song . . . that's done in 6/8 time signature, Charlie Parker's family is not going to sue me for that. . . . If I do a salsa beat right now, I know that Ricky Martin's family is not going to come looking for me." Stressing that differences between Gaye's work and his own should be apparent by looking at the actual notes, Williams saw "no comparison between the minor, bluesy chords he was playing and my major, bluegrass-y chords, and that's very plain to see for anyone who can read music."[31] Unfortunately for Williams and Thicke, the members of an average jury pool are unlikely to possess such knowledge, and instead have to rely on expert testimony. When the case was tried in a Los Angeles district court in March 2015, the experts appearing for Gaye's heirs were apparently more convincing, since the jury decided in favor of the Gaye estate, awarding it $7.3 million (later decreased by the judge in the case to $5.3 million) plus 50 percent of future royalties.

Appealing the jury decision, Williams and Thicke's lawyers argued that the case should never have gone to trial, since there was no substantial similarity between the sheet music for the two songs as a matter of law—and reiterated that a "groove" or "feeling" can't be copyrighted. Their arguments failed to persuade a majority of the Ninth Circuit judges hearing the case, resulting in a March 2018 decision that affirmed the jury verdict on fairly narrow procedural grounds. But the opinion was not unanimous, and Judge Jacqueline Nguyen issued a strongly worded dissent. Showing greater understanding of the musical issues at hand, she insisted that the two works were "not objectively similar," due to differences in "melody, harmony, and rhythm," and she therefore faulted the courts for allowing Gaye's heirs to "copyright a musical style." Accusing their expert of establishing the comparison between the two works on the basis of cherry-picked fragments, she characterized the analysis as "the equivalent of finding substantial similarity between two pointillist paintings because both have a few flecks of similarly colored paint."[32] As opposed to the court bowing down before the jury conclusion, Nguyen insisted, Williams and Thicke should have prevailed as a matter of law, since the finding of infringement turned on claims emphasizing substantial similarity between elements that were both unprotectable and objectively dissimilar.

The potential consequences of the "Blurred Lines" case quickly became apparent when a jury found that Katy Perry's song "Dark Horse" bore too close a resemblance to Marcus Gray's more obscure "Joyful Noise." Although Perry said she had never heard the song, its distribution on YouTube could theoretically have provided access. More to the point, Perry's lawyer argued that the riffs in both songs were so generic that any attempt to copyright them would be akin to "trying to own basic building blocks of music, the alphabet of music that should be available to everyone."[33] As another music attorney summed up the issue, "There are only 12 notes you can work with, and so things are going to sound alike without technically infringing."[34] This logic apparently prevailed, since the jury award against Perry was subsequently thrown out in a 2020 ruling by US District Court Judge Christina Snyder, who found that because the basic sequence of notes at issue was not protectable expression, the infringement verdict failed as a matter of law. Snyder also referenced an important 2020 Ninth Circuit appeals court ruling affirming a 2016 jury determination that the opening riff from Led Zeppelin's "Stairway to Heaven" had not infringed on Spirit's "Taurus." Given that popular music is indeed the basis for a highly organized and lucrative industry, it is not surprising that copyright claims are sometimes aggressively pursued. But cases focused on passing similarities, within the context of widely shared musical structures and conventions, provide ample evidence of ownership culture run amok.

FAIR SAMPLING

It is striking, given the general importance of *Campbell,* that there have been few attempts to extend its articulation of transformative fair use to cover non-parodic sampling.[35] One of the rare cases to push this strategy, *Bridgeport Music, Inc. v. UMG Recordings, Inc.* (yet another of the nearly five hundred cases filed by Bridgeport in

2001), concerned a 1998 song, "D.O.G. in Me" by the rhythm and blues group Public Announcement, which sampled from George Clinton's 1982 "Atomic Dog." The defense was unsuccessful, with a 2009 Sixth Circuit appeals court decision upholding a district court jury finding of infringement for sampling "the phrase 'Bow wow wow, yippie yo, yippie yea' (the 'Bow Wow refrain'), as well as use repetition of the word 'dog' in a low tone of voice at regular intervals and the sound of rhythmic panting."[36] The courts were clearly much more focused on the mere fact of quotation than on how the material potentially gained new meaning from being incorporated into a different context.

A major issue in relation to both sound and video is the increasing use of digital tools to screen for potential infringement. For videos posted to YouTube, the excessive reach of Content ID is indicated by stories about sounds as various as birdsong, public domain classical music compositions, and even static noise becoming the target of takedown notices. It is then up to individuals hit with these claims to push back against an increasingly automated system. The nature of the interface makes it difficult to contest even claims that are clearly absurd—such as the background birdsongs recorded during a nature walk that were tagged as copyright infringement by a licensing and royalty management company called Rumblefish.[37]

Yet somehow, in the midst of a generally conservative attitude toward sample clearance, one encounters the striking exception of Girl Talk, the stage name of Gregg Gillis, who gained prominence for mashup albums that explicitly sampled from multiple sources without requesting clearance. The liner notes for his 2006 *Night Ripper*, released by the Illegal Art record label, left no room for confusion by crediting all 164 artists sampled on the album. Although a review on *Pitchfork* described it as "practically begging for court drama," nothing of the kind actually happened.[38] Why did Girl Talk not become a target for legal action? The answer, according to various commentators, was Gillis's explicit claim of fair use, and repeated statements that he would rely on that principle as a defense if sued.[39] If he had been taken to court, and succeeded with a fair use argument based on his transformation of the original sources, that precedent would have changed the clearance landscape dramatically.

Kembrew McLeod took a similar stand in relation to a 2010 documentary film about sampling called *Copyright Criminals* that he co-produced with Benjamin Franzen, despite being painfully aware of the industry-wide litigious attitude. Had they actually attempted to clear copyright, the underlying claims for each sample would have sent them down an endless hall of mirrors, but luckily fair use standards articulated for documentary filmmaking gave them an alternate option.[40] Perhaps because they were able to link their dependence on fair use to a widely circulated code of best practices, they, too, managed to avoid having to defend their stance in court. What these two examples have in common is an explicit statement of their reliance on fair use, thus announcing to anyone who might consider coming after them that they planned to argue a principle that could, if upheld, have far-reaching consequences for all business models based on demanding payment for samples that have unquestionably been incorporated into new aesthetic or critical contexts. While it is impossible to see into the hearts and minds of the various industry players who chose not to pursue legal action, it is attractive to imagine that just hearing the three words "fair use defense" was sufficient to stop them in their tracks.

CELEBRITY IMAGES, AND IMAGES ON CELEBRITIES

When is your own image not actually yours? Stories of celebrities battling paparazzi are legion, with both privacy and right of publicity laws in the United States governed by a patchwork of state legislation. But federal copyright laws come into play as well, with photographers who take paparazzi images sometimes suing celebrities who post the photos to their own social media feeds. And this is just one of many areas where both laws and norms are only gradually catching up with current practices. The fact that it is increasingly feasible for filmmakers to employ computer-generated imagery to create plausible facsimiles of movie stars is opening up huge questions about who has the right to control such appearances, both during an actor's lifetime and posthumously—as well as the likelihood that studios will push actors to sign away these rights as part of contract negotiations.[41]

There are equally crucial definition questions around what constitutes an advertisement in the social media realm, with US-based "influencers" under pressure from the Federal Trade Commission to clearly indicate when they are receiving some form of consideration in exchange for their online enthusiasm.[42] Obviously one of the allures, but also perils, of social media is the intersection between personal and business interests (with business made to look personal, and personal presence leveraged for financial gain). The potential value of a celebrity endorsement was demonstrated when a fast-fashion company called Missguided attempted to promote their knockoff goods by posting to Kim Kardashian's social media feeds, and she fired back with a trademark infringement case that stressed the price of any validation emanating from her illustrious existence. According to her complaint, "a single social media post by Kardashian can fetch fees of several hundred thousand dollars, and her longer-term endorsement arrangements regularly garner fees in the millions of dollars."[43] But even individuals who are not officially fabulous can hope to glean a modest bit of ad-generated revenue if their YouTube videos attract significant views.

Some of the most interesting tensions appear in the realm of celebrity tattoos. Copyrights for original compositions belong to the tattoo artists, even as it is generally understood that their work will be reproduced whenever the body part in question happens to be exposed to a camera. But the appearance of tattoos in extended contexts, such as video games with characters based on well-known athletes, is another story, with copyright matters intertwined with a variety of publicity rights and contractual agreements.

One of the first major cases, concerning former boxer Mike Tyson's facial tattoo, addressed the status of human skin in relation to copyright's requirement that an original work be "fixed in a tangible medium of expression." The complaint from tattoo artist S. Victor Whitmill concerned the design's replication in the 2011 film *The Hangover: Part II*, where the character played by Ed Helms discovers, upon waking up from a night of hard partying, that he has acquired a facial tattoo similar to Tyson's. Interestingly, Whitmill did not sue over fact that Tyson's own face appeared in the film, but only because the tattoo was replicated on another character. The design was, however, closely based on traditional Māori tattoo patterns, raising other questions about the validity of the western artist's copyright claim in the first place. According to Ngahuia Te Awekotuku, an expert on Māori tattoo traditions quoted in various press reports, "The tattooist has an incredible arrogance to assume he has the intellectual right to claim the design form of an indigenous culture that is not his."[44]

Rather than questioning the originality of this specific design, however, lawyers for Warner Bros. made a general argument against tattoo copyrights, emphasizing a lack of physical separability. "Even if the Court were to find that a human body part may serve as a 'medium of expression' under the Copyright Act," they claimed, "Tyson's tattoo would still not be copyrightable because it adorns a 'useful article'—specifically Tyson's head."[45] David Nimmer, author of the widely influential *Nimmer on Copyright* handbook, provided expert testimony for Warner—although his claim that "a body, even as augmented, simply is not subject to copyright protection" appeared at odds with earlier statements suggesting the opposite.[46] As justification, he outlined various potential scenarios, including the possibility that a tattoo's creator, if it were accepted as art of recognized stature under the Visual Artists Rights Act, might invoke moral rights protection to prevent changes to designs adorning a wearer's body. He also envisioned violations of the artist's rights via media images of Tyson's face. But Whitmill's original complaint was careful to distinguish between Tyson's control of his own identity and Warner's use of the art separate from Tyson. District court judge Catherine D. Perry was generally skeptical of the claims put forward by Nimmer, dismissing most of the defendant's arguments as "just silly," since "of course tattoos can be copyrighted," and this assessment presumably helped motivate the studio to reach a settlement agreement with the tattoo artist.[47] Thus there was no ultimate ruling on the potentially more compelling aspect of Warner's defense, describing the quotation as a form of satire protected under fair use.[48] Although attempts by Warner's lawyers to question the entire premise of copyright protection for tattoo art were highly problematic, the parody defense could have established an important precedent.

Since this was only one of multiple lawsuits prompted by the film, clearly *The Hangover: Part II* was not only a box-office hit, but also a bonanza for lawyers.[49] The issue of parody did become relevant for a suit brought by Louis Vuitton over the appearance of an apparently counterfeit version of one of their signature bags. In the film, the Zach Galifianakis character complains about the bag (actually made by a company called Diophy) being roughly handled, warning, "be careful . . . that is a Lewis Vuitton." Warner Bros. were, however, successful in their motion to dismiss Louis Vuitton's claims of potential confusion, with the judge accepting the studio's freedom of expression rights regarding the incorporation of both trademark and counterfeit goods into a storyline.[50] In this instance of multimillion dollar corporations jousting against one another, sympathy goes to Warner—even if the freedom of expression in question was a rather crude comedy about drunken antics, in a franchise that Tyson told a radio interviewer he only signed onto for drug money.[51]

Alongside general recognition that tattoos qualify for copyright protection, there appears to be a tacit consensus that being tattooed carries with it an implied license allowing individuals to display their tattoos in public, including in media coverage. But digital recreations in the context of video games are another story.[52] As early as 2013, the NFL Players Association began advising players and their agents to get tattoo artists to sign release forms, under threat of requiring players to indemnify the association for any infringement problems if they failed to do so.[53] A common workaround, in the lucrative world of video games based on sports figures, has been to avoid depicting their actual tattoos.

One enterprising company called Solid Oak Sketches entered into agreements with a number of tattoo artists responsible for designs inked on major basketball players, including LeBron James, Stephen Curry, and DeAndre Jordan. The company then demanded license fees from 2K Games, and its subsidy, Take-Two Interactive, for the appearance of those tattoos on athletes in their NBA 2K series of basketball simulation games—reportedly to the tune of just under $2 million for past infringement and future use.[54] Individual tattoo artists do periodically sue—including a copyright claim in another "tribal" tattoo, on wrestler Randy Orton, which was reproduced as part of his character in WWE 2K, from the same company.[55] The actions by Solid Oak, however, are striking because they appear to be a clear instance of copyright trolling, with the original tattoo artists reportedly deceived into signing over rights to their designs as part of a deal that was presented as a planned clothing line.[56]

In a declaration of support for 2K Games, James described his tattoos as central to his sense of self: "My understanding is that the tattoos are a part of my body and my likeness, and I have the right to have my tattoos visible when people or companies depict what I look like. . . . My tattoos are a part of my persona and identity; if I am not shown with my tattoos, it wouldn't really be a depiction of me."[57] For the tattoos in question, James described a collaborative process, including specific content requests and providing source material ranging from a baby picture of one of his children to a lion's head from the back of a deck of cards where he liked the image. What is striking is both the degree to which James was directly involved in the design of the tattoos and—presumably not the intended point—a scenario where some of the tattoos incorporated material that was potentially already under copyright by someone else. In the end, however, the final decision shot down most of Solid Oak's arguments, concluding that the brief and small-scale appearance of the tattoos in the game qualified for a *de minimis* exception. More importantly, the judge determined that there was an implied license for the tattoos to be reproduced as part of the players' likenesses, and that their depiction was protected by fair use, including the transformative standard.[58]

Given the widespread popularity of tattoos, and the many ways that both individuals and corporations are attempting to leverage celebrity status, it is possible that tattoo jurisprudence is still in its infancy. Many tattoos feature borrowed imagery, ranging from motifs potentially subject to copyright protection to celebrity likenesses and brand logos. Perhaps the notoriety and likely condemnation will be enough to prevent anyone from bringing legal action that includes a demand to have a tattoo removed or inked over, but it is not beyond the realm of imagination. A lawsuit against the NCAA, Electronic Arts, and Collegiate Licensing Company by former UCLA basketball star Ed O'Bannon also makes it clear how questions about depicting an athlete's tattoos are bound up with related issues about who gets to exploit an individual's identity. The O'Bannon case concerned who should reap the profits associated with "amateur" college athletics in the United States—and it effectively put an end to a highly successful series of interactive video games based on college sports put out by Electronic Arts. Despite the absence of names, the players depicted in the games closely corresponded to college athletes with respect to jersey numbers, statistics, and even their supposedly fictional home states. Electronic Arts indicated that they were willing to pay players for the use of their likenesses, but the NCAA refused to consider an option that would potentially open up other demands for compensation to college athletes.[59]

Issues raised by battles over the right to exploit celebrity images are part of a larger dynamic that both encompasses and extends beyond IP, regarding the degree to which individuals retain the right to control and profit from all aspects of their identity. Related questions include who benefits from information contained in an individual's genes, to the value associated with the endless volumes of personal data harvested over the course of almost any modern interaction. As laws continue to be updated to deal with new technologies and their consequences, it is important to pay close attention to the web of competing interests at play both in specific cases and in proposals to change the legal framework itself.

#SAVEYOURINTERNET

Recent decades have witnessed a growing awareness of the labyrinthine IP interests shaping all aspects of contemporary life. But it is only since masses of individuals began consuming and often sharing media transmitted in the form of digital files that most people have been forced to consider how these laws intersect with their own lives. Early incidents where media companies pursued huge penalties against individuals who had downloaded music or movies did nothing for the popularity of industry heavyweights, but they certainly grabbed everyone's attention. Most people are aware that they are surrounded by IP, even if they are far less clear on their rights in relation to copyright-protected media or branded products. It has also become increasingly evident that politicians, along with the powerful corporations to which they are beholden, cannot be trusted to uphold the broader goals that IP legislation ostensibly promotes.

Even just a few years ago, it would have been difficult to imagine the outpouring of protests, in the name of #SaveYourInternet, that greeted proposed changes to copyright law under a 2019 European Union directive. A key issue concerned the degree of responsibility platforms are required to assume for user-uploaded infringement. Under a "safe harbor" model, platforms are held harmless if they have mechanisms in place to quickly remove infringing material. Excessive takedown demands are problematic enough, given that the mere accusation of infringement is generally sufficient to get material removed, thereby leaving the person who originally posted in the position of having to argue non-infringement to largely faceless entities. The directive did include exceptions for quotation, criticism, review, caricature, parody, or pastiche—including memes and GIFs—which supporters claimed as a victory for uniform fair use recognition in Europe.[60] But once platforms are forced into the defensive position of proactively blocking infringement in user uploads, the only viable mechanism is algorithm-driven filters, and artificial intelligence tools used for scanning content are notoriously crude instruments. The forces lined up on either side of the issue also succeeded in demonstrating the old truism that politics make strange bedfellows. Support for the change came from the music industry, book publishers, and some news organizations, while tech giants like Facebook, Google, and YouTube (the latter two both subsidiaries of Alphabet) lobbied hard in opposition. Given Alphabet's general resistance to regulation, including running roughshod over privacy rights, there is an obvious irony to landing on their side of the dispute.

Online petitions, followed by spring 2019 street protests, particularly in Germany, indicated a growing awareness of the reach of copyright into everyday life, and the potential threats to many vital forms of parody and satire if preemptive blocking becomes the norm. At issue, as the protesters clearly realized, was far more than the right to create and share memes; rather, it was a question of censorship in general, as it plays out in the context of the proprietary platforms upon which we all rely. The larger threats include the increasingly daunting challenges associated with balancing internet regulation (which can support such worthy goals as the removal of hate speech) and freedom of expression. It also seems telling, given problems associated with campaigns to manipulate online information and opinion, that one motivation for protesters taking to the streets was to prove that they were real, not just a bot army of virtual petition signatures.[61]

Individual cases and conflicts point to larger concerns. Because of the degree to which all expressions and inventions draw upon preexisting forms, claims of originality inevitably come down to matters of degree. Who is able to claim ownership is too often connected to who has the resources to pursue their position, including the ability to assert authorship, from one individual to another, or one culture to another. For all that a key rationale for IP is supporting creativity and invention, its exercise, both in the outcome of specific cases, and in advocacy for changing the legal framework, is inseparable from questions of power. Nor is it simply a matter of individual versus business interests. Rather, there are multiple competing agendas—including corporate forces that would be only too happy to extend the scope and duration of copyright protections, and major technology fortunes based on providing free platforms for users to experience, alter, and retransmit material of all kinds (while encouraging them to give away massive volumes of personal information that can be monetized in other ways).

What's at stake is nothing less than our ability to engage in a dialogue with shared cultural resources, the preservation of that heritage for future generations, and our rights over ourselves. Copyright and all forms of IP were already essential elements of the economic landscape before the changes wrought by digital transmission, but the challenges have been exacerbated by the speed, frequency, and ease of sharing of massive volumes of material, along with far-reaching technological measures to counteract what technology has unleashed. With consumption and production increasingly interwoven, questions about the rights and responsibilities of creators, as well as ownership over every aspect of the media environment, are inescapably relevant to all participants.

4

MORAL RIGHTS AND BEYOND

LET'S ASSUME, FOR ARGUMENT'S SAKE, that artists should have rights over their creations that extend beyond the point when a work changes ownership. If protecting art's integrity is potentially important not only for the original maker, but also for the culture at large, then possession does not mean that property owners can do whatever they wish. Yet even granting this basic premise, there are still plenty of questions about what such rights should encompass. For visual arts, should an artist be able to decide when or how a piece is exhibited? For works that were conceived in response to the dynamics of a particular place, how much control should the artist have over the larger site? Should such rights extend to decisions about photos and video of the work, including where reproductions appear?

Some countries have articulated protections for artists' rights that extend significantly beyond basic copyright, even if they are often part of the same overall legislation. Generally described as moral, personality, or integrity rights, this body of law addresses circumstances when creators can continue to exercise control over their work after it leaves their hands. But there are substantial variations between Anglo-American and European approaches, rooted in historical developments as well as distinctions between common and civil law regimes. Crucial points of divergence include the degree to which moral rights continue after an author's death, whether they are treated as alienable or inalienable, and the extent to which examples of work-for-hire are excluded, with these distinctions connected to underlying differences in how the public domain is articulated. In contrast to the long history of protecting moral rights in many parts of Europe, safeguards conferred in the United States by the 1990 Visual Artists Rights Act, or VARA, are both limited, and relatively recent. It also quickly becomes clear that crafting such legislation raises a whole series of questions about what type of work qualifies for protected status, including attempts to distinguish between commercial and noncommercial, art and architecture, or "culturally significant" as opposed to its opposite—material that is unexceptional, or simply not art in the eyes of the law.

There are a number of interrelated issues. One is the reason for granting rights to creators that extend beyond economic benefits. To the extent that such protections are defined as personality rights, then their motivation is often rooted in a romantic conception of the artist as inseparable from the creative act. Yet there is also public interest associated with efforts to maintain the integrity of significant works, with this concern leaving open the matter of how much authority artists should be granted over the ongoing fortunes of works that have become part of a broader cultural dialogue. Questions about whether it is possible to strike a balance between the creator's desire to protect a work's integrity and the public's ability to respond become even more pressing when a work is situated within a public rather than private space.

Although moral rights are supposed to be distinct from the economic focus of copyright, the two are often intertwined in their deployment. Granting or withholding copyright permission can be used to shape or even censor discourse. Conversely, the authority to designate what is or is not an authentic work of art (explicitly defined as a moral right under some legal codes) can have very real economic consequences. Advocacy for artists' rights has also encompassed provisions for resale royalties, which potentially allow artists to benefit from rising monetary values in the future by providing a percentage of any price increase after a work changes hands. Contracts or certificates may likewise be utilized to specify conditions not set by statute—ranging from the types of documents openly employed by conceptual artists to extend the definition of art, to elaborate behind-the-scenes agreements concerning high-value transactions that tend to come into view only when they are part of a lawsuit.

Because of the specific history of US law, along with the role of New York as a postwar center for artistic production and market activity, dialogue and activism around artists' rights unfolded with exceptional intensity in that context. The United States lagged notably behind other countries in signing onto the Berne Convention, first articulated in 1886, which includes copyright protections with a minimum duration of the life of the author plus fifty years, default copyright automatic upon publication (as opposed to requiring affirmative registration), and an important statement of moral rights in article 6*bis*. Even when the United States eventually joined the convention in 1989 (at a point when seventy-seven other countries had already signed), it did so with severe limitations regarding adherence to the moral rights provisions. Separately from that, default copyright, as well as terms of protection linked to the lifetime of the author, were instituted with the 1976 revisions to the US copyright code (which took effect in 1978). The 1976 requirement that copyright has to be explicitly transferred overturned a common-law assumption that reproduction rights accompanied the sale of an art object—which had meant, up to that point, that creators of works sold in the United States had relatively few tools to prevent gift-shop adaptations or other crass uses of their art.

The first part of this chapter traces key moments in the history of US activism around moral rights that helped bring these issues into focus in the period leading up to the implementation of VARA. One thread concerns advocacy for artists' rights against the backdrop of other political activism in the 1960s and 1970s. Attempts to articulate specific provisions through contractual arrangements, including certain model agreements, also point to the interplay between private and public law in this arena. The second part of the chapter continues the discussion of activism and institutional critique to address recent modes of critical practice informed by a close consideration of the law. Examining gestures that both extend and exceed the boundaries of art, it emphasizes protecting freedom of expression for artists as part of a wider concern for human rights.

CONDITIONAL OWNERSHIP

While circumstances were clearly ripe, a January 1969 demonstration in the Museum of Modern Art in New York provided the immediate catalyst for a wide-ranging discussion about artists' rights and institutional responsibilities. Dissatisfied with MoMA's decision to include a 1960 kinetic work entitled *Tele-sculpture* (which the museum owned) in a survey exhibition called *The Machine as Seen at the End of the Mechanical Age*, Takis physically removed his sculpture. Although the action was largely symbolic, since he took it only as far as MoMA's sculpture garden, the demonstration was accompanied by a flyer calling on artists for unified action, and its theatrical nature attracted free publicity via accounts from reporters who had been alerted in advance.[1]

The MoMA demonstration turned out to be the genesis of the Art Workers' Coalition (AWC), announced soon thereafter via a communique, drafted by Hans Haacke, Tom Lloyd, and Carl Andre, demanding that artists have the right to control their "copyrights, reproduction rights, exhibition rights, and maintenance responsibilities."[2] During an April 1969 open hearing organized by the AWC, far-reaching political concerns were intermixed with targeted criticism of art institutions, as more than seventy participants spoke about artists' rights as well as antiwar activism, racism, and sexism. An antagonistic stance pitting artists against museums and dealers was evident in protests against art-world business as usual, including its many exclusions, and museums provided a strategic backdrop for unauthorized demonstrations less directly related to art. Yet this was also a period when museums and galleries were beginning to embrace art forms that required close collaboration between creator and exhibition venue for their realization.

The statement read by Sol LeWitt at the AWC open hearing was typical in its confrontational stance toward both collector and museum, even as it was expansive in its demands:

1. A work of art by a living artist would still be the property of the artist. A collector would, in a sense, be the custodian of that art.
2. The artist would be consulted when his work is displayed, reproduced or used in any way.
3. The museum, collector or publication would compensate the artist for use of his art. This is a rental, beyond the original purchase price. The rental could be nominal; the principle of a royalty would be used.
4. An artist would have the right to retrieve his work from a collection if he compensates the purchaser with the original price or a mutually agreeable substitute.
5. When a work is resold from one collector to another, the artist would be compensated with a percentage of the price.
6. An artist should have the right to change or destroy any work of his as long as he lives.[3]

LeWitt's list is striking for the interplay between calling for long-term control over art objects and pursuit of economic interests—even as the gender-specific language indicates clear limits to its critique of the status quo. Somewhat surprisingly, integrity rights appear only by implication, via the description of the custodial role of the collector, in contrast to the greater stress on an artist's open-ended right to alter or destroy a work. Frederick Castle went further still but in a radically different direction, calling on the AWC to "make no attempt to enforce the proprietary rights which may be claimed by avaricious artists," and for artists to "renounce all claims to originality and uniqueness in their own work, and devote themselves instead to addressing and directing all the rebellious natures in society because of the privileged position which artists already enjoy, namely that of licensed disturbers of the peace."[4] In sharp contrast to LeWitt's presumption that artists should enjoy certain privileges, Castle effectively called for the dissolution of the entire category.

"The Artist's Reserved Rights and Sale Agreement," which attempted to establish key artists' rights via a contractual document, was drafted by Seth Siegelaub and Robert Projansky in the aftermath of the AWC and published in 1971. While it is clearly similar in spirit to LeWitt's statement, overall the form was somewhat less extreme, articulating a more limited framework of ongoing rights. But it was hardly without provocation, especially with respect to the profit-sharing provision known as resale royalties. As outlined in its preamble, "The Agreement is designed to give the artist: 15% of any increase in the value of each work each time it is transferred in the future; a record of who owns each work at any given time; the right to be notified when the work is to be exhibited, so the artist can advise upon or . . . veto the proposed exhibition of his/her work; the right to borrow the work for exhibition for 2 months every five (5) years (at no cost to the owner); the right to be consulted if repairs become necessary; half of any rental income paid to the owner for the use of the work at exhibitions, if there ever is any; all reproduction rights in the work."[5]

The contract fits with the "aesthetic of linguistic conventions and legalistic arrangements" described by Benjamin Buchloh in a seminal essay on conceptual art where he identified bureaucratic rhetoric as an important aspect of its project.[6] Yet one paradox in the agreement was its focus on control over objects at a time when Siegelaub was championing conceptual practices, including several 1969 exhibitions where the exhibition catalogue took precedence over physical manifestation or even became the exhibition—particularly *March 1–31, 1969*, and *July, August, September, 1969*. It was also criticized for its articulation of art as property, as Lawrence Weiner recounted to Maria Eichhorn as part of a series of interviews she conducted on the topic of the Siegelaub-Projansky contract. Although Weiner acknowledged the "legitimate attempt to rectify the terrible situation of exploitation of an artist's work," he criticized its failure to refuse speculation, stressing that artists "are not stocks and bonds."[7] Even more decisive, however, was resistance from collectors and dealers to its attempts to place limitations on artistic property. While collectors are often eager to obtain documentation certifying authenticity, they are potentially less enthusiastic about agreements that limit rather than facilitate a work's marketability.[8]

Nor was this the only gesture in this direction, with a different version of the artist's contract evident in the "Avertissement" that Daniel Buren developed in 1968–69 in collaboration with Michel Claura. It outlined a set of requirements that had to be satisfied by the owner of a work before it could be attributed to Buren. One of the rights retained by Buren was approval over a work's sale or reproduction. And Buren turned the tables by making the owner sign the form, rather than the artist—though it did include a detachable coupon at the bottom that would be returned with a partial mark, after the entire sheet was sent to Buren's studio. According to Buren, once "you sign a work, you can't easily say it's a forgery," whereas a work accompanied by an agreement signed by the collector is a different matter.[9] This alternate approach therefore helped establish authorship as contingent on collectors fulfilling their side of the bargain—including the possibility, as Alessandra Donati has pointed out, that even a collector's decision to allow an unauthorized reproduction of a work could result in it being stripped of authorship.[10]

Hans Haacke seems to be the only artist to have used a version of the Siegelaub-Projansky contract consistently, and he has insisted that it accompany all works

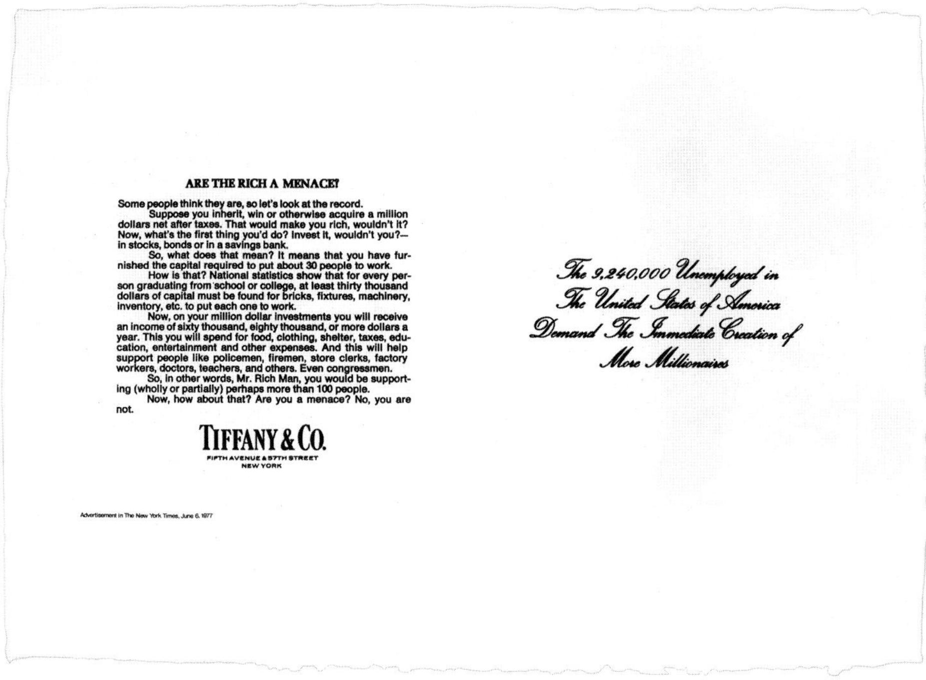

FIGURE 28

Hans Haacke, *Tiffany Cares,* 1978. Photoetching on handmade paper, 29 × 41 in., Edition AP 1. Published by Crown Point Press, Oakland, and printed by Stephen Thomas with assistance from Lilah Toland. © Hans Haacke/Artists Rights Society (ARS), New York. Courtesy the artist and Paula Cooper Gallery, New York.

valued at more than a thousand dollars, even after he became aware of collectors who therefore refused to purchase his work, along with MoMA's rejection of an attempted gift that would have require them to sign the document. The latter case concerned an etching by Haacke, his 1978 *Tiffany Cares,* which juxtaposed the text of a *New York Times* ad celebrating the accumulation of wealth with a statement about unemployment in the United States (figure 28). The print was to be included in a portfolio that the Crown Point Press wanted to donate to MoMA on the occasion of the press's twenty-fifth birthday in 1987.[11] The agreement was also an apparent impediment to Peter Ludwig's interest in purchasing the alternate version of *Manet PROJEKT '74* that Haacke created for a private gallery show after his proposed installation was infamously rejected by the Wallraf-Richartz-Museum based on what it revealed about the provenance history of Manet's *Bunch of Asparagus* (1880). According to Haacke, all communication stopped once Ludwig became aware of the accompanying contract, and he heard later that the collector was "outraged."[12] Yet even though it didn't result in a sale, Haacke's initial encounter with Ludwig was fruitful in a different way, since the attention to Ludwig's overall enterprise formed the basis for his 1981 work *Der Pralinenmeister,* which he in turn refused to sell to Ludwig.[13]

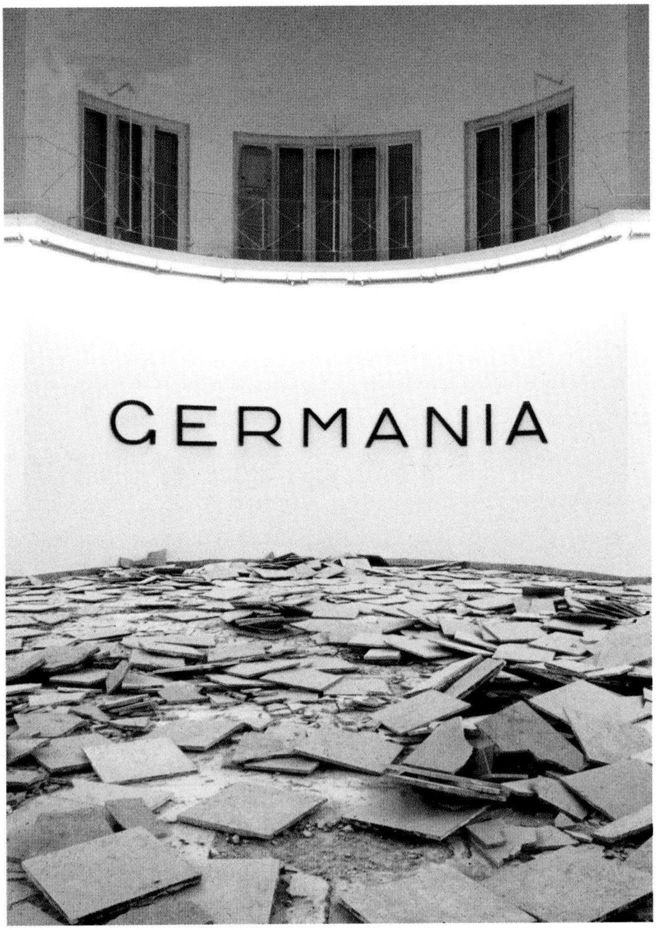

FIGURE 29
Hans Haacke, *Germania,* 1993. Installation view, the German Pavilion, 45th Venice Biennale. Photo: Roman Mensing. © Hans Haacke/Artists Rights Society (ARS), New York. Courtesy the artist and Paula Cooper Gallery, New York.

Haacke has also relied on Siegelaub-Projansky provisions to exercise significant control over where his work is exhibited. Conversing with Eichhorn about the agreement, Haacke mentioned one show that he "nixed" because of its resemblance to a trade fair, and said that he has also tried to avoid having his work flogged at art fairs (which he stopped attended himself, after experiencing the Cologne Kunstmarkt just once, many decades ago, and finding it "enough to make you puke").[14] In another of Eichhorn's interviews about artists' contracts, Ute Meta Bauer recalled Haacke saying that he wouldn't want to be shown next to Jeff Koons—an aesthetic as well as ethical stance one can respect, even as it is possible to imagine how, in certain hands, such a juxtaposition could illuminate interesting art-world tensions.[15]

Given the significance of integrity within the general category of "moral rights," it is also interesting to consider the implications of Haacke's intervention in the architecture of the German pavilion at the Venice Biennale. The components of his 1993 *Germania* (figure 29) included an oversize 1990 deutschemark (referencing the year of reunification as well as late-twentieth-century nationalism centered on currency) positioned where a swastika had once figured over the entrance, followed by an enlarged photo of Hitler's visit to the 1934 Biennale. In the main exhibition space, viewers encountered the destroyed remains of the pavilion's marble floor, which had been in place since a 1938 renovation ordered by Hitler. The vivid act of destruction therefore ensured that visitors would no longer experience, whether knowingly or not, this trace evidence of Hitler's larger agenda. Due to this history, the ongoing physical integrity that Haacke interrupted could be described as amoral, and through his act of demolition, he achieved the permanent removal of a Nazi-era architectural element.

TILTED ARC TO VARA

There is nothing like an act of destruction or willful mutilation to prompt arguments for artists' rights, and two instances frequently cited as part of advocacy for moral rights in the United States would potentially have been prevented by such laws. When Alexander Calder's 1958 *Pittsburgh* mobile was donated to Allegheny County, for installation at the Greater Pittsburgh International Airport, officials decided to give the work a new green and yellow paint job to reflect the county's official colors, as well as making structural alterations that immobilized the free movement inherent to its identity. Isamu Noguchi's 1975 *Shinto,* a large aluminum form commissioned for the Bank of Tokyo's New York headquarters, was destroyed in 1980 when bank officials, citing complaints that it appeared threatening, had the sculpture cut into pieces for removal and storage. But the extensive public debate around Richard Serra's 1981 *Tilted Arc* (figure 30) was particularly important, both for discussions about artists' rights, and for potential challenges when the integrity of the work extends from an object to its relationship to a specific site.

Tensions brought into focus by *Tilted Arc* include the challenging, even confrontational nature of a resolutely abstract form; questions about how to define "the public" for a work of public art; larger issues about how shared space is planned and administered; attempts to define art as something more than, or specifically counter to, an easily transferrable luxury good; and the long-term relationship between artist and work. Installed in 1981, and removed in 1989 by the same government agency that had commissioned the piece, *Tilted Arc*'s relatively brief period of existence coincided with both initial maneuvers to enact US artists' rights legislation and the beginnings of a right-wing campaign to mobilize populist outrage against contemporary art.[16] Serra's inability to prevent its destruction also prompted him to work closely with lawyers on contractual provisions to accompany all his subsequent sculpture.

Although Serra was already well known within the art world at the time of the 1979 commission from the General Services Administration (GSA), the concept of site-specificity was still being articulated—with one important statement, Rosalind Krauss's "Sculpture in the Expanded Field," published that same year. In this essay, Krauss took on the problem of relatively recent work that could only be encompassed by the term

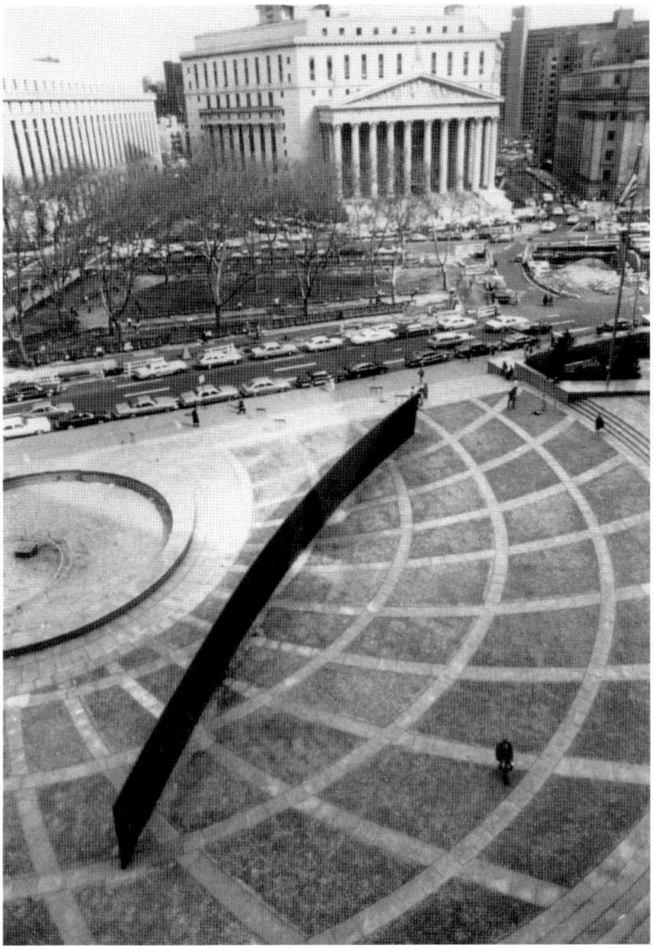

FIGURE 30
Richard Serra, *Tilted Arc*, 1981. CorTen steel, 12 ft. × 120 ft. × 2½ in. Photo Anne Chauvet. Courtesy the artist.

"sculpture" if "the category can be made to become almost infinitely malleable." According to the possibilities arrayed on her frequently-cited diagram, a freestanding, "essentially nomadic" sculpture is neither landscape nor architecture, but there are also "marked sites" embodying "landscape" and "not-landscape" simultaneously; "axiomatic structures" encompassing both "architecture" and "not-architecture"; and at the top, "site constructions," combining both landscape and architecture.[17] As Serra insistently declared, the identity of *Tilted Arc* did not reside merely in the 12-foot-high, 120-foot-long curved arc of steel, but also in the relationship established between the sculptural form and the surrounding space.

Much of what happened later can be attributed to a vehement campaign against the work mounted from within the GSA by William Diamond, who was appointed as a regional administrator subsequent to the original commission. But Serra did himself no favors with his description of his plans in a 1980 interview with Douglas Crimp.

Serra told Crimp that he had "found a way to dislocate or alter the decorative function of the plaza and actively bring people into the sculpture's context," and he went on to say, "After the piece is created, the space will be understood primarily as a function of the sculpture."[18]

Questions about the relationship established to the site became crucial during the public hearing that Diamond convened in 1985 to discuss the fate of the work. Many of those who spoke in favor of the sculpture contrasted its impact to the bland functionality of the Joseph K. Javits Federal Building behind it. But even some of those opposed to the sculpture described a vision for the plaza that it had never fulfilled—one that would include chairs and tables, musical events, and generally promote a sense of community among members of the public who might congregate in the space. Despite arguments that it blocked the functionality of the plaza, however, the space had had, prior to *Tilted Arc*'s installation, little in the way of amenities: there were no chairs or tables, and the fountain had been dry for some time due to problems with blowing spray and leaks into the parking garage below. In other words, it was public space in name only, and many of the negative hearing statements indicated that the sculpture was a stand-in for larger complaints, including a desire for a welcoming space in front of a building seen as uninviting. (Tellingly, one of the immigration attorneys testifying in opposition to the work also referenced a lawsuit against the GSA to allow public access to the bathrooms on the floor occupied by the Immigration Service.)[19]

The oppositional nature of the hearing left no room for more nuanced questions about the role of public art, or public space generally. In his statement, Crimp expressed distress at a manipulation of the process that forced him "to argue for art as against some other social function," and Krauss criticized attempts to dismiss the aesthetic as a "nonuse" of the plaza space.[20] But Diamond's response, when faced with the presumably unexpected result of the hearing—of 180 speakers over three days, 122 spoke for the work, and only 58 against—was to declare that he didn't want to play a numbers game. Rather, he concluded that members of the broader art world who spoke in favor of the work did not have the same authority as building employees who voiced their opposition. Following the hearing, the GSA initially announced plans to keep the work in the plaza until another placement could be found. But no informed institution was interested in the offer of a clearly site-specific sculpture, and the GSA decided to remove the work despite its failed donation attempts.

Serra then took to the courts, where the absence of US moral rights legislation meant that his lawyers had to look for other grounds, including potential violations of Serra's First and Fifth Amendment rights to free speech and due process. But even after acknowledging the possibility of nonverbal forms of speech (such as wearing black armbands), the court of appeals found that Serra had "relinquished his own speech rights in the sculpture when he voluntarily sold it to the GSA."[21] A last-minute attempt to prevent its destruction once the Berne Convention was incorporated into US law in 1989 also failed when it became clear that the Implementation Act had taken

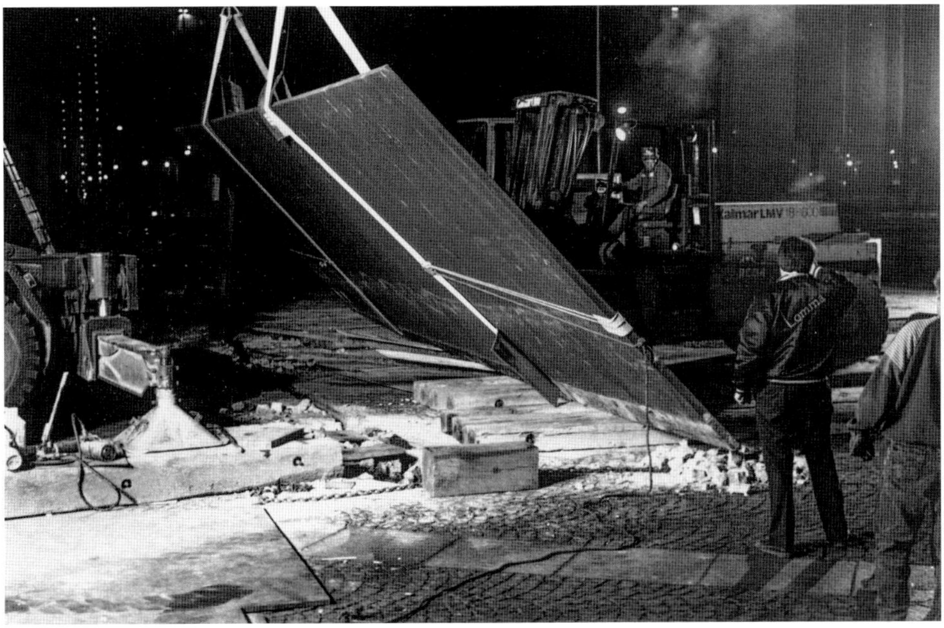

FIGURE 31
The destruction of Richard Serra's *Tilted Arc*, March 15, 1989. Photo: Jennifer Kotter. Courtesy the artist.

a "minimalist" approach to moral rights. As soon as Serra dropped this final bid to halt *Tilted Arc*'s destruction, the GSA removed it, with Diamond himself supervising the late-night action (figure 31).

Looking at the conflict in retrospect, Rosalyn Deutsche underscored claims made in the name of the public, pointing in particular to Diamond's assertion that the removal of the work would return the plaza "to the people," in contrast to Serra's sculptural expression, which Diamond defined as a "private" use of the space.[22] For Deutsche, this was emblematic of cynical assertions of public interest that often served those who were profiting from the gentrification of the city, including a version of public art where usefulness (such as artful benches or tables) was a key criterion. It is therefore telling that the GSA's first gambit, in the immediate aftermath of *Tilted Arc*'s destruction, was to drop some planters and benches into the plaza. That was followed by a redesign of the space by Martha Schwartz, with serpentine benches interspersed by planted mounds, which was completed in 1997. But her design barely outlasted *Tilted Arc* in duration, since the plaza was torn up again following the determination in 2008 that the membrane protecting the parking garage below had failed. The most recent version of the plaza, designed by WASA/Studio A and unveiled in 2013, includes foliage and seating—though the latter, in the form of oval and rectangular marble forms scattered throughout the plaza, may provide places to perch in a city where useable open space is at a premium, but seem designed to discourage lingering.

Tilted Arc's destruction in 1989 clearly needs to be understood in the context of the culture wars of the late 1980s and early 1990s, when campaigns against National Endowment for the Arts funding played a key strategic role in right-wing populism, despite the fact that the overall NEA budget is quite modest when compared to government cultural support in many other countries. But another aspect of *Tilted Arc*'s immediate historical context was the passage, only one year after its removal, of federal moral rights protection in the form of the 1990 Visual Artists Rights Act, or VARA (although it was quickly noted that VARA would provide few safeguards for site-specific works of art, where not just an object, but its entire placement, would need to be preserved).

During an interview where Haacke referenced MoMA's refusal of a donation if the Siegelaub-Projansky contract was required, he recounted that the museum lawyer described signing such a document as "out of the question," because the museum was in the process of lobbying Congress against a bill that would provide such rights.[23] The bill was clearly the legislation eventually realized as VARA. In 1986 (just one year after the *Tilted Arc* hearing extravaganza), Senator Edward Kennedy held an open meeting to solicit responses to the artists' rights bill he was planning to sponsor. Reports detailing Kennedy's meeting indicate that those who spoke in its favor generally emphasized integrity rights, following the argument that a work of art is more than just any form of property that can be altered or destroyed at the whim of its owner. In art historian Irving Sander's somewhat attenuated analogy, art should be understood as more like cats and dogs, rather than chairs or tables, and he accordingly spoke in favor of a statute prohibiting cruelty to art.[24] Provisions for resale royalties (which were eventually stripped out of the bill) helped account for the vigorous opposition from some quarters.

One might expect that the same people who lined up as champions of *Tilted Arc* would support legislation protecting artists' rights. Acting counter to that assumption, however, was Krauss. Her 1985 hearing statement forcefully articulated the powerful visual and corporeal experience established by *Tilted Arc*, but at the 1986 meeting she criticized the proposed legislation on the grounds of its potential threat to publishing for magazines and scholars faced with paying royalties for reproductions—arguing that the enforcement of such rights in France had driven many smaller publishers out of the art book business.[25] Krauss's longtime commitment to fair use was therefore at odds with giving artists the ability to control many aspects of a work's future contextualization, including where it is reproduced.

Attempts to prevent willful destruction or mutilation of significant works of art are easy to support. Yet granting rights to one party generally means curtailing actions by others, as legal scholar Amy Adler has outlined in a trenchant analysis of moral rights protections. Although her key statement in this regard, a 2009 article entitled "Against Moral Rights," casts a rather wide net in its assembly of examples, she asks important questions about whether an artist is the best person to enforce moral rights and, by extension, whether the artist's intent should govern interpretation of a work. One compelling aspect of Adler's essay is her questioning of the assumption that artists, in exercising their moral rights, will act in the interest of the public more generally—since the priorities of artist and public do not necessarily converge.[26] Adler did not mention LeWitt's AWC hearing demand that artists have an ongoing right to alter or destroy their own work at any time, but it would certainly have supported her contention. Or there is Penelope Curtis's account of a special initiative set up at the Tate in order to curtail efforts by Richard Hamilton and John Latham to alter works in the collection, thereby allowing "early works to remain early works."[27]

It also quickly became clear that VARA would offer limited protection for the type of work encompassed by Krauss's conception of an "expanded field." Legal categories tend to be highly specific, with little room for the slippage Krauss was attempting to capture, and VARA is no exception. This exclusion was clarified by a 2006 decision concerning a work that, ironically enough, would seem to embody a vision of public sculpture as corporate amenity, at the opposite end of the spectrum from Serra's aesthetic. The example in question consisted of an array of bronze sculptures of marine life, granite forms, and pathways that David Phillips installed in Boston's Eastport Park at the behest of Pembroke Real Estate. Not long after the work was completed in 2000, Pembroke proposed making changes to the configuration, and Phillips sued to prevent this. In *Phillips v. Pembroke Real Estate,* the First Circuit Court of Appeals did accept the premise that the installation constituted an example of site-specific art. There was a direct echo of Serra in the court's finding that "To remove a work of site-specific art from its original site is to destroy it." Refusing to allow VARA to curtail the rights of landowners to make ongoing alterations to their property as a whole, however, the appeals court held that "VARA does not apply to site-specific art at all."[28]

ART AND MONEY

There is something of an irony in the attention focused on the seldom-used Siegelaub-Projansky contract, given that it has become quite common for art purchases and commissions to be accompanied by extensive written agreements that are typically not made public. Some behind-the-scenes provisions are designed to protect artists and dealers (especially in areas where their interests converge), but other contractual provisions are prompted by client concerns, particularly for art collected as a form of investment. As part of overall strategies to shape both market and reputation, dealers for highly-sought-after artists sometimes place sharp restrictions on resale, along with limiting who is allowed to buy in the first place. Works are ideally not sold, but "placed," in a process that includes wait lists that can stretch for years, sometimes explicit requirements that art be donated to a museum, potential preference for collectors who maintain their own private museums, and blacklists of collectors known to flip works. Although operating in a different realm than copyright law, private agreements prompted by market considerations help pinpoint other ways that artistic expressions make the transition into rarified forms of property.

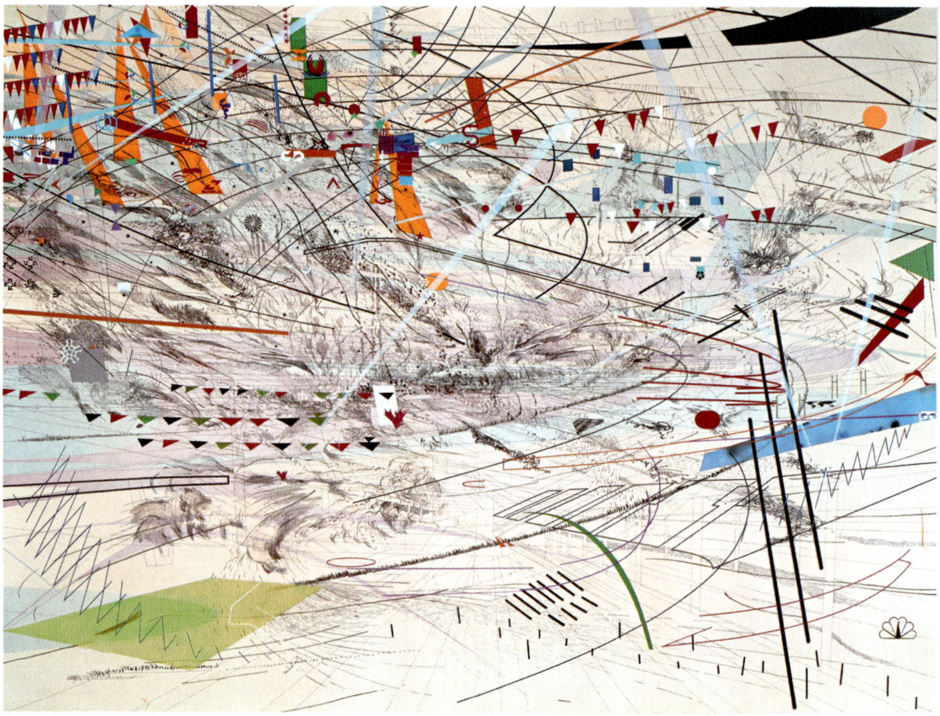

FIGURE 32
Julie Mehretu, *Stadia III,* 2004. Ink and acrylic on canvas, 107 × 140 in. © Julie Mehretu. Courtesy the artist and Marian Goodman Gallery.

Although most art sales are shrouded in secrecy, the intricacies of these arrangements are sometimes revealed by conflicts that wind up in court. One such instance was a 2004 lawsuit by Jean-Pierre Lehmann against a gallery called The Project for breach of contract. Lehmann had provided the gallery with an open-ended, interest-free loan of $75,000, which was supposed to allow the collector to jump to the head of the line to purchase several of the gallery's particularly hot artists: provisions in the accompanying agreement gave Lehmann right of first refusal for any work sold by the gallery, as well as substantial discounts up to a certain threshold. But despite the arrangement, Lehmann was unable to buy key pieces by Julie Mehretu. At the time Mehretu had begun to receive extensive attention for large-scale works on canvas incorporating a dense yet delicate interweaving of architectural diagrams, maps, banners, and other forms to create compositions that were both abstract and evocative—with these characteristics, along with suggestions of mass spectacle, evident in her 2004 *Stadia III* (figure 32). After becoming aware of sales to other collectors, including works from the *Stadia* series to Jeanne Greenberg Rohatyn, Lehmann sued and won a $1.7 million dollar judgment against the gallery, with the monetary figure based on the difference in price between what the collector would have paid, had he been able to buy a group of eight works by Mehretu when they were initially handed off to the gallery, and their estimated market value at the time of the suit.[29] The first order of affront—not being able to purchase art that one wants, even if rich enough to do so—is business as usual in the art world. The more inexplicable matter was the gallery's decision not to sell to someone despite having made a financially advantageous agreement to do exactly that.

Some artists take it upon themselves to pay close attention to how collectors engage with their work, as Craig Robins discovered to his chagrin. Robins, who owned a substantial number of works by Marlene Dumas, was outraged that he wound up on the artist's blacklist after selling one of her works in a transaction he hoped to keep confidential. He eventually sued the David Zwirner Gallery, which handled the 2004 sale in collaboration with Jack Tilton, accusing Zwirner (who did not represent Dumas at the time, but signed her in 2008) of revealing the sale to Dumas. Zwirner countered that, despite Robins's claim that he requested by phone that the sale be kept secret, there was no such written agreement. According to Zwirner, though negotiations leading up to a sale are generally confidential, once sold, "the new ownership of the work is as public or as private as the new owner wishes to make it."[30] Robins also claimed that Zwirner, in a 2005 meeting, agreed to give him preferential treatment in the future—again, without anything in writing. When he was unable to purchase work from Dumas's first exhibition at Zwirner in 2010, Robins sued to stop Zwirner from selling his top choices to anyone else. According to Zwirner's lawyers, "By bringing suit . . . the wealthy Robins has literally made a federal case of not being able to buy what he wants, when he wants," adding further, regarding Dumas's blacklist, that "Zwirner did not put him there and cannot take him off."[31]

Most such disagreements are undoubtedly negotiated behind closed doors, since galleries are presumably loath to sue potential clients.[32] In 2011, however, the Michael Werner Gallery did take action against both collector James H. Rich and Christie's to prevent Rich from selling Peter Doig's 2004 *Red Boat (Imaginary Boys)* (figure 33) at auction. The evocative image of a journey across tropical waters had originally been sold with the stipulation that the "artwork, while purchased privately, is done so with the explicit agreement that the work is to be given as an eventual gift to the Carnegie Museum of Art" (where Rich was a trustee).[33] The gallery insisted that neither they nor Doig would have sold the work at the bargain price of $162,000, absent that provision. However, the gallery reached an agreement with Rich to allow the Christie's auction to proceed, reportedly based on Rich's promise to donate the work if it failed to sell or, alternately, to give a significant new painting by Doig to the museum in the future.[34] Court documents revealed that Rich had initially donated a 10 percent fractional gift of *Red Boat* to the Carnegie in 2005 (and doubtlessly took a proportional tax deduction), but then bought back that gift from the museum in 2007 in exchange for $150,000.[35] His change of plans may have been motivated by tightened restrictions on fractional giving, as of 2006, that reduced tax benefits for such donations. (These rules

FIGURE 33
Peter Doig, *Red Boat (Imaginary Boys)*, 2004. Oil on canvas, 78¾ × 73¼ in. Private Collection. Photo courtesy Michael Werner Gallery. © Peter Doig. All Rights Reserved, DACS 2020.

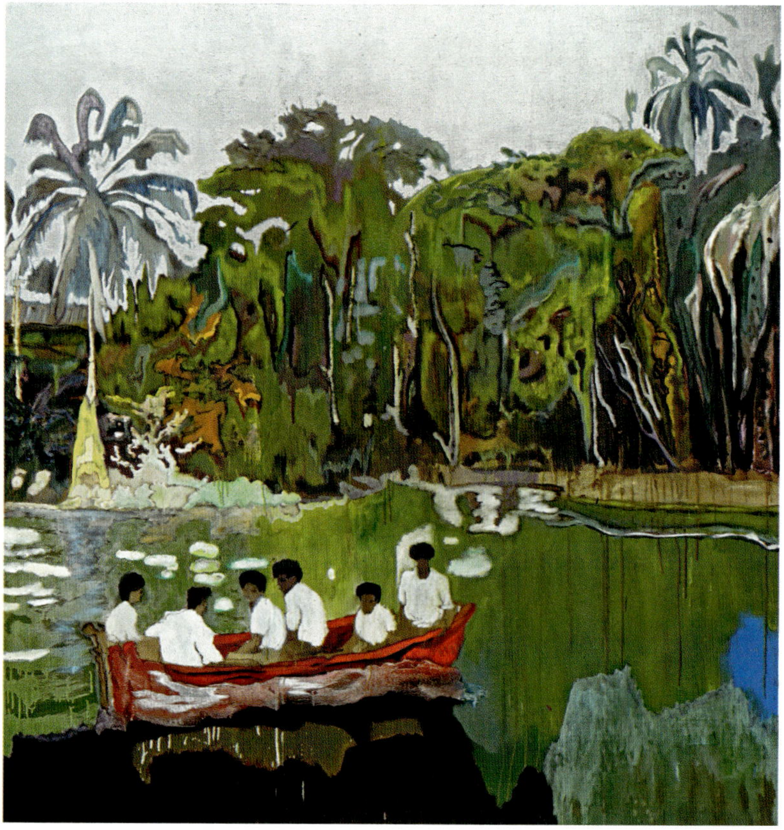

had allowed donors to take tax deductions spread out over a number of years while holding onto the work during that time). Another incentive, however, would have been Sotheby's 2007 sale of Doig's 1991 *White Canoe,* previously owned by Charles Saatchi, for £5,732,000 ($11.3 million at the time), far above the auction house estimate of £800,000–£1,200,000.[36] And Rich's gamble paid off, given that the 2011 auction price achieved at Christie's for *Red Boat* was £6,201,250 ($9.9 million in 2011), against an estimate of £1,400,000–£1,800,000.[37]

A series of back and forth lawsuits between billionaire Ronald Perelman and the Gagosian Gallery give a painfully clear indication of the degree to which the high end of the market is as much about speculation as art. Although the two powerbrokers had once been friends, that was evidently no longer the case by 2012, when Perelman sued Gagosian over issues involving the title and market value for one of Jeff Koons's granite *Popeye* sculptures, which Perelman was purchasing for $4 million via installments prior to the completion of the work. Originally the final payment and transfer of title were all supposed to take place at the same time, in December 2011. But Perelman had begun negotiating with Gagosian in April 2011 to trade the (future) value of his (future) ownership of the sculpture to the gallery for other works, and he was distressed that Gagosian would not set an exchange amount significantly higher than what he had (not yet) paid, based on Koons's appreciating value. After completion of the sculpture was delayed until 2012, Perelman learned about an agreement between Gagosian and Koons that guaranteed Koons 70 percent of any price above $4 million if Gagosian resold the work, and Perelman contended that this secret provision fraudulently depressed the sculpture's exchange value.[38] Perelman's complaint against Gagosian was dismissed in 2014, but clearly he was not over it, since Gagosian's lawyers discovered in 2019 that Perelman had been secretly paying the legal bills for another lawsuit about delayed delivery of Koons sculptures filed against Gagosian by Joel Silver—with this discovery apparently prompting Silver and Gagosian to settle the dispute.[39]

Alexander Alberro has described the Siegelaub-Projansky contract as a form of anti-institutional self-help, which allowed artists to bypass the need for governmental provisions.[40] But its mechanism is surprisingly typical of a marketplace shaped by shared customs and assumptions rather than detailed legal regulations. While it generally takes a lawsuit to reveal provisions negotiated in the highly secretive upper strata of the art world, one striking aspect of these agreements is where they fall in in relation to broader distinctions between public versus private law—with contracts on the private side, as opposed to legislated controls. Although it was a dead end in many respects, the Siegelaub-Projansky contract is therefore an important marker. The proposition that a work of art might remain tethered to its point of origin, even if resisted at first, has become increasingly commonplace. It is also important to consider these developments against the backdrop of larger shifts away from goods sold on the basis of a clean, one-time purchase and transfer, with consumers increasingly pushed to accept required updates along with limitations on independent repair or intervention. Viewed in this light, such transfers can be understood as art sold with an EULA (end-user license agreement) or other TOS (terms of service), akin to the click-through legalese initially associated with software licensing that now accompanies a wide range of transactions.

MORALITY BEYOND MORAL RIGHTS

In an ideal scenario, the rule of law should provide consistent parameters for both protecting rights and settling disputes. Yet even in the best of circumstances it is necessarily an imperfect instrument, reflecting the limits of what can be anticipated or described, and often tilted to the benefit of individuals or entities with the power to advocate for their interests. Both copyright and specialized moral rights legislation are no exception, since attempts to provide safeguards for one type of activity necessarily impede others. Under such conditions, artistic engagement with the rule of law has the potential to demonstrate the limits of its efficacy, both in countries where it is framed as upholding the rights of individuals and in more repressive situations. Moreover, as Joan Kee has argued, artistic integrity is not necessarily synonymous with following the letter of the law.[41] Intersecting with activism around cultural patrimony, freedom of expression, and other basic human rights, such work can highlight and amplify issues that extend well beyond a specific focus on creative authorship.

Evidence of this expanded purview can be found in the rather pointed ways that certain artists have employed behind-the-scenes agreements. Adrian Piper has relied on two contracts to control the circulation and sale of her work. While her transfer agreement was based in large part on the version of Siegelaub-Projansky used by Haacke, her "Solo Exhibition Agreement," developed in the mid-1990s, was far more pointed. This is particularly true of its provision forbidding discounts on the sales of individual pieces, due to the fact that the work "is already subject to the 50% Off Black Artists Discount and the 25% Off Women Artists Discount."[42] In Cameron Rowland's hands, contracts offering certain works of art as rentals rather than outright sales have been part of an extended interrogation of property relations, including histories of slavery and incarceration.[43] But the conscious deployment of a legal instrument is not the only way that artists have used their work to challenge as well as spotlight operations of the law.

In 1976, a staff member of Harvard's Peabody Museum of Archeology and Ethnology opened a long-unattended storage cabinet in the museum's attic, where she discovered a remarkable group of daguerreotype images of US slaves. The photographs had been commissioned in 1850 by Harvard professor Louis Agassiz to support his racist theories of polygenesis, which posited separate origins for people of European and African descent. Working to Agassiz's specifications, a Columbia, South Carolina, photographer named J. T. Zealy took fifteen images of seven different slaves, which presented the individuals as objects of (pseudo)scientific study. Two slaves photographed by Zealy, Alfred and Jem, were shown standing, fully nude, from multiple sides. Five more, Renty, Delia, Jack, Drana, and Fassena, were recorded nude from the waist up, in front and side views. They are part of a larger group of early daguerreotypes at the museum, many collected by Agassiz, which redirected the portrait format to present their human subjects as "ethnic types."[44] Though long hidden from view and apparently forgotten, the Zealy photographs were revealed to the public the year following their rediscovery, via an article by the staff member who made the find.[45]

Harvard did apparently release the images to Brian Wallis, for a 1995 article on photography's role in racial typography that included reproductions of both the daguerreotypes and an early example of Carrie Mae Weems's incorporation of them in her 1992 *Sea Island Series*.[46] However, Harvard's response to Weems's use was somewhat different. When she viewed the photographs in the early 1990s, the museum required her to sign an agreement that she would not use the images without their permission.[47] Zealy's daguerreotypes were certainly no longer covered by copyright, and even if there had been a valid claim, Weems could have made a strong fair use case based on the intensely critical message conveyed by her appropriation. Despite the absence of intellectual property rights, however, Harvard's control over the objects meant that they could insist on a contractual agreement that would supersede relevant copyright provisions.

Weems decided to go ahead and use enlarged photographs of the daguerreotype images in her own work without clearance from Harvard, including in her landmark 1995–96 *From Here I Saw what Happened and I Cried.* The series of thirty-three photographs, each blown up, with text superimposed, opens powerfully with four of the Zealy photos, combined with statements "you became a scientific profile," "a negroid type," "an anthropological debate," "& a photographic subject." When Harvard threatened to sue, Weems has recounted, she ultimately told them to go ahead, so that they could have the discussion in the public forum of a court case. According to Weems, even after they declined to pursue legal action Harvard still demanded payment for the image use if she sold the work. Although Weems was uncertain about her legal standing, she felt that her moral case was another matter.[48]

Nor was that the end of the story. In 2019, descendants of two of the slaves filed suit over ownership of the daguerreotypes. Based on genealogical research, Tamara Lanier connected individuals in the Harvard photos—both Renty and his daughter Delia—to oral traditions tracing her family's ancestry to "Papa Renty." Starting in 2011, Lanier made unsatisfactory attempts to discuss the situation with officials at Harvard, and she also attended a 2017 symposium, "Universities and Slavery: Bound by History," where she was taken aback by how this effort by Harvard to grapple with its past was using Renty's image to promote the event, including his appearance on the front cover of the program. Following the symposium she wrote to Harvard with a new demand that they turn over the daguerreotypes themselves, and she then initiated a lawsuit calling for the same. The suit emphasized the lack of consent by the subjects as the basis for its argument that the photographs were never "lawfully possessed" by Louis Agassiz, his son, or in turn, Harvard.[49]

The issues raised by the court complaint evoke Ariella Azoulay's analysis of the photographs, including her characterization of the terms under which they were made as the result of "negotiations between four white men—[Robert] Gibbes, the scientist colleague and liaison; Agassiz, the scientist who initiated the photographic project; Joseph T. Zealy, the photographer; and [B.F.] Taylor, the slave owner."[50] With the nudity of the individuals dramatizing how they were literally stripped of power, Azoulay has argued, the photographs recorded an acting out of white supremacy. Clearly Lanier perceived a similar message: her initial excitement upon hearing that her ancestors had been photographed turned to disappointment when she saw how they were posed, as well as learning the purpose, and she therefore expressed relief that her mother had never seen the images.[51]

The symposium was one of the ways that Harvard has attempted to address this legacy—but on its own terms.[52] Among the speakers was Ta-Nehisi Coates, who has argued forcefully for reparations. Yet even though he described the image of Renty as "like a hostage photograph" and later indicated that he could see how its featured role in the symposium would disturb Lanier, he admitted that he had not thought about it in those terms at the time.[53] Harvard has stressed its stewardship over the daguerreotypes, which are kept in climate-controlled storage and only taken out twice per year for viewing.[54] Although the income associated with granting reproduction requests for the daguerreotypes has apparently been minimal, Lanier still questioned the role of the university as "the ultimate decider" regarding who gets to see the photographs, and when.[55] Her lawsuit also highlighted the various ways that Agassiz's scientific work continued to be honored in institutional histories, without reference to his racist theories. Reflecting their rejection of this aspect of their legacy, forty-three Agassiz descendants signed a letter to the president of Harvard in support of Lanier's quest for the photographs.[56]

There is an obvious divergence in goals between the wish to honor one's own ancestors and the desire to use the photographs as evidence to demonstrate the horrors of slavery in broad terms. An important precedent for considering the museum's role in this dynamic is the 1990 Native American Graves Protection and Repatriation Act (NAGPRA), which addresses the potential return of both Native American religious objects and human remains held by museums. United States law does not, however, offer equivalent protections for artifacts associated with slavery. And even NAGPRA's provisions do not extend to photographic images, including those taken under duress.

Another suggestive comparison is to the ethics involved in scientific discoveries based on tissue and other genetic material collected from individuals without their knowledge or consent. One of the best known is the immortal cell line, called HeLa, derived from a sample of Henrietta Lacks's cancer tissue that was taken in 1951 when she was being treated at the Johns Hopkins Hospital in Baltimore for cervical cancer. Neither Lacks, an African-American farmer with limited means, nor her descendants derived any financial benefit from this scientifically crucial as well as lucrative discovery; the family only found out about the cell line decades later. In a similar case that was eventually litigated, John Moore unsuccessfully sued the University of California over a highly valuable cancer cell line developed from tissues collected when he was being treated for leukemia in 1976.[57] In that instance, researchers took further material over a number of years while representing their harvesting of the samples as ongoing treatment. Although the California Supreme Court eventually ruled that physicians are required to disclose their research interests, they also concluded that patients do not retain property rights over tissues taken from their bodies, and Moore was therefore not entitled to share in the significant revenue derived from commercial exploitation of his unusual cancer cells.[58]

The Moore case is one of the legal precedents cited by artist Carey Young as reference points for her exploration of intersections between law and business. Her 2005 exhibition *Consideration* (figure 34), mounted at the Paula Cooper Gallery in conjunction with Performa 05, was an important statement in this regard. The exhibition featured "a series of legally-enforceable contracts between artist and viewer" that Young created in collaboration with a team of lawyers credited in the press release.[59] At the entrance to the gallery, visitors were met with a reception desk where, in order to continue further, they not only had to provide a fingerprint, but also had to agree to transfer copyright to Young. The form, labeled at the top with the work's title, *Artistic License,* indicated that the visitor, in signing, granted Young "and her estate the absolute right and permission to use my fingerprints within the resulting work of art, for any commercial purpose, for the duration of copyright (plus any extensions and renewals)" (figure 35).

Those who opted to participate in the work by providing the required biometric information were then confronted with additional participatory situations. For *Donor-card,* an open-ended edition that follows the format of the organ donor cards that people sometimes carry in their wallets, viewers were directed to take a card and transform it into a work of art by signing it. The card references how existing copyright and moral rights laws are generally keyed to the life of the author, but brings the receiver into the equation as well, via its key provision: "In consideration of the donation of this card to me by the Artist, I hereby agree that this object will only become an artwork by her upon the inclusion of my signature, and that it will retain its status as an artwork solely for the duration of the Artist's life, or my life, whichever is shorter." Far more ominously, however, a work entitled *Declared Void* combined lines on the wall and floor setting off a corner of the gallery space with large lettering on the wall that presented a stark admonition: "By entering the zone created by this drawing, and for the period you remain there, you declare and agree that the US constitution will not apply to you."

In all cases participation was entirely optional. The only penalty for declining to provide a fingerprint was the inability to move beyond the doorway to the exhibition, and there was no pressure to step into the "Constitution-free" zone. But both are clearly reminiscent of situations that are far less voluntary. The format for the fingerprint release was based on US immigration paperwork, and *Declared Void* evoked detentions at Guantánamo and elsewhere in the aftermath of the September 11, 2001 terrorist attack. In addition to taking inspiration from the exploitation of genetic information, *Artistic License* drew prescient attention to the ever-expanding corporate appetite for personal data. After all, how many people have unthinkingly followed instructions to register their fingerprints as a means to open their smartphones and other devices, or activated web-based functionality for their wearable technologies, thereby handing off core personal details to corporations intent on amassing and marketing such information?

A more recent work by Young highlights how she has combined her interest in law as a subject with exploring ways that a nuanced understanding of her rights can help her realize her work. In preparation for the filming of her 2017 *Palais de Justice,* shot in the Brussels Palais de Justice courthouse, she initially went through official channels and

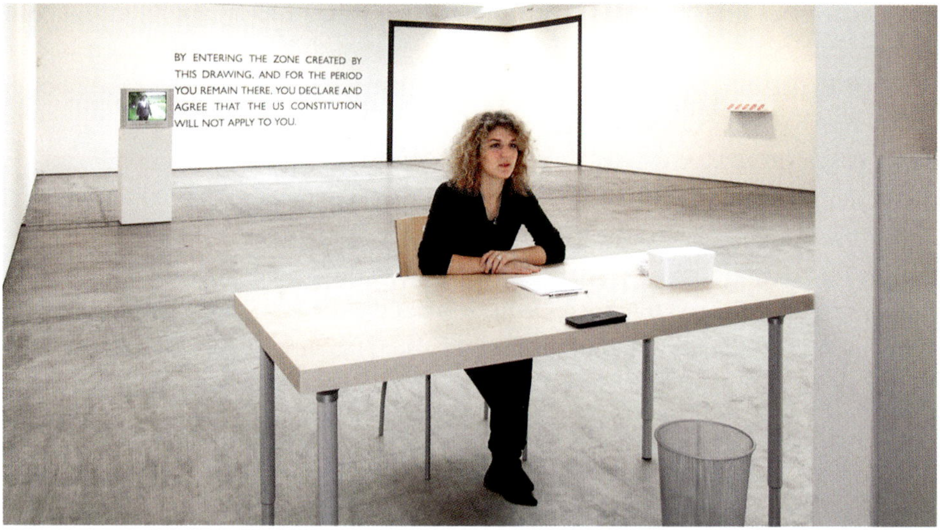

FIGURE 34 ▲
Installation view, *Carey Young: Consideration,* as part of Performa 05 Biennial, curated by Rose Lee Goldberg, Paula Cooper Gallery, 521 W 21st Street, New York, NY, November 16—November 19, 2005. © Carey Young. Courtesy the artist and Paula Cooper Gallery, New York.

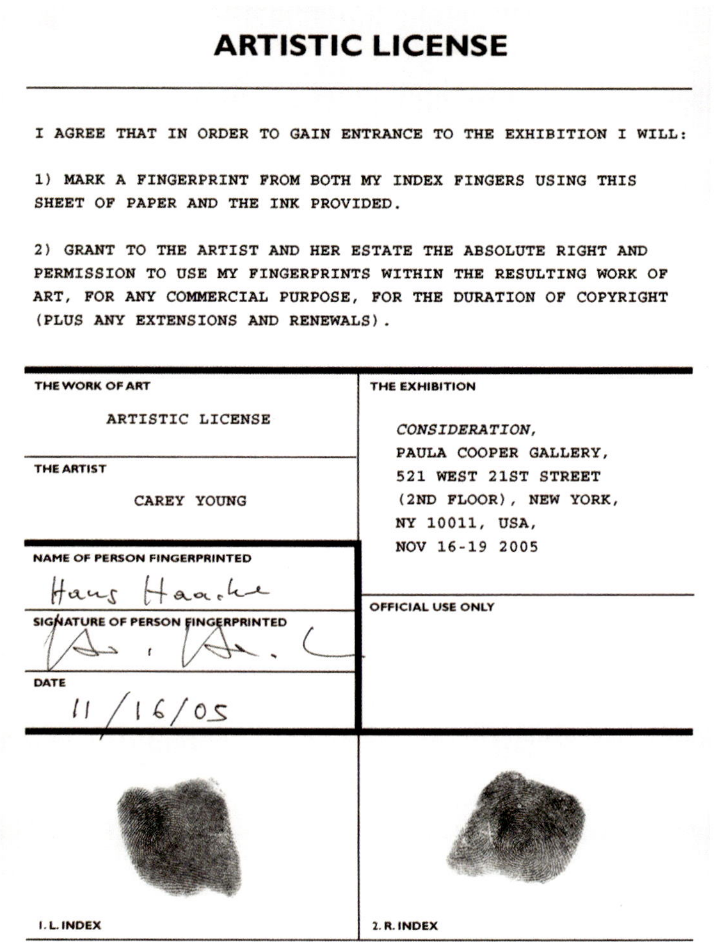

ARTISTIC LICENSE

I AGREE THAT IN ORDER TO GAIN ENTRANCE TO THE EXHIBITION I WILL:

1) MARK A FINGERPRINT FROM BOTH MY INDEX FINGERS USING THIS SHEET OF PAPER AND THE INK PROVIDED.

2) GRANT TO THE ARTIST AND HER ESTATE THE ABSOLUTE RIGHT AND PERMISSION TO USE MY FINGERPRINTS WITHIN THE RESULTING WORK OF ART, FOR ANY COMMERCIAL PURPOSE, FOR THE DURATION OF COPYRIGHT (PLUS ANY EXTENSIONS AND RENEWALS).

THE WORK OF ART
ARTISTIC LICENSE

THE ARTIST
CAREY YOUNG

NAME OF PERSON FINGERPRINTED
Hans Haacke

SIGNATURE OF PERSON FINGERPRINTED

DATE
11/16/05

THE EXHIBITION
CONSIDERATION,
PAULA COOPER GALLERY,
521 WEST 21ST STREET
(2ND FLOOR), NEW YORK,
NY 10011, USA,
NOV 16-19 2005

OFFICIAL USE ONLY

1. L. INDEX

2. R. INDEX

FIGURE 35 ▶
Carey Young, *Artistic License,* 2005. Signed inkjet prints with fingerprinting ink, pins, table and chair, invigilator. Detail: Hans Haacke's agreement, paper size: 8¼ × 5¾ in. © Carey Young. Courtesy the artist and Paula Cooper Gallery, New York.

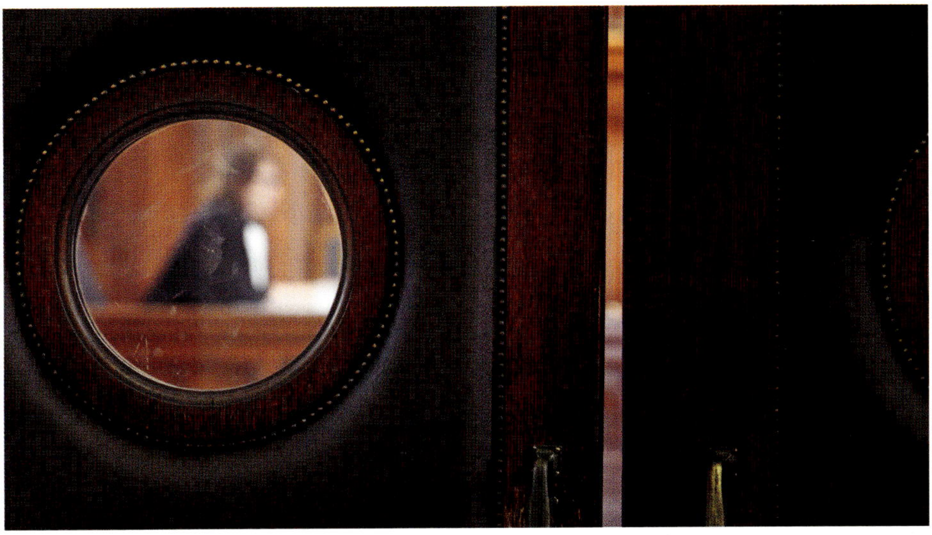

FIGURE 36
Carey Young, still from *Palais de Justice*, 2017, single-channel HD video (from 4K), 16:9, color, quadraphonic sound, 17 minutes, 58 seconds. © Carey Young. Courtesy the artist and Paula Cooper Gallery, New York.

requested permission, which was refused. She then hired a lawyer to determine what standing she might have to film anyway. As Young recounted, "First, she deduced that the building is no longer in copyright and, second, that, although Belgium has very restrictive privacy laws, during a trial, the judges, clerks and everyone facing my camera are considered public figures revealing themselves in public. According to this argument, the project did not need their permission."[60] Young therefore simply set up equipment and filmed through the glass windows of courtroom doors, going back repeatedly over the course of two years (see figure 36). Training her camera on female judges and advocates, she created a subtly subversive record of the exercise of legal power. Only after the work was complete did she alert the individuals to what she had recorded and request their agreement to be included in the project (which she received).

Maria Eichhorn has been equally fascinated by the power of negotiated agreements, including contracts. One aspect of this interest was realized through extensive research regarding the Siegelaub-Projansky agreement and related documents, including the series of interviews eventually published in her important book on the subject.[61] In many instances, however, she has leveraged the type of creative license granted when artists are invited to create a project for an exhibition to explore legal and ethical issues that extend outward, beyond art-world confines. Her version of institutional critique sometimes takes the form of highly targeted attempts to employ the tools of capitalism to sabotage its logic or efficacy. But she has also used exhibition invitations as a framework for important research that might otherwise not receive support.

The Aktiengesellschaft (Public Limited Company) that Eichhorn established in 2002, on the occasion of her participation in documenta 11, was constituted by an intriguingly subversive articulation of corporate structure established on the basis of a 50,000 Euro investment in shares that could neither be traded nor appreciate in value. She then transferred the shares to the company, meaning that it belonged either to itself, or to no one. Yet the presentation rights for the venture, *Maria Eichhorn Aktiengesellschaft,* were acquired by the Van Abbemuseum in Eindhoven in 2007, which repaid the original 50,000 Euro loan extended by documenta GmbH in 2002 and assumed responsibility for operating expenses as well as an ongoing collaboration with Eichhorn to maintain the company's operation.[62] Her interest in using legal structures against the grain was equally evident in the project she pursued as part of her participation in documenta 14. For the section of the exhibition sited in Athens, her Κτίριο ως περιουσία άνευ ιδιοκτήτη / *Building as Unowned Property* (2017), she responded to the financial crisis in Greece by attempting to have a vacant building declared unowned—with the goal of thereby turning a former private house into a form of public property.

The *Rose Valland Institute* that Eichhorn established as part of her participation in the Kassel segment of documenta 14 reflected a different form of site-specific response, as well as another long-term focus of Eichhorn's work (figure 37). Although documenta 14 curator Adam Szymczyk failed in his attempts to present the now-infamous Gurlitt estate to the public as part of the exhibition, Eichhorn's *Rose Valland Institute* drew attention to other aspects of Nazi looting of Jewish property, together with calls for ongoing action.[63] Its nine-part framework included a lengthy video loop of 1935–42 auction records from Berlin, now accessible through the Berlin State Archive, which have provided important evidence for researchers examining provenance history; a series of original documents and facsimiles relating to confiscations from the collection of Kassel philanthropist Alexander Fiorino; and photographs as well as other documents tracing systematic looting of Jewish property in Paris. The centerpiece was a towering, double-sided bookshelf structure, *Unlawfully Acquired Books from Jewish Ownership,* which presented dramatic evidence of looted volumes in Berlin libraries that have been identified through provenance research at the Zentral- und Landesbibliothek that has been ongoing since 2010. Perhaps equally important, however, was her attempt to leverage the visibility of the exhibition to promote further research.

Both the focus on provenance, and Eichhorn's strategic response to an exhibition invitation, reflected a continuation of concerns that motivated her 2003 "Politics of Restitution" at the Lenbachhaus und Kunstbau, Munich (figures 38 and 39). On that occasion, Eichhorn used funds associated with the exhibition to hire a historian to research a series of so-called "orphan" works. Many of the paintings on display, in nineteenth-century figurative styles favored by Hitler, were once destined for his unrealized Führermuseum. By presenting them on free-standing pedestals that allowed viewers to see the labels and other marks on their backs, Eichhorn emphasized their passage

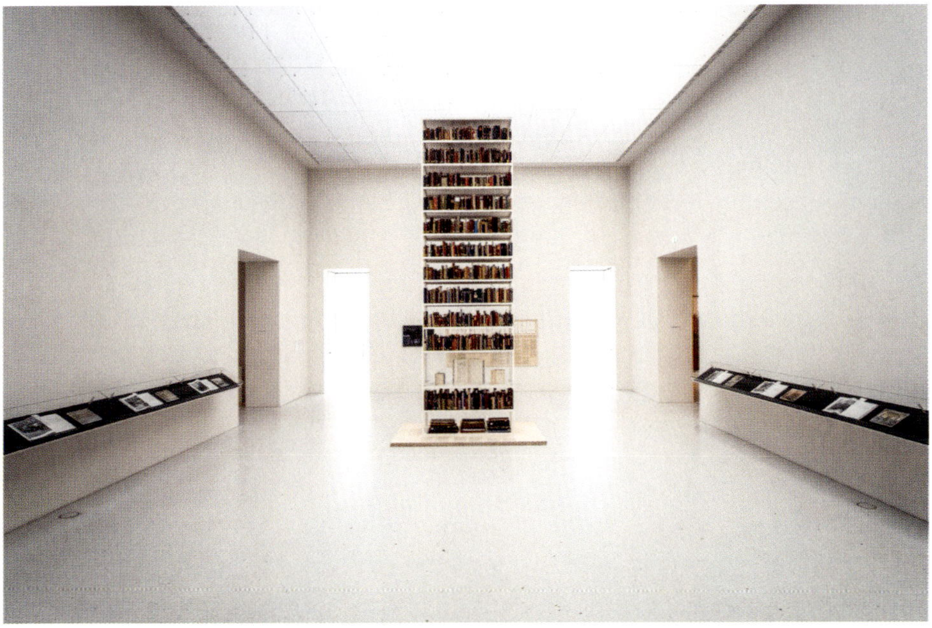

FIGURE 37
Maria Eichhorn, *Rose Valland Institute*, 2017. Exhibition view, documenta 14. Detail: Unlawfully Acquired Books from Jewish Ownership; Album Bundesarchiv Koblenz, B $^{323}/_{311}$; "I distinguish between Germans old enough to have played a role in the war, and the post-war generation." Interview with David Toren (2016–17). Photo: Mathias Völzke © VG Bild-Kunst Bonn, Maria Eichhorn 2020.

through time. Ownership of one of the paintings had been resolved two years earlier. But the other fifteen had remained in limbo ever since being impounded from Nazi holdings by the Allies, and they were listed as "Loan from the Federal Republic of Germany" based on the fact that they were part of a group of over 2,700 paintings that were declared government property in 1962 because their provenance had not been determined.[64] While the research Eichhorn commissioned did free eight of the works from suspicion of looting, ownership records for seven could not be traced to before 1933, and some had clearly been handled by dealers who participated in the transfer of looted art.

German civil code specifies a thirty-year statute of limitations for making claims regarding stolen property—meaning that time limits ran out during the 1960s and 1970s for works confiscated under Nazi rule. Nonetheless, the 1998 Washington Conference on Holocaust-Era Assets established a series of non-binding principles "to assist in resolving issues relating to Nazi-confiscated art," which called for renewed efforts to identify ownership, grant access to relevant archives, provide allowance for potential gaps in the record, create a central registry, and take steps "to achieve a just and fair solution" when prewar ownership is determined.[65] Thus the pressure to return this material goes beyond what is generally specified by law, both in Germany and elsewhere.

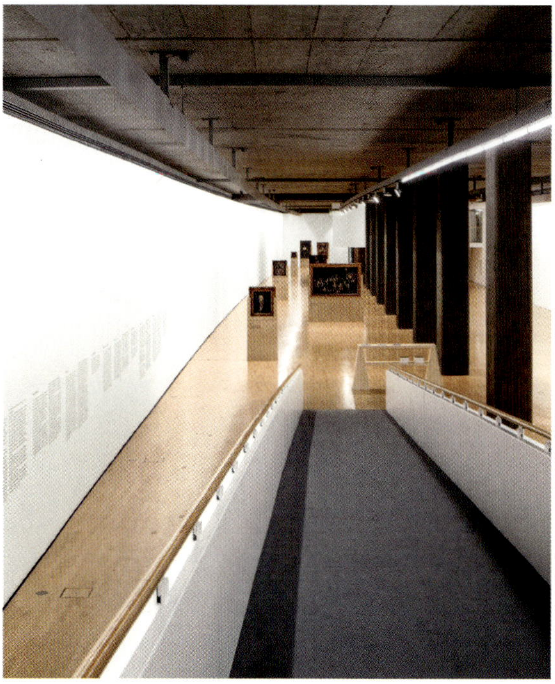

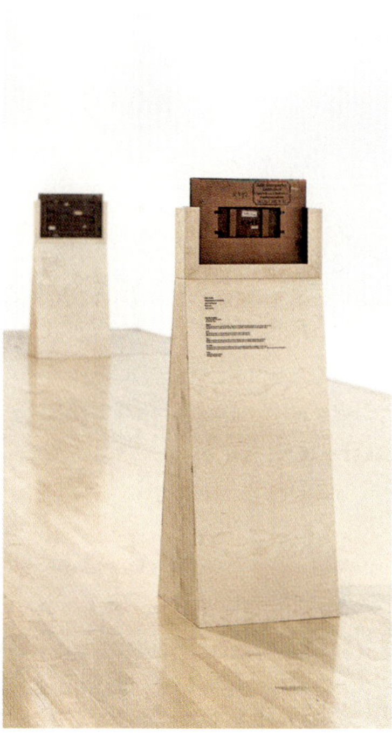

FIGURE 38 ◀
Maria Eichhorn, *Restitutionspolitik / Politics of Restitution,* 2003. Exhibition view, Städtische Galerie im Lenbachhaus und Kunstbau, Munich. Photo: Ernst Jank. © VG Bild-Kunst Bonn, Maria Eichhorn 2020.

FIGURE 39 ▶
Maria Eichhorn, *Restitutionspolitik / Politics of Restitution,* 2003. Detail: displays. Photo: Ernst Jank. © VG Bild-Kunst Bonn, Maria Eichhorn 2020.

The moral responsibility of returning works confiscated as part of the Holocaust—above and beyond explicit legal obligations—is also an important model in relation to other claims associated with forced removal. Greek demands regarding the return of marble sculptures taken from the Parthenon by Lord Elgin are well known (and so far fruitless). However, French President Emmanuel Macron's embrace of a 2018 report recommending the restitution of African works seized as part of French colonial rule set the stage for a series of resolutions regarding the return of such material.[66] These plans denote an abrupt reversal from reliance on the 1970 UNESCO "Convention on the Means of Prohibiting and Preventing the Illicit Import, Export and Transfer of Ownership of Cultural Property," with most institutions previously only recognizing claims for works illegally excavated or exported after the accord's effective date of 1972.

Even as there have been certain steps to address past violence, however, current artistic expression is severely threatened in many parts of the world. PEN, the international organization supporting literary as well as human rights, launched the Artists at Risk Connection (ARC) in October 2017 to address the growing danger of attacks on artists.

Their reports have highlighted acts of repression by a number of different regimes that include arrests, prison sentences, and disappearances, with China, Cuba, and Turkey making repeat appearances.[67] One widely covered incident, the 2018 razing of Ai Weiwei's Beijing studio, was a particularly visible example of a pattern of attacks on artistic expression that echo broader threats to human rights. Although works by Ai were damaged, he expressed more concern about how assaults against art communities reflect a larger agenda to control who is allowed to reside in Chinese urban centers.[68] The official reasons for the studio demolition and other forms of persecution were framed in bureaucratic terms, but there can be little doubt that they were provoked by his challenges to government authority through specific works, including a large-scale installation using rebar salvaged from the rubble after the 2008 Sichuan earthquake, which drew attention to the catastrophic collapse of school buildings. Any hope that his international profile might protect him was shattered in 2011, when he was arrested and jailed for almost three months on charges of tax evasion as he was about to board a flight to Hong Kong, and it wasn't until 2015 that he was again allowed to leave China.

Tania Bruguera has also faced arrest and other forms of detention after repeatedly challenging governmental restrictions in Cuba as part of a far-reaching agenda questioning the exercise of power in political and social realms. To describe her overlay of activism and art, she employs the term "artivist," and in frequently provocative performances or interactive situations she has not been afraid to use the platform provided by exhibition invitations to confront or even startle her audience, including subjecting them to various forms of surveillance or manipulation. While intrinsic to all her work, that activism has been particularly apparent in several long-term projects, including *Cátedra Arte de Conducta* (*Behavior Art School*) in her native Cuba, 2002–9, which used a workshop format, as well as the freedoms accorded to international visitor participants, to explore the boundaries of what could be expressed in the Cuban context. It was also on display in the 2010–15 *Immigrant Movement International*, centered on a storefront in the Corona neighborhood of Queens, New York, which assumed a double role—drawing attention to the plight of immigrants, and providing a street-level resource center.

Bruguera's responses to the Havana Biennial have been particularly pointed. Billed as the biennial for the third world when it was founded in 1984, a key aspect of its mission has been providing a forum for art from outside Europe and North America. Because of its outward-facing nature, it has been relatively free from the censorship woven into Cuban life, and Bruguera took advantage of this dynamic in 2009 to stage her *Tatlin Whisper #6*, an hour-long event in the courtyard of the Centro Wifredo Lam, where members of the audience were invited to come to the microphone for one minute of free speech. But she managed to find the limits of Cuba's provisional openness when she responded to President Obama's December 17, 2014 announcement of plans to normalize relations between Cuba and the United States by proposing a new version of *Tatlin Whisper #6* to take place in the Plaza of the Revolution. Upon arriving

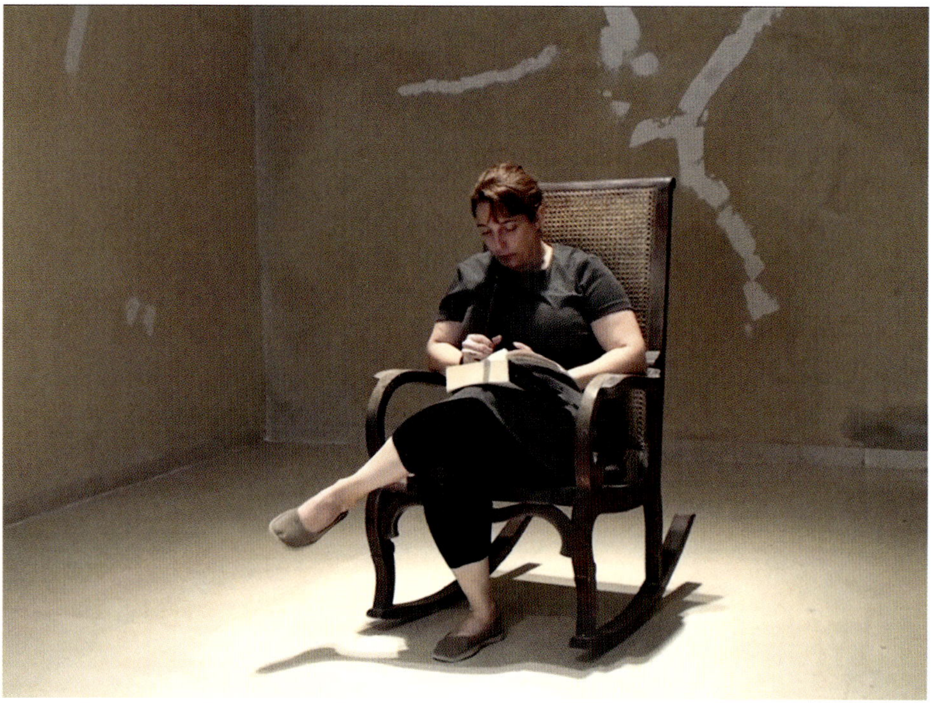

FIGURE 40
Tania Bruguera reading from Hannah Arendt, *The Origins of Totalitarianism,* Havana, May 2015, as part of the Hannah Arendt International Institute of Artivism. Photo: Pablo León de la Barra. Courtesy Estudio Bruguera.

in Cuba later the same month, Bruguera was detained and her passport was confiscated.[69] The prolonged legal limbo that followed meant that Bruguera was still in Cuba when the next iteration of the Havana Biennial opened in May 2015. Running concurrently with the opening festivities, Bruguera staged a one-hundred-hour reading of Hannah Arendt's *The Origins of Totalitarianism* in her Havana home—despite loud roadwork that suddenly started up outside her building, as well as the threat of further detainment (figures 40 and 41). Though she was indeed arrested again immediately following its conclusion, Bruguera did have some small satisfaction in knowing that her interrogators would have to familiarize themselves with the Arendt text.[70] That performance marked the beginning of another long-term project, her *Instituto de Artivismo Hannah Arendt* (*Hannah Arendt International Institute for Artivism*, or INSTAR), planned as a "hub for civic literacy" in Cuba.

While Bruguera's international profile has ensured publicity for her interventions, she is far from alone in mounting acts of resistance in Cuba. Luis Manuel Otero and Yanelys Núñez have created their own series of alternative exhibitions and projects, the most pointed of which took place at the time of the 2019 Havana Biennial. Their title, *Bienal Sin 349* (*Biennial Without 349*), was a reference to Decree 349, issued by the

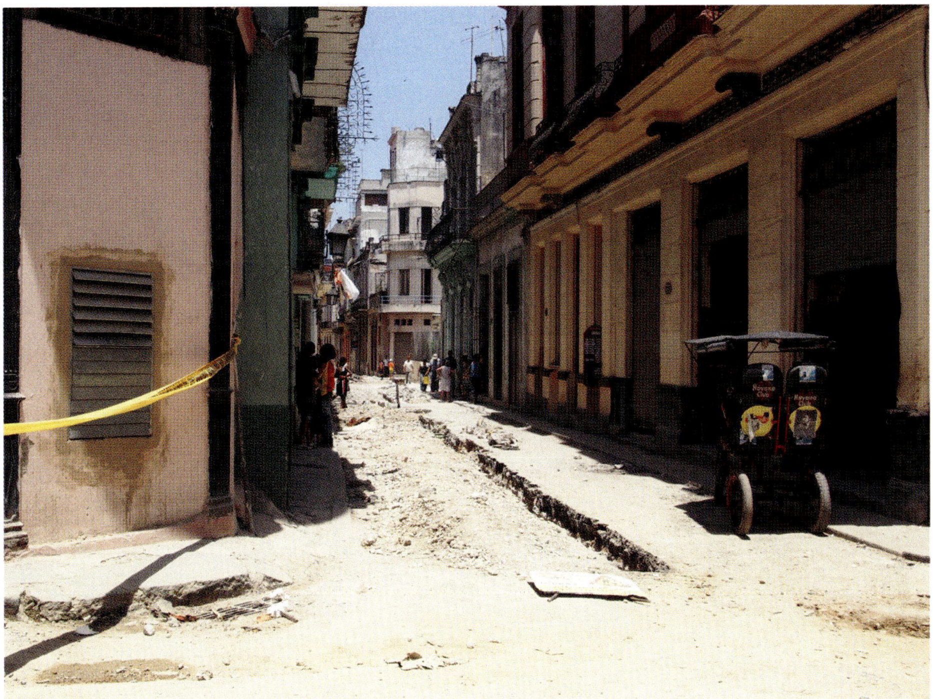

FIGURE 41
Roadwork outside Tania Bruguera's Havana residence, May 2015. Photo: Judith Rodenbeck.

Cuban government in December 2018, which linked an extensive list of prohibited content to a mandatory registration system for anyone providing "artistic services" (including visual and performing artists, along with those supplying equipment or facilities).[71] Key provisions essentially grant the Cuban government the ultimate authority to define what constitutes art by declaring any unregistered activity illegal, giving inspectors power to decide what work conforms to the requirements of the decree, and requiring registration with the "Registry of Fine Art and Applied Art Creators." In addition to the potential for corruption, according to Otero and Núñez, the "agents who grant the permits have no background in art or art history and will subjectively make permit decisions depending on whether or not they approve of the lyrics of a song."[72]

The possibility that art might be defined by governmental authority, evident in some of the lawsuits discussed elsewhere in this book, takes on a whole new significance in relation to Cuba's Decree 349. One response would be to conclude that conflicts about the fine points of authorial rights necessarily pale in comparison to the struggles faced by artists responding to overt governmental surveillance and repression. In such circumstances, attempts to restrict artistic discourse are likely to be only one aspect of widespread campaigns. Yet artistic activism in the face of obvious risks also presents a dramatic case for the overall importance of freedom of expression. The principles at stake should not be dismissed as inconsequential, even in circumstances where the threats are less immediately dangerous.

The global biennial phenomenon is just one marker of an interconnected world that encompasses elaborately interwoven supply chains, overlapping consumer cultures, and pressure on governments to adhere to international IP accords. In regions where censorship is less overt, citizens still need to pay close attention to the corrosive impact when creative expressions, and intellectual activities in general, are appreciated primarily for their property value. Artists who have made the law and its limits an explicit focus of their work help draw attention to ways that legal codes shape all aspects of life. At the same time, artists who never intended to engage with law, but nonetheless wound up caught in its clutches, present another form of cautionary tale, since conflicts resulting from unanticipated transgressions help to demonstrate constraints that might not be immediately obvious.

Specific legal protections for art and other creative work reflect a certain idealism about the nature of creativity as well as the efficacy of law to support its goals. Yet cases that go to court often suggest the opposite, through the intersections of art and money, along with strategic, sometimes cynical attempts to use legal categories or definitions to the advantage of whoever is framing the argument. Lawsuits spawned by market disputes underscore the underlying contradiction of treating certain works of art as investment properties, even as stratospheric prices are justified with reference to art's ineffable qualities. Questions about what creative work should qualify for the safeguards known as moral rights indicate some of the challenges associated with drawing distinctions between artistic authorship and many other closely related pursuits. Taken individually and as a group, the conflicts that wind up in court can help demonstrate a range of options. Some involve raising questions about the role or definition of art, particularly in its many expanded forms. Others indicate ways that the law is out of step with current customs or ideals. Playing with or against assumptions about the power of art can also provide artists with a platform for various forms of activism. It is important to see these possibilities as part of a continuum, within which one important role for artists is making values and tensions visible.

5

PUBLIC MATTERS

A CRUCIAL ASPECT OF THE DIALOGUE around *Tilted Arc* discussed in the previous chapter concerned the role of public space, including the nature of the plaza that it interrupted. Although *Tilted Arc* dated to 1981, the Jacob K. Javits Federal Office Building in front of which it stood was completed in 1969, and the overall dynamics of the site were similar in many respects to plazas associated with private buildings completed around the same time—often public in name only, given their unwelcoming character. Starting in 1961, New York began allowing larger buildings in exchange for the creation of public space (sometimes referred to as "bonus plazas"). Almost immediately, developers pursued designs that would discourage actual use. Richard Roth, of the firm Emery Roth and Sons, described a conscious strategy, realized through water features (such as elaborate fountains in front of a 1969 building at 1345 Sixth Avenue) or sunken plazas (evident in the firm's 1970 Paramount Building), with the latter employed precisely because below-grade areas were known to be uninviting.[1]

During the intervening decades, however, as privately owned public spaces, or "POPS," have continued to play a major role in urban development schemes, businesses have found it advantageous to create environments that seem welcoming even as they remain tightly controlled. A *Guardian* article about the POPS phenomenon characterized London's Granary Square, opened in 2012, as "one of the largest open-air spaces in Europe" but also recounted how restrictions meant that their photographer had to record the site from a distance.[2] Similarly, because London's City Hall is situated within More London, a thirteen-acre POPS along the Thames's south bank, there are constraints on both protests and photography. In 2010, London Assembly Member Jenny Jones described how it had taken eight years of negotiation with More London for politicians to secure the right to conduct television interviews outside the building where they work.[3]

Any engagement with the physical environment encompasses a range of concerns. One is the distinction between public and private—with "public" often synonymous with government-owned, but also applying in varying degrees to many forms of private property accessible to the public. For individuals attempting to create a visual record of their surroundings, there is the danger of crossing not only invisible physical property lines, but also intellectual property, in the form of copyrights over public art and architecture. When recording phenomena within the built environment, the status of the original manifestation as well as purpose of the response can both be crucial, including distinctions between commercial and noncommercial, or art versus architecture. To the degree that certain rights and privileges turn on whether a phenomenon is defined as art, then category assignments can become sources of conflict. Debates about how to articulate public interest have also been provoked by site-specific work ranging from officially commissioned art to unsanctioned graffiti.

Expectations of privacy are equally significant, with individuals traversing publicly accessible spaces subject to various forms of surveillance, governed by regulations that differ dramatically from one country to the next, while everywhere prey to dangerous erosion from new technologies. Seeing how these issues play out in relation to physical versions of public space is vital to understanding their extension and transformation within virtual public realms: in particular, limitations on political speech in the context of POPS should serve as a warning with respect to communication within the framework of proprietary technology platforms.[4] Attempting to understand the tangle of rights and responsibilities associated with both physical and virtual property lines is made even more complex by differences in national laws, along with ongoing changes in both technologies and regulatory frameworks.

FREEDOM OF PANORAMA

The bundle of rights and regulations governing photographic and video records of the built environment is generally known as "freedom of panorama" (FoP), with laws that vary notably in different countries. Under US law, even though architecture qualified

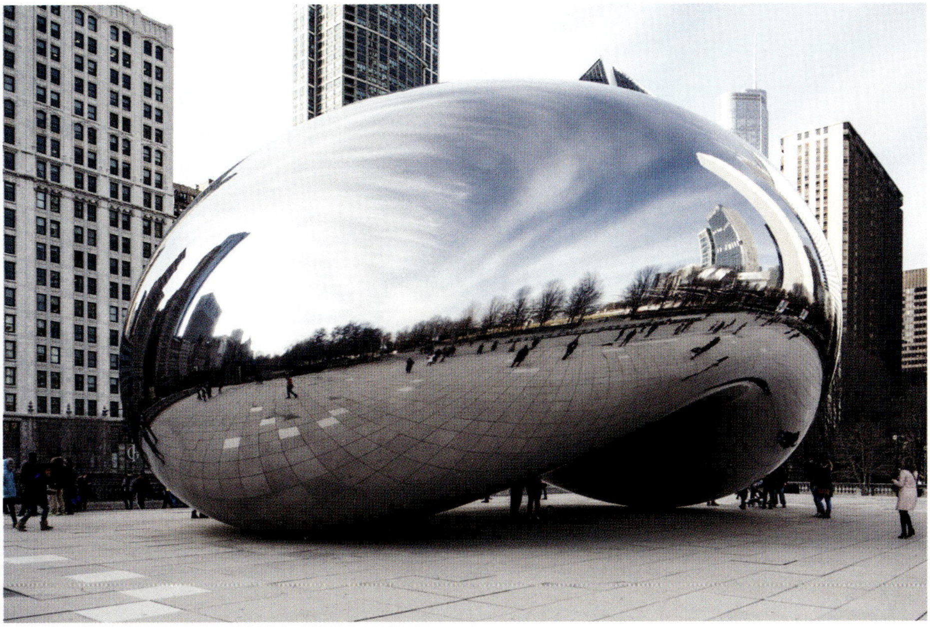

FIGURE 42
Anish Kapoor, *Cloud Gate,* 2004, Chicago. © Anish Kapoor. All Rights Reserved, DACS, London/ARS, NY 2020. Photo: Sharon Mollerus, posted to Wikimedia Commons under Creative Commons license CC BY 2.0.

for copyright starting in 1991, copyright holders cannot limit the circulation of images of publicly visible building exteriors, whereas copyright holders for public art can do so. When the United States extended copyright to include architecture, it provided explicit exceptions for making and distributing representations of buildings located in or visible from public places.[5] Nor are building owners prevented from making alterations due to copyright (though there generally are other limitations associated with zoning regulations, or sometimes landmark status).

For works of public sculpture that become emblematic of a particular place, however, copyright claims by the original author can be dramatically at odds with popular practice in an age of incessant image production and circulation—with Anish Kapoor's 2004 *Cloud Gate* sculpture, in Chicago's Millennium Park, as a notable example (figure 42). Known as "the Bean" due to its curvilinear shape, the work quickly became a lure for countless pictures taken in the presence of its reflective surface. At the same time, however, security guards attempted to enforce city policy requiring paid permits for professional photographers—who could apparently be identified as such due to their camera gear and tripods. The social media response to reported restrictions on photography was to post even more photos, including a Flickr compendium tagged "cloudgate" that quickly came to include thousands of examples. Regardless of such defiance, however, Kapoor relied on his copyright over the work when he sued the National Rifle

Association to block *Cloud Gate*'s appearance in a 2017 propaganda video, *The Clenched Fist of Truth*. The video's excoriation of liberals included a momentary view of Chicago, with the sculpture in the foreground, accompanied by a voice-over claim that "they" (liberals) "use their ex-president to endorse the Resistance." In that context, the view of Chicago, identifiable as such because of the landmark sculpture, evoked Barack Obama's ties to the city, while the "Resistance" seemed to be any form of anti-Donald Trump protest. The NRA initially defended the sculpture's appearance on First Amendment grounds, but ultimately reached an agreement to remove the image and release a new version of the video, rather than pursue a court case.[6]

Via an open letter published on his own website, Kapoor wrote, "I am disgusted to see my work—in truth the sculpture of the people of Chicago—used by the NRA to promote their vile message."[7] Those opposed to the NRA's right-wing mission will presumably applaud Kapoor's desire to contest this use. Yet as a policy matter, it is problematic when a copyright holder can prevent others from responding to a work that is both publicly sited and broadly symbolic of a particular place. These contradictions are evident even within Kapoor's statement, where his shift from describing the work as his own to referencing a larger claim by the people of Chicago suggests potential tensions between individual authors and less clearly defined claims of public interest. Even if one admires Kapoor's position, it is still important to recognize the danger of allowing intellectual property rights in a public monument to regulate discourse.

Kapoor was less successful, however, in his attempts to get Chicago mayor Rahm Emanuel to join him in pursuing legal action regarding a public sculpture installed in the Chinese city of Karamay that was notably similar in material and shape to *Cloud Gate*. The threatened action never materialized, perhaps due to difficulties anticipated by art law expert Daniel McClean, who indicated that chances of success in Chinese courts would be greater if the suit was viewed as an economic or brand issue.[8] But recourse to private law did allow Kapoor to block other artists from access to a new pigment, Vantablack, billed as the "blackest black" due to its light-absorbing qualities, after he entered into a 2016 agreement with the manufacturer providing him with exclusive access.

In places such as the United States, where freedom of panorama applies to architecture but not public art, definition questions are significant. One key case, *Leicester v. Warner Brothers*, involved a Los Angeles plaza complex called Zanja Madre, designed by Andrew Leicester and completed in 1992. When certain details appeared in the 1995 film *Batman Forever*, Leicester sued on the basis of the work's identity as a sculpture. As publicly visible architecture, photography would be allowed; as a sculpture, he could claim copyright protection. Although the Ninth Circuit referenced the possibility of independent copyright for certain elements incorporated into useful articles (e.g., "a carving on the back of a chair or an engraving in a glass vase"), the court focused on the need for "separability," either physical or conceptual. The plaza was judged to be an integral part of the overall architectural vision, and therefore encompassed by freedom of panorama.[9]

Another strategy employed by certain institutions attempting to control representations of distinctive buildings is not copyright, but trademark. According to the Guggenheim Museum's website, for example, not only the name, but all aspects of the distinctive Frank Lloyd Wright building in New York are protected: "The name 'Guggenheim' and the interior and exterior images of the Guggenheim Museum are registered trademarks of the Solomon R. Guggenheim Foundation."[10] In Australia, the Sydney Harbor Opera Trust extended existing trademark claims in 2014 to register a shape trademark for the distinctive Sydney Opera House designed by Jørn Utzon—thus attempting to control both two-dimensional images from all angles and three-dimensional renderings.[11] But such claims do not always hold up, as the Rock and Roll Hall of Fame in Cleveland found when it unsuccessfully attempted to use a trademark claim to prevent photographs of the building exterior from being reproduced in an unsanctioned poster.[12] The courts also sided with makers of the 2002 *Spider-Man* movie, who were subject to a trademark lawsuit by property owners and advertisers over a scene set in Times Square where the backdrop included a mix of actual buildings and certain billboards where the filmmakers had substituted alternate imagery.[13]

Even though it is a bit of an aside, given that it concerns the use of a trademarked name rather than image, it seems worth noting the value associated with the appellation "World Trade Center," which rather surprisingly is not controlled by the Port Authority of New York and New Jersey, despite the agency's ownership of the World Trade Center site. Entities that want to use the name for their own ventures are required to pay a $250,000 initiation fee and $12,500 annual dues to the World Trade Center Association—a private organization established in 1986 with the acquisition of naming rights from the Port Authority for the nominal sum of $10, and initially presided over by a former Port Authority official who drew a notably high salary from the revenue generated by some three hundred association members. Until the unusual deal was revealed, that income stream included substantial dues paid by the Port Authority itself for ongoing use of the name it had handed over to the association.[14] The purported rationale for the highly suspect arrangement was that the Port Authority did not have the resources to protect their trademark name themselves.

Apparently Port Authority lawyers did, however, have time to go after a local business for selling New York skyline dishware characterized by imagery that included the twin towers (as part of a design that was created before 2001) (figure 43). The houseware business, Fishs Eddy, was undaunted by the Port Authority's cease and desist letter, having already stared down lawyers associated with the Chrysler Building over the same product line in 1998. According to Fishs Eddy co-owner Julie Gaines, she asked in response to the earlier demand how it was possible to say they couldn't include the Chrysler Building: "We wanted to do a plate that represented New York City. Leaving off the Chrysler Building would be like leaving off the World Trade Center."[15] When the Port Authority accused the store of trying to benefit from the September 11, 2001 terrorist attack, commentators were quick to point out its own

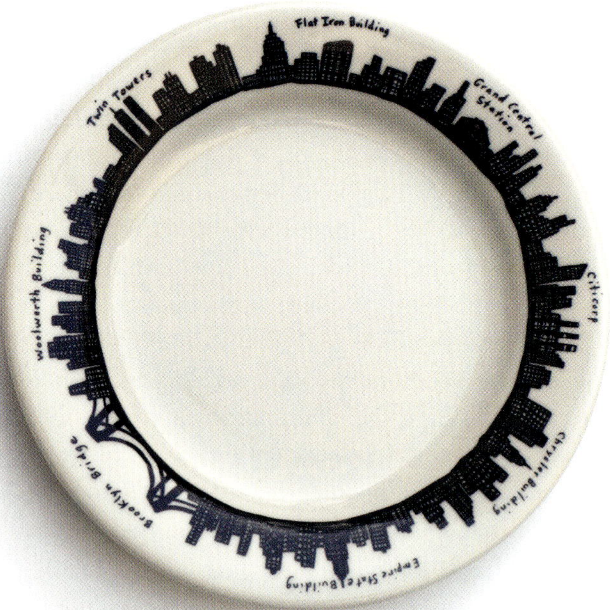

FIGURE 43
212 Side Plate, Fishs Eddy.
Photo: Martha Buskirk.

controversial 9/11 museum gift shop, loaded with merchandise far more explicitly associated with the event.[16]

The US distinction between art and architecture is only one example of widely divergent approaches to freedom of panorama. Some countries allow photography of both art and architecture, including building interiors that are publicly accessible. Germany, known for strong privacy protections, nonetheless has expansive freedom of panorama exceptions to copyright, modeled on laws established in Bavaria when Germany was still a confederation of separate states.[17] Some countries impose restrictions based on whether a photograph was taken from the vantage point of public rather than private property (with the divisions sometimes difficult to discern in relation to private ownership of publicly accessible spaces). Other countries impose copyright controls on both art and architecture. And a few are even more restrictive—such as Italy, which requires permission and fees to publish anything defined as a cultural heritage asset, no matter how old.[18]

Not surprisingly, given its mission, Wikimedia Commons has posted an extensive compilation of what is allowed in each country. The severe disconnect between legal restraints and actual practice (all those selfies!) is one factor cited in frequent arguments for expansive panorama rights. But certain specific dynamics have provoked advocacy in the opposite direction. Regarding the relationship between publicly sited

Māori sculptures, and New Zealand's generous panorama exceptions, Jonathan Barrett has argued for stronger restrictions to protect indigenous works that have been freely shared. Among the examples he referenced are two carved *pouwhenua* (landmarking posts) by Ra Vincent that were donated to the city of Wellington. The works have appeared in Alamy/Getty stock images with no identification of the original artist, even though use of the photographs is tightly controlled and monetized.[19]

Such differences in national law are challenging under any circumstance, but the lack of harmony is especially problematic for online circulation. In one notable instance from 2012, representatives of Claes Oldenburg and Coosje van Bruggen sent the Wikimedia Foundation a takedown notice covering images of public sculptures permanently installed in a number of different countries, including the United States, Germany, Japan, the United Kingdom, Israel, Portugal, the Netherlands, and Spain. According to their lawyer, even though such photographs would be permissible in most of the countries where the works were installed, they constituted infringement in the United States. Wikimedia's decision to comply by removing the photos listed in the notice sparked vigorous criticism by Wikimedia contributors who stressed, in particular, that numerous photos of works installed in Germany were clearly not infringements under German law.[20] The takedown notice hardly put a dent in the number of readily available images of the sculptures in question, as a Google image search for any of the works quickly reveals. But it did knock out a number of photos whose creators shared the images under a Creative Commons license, which typically allows others to republish as long as they include proper attribution. Thus the artists succeeded in shutting down circulation of images presented with care for proper attribution and controlled reuse, while doing nothing to slow the vast numbers of other photos shared via platforms where reliable source information is less likely to be included.

Rather surprisingly, Sweden's supreme court ruled against Wikimedia in a copyright case concerning a collaborative database of Swedish public art, Offentligkonst.se, run by Wikimedia Sweden, which relied on user-uploaded imagery. Swedish law does afford panorama rights for both art and architecture. BUS (Bildkonst Upphovsrätt i Sverige, the Visual Arts Copyright Society in Sweden) nonetheless demanded a licensing fee from Wikimedia for publishing images of works by three artists they represented. When Wikimedia refused, BUS sued, arguing that the FoP exception applies only to printed imagery, rather than online postings, and the Swedish high court agreed. Therefore a postcard image sold for profit in Sweden would qualify for a FoP exception while an online posting, even to a nonprofit web site, is enjoined.[21] The Swedish ruling against Wikimedia notwithstanding, is it easy to find online images of the three works at issue (Thomas Qvarsebo's *Duo;* Johan Paalzow's *Moby Dick;* and Eva Hild's *Binär,* all in Stockholm). These three works, and many more examples of public art, even in places with limited FoP exceptions, can also be surveyed via Google Street View.

Launched in 2007, Street View is a prime example of the disconnect between the patchwork of national copyright laws and the pervasive reach of Alphabet (Google's

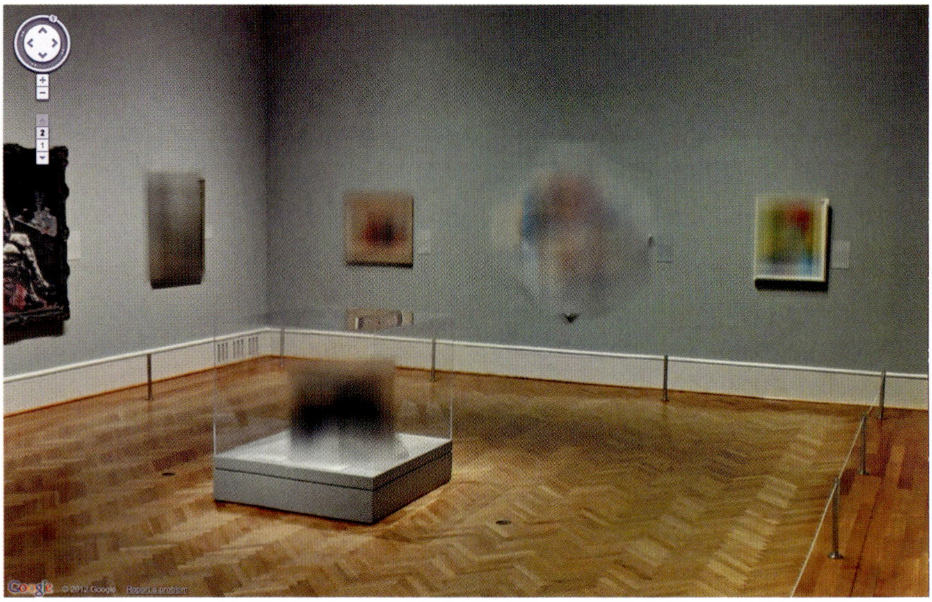

FIGURE 44
Greg Allen/greg.org, *Study for Untitled (Google Art Noguchi Table)*, #2, 2013. Cropped screenshot of the Art Institute of Chicago via Google Art Project, digital print on paper, dimensions variable. Courtesy the artist.

parent company). Despite various restrictions limiting the circulation of images taken in public places, Google has managed to push forward its agenda of capturing a panoramic record of just about everything—sometimes in multiple versions, given their repeated passes through many areas. Copyright concerns seem to have a minimal impact on what is captured in exterior views, including graffiti, where one generally encounters a blurred image only when a face is rendered with sufficient realism to trigger that aspect of the algorithm-driven software.[22] However, their attempt to extend the principle to museum interiors with the Google Art Project, announced with much fanfare in 2011, did not go as smoothly, with virtual gallery tours interrupted by repeated examples of blurred artwork (mostly for copyright, but some for nudity).

Many who explored the early versions of Google Art Project were fascinated by the vagaries of the blurring, with unaltered works sometimes popping in and out of view depending on one's position in the virtual spaces. Greg Allen, in addition to recording his experiences with the interface through screen captures, used those images for a series of artworks where he further distorted the already blurred images with applications of solvent to the physical printout. A study for one of those works (figure 44) shows (or more accurately, doesn't show) a gallery from the Chicago Art Institute where a vitrine with an Isamu Noguchi chess table is positioned in the foreground, with various paintings on the wall behind.[23]

It is therefore notable how completely initial resistance to Google's Street View initiative was framed in terms of potential privacy rather than copyright violations, given attention to freedom of panorama restrictions in other circumstances. Not surprisingly, privacy questions were raised more insistently outside the United States—reflecting stronger limitations on collecting personal data in certain other parts of the world. By and large, however, such concerns seemed to lose their urgency once people became accustomed to yet another mode of pervasive data collection and distribution, pursued with limited transparency and few options for informed consent.

Despite the premise that Google's panoramic view only records what is publicly visible at street level, the fact that the cameras are generally mounted seven to eight feet above the ground means that they are able to see over many standard fences and hedges designed to shield buildings and private outdoor spaces from typical pedestrians and passing motorists. Complaints about initial Street View images captured in Japan in 2009 led Google to lower camera heights by sixteen inches (forty centimeters) and reshoot footage in twelve cities that had already been recorded.[24] In Switzerland, a 2012 Federal Supreme Court ruling also directed camera heights to be lowered, specified certain types of facilities that would have to be blurred, and required advance notice for image capture.[25] Italy mandated preannounced itineraries; Canada and the United Kingdom required Google to develop technology to blur faces and license plates; and Germany insisted on the choice to opt out of having one's private residence recorded.[26]

Clearly attempting to assuage such concerns, Google began to blur faces and license plates in 2008 even where not ordered to do so. Privacy fears were further underscored in 2010, however, when Google was forced to admit that the technology it had been using since 2007 to photograph Street View imagery had simultaneously been scanning and collecting Wi-Fi data from domestic networks its vehicles passed—initially described as the unintended consequence of a programming error in software used for location services, but later revealed to be the result of an intentional plan by a Google engineering team to collect and analyze such data.[27] Equally urgent are the many issues raised by private ownership of this documentation. Although Google has pushed forward with Street View, even in the absence of FoP exceptions in many countries where they operate, the ever-present copyright line at the bottom of the screen indicates their proprietary claim over the user's experience of this virtual public space.

Given the concerns about camera height for Street View, what about drones, one might ask? Existing drone regulations in a number of countries place restraints on the standard tech gambit of "do first, ask for forgiveness later." But Apple's successful 2018 application to begin collecting drone data in North Carolina to improve its Apple Maps could open up a host of new questions. No need to worry about privacy, however, Apple promised, since they simultaneously announced plans to blur such sensitive subjects as faces and license plate numbers.[28]

ART VS. AD

Tensions between the law's typical need for clearly defined categories and the artistic impulse to push boundaries can sometimes be exacerbated by the many areas of overlap, and even collaboration, between artists and a range of commercial interests. With respect to signage, even if it is situated within the confines of private property, there are often strict zoning rules. In circumstances where these same restrictions would not apply to art, distinctions between commercial versus noncommercial messaging can be crucial—even as they are potentially blurred in a cultural marketplace where differences between artists and other "creatives" are often challenging to delineate.

One such instance can be seen in Richard Phillips's 2013 *Playboy Marfa,* which included a sign-like neon outline of a Playboy Bunny mounted on a tall post. It was installed on the edge of a tract of Texas land leased by Playboy Enterprises—the parent company of the magazine known for its nude centerfold images and bunny icon—with the title as well as certain aspects of its form evidently intended to evoke Donald Judd's long-term Marfa installations. To the Texas Department of Transportation, however, it looked like an unlicensed outdoor advertising sign, and it ordering Playboy Enterprises to take it down within forty-five days.[29] Yet the removal order wasn't all bad, since Phillips had an upcoming show at Dallas Contemporary, and the structure was moved to a new location in a parking lot in front of the museum.

If the neon bunny was unauthorized signage rather than sculpture, however, could the same be said of Elmgreen and Dragset's 2005 *Prada Marfa?* The well-known roadside oddity has the appearance of a freestanding Prada boutique, located in the middle of the Texas desert landscape, within a building that is actually a sealed container. As the incident with the bunny suggested, works of art that incorporate commercial logos or other aspects of trade dress are especially prone to category questions when they appear outdoors, potentially intermixed with other commercial messages, rather than in a museum or gallery setting. And it seemed for a time that the clear brand associations would subject the mock store to a removal order as well.[30] However, Ballroom Marfa (one of the art organizations involved in the initial commission) stepped in to save the day: they took over the lease on the land and designated it as an art museum—meaning, in other words, that the site was a museum, with the building as its only exhibit. In this case, the institutional embrace carried sufficient authority to ensure the project's status as art.

The important point, in relation to the threatened transportation department removal order, was to secure the designation of *Prada Marfa* as art. But where, one wonders, does that leave photographs of the work, including the many selfies it has spawned? If the building is a building (architecture), no problem under US law. But if it is art, the artists can claim copyright protection that might limit the circulation of photographs. Ideally that shouldn't prevent someone from publishing an image as part of a critical analysis of the work, assuming the relevant US publisher is willing to assert fair use. But it could limit commercial use—if, for example, Beyoncé decided to use the selfie in front of the work that she posted on her Tumblr in 2012 as part of an album cover.[31] A more expansive argument might even assert that everything posted by Beyoncé and other celebrities on social media is commercial, since the presentation of carefully curated personal information plays an integral role in promotion and publicity.

In another instance of art claims being shot down by public employees, a mural painted by Shepard Fairey in Williamsburg, Brooklyn, resulted in a $15,000 fine leveled by the New York Department of Buildings against the landlord for not having a permit for outdoor advertising. Though the band's name did not appear, the 2014 mural included imagery from an Interpol album cover by Fairey, and Fairey had designed a similar billboard in Los Angeles, promoting the album release (therefore definitely an advertisement). In an initial hearing, the judge sided with the landlord, but following an appeal by the city, a different judge ruled that the mural was indeed an outdoor advertising sign.[32] Nor was this the first time that Fairey found himself in the sights of the New York Department of Buildings: it had issued a 2010 stop-work order and fine for a different outdoor mural deemed an advertisement for his simultaneous art exhibition at Deitch Projects.[33]

Starting in 2010, the city attorney for Los Angeles went even further, filing suit in an attempt to prevent Cristian Gheorghiu, known as Smear, and other graffiti artists from profiting from their street names. The argument put forward by the city was that their graffiti constituted free publicity for sales and other profits related to their brands. It therefore amounted to taking over public space for private gain, while also forcing the expenditure of municipal resources to clean up vandalized property. The American Civil Liberties Union quickly became involved, over concerns about artistic freedom related to both the suit and Gheorghiu's arrest for violating probation, with the latter due to posting about graffiti on his website and the discovery of art-making tools (potentially similar to graffiti tools) in the studio where he was producing work for gallery shows.[34] The ACLU was equally alarmed by the city attorney's decision to go after graffiti artists using legal strategies developed to combat gang violence (including orders against associating with one another in public and curfews), along with charges of unfair competition for reputations built on vandalism.

The status of graffiti also quickly became an issue in relation to a notably idealistic initiative, São Paulo's 2006 Cidade Limpa ("Clean City") law, which mandated the removal of virtually all outdoor advertising and placed sharp restrictions on store signage. When São Paulo city workers began painting over graffiti, including murals sanctioned by property owners, however, complaints quickly resulted in the development of criteria to exempt street art that was not functioning as advertising.[35] Not coincidentally, two of the artists whose work was threatened or inadvertently painted over, Otavio and Gustavo Pandolfo, known as Os Gemeos, were featured in a 2008 street art exhibition at the Tate Modern around the time examples of their São Paulo work were destroyed. In clearly cynical attempts to take advantage of that potential opening, advertisers subsequently tried to find ways to present ads in the guise of graffiti, including a 2015 Converse ad campaign. Claiming to "fight the gray" associated with an ad-free environment, the campaign requested that people "donate their shadows," so that the forms could be transformed into colorful street art. Despite the ad ban, the agency responsible managed to get permission for the silhouettes to remain in place for a month—which ensured plenty of time for the campaign to be amplified via social media.[36]

Still other issues come into play when the messaging is political in nature. In 2004, Hank Willis Thomas transformed a photograph he had taken at his cousin's funeral four years earlier into a pointed version of the MasterCard "priceless" ad campaign. Referring to the act of senseless violence that took Songha Willis's life outside a Philadelphia nightclub, the prices superimposed over the group of African-American mourners (including "9mm Pistol: $80" and "Bullet: ¢60") concluded with "Picking a perfect casket for your son: Priceless." Had the work of art remained within the confines of the exhibition space, its critical message would presumably have been the primary reading. But when the Birmingham Museum of Art presented the image, billboard style, on the exterior of the institution, its scale, combined with the incorporation of the MasterCard logo, provoked a heated response from members of the public who mistook it for an actual advertisement.[37]

Also activating a museum exterior, but without authorization, a group known as The Illuminator was subject to arrest and the seizure of their equipment after projecting "Koch = Climate Chaos" on the outside of New York's Metropolitan Museum during the festivities to inaugurate the David H. Koch Plaza, renamed in honor of a large donation from a prominent supporter of far-right groups, including climate change deniers. The initial arrest was based on a charge of unlawful posting of advertisements, though that was eventually dropped, and the activists filed a lawsuit of their own alleging false arrest and First Amendment violations due to the impounding of their projection equipment. In the view of Grayson Earle, one of the members of the group, they were not looking for commercial gain, in contrast to Koch, who was "permanently inscribing his name on more or less public land, as the Met sits atop Central Park, and doing so obviously benefits him financially, considering he brands his multi-billion-dollar company with his own name, 'Koch Industries.'"[38] Similar to the blurring of distinctions between art and ad, such naming opportunities, essential in the context of US reliance on private rather than government support for cultural institutions, reveal the potential slippage between disinterested cultural patronage and highly targeted forms of elite brand messaging.

STREET CRED

Issues of commercial versus noncommercial, public versus private, and protected versus free for the taking are all forced to the surface by graffiti. Its potentially subversive, noncorporate takeover of public space forces questions about usage at odds with both private property and commercial interests. But graffiti's increasingly mainstream appeal, including associated product lines and endorsements, complicates the narrative of a rebellious subculture.

The story emerging from various lawsuits is one of close attention to authorial rights and interests, extending from the tradition of tags recognizable first of all to other graffiti artists, to using both copyright and trademark law to protect against unauthorized commercialization, and the pursuit of selective licensing deals. Additional issues include the overlap between graffiti created without permission, and the large number of works, often indistinguishable in terms of style and authorship, that are invited, or even commissioned (frequently referred to as street art, or even aerosol art, to acknowledge this distinction). In certain circumstances, evidence of careerism among artists can be read as taking over shared public space for expressions that help further the creator's brand identity.

The relationship to copyright is complex. Andrea Baldini has pointed to vibrant subcultures around unauthorized forms of graffiti as a counterpoint to the foundational arguments that copyright protections encourage creativity.[39] But the dynamics have been altered by popularity, and graffiti artists have increasingly turned to the courts to protect their copyright interests in both authorized and unauthorized examples. They have faced questions regarding their right to exercise such control over unauthorized work, but "unsanctioned" is not a disqualification for copyright protection, and key lawsuits reveal a marked degree of both misunderstanding and opportunism in many quarters. As in the example of the Māori-inspired tattoo discussed in chapter 3, a number of prominent fashion industry figures have treated graffiti as found design that they can incorporate into their work with impunity—which is in some respects simply an extension of business as usual, given the accusations of cultural appropriation prompted by fashion's endless thirst for new sources of inspiration.[40] The use of graffiti as a backdrop in various ad campaigns attempting to appeal to youthful edginess, even if likewise cynical, nonetheless raises important freedom of panorama questions regarding how much control artists should be able to exercise over urban views incorporating their work. It is also notable that one of the few fully litigated VARA cases in the United States involved street art that was initially invited, before being abruptly painted over.

In a particularly brazen example of appropriation, Roberto Cavalli used a 2012 mural created in San Francisco's Mission District by a trio of artists, Revok, Reyes, and Steel (Jason Williams, Victor Chapa, and Jeffrey Rubin) as the source for his 2014 Just Cavalli graffiti collection, which featured clothes, bags, and shoes completely covered with closely corresponding designs. Through their lawyer, the artists demanded that Cavalli stop marketing products derived from their art, and when the collection continued to be sold, the artists sued. According to their lawyer, Cavalli threatened their "outsider 'street cred'" through the association of their work with a luxury brand. But the complaint also highlighted some of the tensions inherent to the professionalization of this ostensibly rebellious activity with its account of extensive exhibition careers, including the Los Angeles Museum of Contemporary Art and the Pasadena Museum of California Art. Adding a form of insult to injury, the appropriation included sections of the mural incorporating two of the artists' names, over which the designer had superimposed "Just Cavalli" in a spray-paint-style signature, thereby "creating the false impression that Roberto Cavalli himself was the artist."[41] Trademark was also in play: regarding Reyes's black-and-white "revolutions" imagery, the complaint asserted a Lanham Act violation based on "false designation of origin" or "passing off," since Cavalli's use of this signature motif could indicate either an affiliation with Reyes, or that Cavalli was presenting the imagery as his own.[42] Following the judge's denial of the defendant's motion to dismiss, which raised serious doubts about key aspects of Cavalli's arguments, the case was settled.

The lesson was apparently lost, however, on Jeremy Scott, Moschino's creative director, since its February 2015 Milan runway show prominently featured clothing incorporating imagery taken from a 2012 work, *Vandal Eyes,* by Rime (Joseph Tierney). As the initial complaint noted, there could be little doubt about the source, since Scott had added Rime's name, in the form of a fake signature, to the clothing. And, once again, the appropriation also included "superimposing the Moschino and Jeremy Scott brand names in spray-paint style as if part of the original work."[43] One major statement piece was a gown worn by Katy Perry to the Metropolitan Museum of Art's 2015 Gala, where she was accompanied by Scott in a jacket adorned with the same motifs. According to the complaint, "Not only did Ms. Perry and Defendant Scott advertise, wear, and display the clothing at the event, they arrived at the event in a spray painted Rolls Royce, and even carried around Moschino branded cans of fake spray paint during the event, as if Defendants were responsible for the artwork."[44] Rime's complaint accused Moschino and Scott of both copyright and trademark violations, the latter based on the misappropriation of "source-identifying" elements, including the artist's pseudonymous name and signature.[45]

Moschino's lawyers began one of the documents filed in response with a rather bizarre analogy between the unsolved Black Dahlia murder case and contemporary graffiti, describing *Vandal Eyes* as "an unapologetic act of vandalism and trespass" and claiming that Rime lacked copyright standing because "felons do not get copyrights in their illegal actions."[46] Yet the original complaint indicated that Rime had been invited to create the mural by the property owner of the Detroit building in question. The case does not fit an insider/outsider paradigm for other reasons as well, since Rime shows his work through galleries; he had collaborated with Adidas and Converse footwear before the Moschino case; and he worked with the VRY WRM brand in 2016 to create a graffiti-print bomber jacket. Here and elsewhere, the arguments against unauthorized commercial use emphasize how carefully street artists have cultivated their own brand identities, such that these situations are framed as one brand attempting to coopt another. But once again the legal issues raised by the clash of authorship interests were left on the table when the case brought by Rime was settled.

Street artists going up against major brands may not have the same deep pockets for lawyers' fees. But they do have various tools at their command, including the ability to harness social media. In one striking instance, H&M apparently didn't think through the contradiction of trying to play up their street appeal and then suing the graffiti artist whose work was featured in their ad. When a lawyer representing Revok sent H&M a cease-and-desist letter concerning an ad showing a clothing model doing a backflip off a Brooklyn wall painted with his graffiti, H&M's first response was to go on the offensive by filing a lawsuit claiming that copyright law would not protect the result of an illegal act. The argument itself was potentially flawed, since the background surrounding a work's creation does not necessarily contradict the fixation requirement at the core of copyright. But far more problematic for the company was the immediate backlash, including calls for a boycott, which were summed up in a drawing posted by KAWS showing a tombstone emblazoned with the text "RIP H&M." The response quickly caused the company to back down, apologizing in a tweet that claimed "It was never our intention to set a precedent concerning public art or to influence the debate on the legality of street art." The case was subsequently settled, with H&M agreeing to donate an unspecified amount of money to Detroit arts organizations.[47]

Another case involving an example of street art as backdrop had the added significance of showing some of the ways that even major legacy companies have been attempting to tap into viral marketing. The image in question showed a Cadillac XT5 parked in front of a mural by Swiss graffiti artist Adrian Falkner, known as Smash 137, who was commissioned in 2014 to create an outdoor mural in a Detroit parking garage. The photo was taken two years later by Alex Bernstein, who had borrowed the car from what GM lawyers described as a "press fleet," loaned for publicity purposes. In exchange, the photographer was asked to provide four photos to Cadillac, with permission to use them on social media.[48] Thus the image, which General Motors circulated as part of an online publicity campaign, was not the result of a traditional ad shoot, but rather part of a widespread and more diffuse strategy of attempting to tap into social media "influencers." It is hardly irrelevant that the US Federal Trade Commission has been putting increasing pressure on influencers to clarify when they are promoting goods that have been provided for that purpose, such that their enthusiasm should be understood as a form of ad rather than a spontaneous preference.

Falkner's initial complaint emphasized the lack of consent; the damage to his reputation due to the association with a mass-market campaign attempting to reach a new demographic; the central role of the mural in the photo in question; and the deliberate effacement of Falkner's signature, or "copyright management information." Citing the 2000 decision in *Leicester v. Warner Bros.* as precedent, GM's lawyers countered by describing the mural as inseparable from the architectural work constituted by the parking garage. In denying GM's bid for summary judgment dismissing the copyright case, however, judge Stephen V. Wilson noted the creative freedom enjoyed by Falkner and the absence of a functional role for the work in relation to the parking garage structure. But the judge did rule against Falkner's Digital Millennium Copyright Act claim that GM had intentionally altered or removed copyright management information simply because the photograph was shot from an angle where the artist's signature was not visible.[49] Once the judge allowed the core copyright case to move forward, however, both sides reached a confidential settlement.

If one takes out certain references to DMCA copyright management information, it is striking how closely the points of contention in many of these cases echo the sixteenth-century conflict between Albrecht Dürer and Marcantonio Raimondi discussed in chapter 1. Like Dürer, who protested the reproduction of his monogram, many of the complaints by graffiti artists concern appropriations that include their tag or other versions of their name. When signatures are not shown, however, including instances where it was simply a matter of how a photographer's vantage point framed a wall, lawyers have characterized the omission as a willful violation. Complaints presented on behalf of the artists also work from two sides of the issue when they protest commercialization as an affront to purity, or "street cred," while simultaneously describing how strategically the artists have chosen their commercial collaborations.

BUFFED

Given the precarious nature of graffiti, including the knowledge that unauthorized forms can be effaced at any time, it is noteworthy that one of the major VARA cases in the United States was provoked by the destruction of street art at a site known as 5Pointz. The conflict concerned a set of warehouse buildings in Long Island City, New York, owned by real estate developer Jerry Wolkoff. In the 1990s, a group called the Phun Phactory began using its walls for graffiti, with his permission, and starting in 2002 he allowed Jonathan Cohen (a graffiti artist known as Meres One) to curate the site (see figure 45). In addition, interior spaces were rented as artists' studios at below-market rates consistent with the general lack of maintenance.[50] According to Wolkoff, authorization to create art on the walls of the building was always understood as temporary—though there was no written agreement specifying the terms. By the time Wolkoff moved forward with development plans in 2013, however, the site had become renowned for the art on its walls, and Cohen made a series of preservation attempts, including seeking landmark status and trying to identify backers to buy the property. When those steps failed, Cohen and sixteen other artists took the developer to court, invoking their rights under VARA.

One significant challenge was the relative scarcity of case law concerning VARA, which has left substantial ambiguity regarding a key provision that its safeguards apply only to art of "recognized stature," as well as the degree of protection it offers to works that are not readily portable. Although the district court initially issued a temporary restraining order on October 17, 2013, it lifted that order November 12, indicating that a written opinion would follow (which it did, on November 20). Judge Frederic Block denied the request for a preliminary injunction based on specific legal

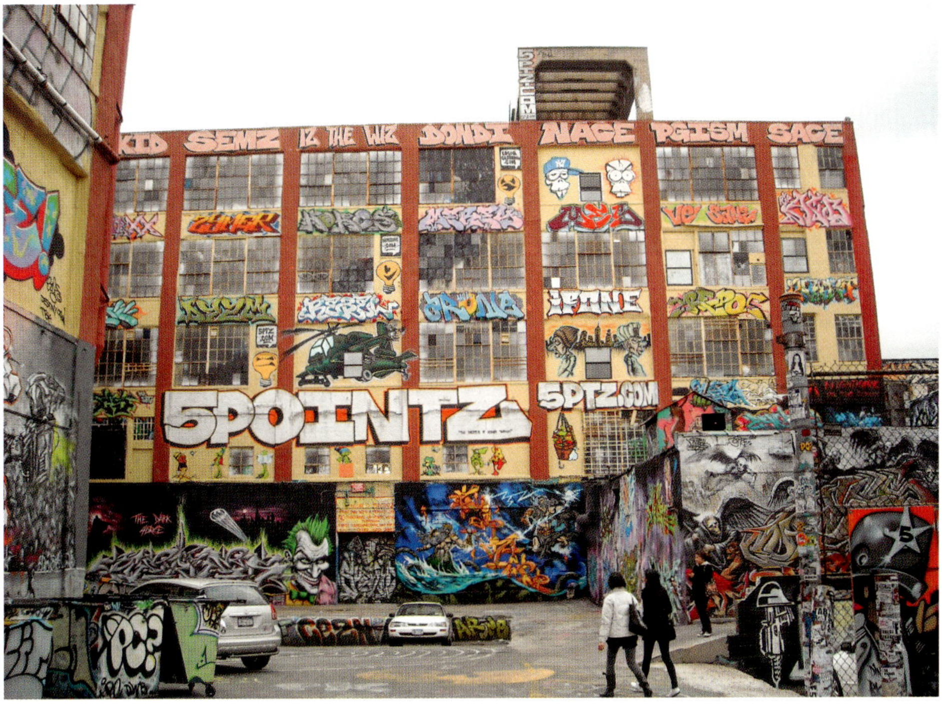

FIGURE 45
Rear of 5Pointz, as it appeared in November 2010. Photo: Eco84—Own work. Posted to Wikimedia Commons under Creative Commons license CC BY-SA 3.0.

grounds, including the likelihood of success and a balance of hardships, in an initial written opinion that distinguished between protecting individual works and preserving the overall site.[51] But during the week between the lifting of the temporary order on November 12 and the written opinion, Wolkoff abruptly denied artists access to the building and had all the works whitewashed, or "buffed," with crudely applied paint. Despite representations from the developer about urgency, however, actual demolition of the buildings did not begin until months later and was not complete until August 2014.

Despite the fact that the work at 5Pointz was destroyed by Wolkoff's preemptive action, the VARA case moved forward and ultimately went to trial. Shortly before the jury proceedings concluded, the litigants agreed that the final decision would be made by the judge. Block nonetheless allowed the jury to remain in place, even though their verdict would be merely advisory, since he was "keen to learn whether the jurors, as members of the community, would view the works as having achieved recognized stature under VARA."[52] The jury awarded damages for thirty-six of the forty-nine works presented to them, and Block added nine more, bringing the total qualifying for damages to forty-five.

The determination regarding recognized stature was based on a number of factors, including Cohen's curatorial expertise, testimony from experts about the quality of the works, and various indications of public impact. Cohen described an organized process, with many examples quickly replaced by new works, but the most prominent walls going to well-known artists whose works often remained on view for years. Efforts by the defense to denigrate their status included expert witness testimony from art historian Erin Thompson in both the initial hearing and the trial. Despite important cultural heritage advocacy in other contexts, Thompson applied a notably narrow standard for determining recognized stature, citing "no dissertations, no journal articles, no other scholarly mentions of the work" (though she did, in her initial testimony, allow that one work, Lady Pink's *Green Mother Earth,* might qualify).[53] But the judge critiqued Thompson's methodology as too restrictive, pointing out that she failed to uncover many online sources featuring the artists and acknowledging "social media buzz" as a potential marker of a work's impact.[54]

The developer's lawyers questioned whether VARA protection would extend to works that were often temporary in nature anyway, given the revolving nature of the overall display, but Block ultimately found that to be a nonissue. Whether the work might have been moved from the site was more significant—particularly since this is an area where VARA is notably ambiguous. Expert testimony indicated varying degrees of removability, and also referenced examples of works created directly on a structure that had been successfully preserved, including graffiti-covered sections of the Berlin Wall.[55] Crucially, Block pointed to case law interpreting VARA as giving artists the right to attempt to retrieve their work, but not an open-ended prerogative to preserve it in place.[56] Therefore the key issue became the developer's decision to ignore VARA's provisions for a ninety-day notification period to allow artists to save potentially movable works.

When it came to assessing damages, Block acknowledged the challenge of assigning monetary value even as he sharply rebuked the developer's willful actions. He stressed that Wolkoff knew, from the moment the lawsuit was initiated, that the artists were pursuing VARA claims. Furthermore, the destroyed work remained partially visible. "The whitewash did not end the conflict in one go; the effects lingered for almost a year," Block found, noting that the "sloppy, half-hearted nature of the whitewashing left the works easily visible under thin layers of cheap, white paint," and that the "mutilated works were visible by millions of people on the passing 7 train."[57] According to Block, "the only logical inference that the Court could draw from Wolkoff's precipitous conduct as soon as the Court denied the artists' preliminary injunction application was that it was an act of pure pique and revenge for the nerve of the plaintiffs to sue to attempt to prevent the destruction of their art," leading him to conclude, "This was the epitome of willfulness."[58]

Based on Wolkoff's willful conduct, Block awarded statutory damages of $150,000 for each instance (increased from a maximum of $30,000 in the absence of such conduct), for a total judgment of $6,750,000, far exceeding what the jury had indicated. Block also repeatedly drew contrasts between the dignified and lawful behavior of the artists, and Wolkoff's unrepentant attitude regarding the initial whitewashing. "If not for Wolkoff's insolence, these damages would not have been assessed," Block stressed, directly linking the amount of the judgment to the developer's arrogance. "If he did not destroy 5Pointz until he received his permits and demolished it 10 months later," according to Block, "the Court would not have found that he had acted willfully." Block further declared that the size of the statutory damages award was important to make VARA viable, since, "If potential infringers believe that they can violate VARA at will and escape liability because plaintiffs are not able to provide a reliable financial valuation for their works, VARA will have no teeth."[59] In addition to moving forward at full speed with his new development, however, Wolkoff quickly contested the judgment, basing his appeal in part on representations that the judge was biased against him.

One apparent message from the conflict concerns potential risks for landlords if they open their doors, or walls, to artists and then face moral rights limitations on how they can use their property. Yet even though the Second Circuit court of appeals upheld the substantial penalty, the developer might still come out ahead, given the contribution of the art to the overall gentrification of the neighborhood. In describing what had been achieved at 5Pointz, Cohen and others highlighted its intense popularity, with benefits that extended to the whole neighborhood, including multiple visitors and events, social media attention, and the willing participation by artists, generally at their own expense. Since there can be little doubt that the project contributed to the value of the property, the developer therefore directly profited from the art that he willfully destroyed. To add insult to injury, the rental tower complex built for Wolkoff by Mojo Stumer Associates to replace the demolished complex used both the 5Pointz name and a graffiti theme as part of its marketing and identity.[60] On top of everything else, construction of the residential tower succeeded in compromising another work of art, James Turrell's 1980 *Meeting*, installed in nearby MoMA PS1, which was closed at Turrell's request when construction scaffolding became visible within the previously unobstructed skyscape (though the tower itself did not intrude once construction was complete).[61]

Despite the cliché of graffiti-tagged walls as a marker of urban blight, many examples that fall on the street-art side of the equation (invited rather than unwelcome) are part of the same process where inhabitation by artists is a first step toward gentrification—as the dialogue around 5Pointz demonstrates. The possibility that certain examples from 5Pointz might have been salvaged raises other issues about the significance of removing such works from their original context. One obvious indicator of graffiti's shift from outsider status to assimilation can be found in the active market for examples of work that could be described as site-specific, cut from the walls where they were painted and sold to the highest bidder. Various protests have clearly done little to impede the enthusiasm for such material, including a 2014 exhibition and sale in

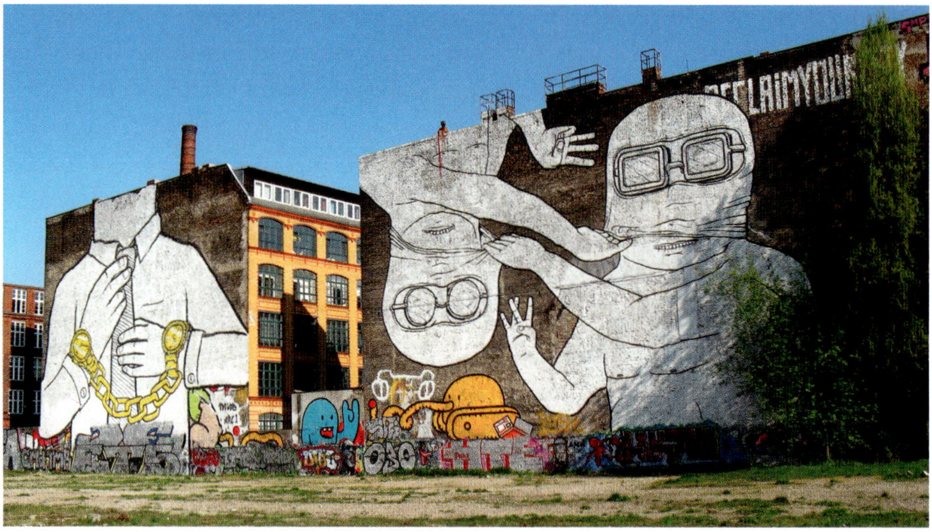

FIGURE 46
Blu, "Cuvry-Graffiti," Berlin-Kreuzberg, April 12, 2009. Photo: Frank M. Rafik from Berlin, stateless person. Posted to Wikimedia Commons under Creative Commons license CC BY-SA 2.0.

London, *Stealing Banksy?*, where the organizers claimed that they were saving the works from decay or defacement by helping facilitate their removal.[62]

It also makes a difference who effaces the work in question. Artists whose works wind up in traditional museums are highly unlikely to have the opportunity to destroy their own creations—despite LeWitt's call for such rights during the AWC public hearing discussed in chapter 4. But the unofficial museum of street art is another matter, as the Italian artist known as Blu demonstrated in both Berlin and Bologna. In Berlin, Blu painted out a major work in the Kreuzberg neighborhood (figure 46) after a developer purchased the site and evicted the squatters who had been in residence. Testament of the work's broad appeal was evident in a Change.org petition supporting its preservation despite plans for a new luxury building. Blu had other ideas, however. On the night of December 11, 2014, workers with crane trucks appeared and began covering the work with black paint, indicating to those who asked that they were there at Blu's instigation.[63] In March 2016, Blu and his assistants embarked on an even more dramatic campaign to efface twenty years of street work in Bologna to protest a controversial exhibition, *Street Art—Banksy & Co* at the Palazzo Pepoli—Museo della Storia di Bologna, which included multiple works cut out from walls. Blu's strategy was not the only response, however, since a significant number of other artists created new works for a counter-exhibition that was actually in the streets.[64]

Blu's decision to act rather than ask therefore included both initially painting the works and later effacing them. The double gesture helps bring into focus various questions. On what grounds did the artist take over publicly visible space in the first place?

And if it could be described as a form of gift to the public (rather than simply personal gratification or promotion), who should get to decide its long-term fate? Both the 5Pointz building as a whole, and Blu's Kreuzberg mural, were doomed when private developers moved forward with plans for new construction. But articulating the conflicts purely in terms of artists versus landowners leaves out the matter of public interest regarding works that had, over time, achieved an unofficial form of landmark status, based on their importance for community identity.

Although they do not address graffiti directly, Eduardo Peñalver and Sonia Katyal's *Property Outlaws* provides an important point of reference: debates about legal principles in the abstract have their place, but acts of civil disobedience can provide actual, as opposed to hypothetical, visions of an alternative to the status quo.[65] Interventions, from messages on the walls to protest marches and the toppling of monuments, present insistent counterpoints to the fiction that current institutions serve all equally. Uninvited incursions help to emphasize the many overlapping as well as divergent experiences of publicly accessible space, as well as the important role of law, not just in establishing property rights, but in articulating priorities that serve the larger good. This balancing act is equally evident with regard to tensions between ownership and access, the blurring of distinctions between commercial and noncommercial, and the complex interweaving of different types of property, ranging from real to intangible. In a culture that encourages individuals to treat all aspects of their self-expression as brand identity—and by extension, a form of property—it is essential to remain focused on the value of a shared public sphere, in both physical and virtual manifestations.

6

AUTHORSHIP AND THE UNDEAD

WHAT DISTINGUISHES AN ACTUAL WORK of art from the dizzying number of objects that look the same, and in some cases may actually be the same? One answer would be that it was made by an artist. That response quickly gives way, however, in the face of information about delegated forms of production, art that becomes art merely through a process of selection or arrangement, art that does not have an enduring physical presence, and many other forms, both historical and contemporary, where a romantic conception of solo and sovereign creation is dramatically contradicted. Yet some mechanism of authorship is almost inevitably involved where modern or contemporary art is concerned, and the more importance accorded to the work, the greater the number of voices likely to be involved in a consensus-driven process of definition that can claim to speak for the artist after the individual in question is long dead. Equally striking are moments when attempts to define or control the work come into direct conflict with living artists who are somehow not adhering to audience expectations.

The general framework of copyright, which enables the transformation of creative expressions into property with a life quite apart from the original author, provides an important precedent for a gamut of estate activities that extend beyond the boundaries of copyright per se. Referring to the potential antagonism between authorship and property, Daniel McClean gives a cogent description of the "bundle of legal rights" brought to bear in the postmortem management of artists' legacies, "including ownership of the actual works and materials (which can be more important than copyright) as well as ownership of the copyrights and moral rights."[1] In a related analysis, Ines Weizman outlines three phases of activity: the first when work is still being produced, under the original author's creative supervision; a second that begins immediately after the author's death and extends for fifty to seventy-five years, depending on the jurisdiction; and a third that commences when material enters the public domain—with the second phase the worst for "games of power and control."[2] Posthumous distortions can range from attempts to regulate the content of scholarship to questionable proclamations regarding authenticity, but perhaps the most troubling concern decisions to continue producing an artist's work.

The sculpture of Auguste Rodin is bound to make an appearance in any discussion of the interplay between artistic originality and ongoing production via replication. One factor is the sheer volume of editioned work produced in his name, both during his lifetime and after his death. There is his incorporation of casts and multiples as an essential aspect of his creative process. Legal instruments play an important role as well, given his major bequest to the French state of authorship rights over his work. But particularly significant is the way that Rosalind Krauss drew all these threads together in order to present Rodin as a central example of her rereading of avant-garde originality through an emphasis on the persistent role of replication, including the possibility of multiple copies in the absence of a singular original. Krauss's interpretation linked critical assessments of his work, Rodin's own creative process, and posthumous production decisions that scholars might be tempted to view as separate from the work's core identity.[3] Doubling down on her reading in response to a letter of protest from Rodin scholar Albert Elsen, she underscored both the large-scale studio operation devoted to different versions of marble sculpture during Rodin's lifetime (which pushed his work in the direction the avant-garde's presumed opposite, kitsch, regardless of the authorized status of many of those derivative objects), and also how his bequest meant that the funding for the Musée Rodin is dependent on the museum's participation in ongoing production of the work they are charged with protecting and preserving (a dynamic that includes a 2014 cast of the *Gates of Hell* that enabled substantial museum refurbishment).[4]

Building on these insights, it is crucial to examine the ways that different phases of reception can actively shape the work in question, and in that sense how decisions made by (or attributed to) individual artists intersect with interpretations of the work that have a direct impact on its ongoing physical form, including conservation strategies, choices associated with posthumous editions, and decisions to uncover official works lurking in the inchoate amalgam of unfinished thoughts and ambiguous gestures that artists frequently leave in their wake. French law codifies in detail who inherits the right to make such determinations (even though there can still be circumstances where the word of an official heir is treated as suspect). Yet greater ambiguity about inherited rights in many other countries certainly hasn't prevented their exercise in relation to the estates of noteworthy artists.

Once an artist is anointed as historically significant—via a process of institutional validation and consensus opinion that is a fascinating subject in its own right—both work and life become subject to intense scrutiny, driven by a web of scholarly and market considerations that are often impossible to untangle. In the process we, the larger audience for the work, are likely to discover further background about the artist's creative life than initially revealed. The digging process begins with interviews and related forms of research while an artist is alive, and it often extends to mining unpublished correspondence, notebooks, sketchbooks, and the like after the artist's death. Typically such scholarship is understood as simply learning more about one's subject, but each new series of revelations exposes or constructs a potentially different artist—one that can contrast in both subtle and dramatic ways with the authorial image the artist initially chose to present. In some instances, heirs may directly contravene an author's instructions, particularly when it comes to commands to destroy material; the decision by Franz Kafka's executor not to burn the unpublished manuscripts for *The Trial* and *The Castle* is one often-cited example. The idea that cultural posterity might be more important than an author's specific wishes implies a shift in ownership, with particular works or objects figured in crucial ways as belonging to society at large. A related tension is already present in moral rights legislation. Creators are granted certain forms of control over their work even after it is sold, based on a belief in its broad cultural significance. Yet one can argue, for the very same reason, that individual creators should not have final authority to make potentially arbitrary decisions about work understood to be part of a shared heritage.

Many of these tensions surface in struggles over artists' estates. Not only do heirs exert control over interpretation by blocking access to research material, but they can reshape the very ground for assessment when they are involved in shifting or extending the scope of an artist's authorized works. It is even more striking, however, when living artists are caught up in disputes about the extent of their right to control their production or authentication of works. While market-driven motivations for these disputes are often patently obvious, such conflicts help to reveal the interplay between a system that emphasizes solo creative authorship and the operative conventions that transform historic individuals into cultural abstractions.

GIACOMETTI'S WAKE

During his lifetime, Alberto Giacometti's exploration of the instability of perception found its expression in an intense search for form that was subject to a potentially endless process of revision. But the half-century following his death in 1966 provides equally dramatic evidence of some of the dynamics surrounding who is authorized to speak for the artist, and thereby continue to fashion the work, over a far longer term. The fact that Giacometti died without a will certainly contributed to the extended legal struggle over his legacy, with tensions based on the initial division of his estate erupting into open conflict after the death of his wife, Annette Giacometti, in 1993. The rather depressing chronicle includes multiple lawsuits, the ill-advised sale of important works from the estate to cover costs associated with the chaotic state of affairs, and, at a particularly low point, the court-ordered removal of documentary records from the association initially charged by Annette with safeguarding his opus. The stakes have only continued to grow as Giacometti's work has commanded ever-higher auction prices during recent years. But even if it constitutes an extreme example, the discord is hardly unique in its demonstration of the many parties who may claim to speak for the interests of the artist, the potential for competing visions of how to safeguard the work, and financial motives that are often difficult to disentangle from even the most passionate defense of an artist's legacy.

As a Swiss artist who spent most of his career in France, Giacometti left heirs in both countries: five eighths of his estate were inherited by Annette, and three eighths were divided among his siblings or their descendants—though Annette, as his widow, retained usufructuary rights over the portion of the estate designated for his relatives.[5] (This term, under civil law, refers to use of property owned by another, as long as it is not altered or diminished). Approximately two hundred plasters continued to be held by Annette, with revenues from their casting shared according to the same formula by which the estate was divided. Therefore Annette had the central role in decisions about further editions of the work, despite the fact that Alberto's younger brother Diego was extensively involved in the production process during his lifetime.

Prompted by the need to sort out Giacometti's sporadically documented production, together with her long-term goal of establishing a catalogue raisonné that would protect his work against the forgeries and unauthorized casts that began to crop up as early as the 1950s, Annette undertook the considerable task of inventorying the contents of his long-time studio. Documentation included extensive photographic records by Sabine Weiss (a friend of Annette's who later became the president of the Association Alberto et Annette Giacometti). Those records encompassed not only the studio contents, but the walls themselves, which were extensively covered with working drawings and paintings. Large sections of those walls, along with marked walls from other sites, were eventually removed and preserved. But the reported refusal of Diego to participate by inventorying plasters he held in storage also foreshadowed later tensions.[6]

Some bronze editions were still in progress at the time of Giacometti's death in 1966, and other plasters had been delivered for later casting. Using her inherited legal authority, Annette continued creating editions from the plasters left in her care as well as some plasters already in private collections (figure 47).[7] Annette eventually began

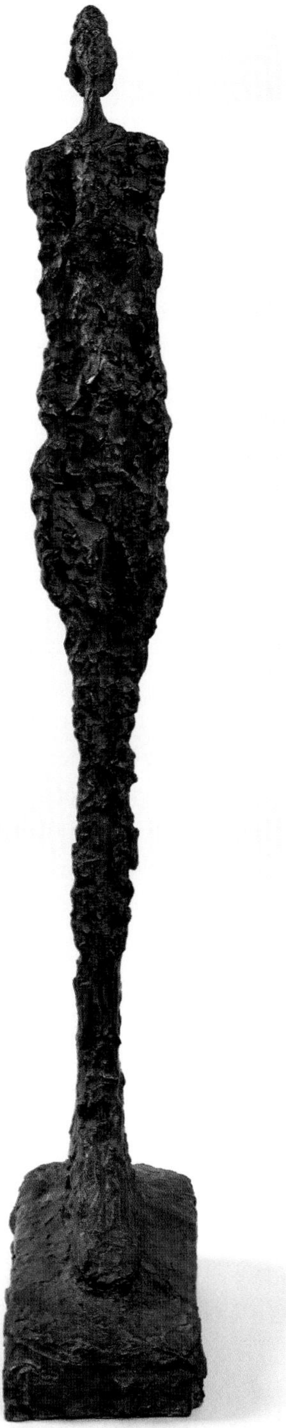

FIGURE 47
Alberto Giacometti, *Woman of Venice III,* 1956. Bronze, 46⅝ × 7 × 13¹³⁄₁₆ in. © 2019 Alberto Giacometti Estate/VAGA at Artists Rights Society (ARS), NY/ADAGP, Paris.

the process of forming a foundation to house and safeguard the estate, establishing an association in 1989 as an interim step because of high hurdles under French law. Although the association was initially slated to last for only five years, Annette's death in 1993 delayed matters, and the Fondation Alberto et Annette Giacometti was not established until 2003. By then the association had already been stripped of assembled documentation pertaining to Giacometti's work on the basis of a 2001 court order obtained by a judge appointed by the French government to oversee the estate. But the association continued to exist as a rival body for over a decade, sparring with the foundation and still authenticating works. Plus there is the Alberto Giacometti-Stiftung in Zurich as well—a foundation established independently in the 1960s by a group of private collectors, but directly involved in estate questions after Giacometti's brother Bruno transferred his inherited rights to the Swiss foundation.

The battles undertaken by the various Giacometti factions turn to some extent on the astonishingly detailed and specific French laws concerning authors' rights. *Les droits patrimoniaux* (concerning economic or property rights) are subdivided into *le droit de reproduction* (the material fixing of the work in any form by which it is communicated to the public), *le droit de représentation* (the right to communicate the work to the public), and *le droit de suite* (resale proceed rights for works sold by a professional). Except for *droit de suite,* these rights can be assigned by contract, and their duration, like copyright, is the lifetime of the author plus seventy years. After the death of the author, not only does the right to exploit the work therefore persist for seventy years, but during that period, a surviving spouse (as long as the spouse does not remarry) has the exclusive usufruct over exploitation rights not otherwise disposed of by the author. There is also the separate but closely related matter of *les droits moraux,* which include *le droit de divulgation* (whether or not to reveal work to the public), *le droit de paternité* (encompassing the right to claim, to disclaim, and to not reveal authorship), *le droit au respect de son œuvre* (integrity rights, including the right to oppose changes made without consent), and *le droit de repentir ou de retrait* (the right of withdrawal, including works already disclosed to the public). Moral rights are both perpetual and inalienable, though they can be transmitted to heirs or a third party after death, and they remain in force even after a work otherwise enters the public domain.

One major player in the Giacometti saga was Mary Lisa Palmer, Annette's long-time private secretary, who became director of the association after Annette's death. In her will, Annette attempted to pass along control over the *droit moral* to Palmer, but this was rejected in a 1995 ruling (confirmed upon appeal in 1997) because the rights were not fully Annette's to bequeath.[8] Although Palmer has sometimes been described as difficult and possessive, her stubborn protection of Giacometti's legacy played an important part in unmasking a major forgery scandal involving fake paintings by John Myatt that were accompanied by elaborately falsified provenance documentation proffered by conman John Drewe—with Palmer holding out against the threat of legal action when she refused to respond to authentication demands.[9] Another divisive figure was Véronique Wiesinger, in her role as foundation director. The fact that the Paris foundation joined forces with the Zurich foundation and the other Swiss heirs in 2004 to establish the Comité Giacometti as a joint authentication body did not stop Wiesinger from suing the Swiss rightsholders in an attempt to obtain sole power to authorize future editions. (This case was decided against the foundation in 2013). These conflicts prevented the initiation of further casts from the plasters Giacometti left behind, though production did continue on editions that were ordered by Annette but not fully executed at the time of her death. It is also interesting to note the interplay between explicit legal rights and art-world customs: despite the court ruling against Annette's attempt to bequeath her moral rights to Palmer, the 2001 confiscation of estate documents held by the association, and the foundation's official control over rights linked to Annette's portion of the estate once it was established in 2003, Palmer retained art-world respect as a Giacometti authority—with the upshot that many collectors and dealers found it advisable to seek authentication from both the association and the foundation.[10]

There is incidental evidence that posthumous production shifted Giacometti's aesthetic in subtle but potentially crucial ways. Giacometti himself willingly accepted certain irregularities—foundry "defects" including small air bubbles and fissures in the surface of the cast bronze.[11] But Annette was reportedly much more exacting regarding the details of the production process, and Palmer in her turn even more so—leading to a lawsuit brought by Swiss dealer Ernst Beyeler over production delays for an edition cast by Giacometti's long-time foundry, Susse Fondeur, which had been authorized by Annette as part of a joint venture between herself and Beyeler.[12] Wiesinger has also described the foundation's gradual formulation of standards for the restoration of Giacometti's plasters, articulated on the basis of accumulated knowledge, but in that respect also circular in their logic, given that they reflected principles derived from the foundation's ongoing practice of making posthumous restoration decisions.[13]

For all their antagonism, however, the foundation and association did wind up united in defense against a lawsuit initiated by Jean-François Grenet, who sued the association after Palmer intervened in a 2000 sale by stating that two bronze editions cast from plasters acquired by Grenet from Diego would not be included in the catalogue raisonné. According to the summary in the 2014 French appellate court judgment, Alberto gave two 1946 plaster sculptures to Diego in 1956, and Diego sold them to Grenet in 1983. Grenet also obtained a statement from Diego in 1984 (therefore shortly before Diego's death in 1985) assigning the reproduction rights. Grenet entered into a 1993 agreement with Leonardo Benatov to cast the two Giacometti sculptures in editions of eight. Although no doubts were raised about the gift of the sculptures themselves, the court did not find it credible that Alberto also gave Diego express rights to exploit the plasters in 1956. If those rights were therefore not Diego's to convey as part of the 1983–84 transaction, the agreement infringed on the rights held by Annette, who had sole prerogative to authorize editions at that time. But even though the appellate court found against Grenet on most points, it did order that the plasters be included in the catalogue raisonné in preparation—and in that respect participated in a process of authentication by court order.[14]

For Benatov, however, the Giacometti edition was only a small part of the often-controversial posthumous production undertaken at his Valsuani foundry, outside Paris, which he bought in 1981. Other editions included the work of Rodin, Amedeo Modigliani, and Salvador Dali, though he is perhaps best known (and not in a good way) for the bronzes he produced from seventy-four plasters attributed to Edgar Degas that he apparently discovered in the foundry at the time of its purchase. The Giacometti bronzes were also not the only edition he produced on the basis of contested authority, with other lawsuits inspired by his Dali editions. But even more provocative is the interplay between his editions of originals (created with authorization from the heirs of the artist in question) and works designated as "reproductions," made after the artist in question has been dead for over seventy years (with multiple copies of Rodin's *Thinker* among the latter). Wiesinger issued a public call for scholars to boycott a 2012 colloquium, "Posthumous Bronzes in Law and Art History," held at the Hermitage in conjunction with an exhibition of the Valsuani Degas bronzes, but reservations about the work have generally taken the form of a conspiracy of silence, undoubtedly due to a fear of being sued.[15] The Valsuani foundry was eventually ordered closed by a French judge in 2016, not because of the still active controversies about the work, but for the more prosaic reason of liquidation to pay off creditors.[16]

One can certainly sympathize with vigorous opposition to fakes and frauds attempting to cash in on the monetary value of artistically significant work, and given the amount of shady activity, it is hardly surprising that the individuals and organizations devoted to the legacies of key figures can develop highly protective attitudes. But the line between defending the work in question and attempting to control all forms of interpretation is easily blurred. A case in point is the action taken by Wiesinger in Italian courts against John Baldessari. She successfully forced the early closure of a 2010 exhibition at the Prada Foundation in Milan where Baldessari presented a series of fifteen-foot tall reinterpretations of one of Giacometti's standing female figures, accessorizing the gigantic, elongated forms to evoke a fashion show (figure 48). According to a statement quoted by an Italian newspaper, Baldessari initially sought permission from the Giacometti foundation to scan an original work and, when that was denied, made his own interpretation in a clay model that was used as the basis for the enlarged sculptures.[17] Wiesinger framed her action against another artist as protecting Giacometti's work from unauthorized reproduction contrary to the spirit of his work, whereas the Prada Foundation characterized their backing of Baldessari's project as support for his artistic freedom.[18]

Elaborating her stance in a 2011 article, Wiesinger provided evidence of the larger issues at stake by arguing for a highly restrictive understanding of copyright.[19] If Wiesinger had her way, artists would need to acquire a license for any form of artistic

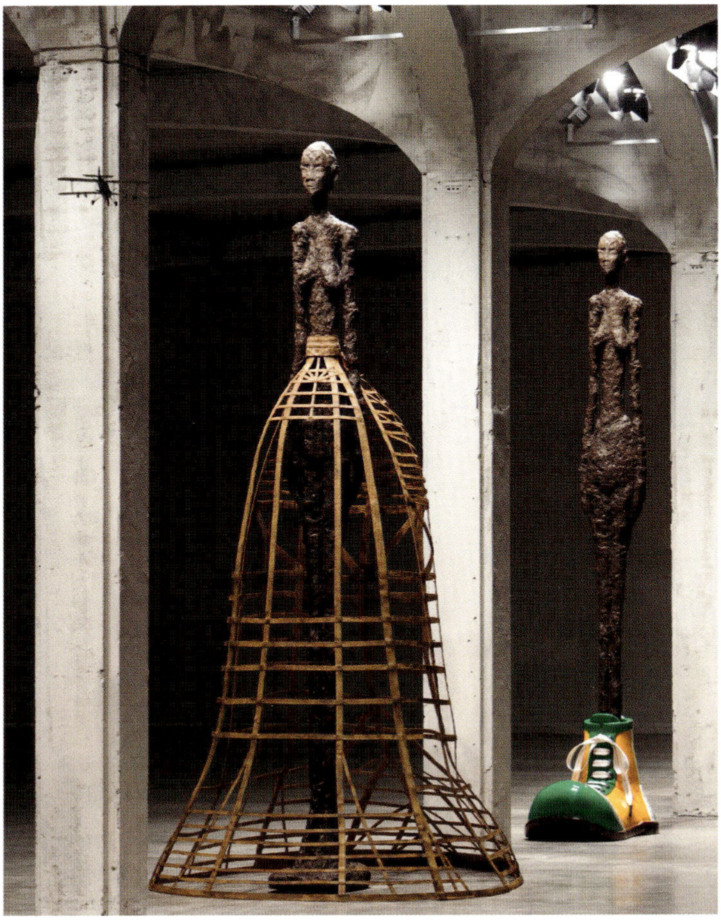

FIGURE 48
John Baldessari, *The Giacometti Variations,* 2010. Nine sculptures: stainless steel armatures, roto-cast hybrid polyurethane resin, cold sprayed bronze, and ceramic clear coat, each ca. 15 ft. tall. © John Baldessari. Courtesy of the Estate of John Baldessari and Marian Goodman Gallery.

appropriation, and she supported her position by suggesting parallels between artistic borrowing and the looting of archeological artifacts. She also applauded a "sensible reconsideration of the issue" in US court decisions that she cited in support of her rather draconian stance. In an interesting irony, however, her two key examples were quickly superseded—with the initial lower court ruling against Richard Prince in the lawsuit brought by Patrick Cariou subsequently overturned by an appeals court that found transformative fair use, and the position inferred from an early anti-settlement ruling in *Author's Guild et al. v. Google Inc.* pointing in a different direction than the later finding of fair use for Google's library scanning initiative.

There is no question that an artist's reputation can be distorted when pretenders are mistaken for the real thing. But it is important to pay close attention to all of the mechanisms that shape the canon of authorized works, including ongoing production and restoration conventions. Detailing controversies may appear to be secondary to serious art historical analysis of the work itself (though there is no denying the potential appeal

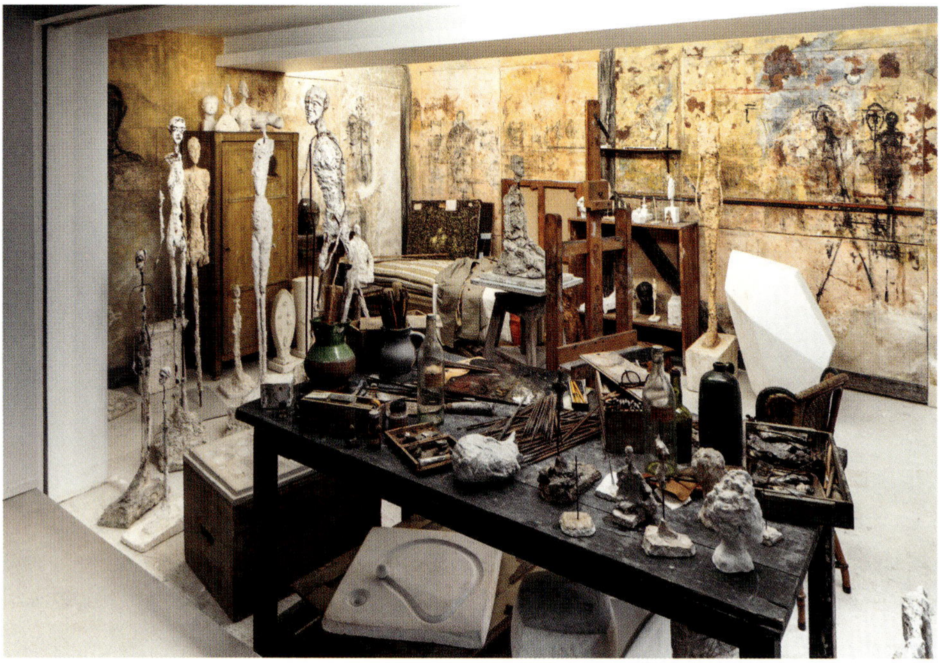

FIGURE 49
View of the reconstruction of Alberto Giacometti's studio at the Institut Giacometti. © 2019 Alberto Giacometti Estate/VAGA at Artists Rights Society (ARS), NY/ADAGP, Paris.

of accounts of bad behavior by privileged insiders), but critical assessments are necessarily dependent on prior interpretive acts taking place behind the scenes, including the sometimes-contentious process of determining what actually constitutes a work. The gatekeeper functions undertaken by an ever-expanding cluster of people and institutions empowered (through a variety of mechanisms that can include self-appointment) to safeguard an artist's reputation, both during the artist's lifetime and after, can have a chilling effect on acts of interpretation that are vital to the larger cultural fabric.

Press reports about the 2014 appointment of Catherine Grenier as director of the Paris foundation eagerly anticipated that the worst of the internal strife among rights-holders might be over, given that the change of foundation leadership was accompanied by the association's decision to disband itself, and because it was heralded as ushering in a new unity between the French and Swiss rights holders. There was also welcome news of revived attention to the long-delayed catalogue raisonné (subsequently published online), and Grenier initiated work on a new research center near Giacometti's long-time studio on rue Hippolyte Maindron, including a reconstruction of Giacometti's studio at the time of his death that opened in 2018 (figure 49).[20] Financing will potentially be an ongoing challenge, however: periodic sale of bronzes from the editions authorized by Annette provided an important funding source during years past, but reports indicated that those were nearly depleted at the time of the leadership change. It is therefore telling that support for the new initiatives came, in part, from the sale of a painting by Joan Miró that he had given Giacometti.[21]

Another thorny issue, lost in all the controversies about multiples, is the status of the large numbers of unresolved or fragmentary works Giacometti had stashed in his studio at the time of his death, including the painted and drawn markings on the studio walls themselves. A 2016 exhibition at the Kunsthaus Zürich, *Alberto Giacometti—Beyond Bronze,* presented numerous estate plasters, ranging from examples left in fragments by the casting process to ones where the absence of casting plans raised questions about their status as finished works. In particular, the decision for the Zürich show to present the plaster remnants of various standing figures, broken apart with the pieces laying horizontally, was a jarring and disconcerting curatorial choice.[22] The inclusion of the preserved wall fragments in a 2007 Centre Pompidou exhibition focused on studio material from the foundation collection raised other issues—given that they were left behind rather than resolved by an artist already known for his tendency to obsessively rework paintings and sculptures as long as they remained in his studio. Their incorporation into the recent studio reconstruction gives a much better sense of their role as part of this open-ended creative process.

Even Giacometti's clearly unresolved material is unquestionably compelling—sharing characteristics in that respect with the canvases and other two- and three-dimensional objects included in the Metropolitan Museum of Art's widely discussed *Unfinished* exhibition of 2016. For many of the examples stashed away the studio, however, Giacometti had not chosen to exercise his right of public disclosure, or the associated right to claim paternity. The sense of fascination that this material inspires means that its public display in exhibition and book form is highly welcome from a scholarly perspective. But presenting painted, drawn, and sculpted objects that might or might not actually constitute works of art alongside examples that Giacometti did choose to release during his lifetime needs to be plainly recognized as a form of posthumous production that carries with it the unmistakable potential to transform public understanding of the artist known as Alberto Giacometti.

MONDRIAN'S FINISH

The possibility that not only the contents of the artist's studio (finalized or not), but the very walls themselves, might be treated as examples of the artist's work was realized to an even more dramatic degree in the case of Piet Mondrian's New York studio. In New York, as in several earlier studios, Mondrian transformed the space into a reflection of the "dynamic equilibrium" he explored in his paintings, mounting colored cardboard rectangles on the walls, and in New York that aesthetic was further complemented by simply constructed furniture composed of basic geometric shapes. The relationship between the paintings and the studio was complex, since Mondrian would alter the studio in conjunction with new aesthetic discoveries. But Yve-Alain Bois has argued forcefully against extrapolating from Mondrian's goals for neoplasticism in

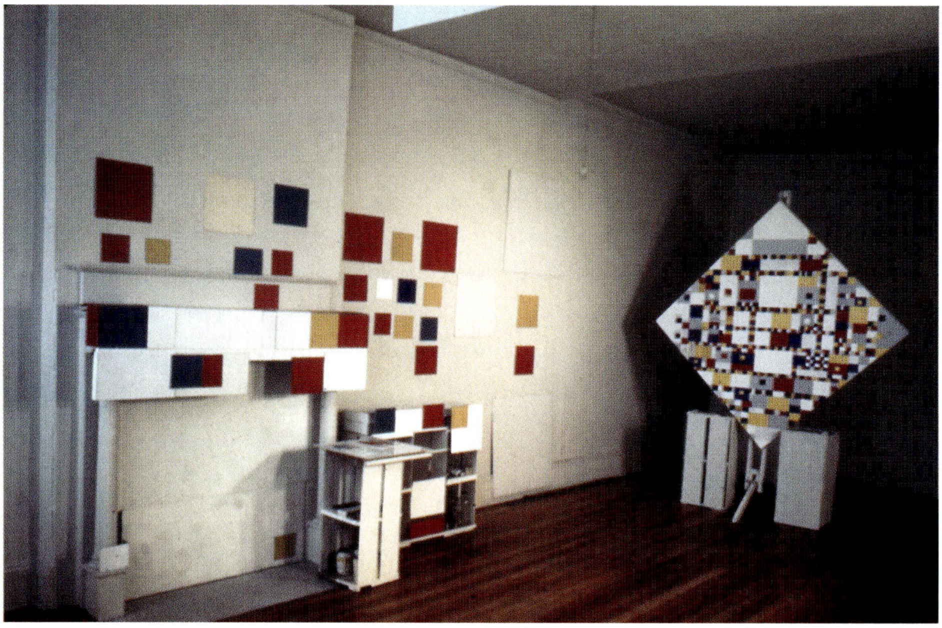

FIGURE 50
Piet Mondrian's studio at 15 East 59th Street after his death in February 1944, with *Victory Boogie Woogie* (unfinished), 1942–44. Photo: Harry Holtzman. ©2019 Mondrian/Holtzman Trust.

architecture to read his paintings as fragments of a larger continuum, describing instead a play of resemblance between different self-contained totalities.[23] At the time of Mondrian's death in 1944 there were therefore two major challenges. One was the status of a number of unfinished works where potential compositions were still indicated with tacked-on strips or blocks of color that Mondrian sometimes employed to explore options prior to realizing his decisions in paint. The other was how to deal with the total environment Mondrian had created for himself and his work.

For years, art historian Nancy Troy has been examining Mondrian through a double lens—studying his paintings while also tracking the mechanisms that shape how the work is treated and defined. Her first foray in this direction, the provocatively titled article "To Be Continued: A Note on Some Recent Mondrians" that she published in 1983 (thirty-nine years after Mondrian's death), revealed the rather dubious attempts by Mondrian heir and executor Harry Holtzman to redefine the studio wall arrangements as stand-alone works of art that he dubbed *Wall Works*.[24]

Mondrian willed his estate to Holtzman, a friend as well as a painter in his own right, who was instrumental in helping Mondrian emigrate to New York. In addition to the paintings included in the bequest (many of them unfinished), there were drawings, the furniture Mondrian had fashioned, other studio equipment, and the studio itself, which Holtzman carefully recorded in photos, a film, and tracings before overseeing the removal of the geometric wall arrangements made with tacked-up colored cardboard (figure 50).

Holtzman's attempts to create official works by isolating sections of the colored cardboard rectangles removed from Mondrian's studio walls (with the results mounted on plywood and displayed behind glass) are particularly noteworthy in their audacity. But far more disturbing, in some respects, is the evidence Troy has uncovered regarding significant reworking of paintings that Mondrian left unfinished. In her early article, and more extensively in her 2014 book *The Afterlife of Piet Mondrian,* she has traced highly intrusive interventions by Holtzman that dramatically transformed the material surface of a number of the canvases that passed through his hands. It is also disconcerting to realize that these interventions might be notable only for the fact that they have been revealed to a broader audience. It is not uncommon for scholars doing in-depth research on a particular artist to discover potentially controversial activities or decisions, but such revelations often remain unpublished, both because they could be construed as peripheral, and due to potential consequences, including blocked access to research material, that might result from airing negative information about estate activities (problems that Troy has fully acknowledged).

The *Wall Works* constitute a dramatic example of posthumous refashioning, but other decisions made regarding the canvases are more insidious, given the circular nature of the interpretive process: ideas about an artist shape conservation and restoration decisions, and the results of those decisions help to establish the baseline for future interpretation. Harry Cooper, for example, has explored how "materialist" versus "idealist" responses to Mondrian have resulted not only in different readings of the artist's work, but also treatment approaches that have altered their physical nature.[25] Many paintings have suffered from flattening of their surfaces during conservation treatments, particularly relining—an approach to preservation involving heat and pressure that has fallen out of favor because of its impact on gesture. Even beyond larger conservation shifts, however, an understanding of Mondrian's work that emphasizes composition as idea potentially gives permission for approaches that are inconsistent with his painstaking approach to paint textures, layers, and relative density—a topic that Cooper and his collaborator Ron Spronk explored in the context of *Mondrian: The Transatlantic Paintings,* a 2001 exhibition that included intensive technical study of paintings that Mondrian brought with him from Europe and generally reworked once in New York. Cooper has also pointed to a similar response to Mondrian's simple wood frames, integral to his conception of the paintings, but often discarded in the course of conservation procedures.[26]

Mondrian's diamond-shaped *Victory Boogie-Woogie* was prominent in studio views recorded by Holtzman. Covered with multiple small pieces of tape and tacked- or pinned-on paper, it reflected a working process that allowed the artist to explore compositional relationships before fixing them in paint. But its unfinished and inherently fragile state did not prevent its sale to Emily Hall Spreckels (later married to Burton Tremaine) in late 1944 for the then sizable sum of $8,000. Nor did it inhibit another high price paid for the work in 1998—newsworthy when the Dutch National Art Collection

Foundation rectified the absence of Mondrian's New York period in Dutch collections by purchasing the work from Si and Victoria Newhouse for $40 million.

Troy has traced the permutations of *Victory Boogie-Woogie*, uncovering a flux that continued after Mondrian's death, including problems posed by pieces of paper falling off the surface on their own, various attempts to stabilize the work, and the surprising production of multiple painted copies. The first painted replica was made at the direction of Willem Sandberg, who was director of the Stedelijk when the work was loaned to a 1946 retrospective exhibition—with permission requested of the Tremaines, but executed despite not hearing back from them. The Tremaines then commissioned two painted copies of their own, with one of their motivations coming from the work's unsuitability for inclusion in a travelling exhibition of the Miller Company art collection (intermixed with Tremaine purchases, and eventually signed over to the Tremaines), which began a multiyear tour in 1947. For the first copy they commissioned Holtzman, with the idea that he could employ Mondrian's own paints for added veracity. Holtzman, however, passed the project on to Perle Fine, who was apparently so careful in her attention to detail that she succeeded in creating something like a trompe l'oeil version of the paper and tape composition, rather than an approximation of the materiality of a Mondrian painting. Although there was an uncertain degree of change to the work before Fine executed her copy, the painted replica was subsequently employed as a document of the work it duplicated. In an even stranger twist, Fine acted as conservator to that original following damage during a loan to the 1958 Brussels Exposition Universelle. Upon receiving both her painted facsimile and the original, Fine decided that the copy also needed restoration, touching up and even repainting whole areas of the replica before she used it as a guide for restoring Mondrian's work.[27]

When works from Mondrian's studio were first shown in 1946 at the Valentine Gallery in New York, a statement in the catalogue, opposite the checklist, indicated that some paintings were not complete (without indicating which ones), but justified their display by describing them as "important documents in the study of Mondrian's work."[28] Troy's scholarship demonstrates how, over time, they began to change status. In the case of *New York City 3* (1941/1977), Holtzman's first step was to order new 3M tape to refurbish the work. Troy indicates that he later replaced the tape with paint, though current listings for the work's materials are inconsistent.[29] In any case, after Holtzman's restoration was complete, Sidney Janis sold the painting in 1983 for $1.5 million. The painting was authenticated by Mondrian scholar Robert Welsh, and Troy reads the clear ambivalence of his equivocal language against his need, as a scholar, to stay on the good side of the person who controlled Mondrian's copyright and therefore associated reproduction rights.[30]

The transformation of the arrangements on Mondrian's studio walls into freestanding framed objects presented as *Wall Works* was far more visible. Yet there was also an incremental quality to the process that implicates all aspects of Mondrian's work. When the *Wall Works* made their debut in a 1982 Sidney Janis show, *Brancusi +*

Mondrian, one example appeared flanked by *Composition with Color Planes 5*, 1917, and *New York City 3*, using its position between the 1917 painting of rectangles on a white field and the reworked painting from a much later period in Mondrian's aesthetic evolution to make an implicit argument for the equivalence of the studio arrangements. Another validation appeared in the exhibition catalogue, where a photograph documenting the colored rectangles in situ, on Mondrian's studio wall, was captioned *Wall Work #5*.[31] *Composition with Color Planes 5* made a repeat appearance in the vicinity of the *Wall Works* for MoMA's 1983 exhibition *Mondrian: New York Studio Compositions*, along with *New York City 3* and *Broadway Boogie Woogie*, which were hung on either side of the entranceway through which the *Wall Works* were visible—though at MoMA the studio fragments were set into the walls, without protective glass, in a strange between-state, neither freestanding, nor part of a full studio reconstruction.[32]

Perhaps the most remarkable transformation of all, however, is the one that overtook the studio furniture. In New York, Mondrian created very simple tables, shelves, and seating from salvaged wood that he assembled into basic geometric shapes and painted white. Some of these elements were saved, in anticipation of a projected studio reconstruction—though two were lost early on when, following their display as part of the 1946 Valentine gallery exhibition, a taboret and shelf unit were mistaken for packing containers and discarded.[33] By the time of their appearance in a 1993 exhibition at the Galerie Tokoro, Tokyo, arranged by Holtzman's son Jason Holtzman (one of the inheritors of the estate after Harry Holtzman's death), the studio furniture had been redefined as sculpture. Even more remarkably, the three furniture items Mondrian had actually constructed (two examples of "Table sculpture" and one "Bench sculpture," each elegantly photographed and reproduced on its own page) were followed by a "Step Stool sculpture" that Mondrian hadn't even made. Rather, the step stool was lent to Mondrian by Holtzman after Mondrian expressed admiration for it.[34]

Thus Mondrian entered readymade territory—but again, via interim stages that included studio furniture that he actually did make as well as the juxtaposition, in the catalogue, with photographs showing the furniture as part of the overall studio aesthetic. The story also has an ironic conclusion. The Holtzman family found out in 2004 that Christie's had managed to lose the furniture (consigned in 1997)—leading to a lawsuit for compensation that was settled out of court. Troy's conclusion: "when they were lost, the items Mondrian made from discarded fruit crates and canvas stretchers may have been inadvertently returned to their original condition as ephemeral, disposable things," even as whatever payment was made to settle the legal dispute would potentially reinforce claims about their status as works of art.[35]

It seems rather implausible that any more Mondrian works are likely to emerge from the studio leavings. But the estate remains doggedly committed to hanging onto rights it can plausibly control. While the website of the Mondrian/Holtzman Trust acknowledges that much of the work entered the public domain in 2015, seventy years after Mondrian's death in 1944, they have pointed out key exceptions in Spain (where protection extends for eighty years), and in the United States, where copyright duration for certain works by foreign artists that were reproduced in other countries between 1923 and 1978 was extended to ninety-five years after the date of first publication by the 1996 Uruguay Round Agreements Act. On that basis, the estate asserted that 45 percent of Mondrian's work remained subject to US copyright protections continuing to dates ranging from 2019 to 2061.[36]

Given the additive nature of the dynamic, where each accepted example validates the next attempt to expand the overall parameters of an artist's work, it is also worth noting the other artist represented in the 1982 *Brancusi + Mondrian* exhibition at the Sidney Janis Gallery, where the *Wall Works* made their debut. Constantin Brancusi's work has been the subject of its own interesting questions about definition and context, including a 1927–28 court case initiated when a shipment of work brought into the country by Marcel Duchamp (wearing his art dealer hat) was assessed import duties by customs officials who refused to accept Brancusi's abstract sculpture as art, and various reconstructions of the studio that Brancusi willed to the French state with the desire that his arrangement remain intact in its original location.[37] Although the current studio reconstruction adjacent to the Pompidou only partially fulfills Brancusi's wishes, the evidence of Brancusi's careful composition of his work as an entire ensemble has been highly relevant for later installation-based practices. One notable response, Scott Burton's 1989 *Artist's Choice: Burton on Brancusi*, was the first in a series where MoMA invited contemporary artists to intervene in the collection. By focusing attention on the role of Brancusi's bases, Burton provided a visual counterargument to assertions that the pedestals were not works of art—a theme further explored in his brochure text, where a quote from Sidney Geist calling the bases "decorative objects of the same kind as picture frames" contained a suggestive echo of the attitude that divested Mondrian's canvases of their artist-built mounts.[38]

Although Brancusi left his studio installation to the French state, Natalia Dumitresco and Alexandre Istrati, a Romanian artist couple who assisted him late in life, inherited the intellectual property associated with his work, and on that basis they began producing a select group of limited editions from Brancusi's original plasters. This aspect of Brancusi's legacy is now controlled by Theodor Nicol, their nephew, and examples from the posthumous editions have been featured in a series of exhibitions at the Paul Kasmin Gallery. In 2013 Kasmin took the occasion of the one-hundred-year anniversary of the Armory Show to present *Brancusi New York*, a gleaming display of five new bronze sculptures, accompanied by a generously illustrated publication. Recounting the story of Brancusi's notorious introduction to American audiences, when his 1912 *Mlle Pogany I* became a focal point for derisive commentary, the 2013 catalogue text by Jérôme Neutres provides oblique justification for the absence of artist-produced bases for the new casts via a reference to how, at the Armory show, "all of Brancusi's sculptures were installed on the same large base."[39] A suggestive connection to the recent editions appears in the description of Brancusi's frequent explora-

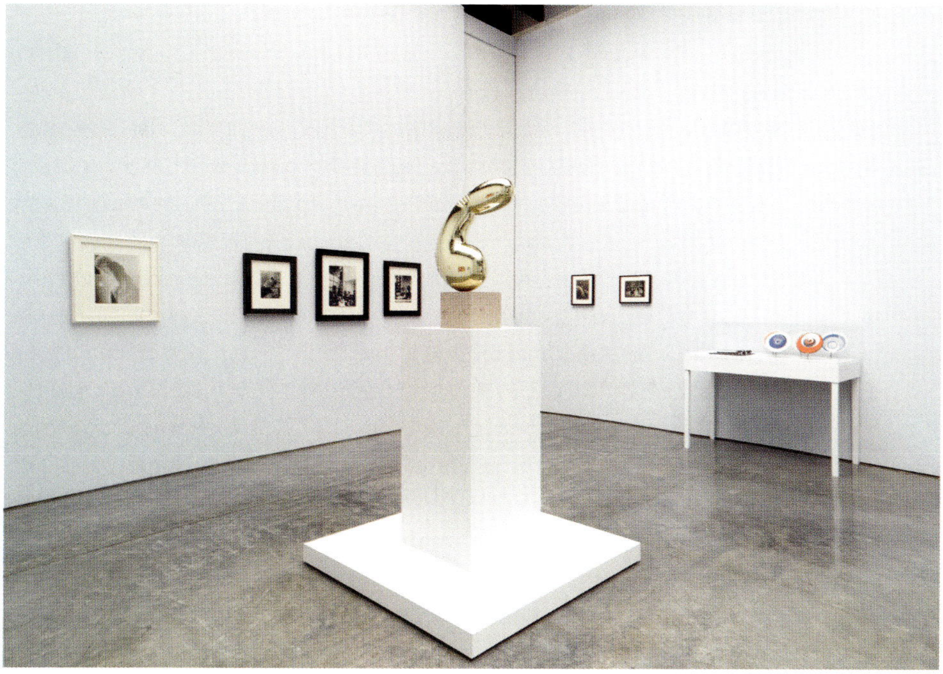

FIGURE 51
Constantin Brancusi, *Princess X,* 1916, featured in the exhibition *Impasse Ronsin* at Kasmin, New York, October 28, 2016–January 14, 2017. © 2019 Succession Brancusi, all rights reserved/Artists Rights Society (ARS), New York/ADAGP, Paris. Image courtesy Kasmin. Photo: Elisabeth Bernstein.

tion of variations on a theme: "With his many *Birds,* his *Muses* made of different materials, his *Columns* of different dimensions, Brancusi created 'models,' which he repeated in the same manner as industrial production, but with variations over the years that often depended on the place they were to be exhibited."[40] In other words, if Brancusi had already established strategies of creation resembling industrial manufacture, that would support further replication.

Kasmin's Armory-themed show was followed in quick succession by further exhibitions that employed the same general strategy. *Brancusi: Pioneer of American Minimalism,* in 2015, was ironic for the much earlier dates of actual production carried by the examples of minimalism surrounding 2013 casts of Brancusi's 1924 *Le Coq* and 1928 *Jeune Fille Sophistiquée.* For *Impasse Ronsin,* 2016–17, work by artists who were drawn to the same locale as Brancusi's long-time Paris studio provided the setting for a 2016 cast of Brancusi's highly suggestive *Princess X* of 1916 (figure 51). And in 2018, *Brancusi & Duchamp: The Art of Dialogue* incorporated both works by Duchamp and photos of Brancusi's studio to provide context for the four posthumous Brancusi bronzes on display. Yet there would potentially be more to say about intersections between the posthumous Brancusi editions and the readymade replicas that Duchamp authorized in the 1960s: the latter were specially fabricated, limited-edition sculptures masquerading as found industrial objects, and thus have their own highly paradoxical relationship to the ethos of the limited edition.

It is also worth noting Brancusi's testimony at the 1927 trial about the steps he took to complete the bronze version of his *Bird in Space* once it was returned from the foundry. "When the roughcast was delivered to me, I had to stop up the air holes and the core hole, to correct the various defects, and to polish the bronze with files and a very fine emery," Brancusi told the court, continuing that "this artistic finishing takes a very long time and is equivalent to beginning the whole work over again." His emphasis on the handmade nature of the work, and his insistence that "nobody but myself could have carried it out to my satisfaction" needs to be read in relation to his testimony's role in a trial contesting the classification of Brancusi's sculptures as industrial products, but the stress on the creative work following the return of the cast object is an important counterpoint to a more hands-off conception of the relationship between artist and foundry.[41]

As it happens, the new versions of Brancusi's sculpture are being generated by the same foundry, Susse Fondeur, that has cast many examples of Giacometti's work, and they are clearly created with similar exactitude. In a highly critical review of *Brancusi New York* in *Artforum,* Robert Pincus-Witten questioned the entire enterprise of posthumous production while nonetheless suggesting that such reservations could well have little impact on the market for belated materializations of otherwise rare and unavailable work.[42] But Kasmin was surprisingly direct: "What we want to come of this," he told the *Wall Street Journal,* "is to know that Brancusi, like many other great artists' estates, is open for business."[43]

UNCOOPERATIVE ARTISTS

The ongoing production of posthumous work understood as authentic—with its status supported by a combination of legal authority and art-world convention—provides compelling evidence of the operation of authorship functions that are surprisingly separable from direct activities of the historic individual associated with certain proper names. But conflicts between collectors or dealers and living artists also present evidence of this principle in action, particularly when they involve efforts to wrest away control over aspects of the work while nonetheless holding tightly to the idea that the artist is its originator. In many cases, such tensions arise from attempts to block artists from tampering with a conception of the artist's work defined by others, often based on market-driven concerns.

In one striking dispute, a collector sued an artist in an effort to prevent him from creating work. The collector was financial executive Jonathan Sobel, and in April 2012 he sued photographer William Eggleston over his decision to create new editions of some of the iconic images he recorded in the 1970s, known for their densely saturated vision of a subtly disquieting American landscape (see figure 52). Sobel had an extensive collection of photos that Eggleston originally produced as limited edition dye-

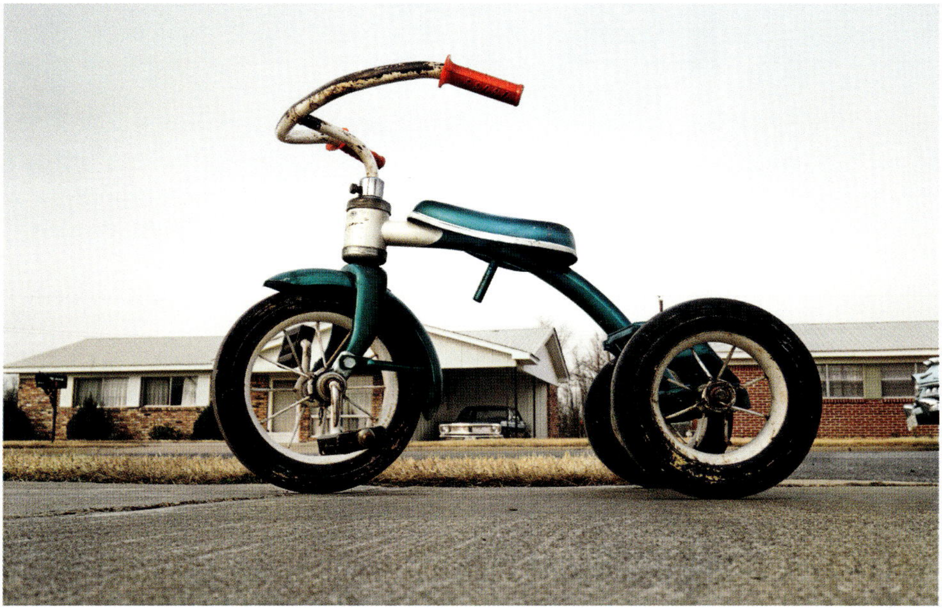

FIGURE 52
William Eggleston, *Untitled (Memphis)*, 1973. Dye transfer print, 16 × 20 in. © Eggleston Artistic Trust. Courtesy Eggleston Artistic Trust and David Zwirner.

transfer prints, and he was apparently not pleased by the popularity of a new series of large-scale digital images (typically 44 in.×60 in. rather than 16 in.×20 in. or smaller), which were featured in a Christie's auction for the benefit of the photographer's charitable trust. Sobel's complaint describes him as a major supporter of Eggleston's career, based on sponsorship of a 2009 retrospective and his willingness to loan works from his collection.[44] One inference is that this investment in the work not only helped Eggleston's reputation, but made Sobel believe that he held some sort of ownership stake, above and beyond the photos he possessed (though he would also stand to profit from any increase in value associated with boosting Eggleston's status). In a world where collectors are much more likely than artists to reap the returns from rising prices, Eggleston managed the feat of directly benefiting from his own reputation when the Christie's auction achieved record prices.

Sobel sought both to prevent any future sales of the new prints and, via a claim for damages, to force Eggleston to pay him a substantial portion of the money he had earned from putting his own work up for auction. In dismissing all counts of Sobel's complaint, however, US District Court Judge Deborah Batts (who had ruled against Richard Prince a year earlier in the lawsuit brought by Patrick Cariou) found that the photo editions, "although produced from the same images," were "markedly different."[45] Perhaps what truly irked Sobel, though it was hardly grounds for a successful lawsuit, was that the new digital prints actually weren't directly competing with the

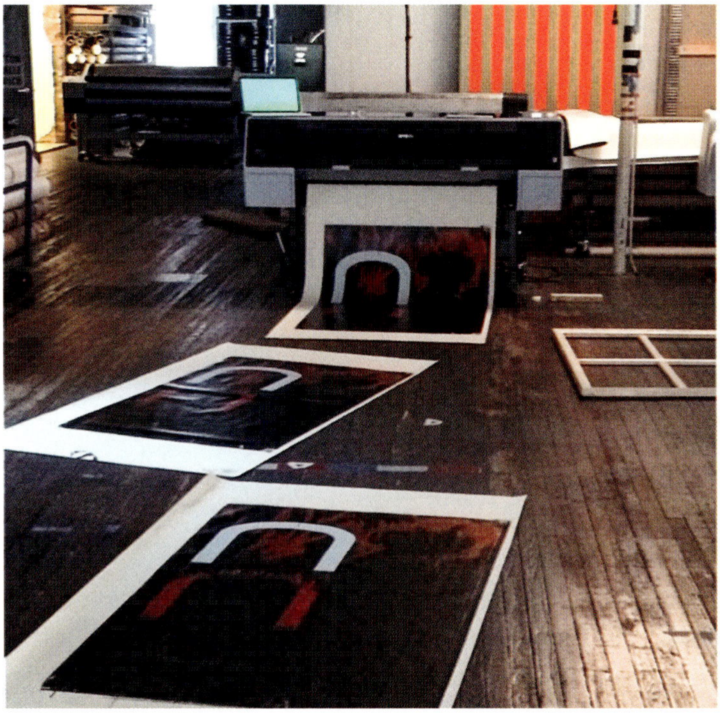

FIGURE 53
Wade Guyton, image posted to Instagram, @burningbridges38, May 2014. Courtesy the artist and Petzel New York.

work he had purchased, but instead were appealing to a different audience. Sobel was a major player in a somewhat specialized realm of photography collectors, whereas the new large-scale images potentially have a broader appeal, in the context of a contemporary art world that is less concerned with medium divisions or the traditional emphasis on vintage prints as a marker of authenticity.

For certain segments of the market, and particularly in relation to artists celebrated for their direct engagement with the ethos of technical reproduction, the artifice of the limited edition can be an ironic capitulation to marketplace demands. But the auction result for a Wade Guyton printed canvas, despite the artist's threat to subject the image to infinite multiplication, suggests that curtailing replication is not necessarily the only relevant issue. Guyton's 2005 *Untitled* was one of a series of large-scale digital inkjet prints on linen depicting red and blue U forms silhouetted in front of an image of dancing flames that he had scanned from a book cover (with the torn edges of the source material visible along the top edge). Trying to make their event-based sales practices into even more of a spectacle, the major auction houses have experimented with curated sales organized around a specific theme. Loic Gouzer, tapped by Christie's, called his May 2014 endeavor at youth-oriented branding "If I Live I'll See You Tuesday" (taken from a Richard Prince joke painting included in the affair), with promotional materials including a video described as "Professional skateboarder Chris

Martin rides through Christie's, giving a behind-the-scenes look at highlights."[46] The auction house hype, plus a *New York Times* feature headlined "For Those Who Can Afford It, Christie's Is Selling Anxiety," were apparently too much for Guyton, whose *Untitled* was featured as one of the works along the skateboard course.

Guyton's response was to create an Instagram account, burningbridges38, where he posted views of multiple versions of the work emerging from his printer and festooned around his studio (figure 53). But the threat of replication clearly failed to dampen auction enthusiasm, given that it achieved the high end of its $2.5–$3.5 million estimate. Nor was anyone deterred when, for the June 2014 Art Basel fair, Guyton provided five different dealers with nearly identical black paintings, made from the same digital information, all of which were priced at $350,000 (even telling them all to hang the works at exactly the same height), since all reportedly sold right away.[47] Guyton is particularly well known for works that, even though generated from digital files, also stand as unique objects due to glitches resulting from strategies that include folding a wide canvas in half vertically before running it through his large-scale printer, and overprinting areas of canvas more than once. But the work sold at Christie's appears to have been produced with little intervention in the printing process, potentially rendering the original up for auction just one of an open-ended series of nearly identical copies.

Even where there is apparent agreement about who is the author of a work (often despite the many hands involved in its production), there is the related matter of responsibility for the artist's reputation—with promotional maneuvers sometimes particularly obvious around emerging artists. The prospect of discovering the work of young artists before they are widely known is in fact a driving motivation for many dealers and collectors. It is hardly uncommon for an artist's early supporters to describe their success in proprietary terms; in the context of a super-heated contemporary art marketplace, the search for the next new thing can be accompanied both by remarkably aggressive hype, largely free from substantive discussion of the work in question, and a host of pitfalls for the artists caught up in this competitive sport. Thus promotional machinations at the beginning of a career are an important bookend to posthumous activities surrounding work by a relatively small number of firmly established figures.

Visitors to the 2015 Venice Biennale who encountered the drama of Ibrahim Mahama's large-scale draping of the entire outside corridor along the south side of the Arsenale with an installation composed from stitched-together sections of jute fabric (figure 54) may well have been surprised to discover that the artist was only twenty-eight years old, the youngest selected by curator Okwui Enwezor for the Arsenale section of the fifty-sixth Biennale. His achievement was striking not only for his youth, but for the fact that, over the course of only a few years, he had already gone from being discovered as the next great thing to being disparaged as a falling star. It seems hardly coincidental that his work was promoted early on by both the Saatchi Gallery and Stefan Simchowitz—each notorious for involvement in forms of art-world collecting

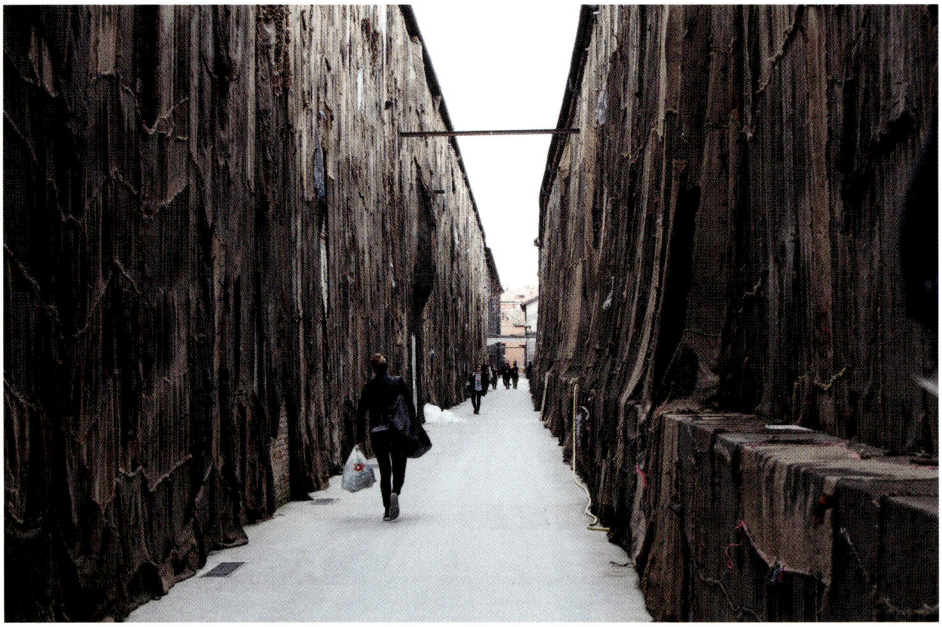

FIGURE 54
Ibrahim Mahama, *Out of Bounds*, 2014–15. Site specific installation, charcoal sacks, metal tags and jute ropes, 56th Venice Biennale. Courtesy the artist and APALAZZOGALLERY.

and marketing that can sometimes resemble a "pump and dump" stock strategy. Of the two, however, the relationship with Simchowitz was far more toxic, shifting from collaboration to lawsuit and countersuit during an interval of only a couple of years.

Although Mahama's material of choice for his early installations was often identified as coal sacks, it has a much more complex and specific history in the context of his native Ghana. Imported from India, Pakistan, and Bangladesh, the jute sacks are initially used for cocoa, a valuable Ghanaian export commodity. But they are only employed for the primary stages of transport, and therefore remain in the country, where they are repeatedly reused for other less valuable commodities sold in local markets: Mahama has mentioned rice, maize, and charcoal in various interviews and statements.[48] Drawn to the material for its associations with labor and trade, Mahama used stitched-together sacks for a series of large-scale installations in Ghana, emphasizing the politics of intervention in the interplay between the different types of buildings he succeeded in wrapping and his production of the work via collaboration with migrant laborers who had moved from countryside to city. The opportunity to create an installation for the Venice Biennale therefore followed a number of realized projects in Ghana and elsewhere, and for Mahama, one of the attractions of the Arsenale was its history as a repurposed industrial building.

At some point in 2012 or 2013 his work came to the attention of Simchowitz, who has been highly controversial for his brash promotion of emerging artists.[49] Simchowitz apparently contacted Mahama through Facebook, and conflicting narratives about what happened next are public knowledge due to a June 2015 lawsuit by Simchowitz and fellow dealer Ellis King against the artist after their relationship soured. According to the complaint filed in California's Central District, Simchowitz and King (owner of a Dublin art gallery) entered into an oral contract with Mahama in October 2013 whereby each paid him £45,000 for six lots of stitched-together jute sack material that would be used in the creation of installations as well as individual works.[50] The latter, made from sections of fabric mounted on stretchers in three standardized sizes, were fabricated by a London artisan hired by the dealers. Dylan Atkins, the artisan in question, produced 294 of these stretched objects, for which he was paid $67,000, and Mahama signed them in Dublin in December 2014.

The complaint summary indicates that the investment paid off well: the initial presentation of the stretched works as part of a December 2014–January 2015 exhibition entitled *Civil Occupation* at the Ellis King gallery resulted in the sale of twenty-seven pieces for an average of $16,700 each, and the complaint therefore valued the remaining unsold inventory at $4,450,000. There were also fifteen more pieces held by Simchowitz in California, stretched but unsigned, for which Simchowitz expected Mahama to provide authentication. But Mahama clearly began to have doubts about the standalone objects produced by Simchowitz and King, along with their demands for exclusive representation. In May of 2015 he wrote to King rescinding the authenticity of the stretched pieces, insisting that they did not have authority to sell his work, and asserting his copyright over all aspects of his production.

The Simchowitz and King complaint itemized the various expenses associated with the exhibition, including the payments to Mahama and the artisan, shipping, and promotional expenses, and it asserted that they had done "all the work," whereas "Mahama was not required to do very much" other than to "approve and sign the stretched pieces created by Atkins."[51] The dealers also objected to the fact that Mahama was actually continuing to make work himself, having created and sold other pieces that they viewed as similar to the ones fabricated under their supervision. Over and over, the complaint presents Mahama as a product of Simchowitz's efforts. According to its narrative, he had few sales and little exposure outside Ghana prior to being contacted by Simchowitz, while Simchowitz was "a renowned cultural entrepreneur" with "significant success in discovering, financially supporting and promoting unknown artists, guiding them from obscurity to international prominence."[52] But the legal case also outlined contradictory versions of their relationship. Mahama, in their telling, was a provincial, "a virtually unknown Ghanaian man in his twenties" transformed by his dealers "into an internationally successful artist." Yet he was also so sophisticated in his deception that they were "fraudulently induced into investing substantial sums of money to bring him into the Western art world," only to have him discredit the work in question "to their considerable financial detriment."[53]

In addition to wanting payment to cover the potential loss in the declared value of the signed works following Mahama's denunciation, the lawsuit sought to compel Mahama to authenticate the fifteen unsigned objects in Simchowitz's possession—or to pay Simchowitz for the difference in price based on his signature. In a striking demonstration of the author function in operation, the complaint described the unsigned examples as "simply jute coal sacks mounted to wooden frames, which impacts their commercial value."[54] Mahama responded with a March 2016 countersuit claiming that the chopping up of the material to create the individual works was a form of mutilation prohibited by the 1990 Visual Artists Rights Act, and asserting that he repeatedly told the two dealers that he wanted to keep his work intact. Although Mahama's lawyer insisted that he signed the stretched objects under duress, presumably the fact that he did so at all would have been an issue had the matter gone to trial.[55] As it was, however, the suit and countersuit were settled out of court, so the final terms are unknown.

The conflict provides evidence of deeply intertwined issues of authorship and branding, with art promoted both on the basis of the artist's achievement and on the reputation of the dealer. For Simchowitz, it was a matter of claiming priority for trendspotting, and his consequent ability to market work based purely on his seal of approval. "I've sold Ibrahim's work to ten of my best collectors without telling them what they will be getting," he told the *Los Angeles Magazine*. "I called it the Simchowitz Trust-Me Special. He is going to be huge."[56] Drawing parallels between speculating on artists and the stock market, he compared his relatively modest initial investment in art he hoped to sell to the returns enjoyed by early Facebook investors.[57] And according to him, the artist was basically doing the same thing—buying low (raw materials) and selling high (authored works). "It wasn't lost on people that Ibrahim bought these for pennies," was Simchowitz's take on the jute sacks, elaborating that "He made $150,000 and he's basically saying, 'Go fuck yourself.'"[58] Despite their conflict, however, both Simchowitz and King nonetheless had reasons to maintain enthusiasm for the artist they were suing, if they wanted to sustain the declared value of the objects still in their possession—and they therefore may not have been pleased by a 2015 *New York Times* story headlined "Emerging Art Cools Down," where Mahama and other young artists were discussed like so many stock futures.[59]

In his recent work, Mahama's exploration of an increasing variety of evocative materials and collaborative processes has included the creation of installations that range in scale as well as how they engage with the context of their display. Representation by APALAZZOGALLERY in Brescia, which provided crucial support for his 2015 Venice installation, together with shows at London's White Cube starting in 2017, suggest that his ongoing career will be supported in a far more responsible manner.[60] But its early stages open a window onto the strange machinations of today's global art market. What comes into view is a young artist already quite sophisticated in his consideration of the issues and motivations for his work, and fully capable of realizing large-scale projects, prior to his association with an aggressive dealer whose sales pitch appeared to consist of little more than claiming greatness for his choices while showing negligible respect for the actual nature of the work.

AFTERMATH

In order to ensure that the physical realization of their work conforms to their expectations, many contemporary artists have begun to rely on accompanying certificates or contracts that contain instructions or even require that collectors agree to specific conditions. One prototype, arising in the context of conceptual art, appears in the wall drawings that Sol LeWitt pioneered in 1968, where the only permanent aspect of the work is the set of instructions for markings that have to be redone each time the work is exhibited. For LeWitt's wall drawings, as well as for such works as Felix Gonzalez-Torres's candy piles and paper stacks that rely on similar documents, these procedures result in art that is eternally new, since the instructions have to be freshly interpreted each time it is shown. Many other artists use certificates or contracts to specify permissible degrees of change or alteration in the face of variable installation conditions or obsolescent technology. But regardless of how it is generated, the appearance of the work under a single name can mask a great deal of collaborative activity. Except in cases of conceptual art where generative documentation is foregrounded, viewers typically have little information about how the works they encounter reflect behind-the-scenes interpretations that can have a profound impact on the work's physical manifestation.

Any perception of past art is necessarily framed by the present tense of the viewer's experience. It can therefore be difficult to discern the many ways that historic objects have been pushed into conformity with the expectations of a later moment. These forces include the process of selection, as some artists go out of fashion and are relegated to museum basements, while others are subject to renewed attention. Less obvious is the impact of conservation, when older works are brought into conformity with contemporary expectations via treatment decisions that are themselves subject to shifting principles over time. Various forms of posthumous production, ranging from redefinition to full-fledged fabrication, are particularly insidious in this respect, since there are many incentives to focus on the aspects of an artist's work that will be most appealing to later audiences, and to emphasize production standards that will conform to contemporary expectations. The incredible precision of recently realized versions of painted steel sculpture that Tony Smith articulated via small-scale models or plywood mock-ups provides one more case in point of how art from even the relatively recent past is brought into conformity with standards driven by extravagant prices, and therefore expectations for high-end finish, in today's market. A truism about forgery is the way that it plays to contemporary taste, with many highly successful deceptions appearing remarkably unconvincing to later viewers. Restorations and posthumous productions are shaped by similarly shifting expectations, but are less likely to be subject to the dramatic unmasking that can overtake a forgery once it is perceived as such—whether because the changes are incorporated into the substrate of an accepted original, or because posthumous examples retain their officially authorized status.

If one's understanding of an artist is incremental, with the experience of each work adding to an overall impression, what is the impact of adding a Mondrian heavily manipulated by Holtzman, or one of the recent Brancusi bronzes floating free of any type of handcrafted pedestal? Brancusi did make many bronzes, after all, and his sculpture was not necessarily accompanied by a corresponding base. But he explored his recurring motifs in multiple materials, with polished bronze complemented by versions in different types of stone, plaster, and even wood. The new examples, all made solely from bronze, potentially shift the balance regarding what type of material one is likely to encounter as a Brancusi. The interventions in Mondrian's unfinished canvases are even more problematic, given the already common tendency to overlook the painterly materiality of Mondrian's work. There is also the ever-present tension between rarity and abundance. Pressure to produce more, whether in the form of posthumous multiples or demands for a greater volume of saleable material from living artists, is largely a function of the economies of desire prompted by already extant examples. Yet overproduction of one type of work can easily alter the entire balance, with new material shifting how all is perceived.

Our culture endows artists with a strange form of power: the ability, whether through physical manipulation or mere selection, to transform raw materials into works of art. Yet there are also interesting limits on how much control an artist is able to retain over this process once it is initiated. Evident tensions or conflicts, including those that wind up in court, help reveal the many functions in operation, both enabling and limiting authorial prerogative. It is important to be alert to evidence of a constantly fluid process of definition that includes where the individual work begins and ends, as well as the overall determination of what constitutes an artist's recognized oeuvre. Discerning the mechanisms governing how a name attaches to a particular manifestation, and what qualities are associated with that designation, will provide answers to certain questions. But acknowledging the existence of these functions is only the first step in understanding their relationship to the larger social, cultural, and economic forces within which they operate.

7

STATUS SHIFTS

WHAT HAPPENS TO AN OBJECT when its status as art is questioned for various reasons, including damage, doubts about authenticity, or even misrecognition? To what extent can a compromised work be saved? Even though it is relatively unusual for art-world disputes to require court intervention (since pursuit of that expensive and often unsatisfying route usually means that all other attempts to resolve matters have failed), tensions that move beyond the secrecy of backroom dealing help illuminate not just specific quarrels, but certain aspects of art-world business as usual. Moral rights legislation can be relevant in some circumstances, but conflicts are just as likely to turn on other legal principles, including contract law and fraud, even if the artist's right to authorize often remains key. The larger set of issues concerns the significance of art as a category, including rights and privileges with respect to how the work is treated and valued, along with associated tax advantages—all of which are brought into focus by situations where that status is somehow threatened.

Typically artists are presumed to hold ultimate authority over their art. Therefore some of the most intriguing situations arise when artists are unwilling to authorize, despite pressure to do so, or when they are perceived to be acting against the interests of dealers, collectors, and institutions invested (both literally and figuratively) in their work. Building on issues addressed earlier, this chapter considers a series of interrelated areas of disagreement and misrecognition, including denunciations by artists, doubts or complaints by others, art not acknowledged as such by bureaucratic officialdom, and questions about the future of damaged objects. One running theme is the problem of trying to define art by court order.

UNFINISHED

The Metropolitan Museum of Art's 2016 exhibition *Unfinished: Thoughts Left Visible* presented ample evidence that incomplete works can be appreciated, even esteemed, for the evidence of an artist's vision and process they reveal. But it is telling that the genuinely unresolved works on display were predominantly by long-dead artists, whereas the contemporary pieces typically involved more self-conscious riffs on the idea of finish. To a large extent this divide can be attributed to artists or their estates being around to object to the display of examples that were not intentionally released to the world. But changes in the nature of art, with various forms of post-studio production often supplanting a studio-based process of hands-on making, can cause the transition from non-art to art to become quite abrupt.

One of the relatively rare cases to be litigated on the basis of the US moral rights statute known as the Visual Artists Rights Act (VARA) turned on both a poorly articulated partnership and rights over the unfinished work that resulted. Planned as a dense, monumental, and disorienting installation that would evoke both the simulated environments sometimes used for military exercises and sociopolitical tensions in American society, Christoph Büchel's major installation, *Training Ground for Democracy,* was supposed to open at the Massachusetts Museum of Contemporary Art in December 2006. But the work remained unfinished once the collaborative process between artist and museum broke down. The resulting conflict turned on the artist's right to complete the work as envisioned and to restrict visitor access before that point. Tangled up in the moral rights claims were questions about the moment when something becomes art, what it might mean for a museum to display objects or material not officially sanctioned as such, and who gets to say.

Although MASS MoCA had acquired many of the key elements for Büchel's installation, disagreements between artist and institution delayed the opening date and left the unfinished accumulation lurking in the museum's largest gallery well into the next year. In spring 2007 the museum made the surprising decision to sue the artist in order to gain the right to show the material already in place. Although they won a September 2007 ruling that would have allowed them to open the gallery to visitors, they bowed to the court of public opinion and disassembled the installation without doing so. Even though the source of contention had been removed, however, Büchel appealed the district court decision as a matter of principle, and he achieved a partial victory when the US Court of Appeals for the First Circuit ruled in January 2010 that VARA protections could potentially apply to an unfinished work. The appeals court ordered a jury trial to determine whether indeed Büchel's rights had been violated, but before it could take place the artist and museum reached a settlement in December 2010.[1]

The status of the accumulated material was central to the dispute. There was no question that the installation, in its arrested state, did not reflect Büchel's vision. The district court's 2007 ruling called for a disclaimer to be posted at the entrance to the gallery indicating that the "exhibit constituted an unfinished project that did not fully carry out the installation's original intent," without specifying the artist's name.[2] Büchel evidently recognized that the proviso would hardly be sufficient to disconnect him from the raw material (including vehicles and buildings) that had not been fully transformed into the work he envisioned. But his lawyers had to contend with a basic philosophical question: if the assembly of stuff had not yet become a work, could the artist rely on VARA's protection against harm to his reputation for showing a distorted version of the installation? As K.E. Gover has stressed, the museum paid for most of the material in the space, so in that respect owned its physical manifestation, even if the resulting work would have been Büchel's.[3] The artist's lawyers argued both that Büchel had disowned the installation because it was never fully realized to his specifications (therefore never becoming art), and that VARA protections should apply to an unfinished work—though Virginia Rutledge has pointed out that it is standard legal procedure to argue in the alternative.[4] MASS MoCA's initial arguments were even more riven, with their lawyers simultaneously contending that the material accumulation was insufficiently original to merit copyright (and therefore VARA) protection, and that MASS MoCA's collaborative production meant they should share ownership of the copyright with the artist. Although the appeals court did establish that an unfinished work could be eligible for VARA protections, it left the final resolution for a jury to decide. Therefore the appellate court did not rule on whether the more problematic issue was the museum's decision to keep adding to the installation after the artist's departure, without full certainty regarding his plans, or the attempt to exhibit something that was clearly unfinished.[5]

One of the more astonishing aspects of the case was the decision by the museum and artist to embark upon an installation of such magnitude without having a written contract spelling out budget and responsibilities. In addition to its obvious practical role, such an agreement might have helped clarify exactly when the raw material would officially achieve its new identity as art. In the context of studio-based practices, unfinished works tend to remain sequestered: despite external pressures that can force artists to hand off works before they are entirely satisfied, the shift from studio to exhibition typically indicates some form of endorsement or closure. The objects assembled for the purpose of becoming Büchel's *Training Ground for Democracy* moved directly from the surrounding environs to the museum without achieving art status prior to arriving in the space of display. The dissolution of the collaboration between artist and institution left many of the physical components already in place, poised for exhibit, without undergoing a formal transformation from accumulation of stuff to authored work of art.

DISCLAIMERS

Cady Noland is well known both for the dark vision of psychopathology and violence evoked through her sculptural assemblages and screenprints from the last two decades of the twentieth century and for her abrupt withdrawal from the art world. Since her last exhibition of new work in 2001, however, she has paid close attention to her work's afterlife, attempting to control where and how it is displayed, and to prevent the circulation of damaged pieces. Her main weapon has been the threat of renunciation, with her disclaimers causing a ripple effect of legal activity due to the consequent devaluation of the work. Although she has invoked the authority of VARA, her exercise of a more nebulous form of artistic license may have greater impact than any court decision. Two works by Noland have been the focus of extended lawsuits, but the grounds on which the cases were argued indicate the potential slippage between the power of the artist's disclaimer within the consensus-driven edifice of the art world, and her ability to invoke conclusive legal authority to back up her acts of renunciation.

In February 2012, dealer Marc Jancou sued Noland and Sotheby's over the decision by the auction house to withdraw Noland's 1990 *Cowboys Milking* from a November 2011 auction. The problem was damages—specifically bending to the corners of the once pristine (though inherently fragile) aluminum surface that had been screen-printed with a combination of image and text. Unlike Büchel's assembled material, there was no question that the piece had initially been a 1990 work by Noland. The status shift enacted by her performative statement happened more than two decades later when, confronted with what a number of observers described as relatively minor damage, she used the intermediary of her lawyer to withdraw authorship. In support of Noland's prerogative to denounce the work, her lawyer cited the provision of VARA that gives an artist "the right to prevent the use of his or her name as the author of the work of visual art in the event of a distortion, mutilation, or other modification of the work which would be prejudicial to his or her honor or reputation," but the legal case itself turned on contract law.

The problem for Jancou was the impact of Noland's attempts to exert ongoing authority over her work on its monetary value. The auction house catalogue was already in print when the lot was withdrawn following Noland's disavowal. After Sotheby's exercised its right to remove a consigned work in the face of doubts about authenticity or attribution, Jancou sued both Sotheby's and Noland for "breach of contract and for tortious interference with contractual relations."[6] No doubt part of Jancou's resentment was due to the fact that another work by Noland, her 1989 *Oozewald* sculpture, achieved a record price the day before the sale where his piece was originally scheduled, even though it was awaiting a replacement from Noland for its missing stand.[7] Because the lawsuit was ultimately decided against Jancou on the basis of relatively straightforward contractual issues, the court did not make a determination about the validity of Noland's VARA claims (and could not have done so, since it was litigated in state court, whereas VARA is a federal law). Yet there can be no doubt that Noland's disclaimer dramatically changed both how the work will be viewed, and its monetary worth.

Cultural issues, legal questions, and market considerations are all bound together in this example. It is easy to support the idea that artists should have the final say when it comes to determining the integrity of their work. Yet protections that supersede absolute property rights are based on a presumption of art's shared cultural significance, and it is therefore important to pay attention to whether authorial control coincides with the public interest in works of art. For Noland, maintaining pristine surfaces is obviously an important counterpoint to the charged thematic content of many of her works. Museums are nonetheless filled with examples that are celebrated despite their damaged state, and it is not necessarily obvious when that aging process is officially allowed to begin.

A second case involving Noland went much further, both in the pursuit of the conflict through the courts and in the philosophical issues it suggested about the status of the work as such. Although not a readymade, Noland's 1990 *Log Cabin* (one of two log cabin sculptures she created) employed a familiar vernacular form, and it was constructed for the artist by outside fabricators. Its subsequent treatment indicated both the significance accorded to the piece as a major example of Noland's work and a surprising disregard for its physical material, evident in the collector's rather convenient decision that it was conceptual in nature once the wood was damaged.

The sculpture was first shown at the Galerie Max Hetzler, Cologne, and acquired directly afterward by Wilhelm Schürmann. For a period of approximately ten years, starting in the mid-1990s, Schürmann loaned the work to the Suermondt-Ludwig-Museum, Aachen, where its display in an outdoor courtyard caused substantial deterioration. Without consulting Noland, Schürmann authorized the replacement of all the wooden components of the structure by the simple expedient of going back to the company that made the first version of the façade and asking them to follow the same blueprints. He then offered the work for sale via the Michael Janssen Gallery, and American collector Scott Mueller entered into a purchase agreement. But the provisions included various clauses to refund the price if Noland denied the legitimacy of the work, disassociated her name from it, or claimed that her moral rights had been violated. Upon being contacted by Mueller, Noland did exactly that, in a faxed message that juxtaposed questions about why she had not been consulted about the conservation decisions with the categorical statement "This is not an artwork." Via a 2018 affidavit filed in association with the case she elaborated, "I feel very strongly that the unauthorized copy of Log Cabin robs my Work of a quarter century of history and denigrates my honor and reputation. The Log Cabin that I created does not exist."[8]

The initial legal salvo concerning *Log Cabin* was again a fairly basic contractual matter involving a demand for repayment, and it was ultimately dismissed after Mueller's lawyers failed to serve the German dealer with the required legal paperwork. Noland nonetheless decided to force the moral rights issue by filing her own lawsuit in July 2017, shortly before the statute of limitations was due to run out following her discovery of Schürmann's replica. One key aspect of the case was Noland's complaint that, because they had refabricated the work, the defendants had "conspired to infringe Noland's copyright by making or authorizing others to make an exact reproduction of Log Cabin without Plaintiff's knowledge or consent."[9] Yet Noland's lawyer was unable to secure copyright registration for the work with the US Copyright Office. Apparently Noland's artistic authorship, widely recognized for the originality of her disquieting redeployment of familiar objects and images, did not mesh with legal criteria, since the Copyright Office rejected the application (twice) on the basis of insufficient "original and creative artistic or graphic authorship."[10]

Even though moral rights are traditionally understood as distinct from the economic interests protected by copyright, the two are deeply intertwined in the US copyright code's definition of a work of visual art (crucial for VARA purposes), which excludes "any work not subject to copyright protection under this title."[11] Moreover, even if all other conditions had been satisfied, the defendants' lawyers argued, the work was not copied, simply restored via the replacement of the rotted wood. There were a few other arguments thrown in for good measure, including the claim that the technical blueprint which accompanied the original sale, "in combination with the Work's conceptual nature, would be deemed to have constituted an implied license for the purchaser to re-fabricate the structure if and as necessary."[12] But for all the twists and turns, Noland's attempts to contest the extreme intervention in her work were ultimately doomed by two crucial issues: the transatlantic sale (since much of the relevant activity took place abroad) and the fact that the work was created in 1990, before VARA's effective date of June 1, 1991.[13] Perhaps the most ominous passage in the case mounted against Noland, however, was the accusation that she was attempting "to impermissibly exert control over works she previously sold."[14] Given that her "control" consisted of statements about the viability of the work's restoration, this could be understood as an assertion that she should not be allowed to speak about the condition of her own work.

Taken together, the two cases raise a series of provocative issues. One piece is still the original object, but damaged. Given the existence of a conservation report describing the overall condition as good, except for the irreparable damage to the corners, there is an open question about how much the impact of *Cowboys Milking* has been compromised by the fact that it is no longer the fully immaculate surface that Noland originally screen-printed. *Log Cabin,* on the other hand, has been rendered newly flawless, with all unfortunate signs of aging erased by the replacement of most of the material that initially constituted the work. Presumably its visual impact is similar to what viewers experienced in 1990, but very little of the that object remains. Most museums are filled with revered historical examples that are valued despite the fact that they are no longer pristine. Therefore one question concerns how much damage an object can sustain and still be considered a viable expression of the original work. Another is the degree to which potentially replaceable elements should be simply exchanged rather than repaired. Perhaps most importantly, however, there is the matter of who gets to decide.

According to a model of artistic creativity where production takes place primarily in the artist's studio, a work's creation follows a series of steps, with initial conception and physical manufacture insufficient to establish its existence absent the artist's decision that it is ready to enter the world. It is often painful, during a studio visit, to hear an artist's plans to rework or destroy something that appears quite wonderful to everyone else, but few would question the artist's right to do so. In various forms of post-studio production, the artist might be less directly involved in physical creation, but will nonetheless exercise authorial decision-making in the designation of the work as such. Once delegated fabrication is part of the mix, however, the terms through which the artist's authorization are articulated become far more critical, and misunderstandings can quickly become grounds for dispute.

Accepting the principle that an artist should have the final word about when a piece of art is complete, how far should the right of retraction extend once a work has changed hands? To what extent does the definition of the work reside in the initial object? And what is the impact of any given statement? The enthusiastic endorsement of Noland's power to declare a commercially fabricated log-cabin façade as her work of art abruptly gave way to a market-driven push to limit Noland's ongoing ability to define what physical material constitutes its identity. The façade's imposing physical presence is crucial to its impact, but that did not stop its owner from replacing and then discarding most of the original material structure that Noland had designated as the work. Conservation decisions are just one of the many circumstances where the artist's ability to delineate the work is potentially usurped by others, some claiming to speak in the artist's name, and some with different assertions of expertise. Once such matters become contested, further questions arise regarding the authority of the court system or other government agencies to administer artistic authorship. Yet even if Noland's disclaimers are not officially affirmed by legal judgments, they cannot be ignored, and they will certainly shift how her work is received by informed viewers and collectors.

"I AM NOT AN ARMADILLO"

Questions about an artist's power to designate are particularly likely to arise in relation to delegated fabrication. But occasionally they involve an undeniably genuine work (one made by the artist) that does not fully conform to collecting conventions. Tensions in two intriguing cases were associated with the existence of more than one version of the work. During an earlier era it was common enough for a collector to commission a copy of a desired painting, sometimes even from the same artist or artist's workshop, with the proliferation of such variants providing secure employment

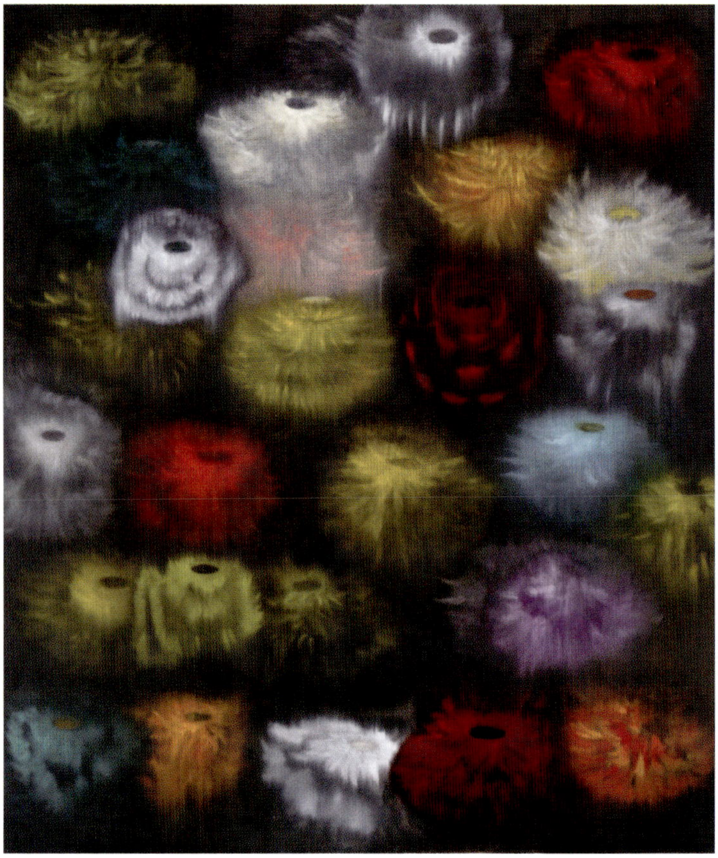

FIGURE 55
Ross Bleckner, *Sea and Mirror,* 1996. Oil on canvas, 84 × 72 in. Courtesy the artist and Petzel, New York.

for generations of connoisseurs once museums and collectors began to prioritize a version of art history organized around proper names and unique originals. Two relatively recent cases where collectors were not pleased to discover the existence of multiple iterations indicate the range of motivations that can come into play.

Actor Alec Baldwin was outraged when he rather belatedly recognized that Mary Boone had satisfied his pursuit of an unavailable 1996 Ross Bleckner painting entitled *Sea and Mirror* (figure 55) by supplying him with another version of the same colorful yet ethereal apparition of forms that appear to float to the surface from a somber surround. The Bleckner painting at issue was definitely created by the artist, but was arguably not the work the dealer declared it to be, since it was evidently painted at a later date, and in that respect akin to the copies that were a frequent response to this form of desire through the nineteenth century.[15] In both the earlier Noland examples and this one, owners took to the courts in response to artists saying the opposite of what they wanted to hear—Noland asserting that something was no longer the work in question, and Bleckner at least tacitly allowing Baldwin to believe that he had purchased the painting he had been seeking.

As outlined in the initial complaint, Baldwin became enamored of the painting after seeing it reproduced on the invitation card for a 2006 exhibition, and in 2010 he asked Boone to obtain it for him. Although it had been sold at auction in 2007, she claimed to be in touch with the owner in Los Angeles, who reportedly wanted $175,000 for the work (an increase over its $121,000 auction price), with the final amount of $190,000 also including a $15,000 commission for Boone. When Baldwin received the painting that same year, however, he noted "that the work appeared brighter and smelled different than he would have expected."[16] Boone countered that she had the painting cleaned as a courtesy, based on its previous owner being a heavy smoker, and that explanation, plus a gallery inventory number corresponding to the original work, temporarily convinced Baldwin that he had the painting he was after. In 2016, however, he happened to speak with art experts who indicated that the cleaning Boone described would be highly unusual, and Baldwin's insistent questions to Boone and Bleckner eventually revealed the substitution. He then filed a lawsuit against both gallery and artist, alleging fraud and deceptive business practices. During oral arguments, Boone's lawyer focused on Baldwin's initial suspicions, suggesting that the substitution was clearly evident, and therefore the statute of limitations had run out. In other words, because it was such a poor facsimile, Baldwin should have recognized the problem immediately, and therefore Boone should not be penalized. Yet Baldwin's lawyer recounted Boone's various subterfuges, and the judge summed up what he had heard: "the painting he was given was not the painting that he desired. . . . it was a Bleckner, but not 'The Bleckner'. It was a *Sea and Mirror,* but not 'The *Sea and Mirror*' Mr. Baldwin sought."[17] Apparently not trusting the force of her side's arguments in a jury trial, Boone wound up settling the civil fraud case by giving Baldwin what news reports described as a "seven figure check," and Baldwin still got to keep the contested work.[18] Well before that, however, a disclaimer of a different order emerged from the conflict. "I am not an armadillo" was Boone's rejoinder to Baldwin's complaints about her thick-skinned willingness to pursue a sale.[19]

The Bleckner conflict had a degree of clarity, due to the fact that one version of the painting was passed off as another. But other circumstances can be far more ambiguous. If a work is conceived one year, but physically realized at a later point, what date should it carry? It is not uncommon for editions to be produced over many years, based on demand, while using the initial date throughout. Works that have to be adjusted for different sites, or updated with new technologies, may also be presented under their original date. These seemingly minor decisions can become significant points of contention—for artists insisting on primacy within any given narrative, and for markets that prioritize genuinely historical examples. Artist have broad powers when it comes to establishing a particular manifestation as art, but how far do their declarations extend when it comes to a work's history?

An earlier case involving a work by Frank Stella is striking for the number of canvases that could be understood as embodying his 1960 *Marquis de Portago* (figure 56). Even though there was no intent to deceive, the identity of the painting from his aluminum

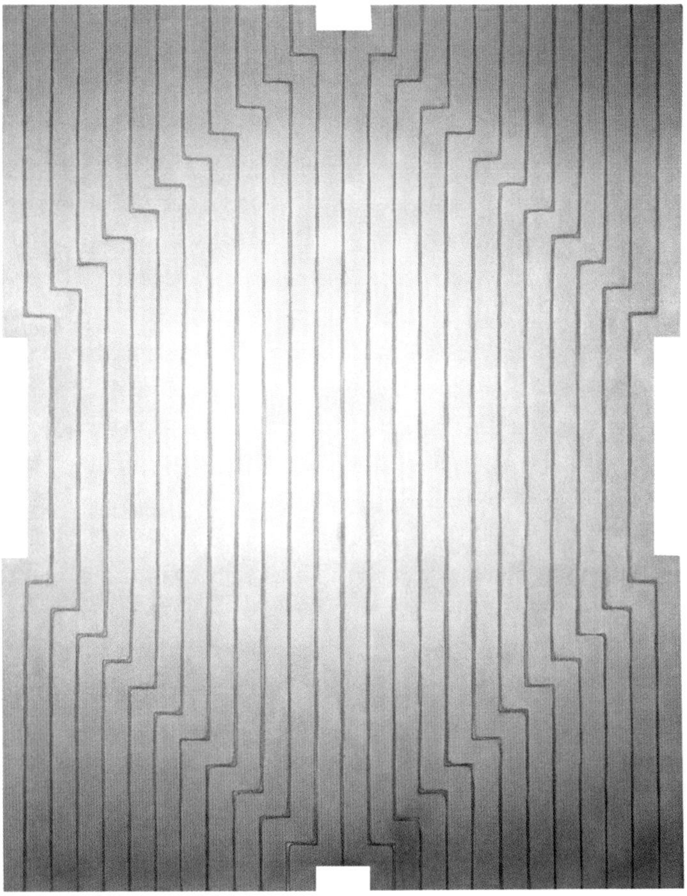

FIGURE 56
Frank Stella, *Marquis de Portago* (second version), 1960. Aluminum oil paint on canvas, 7 ft. 9½ in. × 5 ft. 11½ in. Photo courtesy Marianne Boesky Gallery. © 2019 Frank Stella / Artists Rights Society (ARS), New York.

series (consisting of shaped canvases defined by parallel lines of aluminum paint) bifurcated in surprising ways, including both multiple versions of the work and repeated interventions into the objects presented under that title. The odd twists and turns of the case shed light on Stella's own practice, the impact of increasing value on collector expectations, and the many unheralded conservation campaigns that may become part of a work long after its official date of completion.

The overall series comprised eight different shapes. Stella painted three works using one type of aluminum paint. He then changed his mind and began using a different oil-based aluminum paint for the remaining five, and once they were complete, he also repainted the first three using the same paint. He kept the initial three (with the different paint) in his studio and eventually traded each of those to other artists in exchange for their work. *Marquis de Portago* was one of the first three shapes, so there were two versions as of 1960. Version 1 was traded to Larry Poons in 1963, and version 2 was shown at Castelli as part of an exhibition of the entire series in fall 1960. Castelli then sold version 2 to Irving Blum of Ferus Gallery in Los Angeles for $1,200 (a dealer discount of $300 from its $1,500 price), and Blum sold it to Donald and Lynn Factor. Version 2 of the painting, owned by the Factors, was included in a number of exhibitions in the early 1960s, including *Post Painterly Abstraction* at the Los Angeles County Museum of Art in 1964, where it had the misfortune of being damaged by "a hole kicked in it by a curator."[20]

According to an account produced by lawyer Jerald Ordover in 1973, Stella spoke to the Factors about having the damaged area repainted, and they wanted to know if the repair would show. When Stella indicated that it would, they asked him to repaint the entire work. Stella recollected to Ordover that he was reluctant to do so but eventually agreed. He told the Factors that he could make the replacement (version 3) either in the oil-based aluminum paint used for their work, which had demonstrated some problems with cracking and peeling, or with Liquitex, a paint with metallic pigment suspended in emulsion that he was then using for his *Running V* series, and they chose the latter. Once that version was complete, Stella had therefore painted the work three times—twice in 1960, and again in 1965, when he used a significantly different type of paint. It was, however, their subsequent history that made these works the focus of a lawsuit.

In exchange for painting the replacement in 1965, Stella was paid the total amount of the insurance settlement due to the Factors, $2,400, which left the insurance company as the official owner of the damaged work, although the canvas remained at the museum. In 1966 LACMA curator Maurice Tuchman negotiated, via the museum's insurance broker, to take possession of the damaged painting (version 2), which at that point was classified as having no value. Three years later, in 1969, Tuchman nonetheless arranged with Stella to trade the damaged painting for newer work.[21] Once they reached the agreement, version 2 was shipped to New York in September 1969 and sent immediately to the conservation studio of Daniel Goldreyer, where it remained for the next nine years.[22] As of 1973, Ordover indicated that Stella planned to retain version 2 for his personal collection. Stella would later state that the decision to conserve the work was based in part on advances in restoration techniques subsequent to the initial damages. And Tuchman claimed that he instigated the process of regaining possession of the painting from the insurance company because "Sometimes these types of damaged works end up in embarrassing places."[23]

While this series of events was playing out elsewhere, Larry Poons decided, in fall 1968, to sell his *Marquis de Portago* (version 1) through Lawrence Rubin, his own dealer. Rubin contacted Stella first, offering him the opportunity to buy back the painting, but Stella did not want to pay the asking price. Moreover, according to Ordover, version 1 needed expensive restoration work, which was undertaken by Goldreyer (during 1968–69) at a cost of $2,300. That *Marquis de Portago* (version 1) was then acquired by Carter Burden for over $25,000. Burden loaned the work to Stella's 1970 MoMA retrospective—an exhibition that was both noteworthy and controversial for the fact that Stella was thus honored when he was only thirty-three years old.

The Factors decided to sell their 1965 painting (version 3) at Parke-Bernet's November 1970 auction in New York, where it went for $17,000 after the reserve, initially set at $38,000, was lowered to $15,000. According to Barry Siegel's account in the *Los Angeles Times,* just two days before the auction, "news flashed through the New York art world" that another version of the work was owned by Burden, and Siegel attributed the lowered auction estimate to that revelation.[24] Ordover also recounted that Lynn Factor's father, a lawyer named Morton Harper, learned that another *Marquis de Portago* had been displayed at MoMA when he was in New York for the auction. The Factors concluded that the work in the retrospective was their damaged painting, subsequently restored, and they blamed the alternate version for the reduced reserve as well as what they believed was a suppressed auction price. Harper then joined forces with Los Angeles lawyer John E. Glover and filed suit against Stella, Blum, and Castelli in California Superior Court for fraud, seeking both actual and punitive damages.

The sequence of events recounted in the Factors' initial court complaint indicated that Stella had described their painting as too damaged to be repaired, and therefore without value. But they believed that the damaged work had been shipped to Stella so that he could paint an exact copy, whereas Tuchman stated categorically that version 2 remained in Los Angeles from 1964 to 1969.[25] The Factors concluded that Stella, after receiving the insurance money in exchange for painting the new version, had turned around and repaired the damaged canvas, allowing him to sell it for what the complaint described as "a secret profit."[26] During the years that the Factors' legal action was underway (filed in 1973, and decided in 1978), Stella had not resold the damaged canvas (version 2), but he evidently did so later, since version 2 was owned by Ann and Graham Gund when it appeared in a 1983 exhibition at Harvard curated by Caroline Jones. In a rather striking irony, Jones has also reported that version 3 (the second painting owned by the Factors), was damaged during shipping sometime in the 1980s, in approximately the same place as the injury to their original work (version 2).[27]

Given that the real issue was money, another important date in this narrative is therefore 1973, when the auction sale of the Scull collection set new benchmarks for contemporary art prices. When asked about the multiple versions, Leo Castelli admitted to vague knowledge about the duplication, while saying that, at the time, "those things didn't matter. You couldn't give away a Stella painting."[28] The 1978 ruling by Judge Jack Ryburn cleared Stella of attempting to defraud the Factors by creating more than one example of the work, and he did not find credible evidence that the multiple versions caused the lower-than-desired auction price. But Ryburn did include an admonishment separate from his judgment: "An artist has a duty to the purchaser of his work to inform the purchaser of the existence of a duplicate work which would materially affect the value or marketability of the purchased work." Furthermore, he added, "Stella's failure to inform the Factors of the existence of another 'Marquis' . . . is a violation of his duty to them."[29]

One of Stella's famous quips, regarding the aluminum series, was his claim, "I tried to keep the paint as good as it was in the can."[30] One might extrapolate from that to a more common, if unattainable conservation goal—to keep the paint as good as it was right after it was applied to a specific canvas. It therefore seems important to note that versions 1 and 2 of *Marquis de Portago* were treated by Goldreyer, with one of the Stella canvases (version 2) reportedly in Goldreyer's studio for nine years. Goldreyer later became notorious for his work on Barnett Newman's *Who's Afraid of Red, Yellow, and Blue III* after it was slashed by a deranged visitor to Amsterdam's Stedelijk Museum in 1986. Criticisms about Goldreyer's use of an irreversible alkyd varnish, along with the accusation that he had largely overpainted the Newman canvas (some claimed with a roller), led to a series of suits and countersuits. Art historian Ernst van de Wetering suggested that the conserved work "looks like a reproduction of itself" and was rewarded by being named, along with Elisabeth Bracht, chief conservator at the Stedelijk, in a Goldreyer lawsuit accusing interference with contractual relations, based on the assertion that their derogatory comments prompted Stedelijk director Wim W.A.L. Beeren to decline to make a public statement announcing the painting's successful restoration.[31] In addition, Goldreyer sued multiple publications for libel in response to stories that raised doubts about the restoration, as well as for slander against one conservator quoted by *Time* magazine.

The Stella catalogue raisonné makes it plain that there are three versions of *Marquis de Portago,* so at this point there can be no question of deception. But somehow that information does not entirely clear up the identity of the work presented under that title. There are three examples currently in circulation, each painted by the artist in a distinct paint. The various contenders to occupy the role of *Marquis de Portago* typically appear individually, each performing the function of the painting by that title at different times. It is not evident that any of the canvases have been in the same place at the same time after the first two left Stella's studio, other than the possibility that versions 1 and 2 crossed paths at Goldreyer's in 1969. The 1965 version 3 was also not really a copy, since it was painted without direct reference to either version 1 (traded to Poons in 1963) or version 2 (which remained in Los Angeles until 1969).

In addition to the two acknowledged dates, 1960 and 1965, there have been other campaigns of activity. Each version of the painting now presumably contains a combination of paint applied by Stella and other treatments by later hands. Here, as in most instances, those further interventions are not indicated by the dates assigned to the works. Another important aspect of this narrative is the fluctuating valuations. Based on the insurance payout, version 2 was briefly classified as having no value, which should perhaps be taken to mean that it had also lost its status as art. But even in its damaged state it did carry enough exchange value to be traded for other art, and after conservation treatment, it once again became an official work. Version 3 reveals something else as well: Stella's own shifting priorities, reflected in the fact that the same artist, following the same basic template, and labeling it with the same title, produced a noticeably distinct painting only five years later.

DAMAGED GOODS

There is no single standard for determining when a work is so altered that it is no longer viable. Going by the large number of evidently fragmentary works in the ancient galleries of any historical collection, it is obviously acceptable to show certain works with extensive damage, and the current ethos emphasizes showing fragments rather than dramatically altered restorations, as well as making it clear where infill has been added. Yet it is not entirely apparent how old a work of art has to be before it is allowed to show signs of age, and recent examples with "condition issues" tend to languish out of view.

For works requiring conservation treatment, the many types of materials and procedures used by modern and contemporary artists require an equally varied series of approaches. In situations where the identity of a work remains inseparable from a particular physical manifestation, the obvious answer is repair, via a conservator, even if the results may still be visible. For certain types of work involving readymade elements, components might be replaced—hopefully with the artist's involvement, or based on guidelines the artist helped establish, but sometimes in more attenuated circumstances. A work might not receive treatment for a variety of reasons, including the nature of the damage or the willingness of various parties to pay for expensive interventions. If a particular example can no longer be recognized as the work of art it once was, that determination raises a host of other questions about what should happen to the compromised remains.

Heroic conservation measures often reflect a shared desire not to allow a notable work to slip into invisibility. A major series of murals that Mark Rothko painted for a dining room at Harvard University was largely consigned to storage after strong sunlight in the penthouse space caused their red paint to fade dramatically. While still considered important, the paintings were too far removed from their original state to be shown on a regular basis. In 2015, however, the Harvard Art Museum presented a dramatic but completely reversible intervention that allowed viewers to experience at least an approximation of the original color (figure 57). By projecting pixel-by-pixel color corrections onto the paintings, a semblance of their initial vibrancy was restored, at least as long as the lights were on. Yet the result was only partially satisfying, since the projections made it difficult to see subtle brushwork that could be more readily discerned during the one hour each day when the projectors were turned off.[32] The initiative was thus an ambitious yet unsettling response to a dramatically compromised work, since it involved attempting to correct the losses by using the painted canvases as projection screens for the color compensation images. Additionally, given the demanding technical requirements, including precise calibration to the room in which the work was presented, it is not clear when the series will be displayed again.

It is equally important to recognize that some status shifts occur for bureaucratic rather than aesthetic reasons. When work is paid off as a total loss, not only does it suddenly carry an official monetary value of zero, but since the insurance company

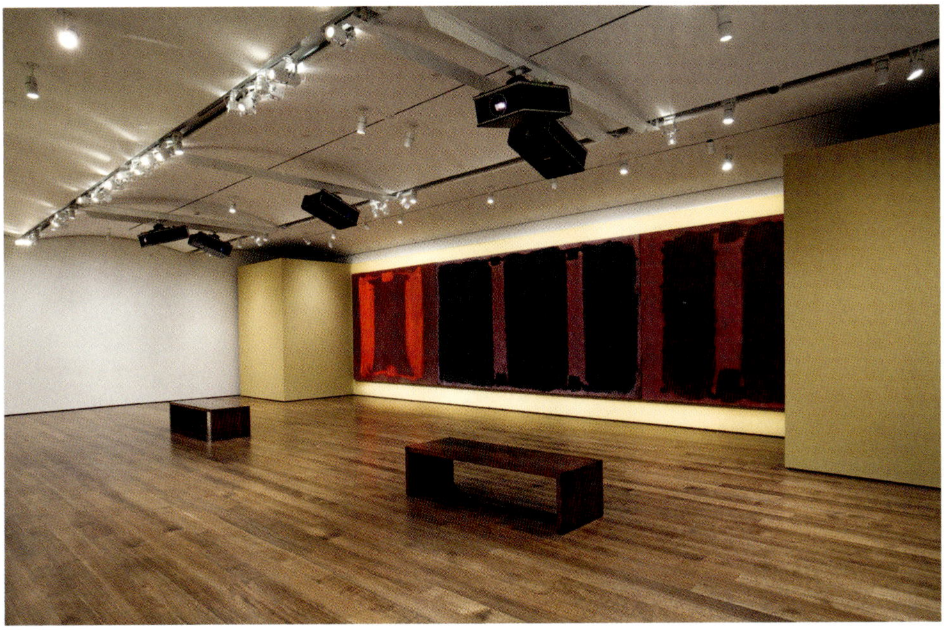

FIGURE 57
Mark Rothko, *Harvard Mural Triptych*, 1962. Harvard Art Museums/Fogg Museum, Transfer from Harvard University, Gift of the Artist. © 1998 Kate Rothko Prizel & Christopher Rothko/Artists Rights Society (ARS), New York. Photo: © President and Fellows of Harvard College.

typically takes possession of the demoted object, it can disappear into the void. A telling exception appeared in the 2012 exhibition *No Longer Art*, presented under the auspices of Elka Krajewska's "Salvage Art Institute" (SAI) (figure 58). The exhibition featured a series of works that had each been written off as a "total loss" by the AXA insurance company. The insurance payout left the company holding the objects, and by soliciting their donation to her SAI, Krajewska brought them back into some form of visibility while also providing guarantees that they would not reenter the market. Some were heavily compromised, others less so, and for a few, the damage was barely perceptible. All were displayed, however, in a manner that denoted their shift in status—from valuable works of art to something else: they were presented on wheeled carts that allowed viewers the freedom to shift the objects around within the exhibition space, or even handle them. The fact that they had been stripped of exchange value also meant that they could be shipped without worrying about insurance. There is a deep paradox in the evocative power that many of the demoted objects still retain, and Jeffrey Weiss contrasted these officially damaged works (including ones where the injury was barely perceptible) with the generally unacknowledged but often extensive alterations that can be part of conservation campaigns designed to maintain a work's uninterrupted identity.[33]

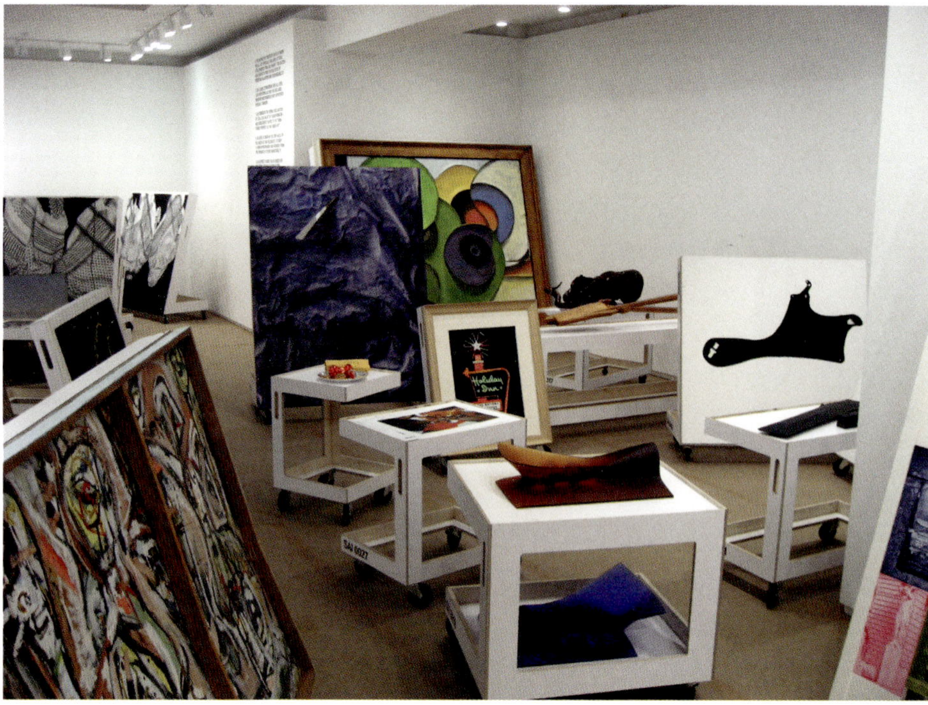

FIGURE 58
Salvage Art Institute, *No Longer Art,* 2012. Photo: Martha Buskirk.

In his discussion of the SAI initiative, Weiss referred to the "decommissioned art object."[34] But that terminology took on new significance in the context of a multiyear initiative that he and Francesca Esmay led to assess the viability of some of the evidently compromised examples in the significant collection of minimal and conceptual art that the Guggenheim Museum acquired from Italian collector Giuseppe Panza in 1991 and 1992. Many of the issues were evident at the time of the acquisition, given the public arguments that had erupted between Panza and certain artists. As an early enthusiast, Panza began collecting both minimal and conceptual work at a time when artists and dealers were only just starting to establish conventions for how to market art embodying various forms of delegated fabrication or dematerialized identity. Panza's tendency to conflate the two led to some of the tensions, with Donald Judd particularly incensed by fabrication decisions in relation to works that Panza had acquired on the basis of plans rather than realized objects. Following Weiss and Esmay's project, the Guggenheim decided to resolve the issues by creating a new category of "decommissioned" work.[35] With this designation, the museum adopted a strategy of essentially holding works deemed not viable in suspension. In most instances the museum will retain all the physical material, and indeed treat it with the same care accorded to recognized works, but the compromised examples will be largely taken out of circulation.

The examples in the Guggenheim's "decommissioned" category are interesting in the sense that they were acquired by Panza as genuine works, directly from galleries representing the artists, and typically for fairly substantial sums of money. Some of the initial transactions were, however, not backed up by viable manifestation or, alternately, clear parameters for how a physical object would be established at a later date. Objects representing the now-decommissioned examples have even been exhibited, including in major museum shows. Yet that history of being presented and viewed as art has now been bracketed off, as something other than a fully valid experience of the work in question.

FAILURE OF RECOGNITION

A few of the more paradoxical status questions have arisen in the context of customs disputes, where government officials, faced with works that do not fit conventional categories of artistic production, have refused to recognize them as such. Yet in many of these same instances, bureaucratic illogic has assessed tax liabilities based on values the objects would only merit as works of art. In a well-known 1926 incident, a US customs official determined that a group of Constantin Brancusi sculptures that Marcel Duchamp was importing into the United States for a New York exhibition did not qualify as art, and therefore should be taxed at 40 percent of their declared value. That decision was contested in a 1927–28 trial that turned in large part on whether the court would acknowledge Brancusi's polished bronze *Bird in Space* as a work of abstract sculpture rather than an "article of utility."[36] A number of less-well-known subsequent cases have involved surprisingly similar issues, including the denial of art status while nonetheless holding onto the declared value for the purpose of assessing tariffs.

In 1982, German collector Reinhard Onnasch attempted to import a work by Claes Oldenburg, identified in court documents as *Modl. Motor Section—Giant Soft Fan,* under the Common Customs Tariff heading for sculpture. Although the work of art was designed to resemble an object from the world of consumer goods, the problem was its materials rather than its form, turning on Oldenburg's use of polystyrene and cardboard instead of rigid sculpture material or traditional sculpting techniques. As an original sculpture, it would have been exempt from duties, but its reclassification by German customs authorities meant that it would be taxed at 14.2% of its declared value of DM 7500. The collector's appeal was successful, however, with the European Court of Justice ultimately affirming the object's status as sculpture.[37]

The Oldenburg case, *Reinhard Onnasch v. Hauptzollamt Berlin-Packhof,* became a precedent, in turn, for one concerning a László Moholy-Nagy painting on metal, initially classified as "other ornaments, of base metal" rather than painting by German customs. In an irony presumably lost on the official, the work at issue was Moholy-Nagy's 1923 *EM 1 (Telephone Picture)*, one of a group of works he famously claimed to have ordered over the phone from an industrial sign factory (figure 59).[38] The initial determination was overturned by the European Court of Justice in a 1990 ruling that

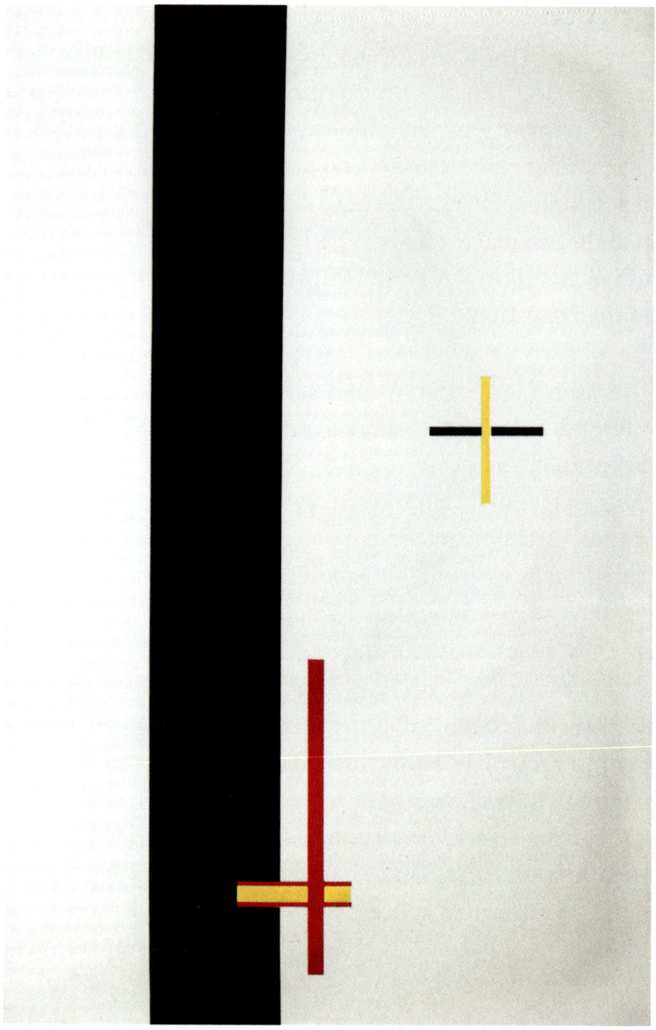

FIGURE 59
László Moholy-Nagy, *EM 1 (Telephone Picture)*, 1923. Porcelain enamel on steel, 37½ × 23¾ in. Collection Museum of Modern Art, New York. © 2019 Estate of László Moholy-Nagy/Artists Rights Society (ARS), New York.

referenced *Onnasch*. The court found that the headings under Chapter 97 of the Common Customs Tariff (those pertaining to art) "must be given a liberal interpretation," and further, that "if the rate of customs duty laid down for the material used were applied to a value for customs purposes fixed on the basis of the work's artistic nature, duty payable would be out of all proportion to the cost of that material."[39] In other words, the court came to the reasonable conclusion that it should be recognized as art, but that a material object not accorded that designation for import purposes should not be taxed according to its art-world value.

Unfortunately that logic fell by the wayside in the final outcome of a 2006 case involving import duties assessed on works by Bill Viola and Dan Flavin. The British customs authority (Her Majesty's Revenue & Customs, or HMRC) rejected the sculpture classification under which the Haunch of Venison Gallery was attempting to import the works, but still assessed the substantially higher VAT duty on the art value declared by the gallery. When the gallery appealed the ruling, HMRC defended their decision by arguing that the component parts were not art when they were disassembled for shipping and, further, because they identified the artistic aspect of Viola's work as the video data and the resultant flat video image, it would not qualify as sculpture.[40] But the gallery scored an apparent victory in 2008, when its arguments before the British tribunal considering the appeal were persuasive, seemingly in part because of the impact of a visit to the Tate Modern to view similar work first-hand.[41]

A crucial issue was Chapter 97 of EU customs law, pertaining to "Works of Art, Collectors' Pieces and Antiques," which does not have a general category for art, but rather subcategories for paintings and drawings, prints, and sculptures. Rather surprisingly to all, the European Commission reversed the British tax tribunal, deciding in 2010 to again declare that the Viola and Flavin works were not art, but nonetheless subject to the substantially higher VAT duties on the declared value.[42] The decision reasserted the proposition that such determinations should focus on the component parts, finding, with respect to the video players and speakers associated with the Viola work, that "the components have been slightly modified by the artist but these modifications do not alter their preliminary functions." Regarding Flavin's work, the commission determined that "it is not the installation that constitutes a 'work of art' but the result of the operations (the light effect) carried out by it."[43]

The tangled reasoning of the European Commission prompted one of the lawyers who represented Haunch of Venison during the earlier British hearing to ask, "Does this mean that if a Flavin is switched on, it is a work of art, but if switched off, it is not?"[44] Obviously this question was meant rhetorically. But even though few would suggest that Flavin's fluorescent light sculptures are immediately stripped of their identity when powered off, they do fail as exhibition objects if not fully illuminated. They also periodically require new bulbs, which presumably are not art until they are mounted in the fixtures, and cease to be once they burn out. In addition, there is an interesting historical precedent in Panza, who took advantage of this potential slippage by having some of the Flavin works he acquired in the 1960s shipped to Italy as lighting fixtures rather than art.[45] Even though the European Commission decision was highly problematic, then, it did reflect a crucial underlying ambiguity for many versions of post-studio art. Where artistic creation tips in the direction of designation rather than direct manipulation of materials, it is not always clear how closely or continuously the work, as such, adheres to any particular physical manifestation.

RESIDUE

Unmasked forgeries are another category where one's presumed experience of a work is subsequently retracted. Even though fakes differ in their initial circumstances and

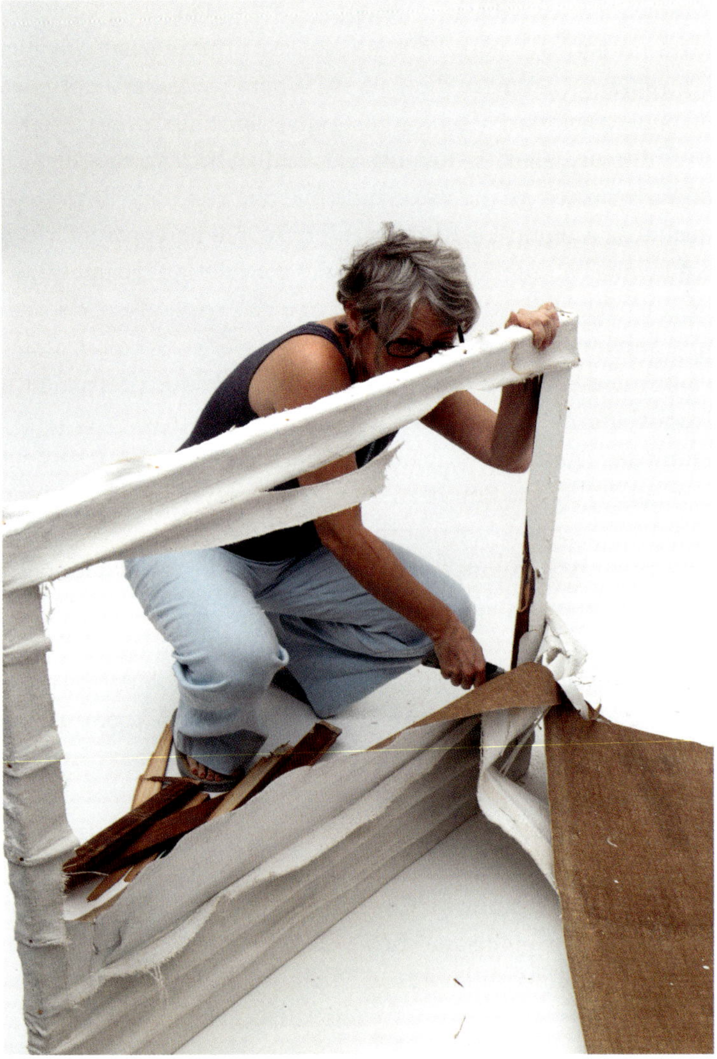

FIGURE 60
The destruction of forgeries purporting to be by Piero Manzoni, 2017. Photo: Bart Herreman. © Fondazione Piero Manzoni, Milano.

motivations from severely damaged works, one point of similarity concerns the challenge of what to do with the demoted object. Both auction houses and law enforcement agencies tend to wind up with collections of fakes by default, and there can also be a strong desire to definitively remove such material from circulation. French law allows for the seizure and destruction of works deemed fake. In Italy, the Piero Manzoni Foundation has not only sought court authorization to destroy rejected works, but has released documentation of those acts. In addition to photographs (see figure 60), a rather disquieting video shows something that looks disturbingly similar to an authentic Achrome painting being torn from its stretchers with ruthless efficiency and quickly reduced to a pile of wood and fabric scraps.[46]

One case involving works submitted for authentication by Giuseppe Zecchillo indicates the potential vagaries of using the court system to affirm or overturn authenticity decisions. Zecchillo claimed to have purchased the works directly from Manzoni and friends in his circle. After the foundation rejected thirty-nine of the examples that Zecchillo presented for authentication in 2000–02 as fake, he sued the foundation. Based primarily on graphological analysis of the signatures, a civil tribunal in Milan declared the works fake in 2006 and ordered their destruction, pending appeal. A separate criminal case in 2009, accusing Zecchillo of having forged the apparently fake works, came to a dramatically different conclusion when the judge rejected graphological evidence as unscientific and acquitted Zecchillo on all charges. Following Zecchillo's death in 2011, however, the Manzoni Foundation made a civil court application for the 2006 verdict to be passed into judgment. Moreover, this was just one of seventeen cases that the foundation has fought successfully, resulting in the destruction of sixty-five rejected works.[47]

Obviously an outright forgery falls into a very different category than art that has been compromised by physical damage. And both are potentially distinct from readymades or examples of conceptual art where status is secured by an external statement or certificate rather than inherent physical evidence. But in all of these scenarios a specific physical manifestation can be subject to dramatic changes in status, based on declarations put forward by artists and a range of other experts. Presumably the artist's word should be final, but examples discussed above and in the next chapter indicate certain circumstances where even that authority can be called into question. Far more complex are the many scenarios where individuals and institutions extend or usurp the artist's role in determining what constitutes the work of art.

It should be readily apparent that these questions are not being pursued for the sake of abstract philosophical inquiry into the nature of art, even though many of the conflicts are indeed interesting for the theoretical issues they suggest. Money comes into play early in the process, since the point of initial transfer can be crucial to defining the work as such, distinct from the flux of other possibilities. Yet the moment of exchange is hardly the only way a work of art comes into being or, in relatively infrequent instances, falls out of that rarified category. The tangle of motives encompasses many acts that reflect genuine concern for a work's aesthetic or cultural significance. But ultimately decisions regarding resources devoted to conserving, authenticating, and otherwise ensuring that a certain select group of phenomena are secure in their status as art are inseparable from the monetary valuations riding on what can appear to be highly esoteric considerations. Nor is the artist the only actor who makes such determinations. Particularly for art anointed as culturally significant, its afterlife is filled with many voices.

8

FROM AUTHENTIC TO FAKE

EXTRAPOLATING FROM AN ANECDOTE ATTRIBUTED to Picasso in the Orson Welles movie *F for Fake*, "I can paint false Picassos as well as anybody," Yve-Alain Bois pondered the question of whether such a move would be possible. "A self-parody, certainly," Bois surmised, while also wondering, "Could Picasso actually paint a fake Picasso?"[1] Obviously there are a great many things made, written, or otherwise manipulated by artists that are not defined as art. Yet the boundaries of what constitutes a "work" can become remarkably blurred. French law is clear about an artist's right both to decide when something is a work of authorship, and to withdraw that association, but many other countries are far less specific, and the customs (as well as machinations) of the art world are yet another matter. With the passage of time, works by many artists are quickly forgotten, even as the spotlight on a select few renders every last scrap of potential interest.

The examples that Bois proposed as "genuine 'non-works'" indicate varying degrees of unfounded optimism and outright greed. One was an Ellsworth Kelly "drawing" that turned out to be a paper kite he had made for a friend's son. Bois also described his encounters with two different objects painted by Barnett Newman that clearly should not have been considered "works." The first was a painting Newman had abandoned. His widow, Annalee Newman, did not consider it an object of value, even telling a conservator after canvas samples to cut out pieces. Bois was therefore shocked to discover it hanging in the Menil Collection, in the midst of paintings validated by Newman. As a definitively abandoned painting, Bois saw it as distinct from other examples by Newman that were merely unfinished. But another, even more dubious, object turned up shortly after Newman's death. That painting was characterized by certain physical qualities that made Bois and fellow Newman expert Carol Mancusi-Ungaro believe that the artist had in fact made it, even though it employed a highly unusual color pairing. The object was owned by a conservator who described it as a gift from Newman, but it eventually emerged that Newman had painted it as a sample, so that the conservator could experiment with preservation strategies without intervening in an actual work. In determining that this example could indeed be described as a form of non-work, or even fake, Bois concluded, "its maker is not the forger."[2]

A little over a century ago, when Marcel Duchamp came up with the playfully provocative gesture of the readymade, transforming everyday objects into art simply because he said so, he simultaneously asserted and undermined the role of the author. But the gesture would hardly have been accorded its retroactive significance if the reverence for proper names, already well established in the intellectual and marketplace dynamics of Duchamp's own day, had not accelerated dramatically since. In the intervening years, and particularly since the 1960s, many of the ways that artists have played against authorship expectations—including appropriation, delegated fabrication, and a host of conceptual strategies—have been readily absorbed by a remarkably voracious market for contemporary art.

Where internal evidence that a particular object should be understood as a work of art is insufficient, a range of statements and documents take on particular significance. Duchamp's gesture, creating art by declaring it so, evokes J.L. Austin's concept of the performative, which references statements that have the power to enact rather than just describe.[3] Yet Austin also cited important caveats regarding the necessary conditions for what he described as the efficacy or "happy" functioning of a performative utterance, including the authority of the speaker. And he pointed to the obvious exception of a performative in a theatrical setting, where it is actually "*parasitic* upon its normal use," even though the appearance of the statement may still serve the purpose of drawing attention to its operation elsewhere.[4] Taking into account the larger context is clearly necessary for distinguishing different orders of renunciation by artists, including those where the purpose appears playful or ironic, such as Robert Morris's well-known 1963 *Statement of Esthetic Withdrawal.*

There are the artist's assertions, both actual and implied (the latter evident, for example, in the decision to release a work to a gallery to be exhibited as such). Many other types of statements or documents can become increasingly significant with the passage of time, including background correspondence, claims made about a work by heirs or estates, and certificates or other authenticating documents issued by experts. Philip Auslander's interrogation of performance art documents in relation to Austin therefore has potentially wider relevance. Due to their role in defining the parameters of the work for later audiences, Auslander argued, documentation of ephemeral actions break down Austin's distinction between performative and constative or descriptive: the document becomes a crucial element in producing the event as a performance.[5]

Certain artists do pay close attention, during their lifetime, to keeping records of their work. But such documentation is challenging to maintain in any event, and it can be at odds with the creative process, given that the moment when a series of ideas and gestures resolve themselves into a completed work of art is often neither punctual nor easy to define. The occasion of exhibition is one such marker, yet it is hardly uncommon for artists to be unsatisfied with what they have shown, and to continue to rework pieces if given the opportunity. A work's sale is potentially a sharper delineation, but even then, ambiguity can remain, particularly for works where elements that have to be remade or reconceived for changing circumstances require ongoing involvement from an artist or artist's studio for their future realization.

The role of the document is particularly significant for works where the manifestation experienced by a viewer is based on directions contained in an artist's instructions or certificate, with Sol LeWitt's wall drawings as a paradigmatic example. For all their importance as a pioneering instance of delegated production, these documents are often insufficient as a roadmap to realize the work, if viewed in isolation from other customary practices. It quickly became typical for LeWitt's wall drawings to be realized by artists associated with LeWitt's studio and subsequently his estate. Artists' certificates are also potentially inadequate as legal instruments, as Joan Kee has argued with respect to the certificates issued by Felix Gonzalez-Torres. Despite their contract-like nature (including a requirement for the collector's signature in later versions), Kee has found Gonzalez-Torres's certificates more convincing as extensions of his artistic vision than as legal documents.[6]

One crucial secondary document is typically the catalogue raisonné—sometimes produced in collaboration with an artist, but often the work of individuals or committees operating posthumously. Gonzalez-Torres's involvement with this process of definition, via the 1997 catalogue raisonné of his oeuvre that was published the year following his death, resulted in certain material held in a form of suspension. In addition to the listing typical of such publications, there are two additional categories: "Catalogue of additional material," which enumerates objects that were generally given away or traded, sometimes even with the artist's signature, but ultimately not designated by Gonzalez-Torres as official works, and "Catalogue of registered non-works," encompassing examples that might appear to be art based on their exhibition history, but were later rejected as such by the artist.[7] Gerhard Richter's catalogue raisonné has similarly excluded various early figurative examples from his official oeuvre, even though he does not deny having painted them.[8] Both of these catalogues reflect the artists' own declarations, but many others are created posthumously, and the superheated art market of recent decades has resulted in increased scrutiny of all efforts to define the scope of an artist's oeuvre.

WHO SAYS?

Lawsuits attempting to contest authentication decisions demonstrate a crucial pitfall, which is the limited efficacy of defining art through a court order. In one noteworthy case, the purchasers of a purported Alexander Calder mobile, *Rio Nero,* filed a lawsuit to reverse the sale after Calder expert Klaus Perls declared it a forgery. Following a 1993 nonjury trial, however, the judge in the case overruled Perls and, in finding for the defendants, concluded "it is more likely than not that the mobile is not a forgery but the original Rio Nero."[9] When the object remained unsold, however, Ronald Spencer concluded that the judge's opinion failed to sway the art world.[10] Perhaps for this reason, other judges have been more reticent to weigh in so directly on matters of authenticity, including the judge in a different case involving Calder.

A 2009 lawsuit concerned stage sets, apparently made with Calder's approval from his designs, that the foundation declined to include in the Calder catalogue raisonné. The opinion of Judge David Saxe, of the New York State Appellate Division, First Department, is worth quoting at length, for its assessment of the ineffectual nature of the plaintiff's quest:

> The point is that a declaration of authenticity would not resolve plaintiff's situation, because his inability to sell the sets is a function of the marketplace. If buyers will not buy works without the Foundation's listing them in its catalogue raisonné, then the problem lies in the art world's voluntary surrender of that ultimate authority to a single entity. If it is immaterial to the art world that plaintiff has proof that the sets were built to Calder's specifications, and that Calder approved of their construction, then it will be immaterial to the art world that a court has pronounced the work 'authentic.' Plaintiff's problem can be solved only when buyers are willing to make their decisions based upon the Work and the unassailable facts about its creation, rather than allowing the Foundation's decisions as to what merits inclusion in its catalogue raisonné to dictate what is worthy of purchase.[11]

Some countries do specify authentication as an aspect of moral rights that can be passed to an artist's heirs. But even though that is not the case in the United States, it is indeed striking how this type of authority is asserted through mechanisms that include activities by heirs and access to archival resources, with their influence reinforced by auction houses and art fairs.[12]

The Mayor Gallery of London responded to this insurmountable barrier with a 2016 suit filed in New York over the exclusion of a group of thirteen works from the Agnes Martin catalogue raisonné, since their omission made it impossible to sell the work through either Sotheby's or Christie's. According to the original complaint, "[Arne] Glimcher has installed himself and the Agnes Martin Catalogue Raisonné and the Authentication Committee as the final arbiters of whether an artwork will be accepted for auction or for private sale anywhere in the world. Defendants [sic] decisions can render worthless an artwork purchased for millions of dollars."[13] Although the complaint concerned multiple works, the central focus was a piece called *Day & Night,* with a claimed date of 1961–64 and a pencil inscription as well as signature. The painting had been sold to Jack Levy for $2.9 million, but after Levy submitted it to the Martin committee and it was rejected, he returned the painting to Mayor for a refund. The Mayor Gallery then resubmitted the work, claiming to have corrected a number of errors in Levy's submission.[14] (Levy had already succeeded in getting a refund for a fake Jackson Pollock painting sold as part of the Knoedler forgery scandal discussed later in this chapter, which suggests that he was some combination of astute about protecting his interests and remarkably unlucky.)

Not only did Judge Andrea Masley dismiss Mayor's claims, but she awarded the defendants the cost of their legal fees. In her response to Mayor's second amended complaint, she echoed the same logic—art world, solve your own problems—as the earlier Calder judge. Noting that a catalogue raisonné is not "controlled by any governmental regulatory agency," the judge found that "whether any catalogue raisonné's inclusion or non-inclusion of an artwork has any bearing on the work's value has been recognized by New York courts as a function of the art marketplace, and it is not for the court to determine what the art market should or should not credit as reliable."[15] The memorandum of law submitted by the defendants even suggested that Mayor would be free to go ahead and initiate an alternate catalogue raisonné—though undoubtedly with the full knowledge that it was hardly likely that anyone else would undertake another version of this massive project, which would have little chance of moving forward without the participation of the estate and even less likelihood of being taken seriously by art-world insiders.[16]

One notorious and ruinously expensive case resulted from a decision by the since-disbanded Andy Warhol Art Authentication Board, Inc., to reject a 1965 Warhol self-portrait owned by Joe Simon-Whelan that had been created through a more hands-off process of delegation than Warhol typically employed, even though it did fall under the broad umbrella of his studio activity. Perhaps the most striking aspect of the case was the information that the board had rejected another example from the series, despite the fact that it had been dedicated by Warhol to Bruno Bischofberger. The letter sent by the board in that instance included the remarkable line, "It is the opinion of the authentication board that said work is NOT the work of Andy Warhol, but that said work was signed, dedicated, and dated by him."[17] Although Simon-Whelan was eventually forced to settle in 2011, when the costs of pursuing the court case became too high, the expenses associated with the defense (reportedly over $7 million) also led to the dissolution of the authentication board soon thereafter.

The United States is not the only place where such matters are being debated and litigated. In France, a 2014 decision by the Paris Cour de Cassation (the high court of appeals) upheld the right of Bozena Nikiel, who was writing the catalogue raisonné on Jean Metzinger, to refuse to authenticate a work. The ruling overturned a lower court decision that went against Nikiel, despite the fact that she was also the official holder of the moral rights pertaining to attribution.[18] And when multiple parties are involved in a high-end transaction, sometimes decisions about how to proceed can become remarkably tactical. Potential complexities are demonstrated by a 2016 lawsuit brought by Asher Edelman regarding a 1969 Pier Paolo Calzolari sculpture, *Cinghie (avido, mio nome, ripetuto, nebuloso, farfallesco)*, made from leather and neon, which was severely damaged after Edelman consigned it to the Geoffrey Diner Gallery in 2015. Edelman wanted to ensure that the repairs would be done through the artist's foundation in Italy, so that the artist would not later rule the work inauthentic. But he also sought to protect his interests if, due to the extent of the damages, the artist disavowed the work when it was presented to the foundation. Since the foundation requires anyone submitting work to waive their right to sue, one goal of Edelman's lawsuit (ironically enough) was to require both insurance companies involved to participate in that agreement.[19]

The ever-present risk of legal action reflects the fact that determinations of authorship are not a theoretical exercise, but rather a major market consideration. Once the authority of an individual or authenticating body is widely accepted, then it is impossible to auction a work without that approval, or to present it at some of the major art fairs. Yet that same presumed authority has put the entire enterprise in danger. Threatened with potential lawsuits over rejecting works, excluding examples from an artist's catalogue raisonné, or even simply refusing to issue a ruling, a number of estates or foundations have ceased authentication activity. Notable closures, in addition to the Warhol board, include authentication committees for Jean-Michel Basquiat, Alexander Calder, Keith Haring, Lee Krasner, Roy Lichtenstein, and Jackson Pollock.

THE ARTIST TESTIFIES

Anyone familiar with art historical literature will be aware of how the process of interpretation is shaped by the artist's words, ranging from published statements and interviews to unpublished notes or letters, and in certain circumstances such statements will play a role in defining the contours of the work itself. In relatively rare instances artists can also be called upon to testify in a legal sense, sometimes about the identity of the work directly, but more typically in cases involving actions by others.

When artists are required to address the court, it is important to consider the function of this highly specialized type of artist's statement. Jasper Johns wound up having to perform this task in 2014 after being faced with two different forgery scandals involving examples that were only a few degrees removed from authentic. The outright forgery was a bronze sculpture made from a mold that had been used to form a wax cast at Johns's behest. But foundry owner Brian Ramnarine retained the mold and made a bronze flag sculpture from the matrix. A second order of forgery followed when he attempted to sell the bronze, since he backed up his claim that it was a gift from the artist with a fake letter from Johns.[20] Ramnarine pled guilty on the fifth day of the jury trial, but not before hearing testimony from the reclusive artist. Although he characterized Ramnarine's casting work as "excellent," Johns was quite clear that the signatures on the back of the bronze and the authenticating documents were all forgeries.[21] Far closer to home, a longtime studio assistant to Johns named James Meyer plundered a drawer of unfinished works, created false inventory numbers and other forged documentation, and sold them with the representation that they had been gifts from Johns (activities he attempted to keep quiet by stipulating that they could not be resold or exhibited for at least eight years).[22] In addition to the massive violation of trust, Meyer's scheme demonstrated the gulf between a fully-fledged work and closely related material that an artist has not chosen to divulge. The only small silver lining was Meyer's guilty plea early enough in the process to prevent Johns from having to testify a second time.

Even if having to appear in court was intrusive, Johns's role in the Ramnarine case was fairly straightforward, with the artist simply confirming the charges that had been lodged. But a far more unusual spectacle unfolded in 2016, when Peter Doig was forced to defend his prerogative to say that he had not painted a canvas. The case was brought in a Chicago court against the Scottish artist known for his engagement with landscape and figurative traditions, and it concerned a work painted in Canada during a time when Doig was living there as a teenager. The owner, a former corrections officer who had purchased it from an artistically inclined inmate with a similar name (spelled Doige, and signed with that spelling), later became convinced that he had managed to acquire a youthful work by an important artist. Rather surprisingly, he was able to convince a federal district court judge in Chicago to grant a trial over his demands to have the work authenticated by court order and to require Doig to pay him $5 million in damages. Yet the call for monetary damages, in addition to an authorship ruling, presumably reflected his recognition that a legal judgment of authenticity would hardly be sufficient to ensure art-world acceptance of the canvas as a recognized work.

In his authorship essay, Michel Foucault speculated on the uneasy relationship between proper names and the individuals thus designated—conjecturing about what types of biographical information would or would not call authorship into question, as well as its relative importance in comparison to assessments of stylistic consistency. It was therefore striking that Doig's lawyers were compelled to argue that the artist was not, as the painting's owner claimed, incarcerated at the Thunder Bay correctional facility in his youth, having spent his teenage years in a different part of Canada. (The plaintiff countered that the supporting documentation proffered by the artist for that part of his life was insufficient to prove that he was not the person he said he wasn't.) The court also heard testimony from Doig himself about his approach to painting. While the owner ultimately lost the case, art-world commentators expressed shock that it had gotten so far, particularly given the fact that a win, even if unconvincing to a knowledgeable collector, would have endorsed the premise that someone other than the artist could preempt Doig's authority to say what he had or had not painted.[23]

And what will become of the paintings presented as evidence in a South Korean case involving Lee Ufan's work based on systematically repeated gestures? Around the same time that Doig's case was underway in Chicago, Lee was in a Seoul court addressing the authenticity of paintings at the center of a criminal case brought against a gallery dealer charged with trafficking in forgeries related to his early *From Point* and *From Line* series. Experts had weighed in that the works were fake and, according to published reports, the suspect even confessed to police that he had commissioned the forgeries. Lee's role was clearly meant to be a final confirmation, similar to that played by Johns. But to everyone's great surprise, when Lee was called to testify he examined the paintings at issue and declared them genuine. It remains to be seen whether the statement will be sufficient to affirm the contested canvases as valuable examples of his work, given that his assertion of authorship ran counter to both expert opinion and the alternate declaration by the accused dealer. Even after Lee's court appearance, the dealer and an associate were sentenced to jail based on the court's determination that at least four of the canvases Lee declared genuine were fake.[24]

If indeed the works Lee authenticated were forgeries, it would not be the first time that an artist has been convinced to authenticate fakes that appear to be examples of their earlier work, though it is certainly one of the more noteworthy. Given the art world's willing embrace of many forms of delegated production, perhaps Lee's assertion of authorship should be accepted whether or not the paintings were made by other hands. The intriguing issues raised by a well-executed forgery were also amusingly demonstrated by Frank Stella. His response to certain requests to authenticate purported early works that he had not painted was to confiscate the objects in question—and to hang them in his own home. Although he hadn't made the works, he told an interviewer, the forgers "know what they're doing."[25]

MISDIRECTION

Without initially setting out to leave behind a series of riddles about his work, Giorgio de Chirico managed to bring together many issues regarding potentially unreliable claims made by an artist about dubious activities by others. The remarkable tangle of competing interests and assertions includes multiple fakes, produced by both his surrealist contemporaries and later forgers; willful misdating and misdirection from the artist himself; legal action against the artist for disowning possibly authentic work as fake; forgeries that were confiscated and destroyed, while still more apparently remain

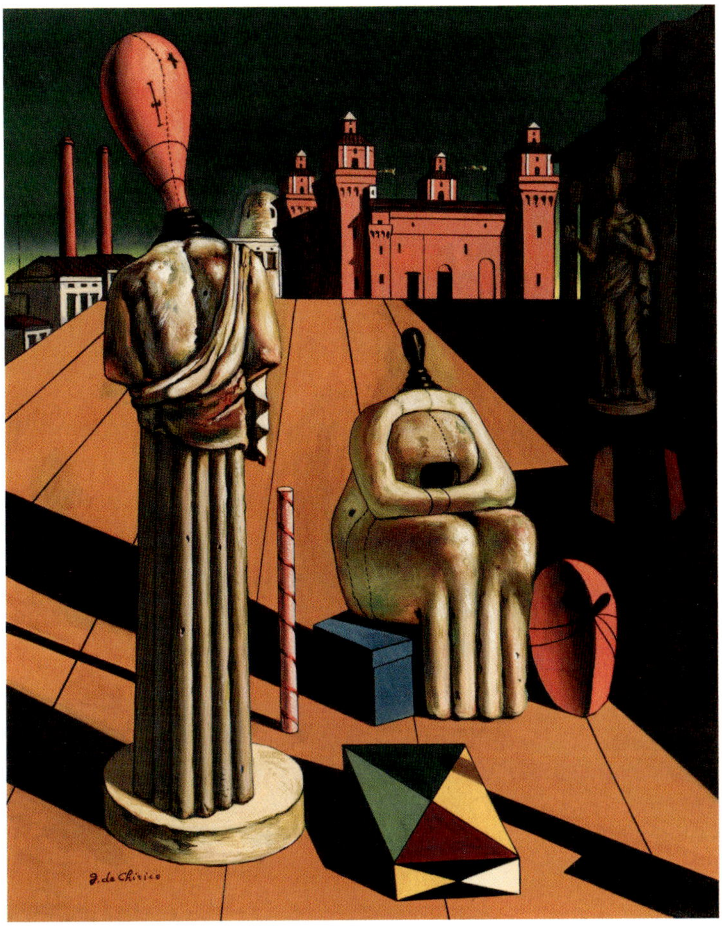

FIGURE 61
Giorgio de Chirico, *Le Muse Inquietanti*, 1951. Oil on canvas, 31½ by 23⅝ in. © 2019 Artists Rights Society (ARS), New York/SIAE, Rome.

in circulation; and sharply divergent assessments among members of the art world about which works are and are not authentic.

A number of ongoing tensions and conflicts were brought to the surface by the sale of a 1951 version of de Chirico's *Le Muse Inquietanti* (figure 61) at Sotheby's in October 2013. Sotheby's ended their catalogue note with a 1911 quote from de Chirico: "What shall I love if not the enigma?"[26] But doubtless they were attempting to direct readers to the subject of the work, with its reference to the artist's early metaphysical paintings, including his first version of the theme in 1917. The price would have been far higher had it been one of those rare early works, but it still sold for £395,500 ($637,281 at the time). After winning the lot, however, the collector balked at paying when he discovered that it was on a list of 117 works in the catalogue raisonné that the notorious forger Renato Peretti claimed definitely or possibly to have painted. Paolo Picozza, president of the De Chirico Foundation, described Peretti as a "mythomaniac" and declared that they held clear evidence that this and many other works on Peretti's list were genuine.[27] Renewed attention to Peretti's claims was prompted by a post on the website of the Archivio Dell'Arte Metafisica, whose principal representatives, Paolo Baldacci (a former foundation board member turned antagonist) and Gerd Roos, have questioned the foundation's attributions. Picozza countered with documentary evidence supporting the authenticity of the work, while nonetheless noting that both the measurements and date listed in the catalogue raisonné were incorrect.[28]

At various points de Chirico denounced fakes presented under his name, but he also contributed to the potential confusion with his production of *varifalsi* ("real fakes"): subsequent works that he passed off as early metaphysical paintings. To add to the uncertainty, their style varied, with some backdated examples obviously related to later work characterized as neo-baroque, but others more closely imitating the early paintings.[29] A request made by Paul Eluard in 1924 for two metaphysical works that had already been sold prompted de Chirico to offer to paint copies, with that incident often cited as the beginning of his self-replication, and the artist's decision to provide the market with versions of sought-after early work helped create openings for additional pretenders. Other artists around André Breton also began producing early "de Chiricos," particularly Oscar Domínguez. While still a board member at the De Chirico Foundation, Baldacci published a book in which he identified multiple works attributed to de Chirico as Domínguez fakes.[30] According to William Robinson, when the International Foundation for Art Research (IFAR) set out to test these arguments based on technical as well as stylistic analysis, they found that one of the works Baldacci identified as a Domínguez forgery, the Cleveland Museum's *Metaphysical Interior*, thought to be from 1917, was more likely a de Chirico circa 1935–45, or possibly a forgery by Max Ernst. But they did agree that another related painting, the Sprengel Museum's *Metaphysical Interior with Italian Piazza*, was probably a Domínguez.[31]

De Chirico may also have renounced certain works that he actually painted. After de Chirico denied the authenticity of a *Piazza d'Italia* dated to 1913, the owner sued and won a judgment against him in 1947, due in part to testimony from a collector who claimed to have bought the work directly from the artist. That verdict was later reversed on appeal, rendering the work officially fake. Baldacci and Roos have concluded, however, that it was an authentic de Chirico with a fake date, made in 1933 shortly before its appearance in his retrospective that year at the Kunsthaus Zürich.[32]

By the time de Chirico presumably painted the work offered by Sotheby's, he had therefore been producing pastiche versions of his early metaphysical canvases for at least a quarter century. And not only have multiple works by that title appeared at auction, but Sotheby's participated in the thematic recycling by simply duplicating the catalogue description from another *Le Muse Inquietanti* sold the year before.[33] The general obfuscation helps account for the lingering impact of Peretti's list, prepared after his career was brought to a halt by his 1976 arrest, and not long before his death, prior to the end of his trial. In it he claimed no fewer than sixty paintings from the catalogue raisonné as works that he was certain he had painted and another fifty-seven, including the work sold at Sotheby's in October 2013, where he said he could not be sure without examining the physical object. The list was first published in 1979 by the Italian art magazine *Bolaffi Arte,* together with a suggestion that Claudio Bruni Sakraischik, author of the catalogue raisonné, might have made mistakes because he relied too heavily on photographs rather than viewing works in person.[34] Given that Peretti was a prolific forger, there is no reason to trust the veracity of his final intervention in de Chirico's oeuvre. But it is equally impossible to ignore the long shadow cast by competing assertions of authorship.

COLORFUL CLAIMS, SERIOUS BUSINESS

Stories about forgery have a seductive appeal. The central characters are often amusingly wily, playing inflated markets to their advantage. The rogues frequently start their careers within the fold of the art world, including artists frustrated with the lack of recognition for work they put out in their own name and individuals with conservation experience who take their knowledge about techniques and materials to the dark side. Yet it is important to keep in mind the subtle and not-so-subtle ways that artistic reputations are distorted by the introduction of fraudulent material, ranging from art works to documentary records.

Reports sporadically surface about entire collections filled with fakes, such as the assembly of works by Chagall, Derain, Bonnard, Modigliani, and other canonical masters acquired by Texas oil millionaire Algur Hurtle Meadows, which were almost uniformly reattributed to the prolific forger Elmyr de Hory, or more recently, a whole museum in China—with the latter emblematic of problems with fakes that followed the rise of a Chinese art market.[35] Typically, however, successful fakes manage to infiltrate collections of otherwise secure works. Occasionally forgeries redirect the narrative in dramatic fashion, as in Han van Meegeren's fake religious paintings by Vermeer, suddenly "discovered" in the 1930s and 1940s, but usually their impact is less notable. Forgers generally follow the market, so distortions usually take the form of additional works by popular artists in their best-loved styles. Because of conscious or unconscious responses to tastes during the time when they were made, forgeries are often unmasked a few decades later, when contemporary preferences have moved on and they suddenly appear remarkably implausible. But, as many are quick to point out, the most skillful fakes are the ones still hanging in museums, unquestioned. Nor is it uncommon for forgers, once exposed, to revel in the sudden spotlight, after years in the shadows, by making broad claims about works in museum collections. While it is occasionally possible to disprove such assertions of authorship decisively, all have a disruptive power. Another running theme is glee at embarrassing experts as well as prestige-driven collectors, evident both in stories told by forgers themselves and in chronicles produced by others.

The case of de Hory was particularly notable, not just for the impressive volume of forgeries he produced, but for the narratives surrounding his activities. One of the most remarkable twists was his involvement with novelist Clifford Irving, who was his neighbor in Ibiza. Irving immortalized de Hory in his 1969 book *Fake: The Story of Elmyr De Hory, the Greatest Art Forger of Our Time,* and scenes of the pair cheerfully recounting de Hory's misdeeds as they relax with friends in Ibiza play a central role in Orson Welles's 1973 *F for Fake.* But the initial inspiration that Irving's book provided for Welles took a new turn when it became evident that Irving was plying the trade himself, in his fraudulent creation of a ghostwritten Howard Hughes memoir that he pitched to McGraw-Hill as made possible by Hughes's admiration for *Fake.* Irving had somehow convinced himself that Hughes was too far off the grid to appear and deny the work—and in fact when Hughes contacted McGraw-Hill they initially thought that he was the imposter. Moreover, as Jonathon Keats points out, Irving's fake memoir extrapolated from extensive research, and was in that respect far more accurate than his de Hory bio.[36]

Welles's film presented de Hory as an appealing bon vivant, and it showcased his facility by filming him drawing and painting a series of works in the style of Picasso, Matisse, and Modigliani, most of which were immediately destroyed by being tossed into a roaring fire. Yet it is important to keep in mind various ways that he and his associates tampered with the record, with his partners in crime, Fernand Legros and Réal Lessard, bribing experts, faking official stamps, and even convincing the aging Kees van Dongen to authenticate a forgery of his own earlier work.[37] Clearly reveling in the publicity following his unmasking, de Hory enjoyed pointing out previous successes, including a purported Matisse, *Figure with Flowers,* that the then venerable (and recently infamous) Knoedler Gallery featured in a full-page 1958 ad in the *Art News Annual.* Yet de Hory also claimed examples from the history of art that are unlikely to be his handiwork, perhaps most notably Matisse's 1939 *Mademoiselle Roudenko (Dancer of the Ballets Russes),* at the Harvard Art Museum. In that instance the provenance appears to dispel any doubts, with the set of drawings sold directly by Matisse to Maurice Wertheim in 1948 and transferred to the museum as part of a bequest only three years later.[38] De Hory did not derive direct income from the publication of *Fake* (as he had initially hoped), but the notoriety did create a market for acknowledged de Hory paintings and drawings, leading to eventual problems with fake de Hory fakes, together with further competing authorship claims when Lessard attempted to take credit for de Hory's earlier forgeries via his own memoir.[39]

Eric Hebborn's career was equally mythologized, largely due to autobiographical accounts, but it was also pernicious for the doubts he made sure to plant after he was largely unmasked in 1978.[40] Like a number of eventual forgers, Hebborn got his start in the art restoration business, where he progressed from filling in voids to adding elements that would greatly increase the interest in a work (a cat in the foreground or a hot air balloon floating through the sky) or "missing" signatures, progressing to the point where he could "'restore' a whole painting—from nothing at all."[41] This was an area where an artist interested in traditional styles could excel, with the added benefit

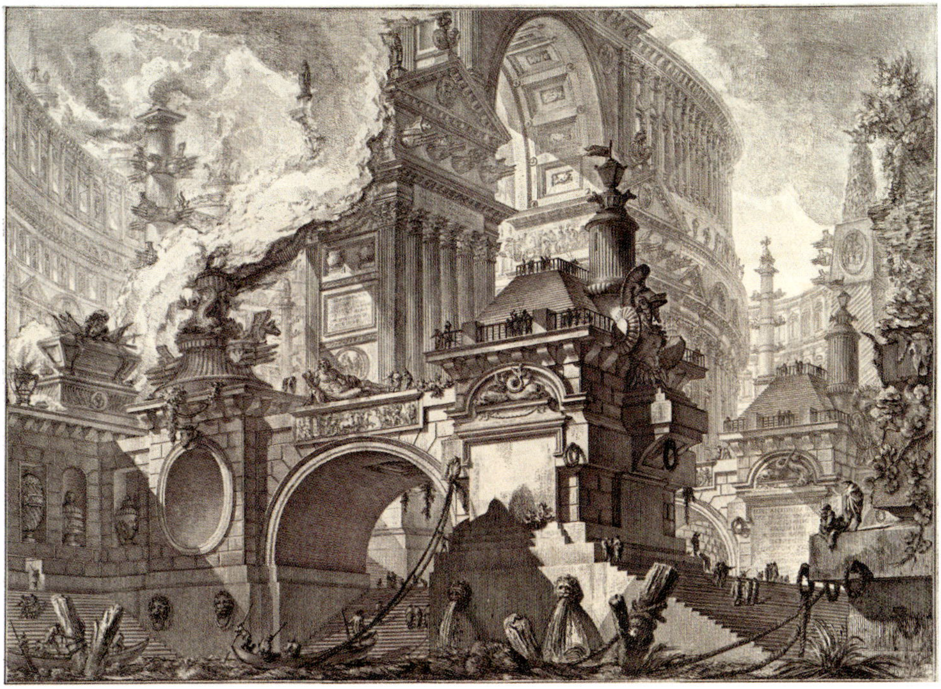

FIGURE 62
Giovanni Battista Piranesi, *Part of a Spacious and Magnificent Harbor Used by the Ancient Romans*, ca. 1749–50. Etching, engraving, drypoint; plate 15¾ × 21⁷⁄₁₆ in. Metropolitan Museum of Art, CC0 1.0, Public Domain Dedication.

of having it over on an art world unappreciative of such skills. As he expounded during a 1991 BBC documentary on his dubious achievements, he was artful at creating works that would neatly slot into the existing historical record. One example was a "Piranesi" drawing bought by the National Gallery of Denmark, where Hebborn corrected weakness he perceived in an existing print, *Part of a Spacious and Magnificent Harbor Used by the Ancient Romans* (figure 62), which he judged too cramped. He therefore created a more expansive drawing, claiming the result as what the work should have looked like, if Piranesi had not been constrained by the dimensions of the copper plate.[42]

In a form of obituary published after Hebborn's unsolved murder in 1996, Denis Dutton described a temporary crash in the market for old master drawings once the extent of his forging activities became apparent. And like others before him, some of Hebborn's wide-ranging authorship claims have been contested, by both authorities in the field and his long-time partner, Graham Smith.[43] Sometimes his motivations seem obvious, as in apparent wounded pride at not being included in the major 1990 British Museum exhibition *Fake?* that led him to claim authorship of a van Dyke work, *Crowning with Thorns*, in the museum's collection.[44] Yet it is important to keep in mind the larger principles at stake. According to Dutton, Hebborn's greatest crime "does not involve the misfortunes of the rich in their attempt to use Old Masters as secure investments," but rather, the potential of his forgery to "subtly distort our grasp of our ancestors' understanding of their world."[45]

Self-aggrandizement is equally evident in other recent cases. Deprived of the publicity of a criminal prosecution, Ken Perenyi did his own unmasking with his 2012 book *Caveat Emptor*, describing his self-trained entry into art forgery after the statute of limitations had passed.[46] His account is mainly notable for the overall degree of hucksterism and larceny pervading all aspects of the art and antique markets that he encountered, including Anthony Masaccio, aka Tony Cha-Cha, who encouraged some "Calder" works on paper and turns up again in the Knoedler forgery saga. Wolfgang Beltracchi, primarily active in Germany, was equally eager to tell his story following his arrest and 2011 conviction (together with his wife, who fronted the sales) for forgeries purporting to be the work of Max Ernst, André Derain, Max Pechstein, Georges Braque, and other twentieth-century masters. He seems to have pulled off a successful second act, with a 2014 movie and other publicity resulting in a new career selling art under his own name.[47] Notably, art historian and former museum director Werner Spies was ensnared in the fraud after being fooled by Beltracchi's forged Ernst works, including at least one example that made it into the 2005 Metropolitan Museum of Art retrospective.[48] It looked for a time like Spies would be financially liable for his mistaken authentication of a Beltracchi "Ernst," *Tremblement de terre (Earthquake)*, which he had certified in 2002 along with indications that it would be included in the catalogue raisonné. It sold for at Sotheby's for $1,142,500 in 2009, but once the forgery was revealed the consigner sued both the previous owner and Spies. A French court ruled in 2013 that they would have to repay the consigner's purchase price, but that judgment was overturned by the Versailles Court of Appeal in 2015.[49] Another "Ernst" entitled *The Forest (2)* purportedly fooled both Spies and painter Dorothea Tanning, who had been married to Ernst.[50] However, Chief Inspector René Allonge, the lead detective investigating Beltracchi, was quoted in *Vanity Fair* as having little sympathy for Spies, based on substantial fees he received from the Beltracchis for his authentications.[51]

Many forgeries are introduced into the market accompanied by forged documentation. In a few cases, however, the fraudulent activity has encompassed tampering with shared archival resources: one of the most sustained campaigns resulted from the collaboration of a down-on-his luck painter and a slick conman who took it upon himself to alter provenance records, sometimes quite pervasively. John Myatt's forgeries were apparently passable enough, even though, rather remarkably, he made few attempts to find appropriate materials (producing many of his works with ordinary house paints mixed with a sexual lubricant that reportedly facilitated fluid brushwork).[52] The far more elaborate fraud was perpetrated by John Drewe, who insinuated himself into market and institutional networks by posing as a wealthy collector and potential patron. As recounted by Laney Salisbury and Aly Sujo in *Provenance: How a Con Man and a Forger Rewrote the History of Modern Art*, Drewe presented himself as a supporter who would be willing to fund the preservation of poorly maintained records and, by so doing, gained remarkably unsupervised access to the archives of the London Institute of Contemporary Art, from which he stole significant original material. At the Tate he ensured his admittance, despite arousing the suspicions of one of the archivists, by backing up his façade with an actual donation of 20,000 pounds, along with the promise of much more to come. In addition to his thefts Drewe created new, entirely fake versions of early exhibition catalogues that he slipped into the archives. "Don't worry," Drewe reportedly told Myatt. "Archives are on the lookout for people taking material out, not for people putting it in."[53]

To shore up Myatt's "Giacometti" paintings, Drewe targeted records of the Hanover Gallery in the Tate archives, where he added new pages with fakes to the gallery's historic photograph albums. He also attempted, under his own name and using various aliases, to get the Giacometti association to issue certificates for Myatt's paintings. When Armand Bartos went back to Drewe's representative demanding answers about provenance inconsistencies for the "Giacometti" he had purchased, the representative suggested hiring an independent researcher from a firm called Art Research Associates to recheck the provenance material. That researcher, who turned out to be Drewe in still another guise, provided a copy of a fake Hanover Gallery catalogue documenting the work's early exhibition history. Bartos was even more persistent than Drewe in his campaign for certification from the Giacometti association, expressing disbelief that Mary Lisa Palmer was stonewalling his requests given the work's extensive provenance documentation, and even threatening legal action if the association failed to act. Once Palmer went to the Tate to check the Hanover Gallery archive herself, however, she found that even though Drewe had backed up his new album pages with corresponding alterations to the gallery's sales legers, he had missed the more obscure gallery daybooks.[54]

Drewe concocted other versions of early exhibition catalogues, including one for the O'Hana Gallery that he inserted into a bound volume of O'Hana publications in the archives at the Victoria and Albert Museum's National Art Library, from which he had removed a somewhat related original publication. The eventual legal case against him was helped by the fact that he was unable to gain access to a duplicate bound volume that still contained the original. Overall, however, the depths of Drewe's forgery posed various challenges when it came to untangling the mess in court. Jonathan Searle, the detective in charge of the investigation, focused not only on the works with the strongest evidence, but also those most likely to sway a jury. Therefore Myatt's fake Jean Dubuffet paintings were out, in part because Drewe had succeeded in getting them authenticated by the Dubuffet Foundation (thereby creating potential ambiguity about their status as fakes in the first place), yet also out of fear that a jury might not be sympathetic to collectors duped into paying too much for works that imitated Dubuffet's purposely crude and child-like painting style.[55]

In his study of forgery's place in art history, Sándor Radnóti has traced the central role that fooling the experts plays in such narratives, from the classic story of

Michelangelo's fraudulent version of classical antiquity, told by Vasari, to recent examples. As somewhat of an aside, however, he also observed how a couple of major twentieth-century exhibitions of fakes could be read as histories of collecting.[56] To the extent that successful forgeries reflect the assumptions and desires of art audiences at a particular moment, they can indeed be highly revealing. Forgeries are a disruptive force, potentially inflicting extensive collateral damage, in addition to the harm they cause to whoever acquires them under false pretenses. Once forgeries are unmasked, however, the details of how they were initially promoted can provide an unexpected window into otherwise secretive business dealings. As the dramatic and sudden demise of the Knoedler Gallery in New York clearly demonstrated, without the distorting force of a market that has both everything and nothing to do with appreciation for art, forgers would have far less incentive to ply their trade.

KNOEDLER FIASCO

The fall of the Knoedler Gallery happened with remarkable speed, despite a venerable history stretching back to 1846, well before the founding of the Metropolitan Museum of Art. On November 30, 2011, owner Michael Hammer announced that the gallery would close, effective immediately. On the surface of things there was little to indicate that such a move might be coming: they were in the middle of an exhibition, and their space had recently been renovated. But behind the scenes, problems had been evident for some time. The precipitating event was Pierre Lagrange's refund demand for a painting represented as a Jackson Pollock, *Untitled,* 1950, that he purchased in 2007 for $17 million. The lawsuit Lagrange filed on December 1 and a *New York Times* article on December 2 provided the first major indications that Knoedler had been marketing a series of purported modernist paintings with murky provenance information and improbable pigments.[57] As if the sudden closure were not dramatic enough, the news dropped just as the Art Basel Miami Beach art fair was opening (where Knoedler also abandoned its planned booth), ensuring maximum impact as a topic of discussion among closely connected circles of high-end dealers and collectors.

The series of lawsuits that followed have helped draw back the curtains on the elaborate and generally secretive deals through which wealthy collectors were convinced to part with major sums of money for works of art with very thin provenance information. While the court documents expose the specific mechanisms of the forgery scheme, they also trace a revealing picture of an art world where museum and commercial gallery interests are closely linked. Nor would the activities have been quite so likely to succeed if fear of lawsuits had not silenced many experts in the field.

The seeds of Knoedler's ultimate downfall date to the mid-1990s, when Ann Freedman, who worked her way up the ranks before becoming gallery director, met with Glafira Rosales to discuss a trove of Abstract Expressionist work to which Rosales could provide access. Potential red flags included Freedman not being familiar with Rosales prior to their meeting; the lack of documentation associated with the works;

their low prices (in relative terms); changing stories about their source; reservations voiced by experts over the years; and the sheer number of works that began to emerge—with approximately forty Rosales works sold by Knoedler, and another twenty or so offered by Julian Weissman, a former Knoedler employee.[58] Rosales would reveal little about the supposedly secretive collector, with homes in Switzerland and Mexico, who purportedly had bought the works directly from the artists' studios, or the son who inherited the works, with the collector therefore known as "Mr. X" at Knoedler. The back story, which shifted over time, included the use of known intermediaries. Initially artist Alfonso Ossorio was invoked and after that was questioned, the explanation pivoted to reliance on advice from David Herbert, who had worked at two galleries that showed Abstract Expressionist work in the 1950s before opening his own gallery. A later embellishment that Herbert and Mr. X might have been lovers gave a potential motivation for Mr. X's desire for secrecy (given the need to keep that information from his fictitious family).

Freedman resigned from Knoedler in 2009, not long after the gallery was served with a grand jury subpoena related to Rosales's activities. But until Rosales pleaded guilty to a host of charges associated with her role in the forgery scheme in fall 2013, Knoedler continued to express confidence that the works were genuine, with that question remaining a matter of contention in early lawsuits. Freedman in fact filed a 2013 defamation suit against another gallery owner who had accused her of not doing due diligence, thereby forcing him to issue a retraction.[59] Attacks on James Martin, of Orion Analytical, who questioned pigments used in the fakes, were also part of the gallery's defense strategy.[60] The main source for the forgeries turned out to be a Chinese painter, Pei-Shen Qian, who was living in Queens at the time and received nominal amounts of money for the paintings he handed over to Rosales and her co-conspirators.[61]

As early as 1994, family members and at least one expert expressed hesitations or doubts about a couple of purported Richard Diebenkorn paintings that had come from Rosales, and when pressured, Rosales eventually provided highly improbable provenance history associated with a gallery in Madrid.[62] In 2003 Knoedler had to reimburse Jack Levy the $2 million he paid in 2001 for a "Pollock," *Untitled,* 1949, because Levy was wise enough to insist, as a condition of sale, that it be evaluated by the International Foundation for Art Research (though it is not clear what happened with four other less pricy forgeries he also acquired). According to their report, "IFAR believes that too many reservations exist to make a positive attribution to Jackson Pollock"; they noted "disturbing" differences between the paints in the work and the materials in a securely identified Pollock from the same year; and they stated that it was "inconceivable" that Pollock sold the work through Ossorio.[63] After the return of the faux Pollock, the gallery tried to sell it to Nicholas and Eugenia Taubman, without disclosing the IFAR report and still claiming that it was due to be included in the revised catalogue raisonné. That sale fell through in 2007, however, when the Taubmans' lawyer insisted on a contract attesting that there had been no questions about the work's attribution or authenticity—though the Taubmans did acquire a $4.3 million "Clyfford Still" in 2005 for which Rosales was paid $600,000 by the gallery.[64]

The Dedalus Foundation, which oversees Robert Motherwell's legacy under the leadership of art historian Jack Flam, became increasingly suspicious of purported Motherwell paintings they were being shown, and in 2008 they insisted that two be submitted for technical examination. Martin's Orion Analytical discovered traces of paints that only began to be manufactured after the claimed dates of 1953 and 1955, as well as evidence of an electric sander, which Motherwell was not known to have used.[65] At that point the narrative regarding contact between Mr. X and the artists whose work he had acquired seemed to change, extending into the 1960s, which would potentially account for pigments Motherwell had not used until later.[66] The Dedalus Foundation nonetheless concluded that it was "significantly unlikely" that the paintings were by Motherwell, and they would therefore not be included in the catalogue raisonné.[67] Regarding one Rosales "Motherwell," a purported 1953 *Elegy* sold by Weissman, the agreement settling the lawsuit brought by its owner included a provision that the back of the painting would be indelibly stamped "AFTER PHYSICAL EXAMINATION AND FORENSIC TESTING, THE ROBERT MOTHERWELL CATALOGUE RAISONNE PROJECT OF THE DEDALUS FOUNDATION, INC., HAS DETERMINED THAT THIS PAINTING IS NOT AN AUTHENTIC WORK BY ROBERT MOTHERWELL BUT A FORGERY."[68]

Despite issues that had begun to emerge, the secretive nature of the art market meant that information about cancelled sales was not widely known, and the ever-present danger of legal action made authorities reluctant to share their doubts. It also took a while for the sheer volume of newly discovered work to become evident, even to specialists. Following the closure of the gallery, each of the multiple lawsuits filed by distressed owners revealed a bit more about the scheme, but because all were eventually settled, much remains hidden. There was even a passing suggestion that Knoedler might have also been sourcing fakes from elsewhere: Martin and Sharleen Cohen managed to buy both a Rosales "Rothko" (acquired via the Rosenfeld Gallery, in same-day flip from Knoedler) and a Tony Cha-Cha "de Kooning" from Knoedler directly.[69]

Yve-Alain Bois has told the story of looking at a purported Barnett Newman on offer by the Knoedler gallery in 2006, together with Carol Mancusi-Ungaro, but neither of them voicing their opinion of it, based on advice from the Barnett Newman Foundation, in order to avoid the danger of being sued. Two years later, caught off guard by another Newman fake hanging in the Beyeler Foundation amid genuine works, he did call out the work and told a museum curator that they were being used by Knoedler "as a legitimizing instrument."[70] Bois was willing to tell this story in a 2016 article because by then not only had his private email correspondence with the Beyeler somehow been obtained and quoted in a *New York Times* article, but the subsequence collapse of Knoedler under the weight of the massive forgery scandal had reduced the lawsuit danger.[71]

It turned out that the Rosario "Newman" at the Beyeler was being offered for sale to another museum, the Kunstsammlung Nordrhein-Westfalen in Düsseldorf, for $18 million, with Beyeler curator Oliver Wick acting as the intermediary. After Bois contacted the Beyeler to let them know about his concerns, the work was taken down.[72] But this was not the only time that both the Beyeler and Wick played a role in validating Knoedler forgeries. A "Rothko" which Knoedler bought from Rosales for $750,000, then sold to the Martin Hilti Family Trust in November 2002 for $5.5 million, had been displayed at the Beyeler during summer 2002. Michael Hilti visited Knoedler to inquire about Sean Scully's work when he was in New York in October 2002 but was redirected by Freedman to the "fantastic Rothko" he had already seen at the Beyeler.[73] The "Rothko" purchased by Domenico and Eleanore De Sole in 2004 for $8.3 million had not yet been showcased at the Beyeler, but they were told that the museum planned to request the work on loan. The work was indeed displayed at the Beyeler soon thereafter, accompanied by a pamphlet written by Wick that repeated the Herbert provenance supplied by Knoedler—with that pamphlet in turn becoming part of the evidence Knoedler used to confirm the back story for other works.[74] Wick was even more closely involved in the sale of a "Rothko" acquired by Frank J. Fertitta III for $7.2 million after it was featured at the Beyeler in 2008. For his assistance with that transaction, he received $300,000 from Knoedler and a $150,000 commission from Fertitta. That same year Wick tried to sell Fertitta another Rothko that he described as a "perfect match" for the one he had already acquired.[75]

Other individuals and institutions were pulled into the general orbit as well. The invoice for the purported 1956 Rothko sold to the De Soles specified: "To be included in the forthcoming supplement to the 1998 Rothko catalogue raisonné under preparation by the National Gallery of Art, Washington, D.C."[76] The statement was supported by a letter from the manager of the catalogue raisonné project to that effect—which a spokesperson for the NGA later said had been taken out of context, since "the NGA does not authenticate artworks."[77] The listing for a "Rothko" *Untitled*, 1959 (oil on paper) offered by Christie's in May 2009 likewise represented that the work was being "considered for possible inclusion" in the NGA catalogue raisonné.[78] A fake Newman was featured in the 2008 inaugural exhibition for the Haunch of Venison Gallery's New York branch, curated by David Anfam. In the catalogue, *Abstract Expressionism—A World Elsewhere,* Anfam waxed eloquent about the painting: "A hitherto almost unknown Newman from his *annus mirabilis* of 1949 [pl. 34] is dense with the inky blueness that expanded into the epic panorama of *Cathedra* (1951)."[79] Two things stand out about the corresponding checklist entry, however. One is the line, "Private Collection, Courtesy Knoedler & Company, New York," which viewed in retrospect clearly connects the painting to the forgery scandal. The other oddity concerns what is not included. Listings for three other Newman works right above it carry the line "©2008 The Barnett Newman Foundation, New York/Artists Rights Society (ARS), New York."[80] The fact that the foundation did not assert copyright over entry number 34 might be a subtle hint that they were distancing themselves from attributing the painting to Newman.[81] Anfam recommended that "Newman" to the Albright-Knox Art Gallery for acquisition, and he suggested to Freedman that she should think about "some measure of recompense for my endeavors" (though he apparently never received any sort of payment from the gallery).[82] Abstract Expressionism scholar Stephen Polcari was enlisted to write glowing descriptions of ten of the Rosales canvases in research essays commissioned by Knoedler—with the additional embarrassment of having to admit, under questioning, that he had once said you can't tell one Rothko from another. Polcari justified his enthusiasm with the claim that they were "very good works" that "just happened to be done by other artists."[83] More impressive, perhaps, was how little he managed to make from the scam, compared to others, since he was paid just $300 per essay.

From the standpoint of public interest, it is unfortunate that all of the disputes were ultimately settled, with undisclosed terms. The case that went the farthest was the lawsuit by Domenico and Eleanore De Sole: a jury trial was underway, with extensive expert testimony already presented, when a settlement agreement was reached just before Freedman was due to take the stand. The De Soles had also gone to Knoedler wanting to buy a work by Scully and were told that nothing was available. Freedman was clearly eloquent in her praise of the "Rothko" they did acquire, but they were wise enough to ask her to put the statements she had made about the work in writing. A December 11, 2004, letter from Freedman to their daughter, Laura De Sole, repeated the Herbert provenance; declared that the painting would be listed in an upcoming supplement to the Rothko catalogue raisonné; and described the work as having been "viewed" by a long list of experts, including David Anfam, E.A. Carmean, Jr., Bonnie Clearwater, Dana Cranmer, Jack Flam, Laili Nasr, Stephen Polcari, Earl A. Powell III, Christopher Rothko, Irving Sandler, and Oliver Wick.[84] In testimony, however, it became clear that most had been quite noncommittal about what they were seeing, with observations that were far short of official authentication. According to Christopher Rothko, he said that the painting was "beautiful," but nothing more, "because I didn't want to be sitting here today," and he also stressed that he steered clear of authenticating his father's work as a general rule.[85] One of the most powerful aspects of the courtroom proceedings, however, was the display of the object itself. As described in *Artnews*, the presentation of the fake Rothko in court dramatized its precipitous fall from grace: "The painting had hung in the De Soles' house for about six years, behind expensive glass casing and rigged to an alarm system; in the courtroom, it was handled roughly, like a piece of cardboard."[86]

FALLOUT

It is difficult to know how much impact the Knoedler scandal will have on art-market practices, given the secretive nature of the business. But documents that have surfaced in various lawsuits indicate that sales at the top end of the art market are increasingly likely to be accompanied by a whole series of provisions ranging from statements of authenticity to assurances regarding clear title. Sotheby's took the proactive step of acquiring Martin's Orion Analytical, based on the conservation studio's reputation for forensic research.[87] (Martin is, however, quick to point out that he doesn't authenticate work; rather, he tries to look as exhaustively as possible to determine if any evidence is inconsistent with a particular attribution.)[88] Other recent developments include a new catalogue raisonné association that will, among other functions, provide members with discount legal advice, and an ongoing initiative to establish an international court of arbitration to mediate art law disputes.[89]

Viewed in retrospect, the forgeries promoted by Knoedler seem stunningly obvious, from the implausible provenance information to the misspelling of the signature on one of the fake Pollocks (rendered "Pollok"). Yet the scandal also highlights the distorting effect of the art market even for genuine examples by the same artists, with work that is interesting for a range of qualities entangled in market speculation that singles out a relatively small subset of artists for their investment potential. The transformation of art into trophy acquisition or market instrument can silence the voices capable of assessing the very qualities on which value is presumably based, with this suppression of expertise potentially threatening the whole speculative edifice.

It is hardly coincidental that most of the canonical works subject to this type of speculation were created by male artists associated with art-world activity in Europe and the United States. A few museums are beginning to respond to this dynamic in unexpected ways. Both the San Francisco Museum of Modern Art and the Baltimore Museum of Art have begun selectively selling a few examples by artists in this rarified group in order to diversify their collections. While there are potentially valid arguments against any plan to remove a historically significant work from a public collection and send it into the private marketplace, SFMOMA was able to acquire work by an impressive list of artists after selling a Rothko painting at Sotheby's for $50.1 million in 2019.[90] The Baltimore Museum's sale of seven collection works at Sotheby's in 2018 for $7.5 million likewise facilitated a series of new acquisitions, as part of an overall programming initiative that included dedicating all of their 2020 exhibitions to female artists.[91] The Rothko that provided SFMOMA with their acquisition budget windfall was indeed a classic example of the artist's work, and its auction price undoubtedly benefited from the prestige of its source. It was nonetheless only one of a number of important Rothko paintings in the collection, and the diverse range of material they were able to acquire afterward provides clear evidence of a market warped by speculative focus on a narrow band of "blue-chip" artists.

WIDER PURVIEW

The classic narrative, where a forger roguishly claims authorship of museum masterworks, takes an interesting twist in the case of Zhang Daqian, a twentieth-century Chinese artist who was likewise active as both a collector and a forger. There are various stories of Zhang gleefully claiming revered historical museum pieces as his

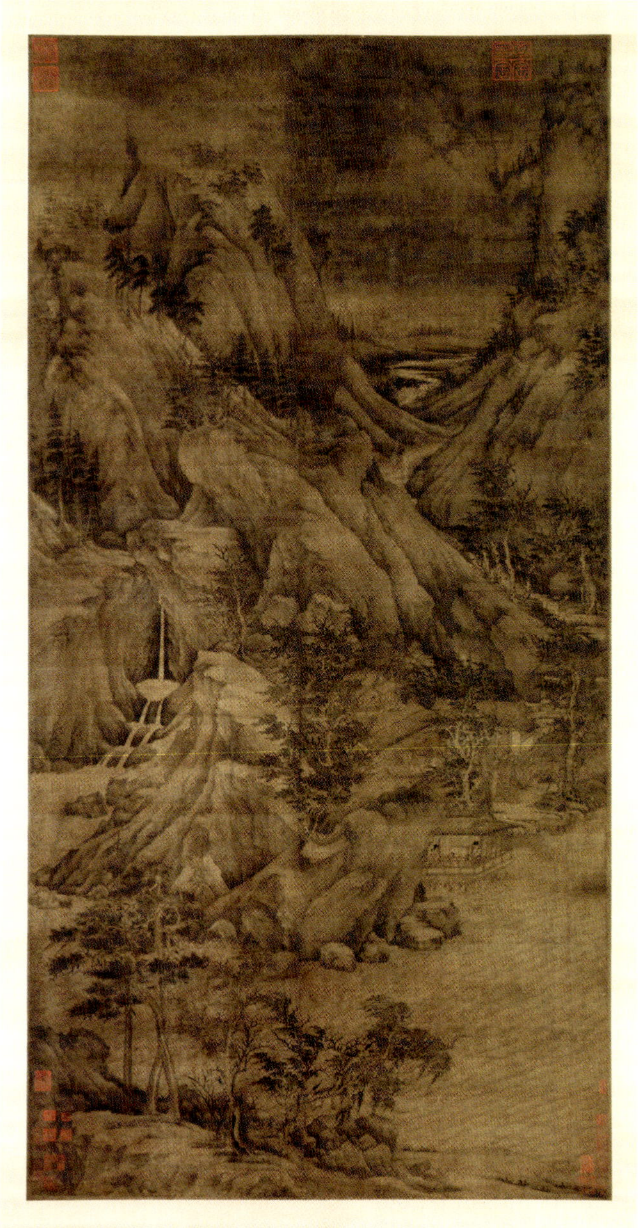

FIGURE 63
Attributed to Dong Yuan, *Riverbank*, Southern Tang dynasty (937–76), China. Hanging scroll; ink and color on silk; image 86¾ × 43 in. Metropolitan Museum of Art, CC0 1.0, Public Domain Dedication.

handiwork, yet his engagement with traditional Chinese painting was also the basis for highly popular work produced under his own name that continues to be avidly collected (and in turn forged) within the Chinese art market. One notable instance concerned the possibility that Zhang was the author of a hanging scroll in the Metropolitan Museum of Art attributed to the tenth-century Southern Tang dynasty artist Dong Yuan (figure 63). While there seems to be little question that the work was once owned by Zhang, there is less consensus about its origin. During a 1999 symposium held by the Met to debate the issue (which was followed by publication of the proceedings), art historian James Cahill forcefully stated the case for Zhang's authorship, but many others have remained confident in its authenticity, and it has continued to be exhibited as a tenth-century masterwork, with that attribution reinforced by the Met's declaration of its public domain status.[92]

The Chinese context is multifold, including the ongoing popularity of works referencing traditional styles, a longstanding culture of copies, and the relatively recent development of a significant art market (which in that respect resembles the compressed history of modern Chinese IP legislation referenced in chapter 1). A major *New York Times* feature from 2013 detailed how exponential growth in the Chinese art auction trade was initially accompanied by few regulations concerning either responsibility for selling fakes or accurately reporting which sales were actually completed.[93] Yet the complicated relationship between original and copy explored in Winnie Wong's analysis of the Dafen copy village, including various artists from around the world who have incorporated Dafen commissions into conceptually driven projects, is just one marker of a series of cultural intersections where an admixture of global information sharing and locally developed traditions can yield unexpected results.[94] A slightly earlier article by Wong on anti-counterfeiting activism in China by Zhao Bandi and Wang Hai also indicated a far larger framework for concerns about authenticity, extending throughout the world of consumer goods.[95]

Anxieties about fake consumer goods are hardly limited to China, with attempts to guard against counterfeit products, from luxury handbags to electronics, as a point of intersection between a rarified art trade and other forms of commerce. A multicountry survey of "Gen Z" (people born 1995–2000) conducted by the International Trademark Association in 2018 found, rather unsurprisingly, that the main reason to knowingly purchase a counterfeit was the inability to afford the real version of a luxury good, while motivations for avoiding fakes included concerns about quality, safety, and ethics.[96] But perhaps the most interesting tidbit was the high degree of intellectual property awareness, with a majority of respondents finding IP rights to be as important as physical property, even as they perceived the sale of counterfeits as widespread.

There are many important parallels between art-world authentication and wider forms of consumer culture. Within the various markets that encompass both "collectibles" and goods purchased for use, signs of authenticity include provenance, material consistency, and secure association with a specific brand name. This continuity was emphasized by a 2017 Winterthur Museum exhibition that opened with one of the Rothko forgeries sold by Knoedler, but also presented a range of other unmasked fakes, including a Chanel suit, a 1787 bottle of Château Lafitte wine that was supposed to have been owned by Thomas Jefferson, a Hermes Birkin bag, a Stradivarius violin, a Tiffany lampshade, and a Babe Ruth baseball glove, with some of the examples on loan from the Federal Bureau of Investigation.[97]

The world of luxury goods also includes certain types of brand signaling that are every bit as arcane as art-world authorship. Large logos are often found disproportionately on the inexpensive items in a fashion company's line, supplanted by subtle indicators on high-end items. There are even versions of the Richard Prince appropriation dynamic (where his repackaged imagery sells to a completely different market, at a dramatically inflated price point). Ikea reacted with humor when Balenciaga made a $2,145 version of the blue tote bag available at Ikea stores for ninety-nine cents, but others were less entertained by seeing luxury quotations of their modest merchandise.[98] Balenciaga was sued for copyright violation (and settled out of court) over its 2018 resort collection, which included clothing and bags priced at thousands of dollars that clearly evoked a line of similar New York City souvenirs printed with a kitschy mix of landmarks beneath a pink sky and a cursive-style city name.[99] The company was also taken to court over $275 keychains that mimicked tree-shaped car freshener devices typically encountered hanging from the rearview mirrors of old-style taxicabs.[100]

It is surprising, yet somehow fitting, to end a chapter on fakes in the same place where the history of copyright begins, with counterfeit books. Unauthorized reprints are making a dramatic comeback, enabled by access to scanning technologies, print-on-demand services, and Amazon's role as an umbrella organization for a vast network of both reputable and unscrupulous resellers. Recent book counterfeiting includes poor-quality reprints that have wound up intermixed with the real thing due to the structure of the Amazon marketplace, as well as content copied from self-published books and then presented under different titles and authorship. (The latter apparently are worthwhile, even if only a small number are sold, since so little human labor is required for production and distribution.) Amazon has been criticized for having few checks in place to prevent such infringement until it is drawn to their attention by those suffering the damage. Rather than being punished for its role in facilitating this commerce, however, Amazon is potentially rewarded, since the main recourse available to many small publishers who want to see their authorized goods given priority is to pay the fees necessary to have official vendor status or to run advertisements on the site.[101]

There is a core similarity between recent counterfeiting and early book piracy: someone is attempting to benefit, through replication, from the reputation or labor of others. Yet the global supply chains, production technologies, and communication networks behind these new versions of fakery are dramatically different than the localized and labor-intensive book-printing operations that inspired the first copyright legislation in eighteenth-century England. What has also changed is the extent to which individuals are attuned to, and potentially caught up in, issues of authorship and branding. Cynical behavior can be found in all sectors of the economy where cultural statements are transformed into marketable goods. Given the obvious excesses and opportunism, it is that much more important to consider the underlying value of cultural expressions, including the shared dialogue from which they emerge.

Legal cases that involve conflicts over artists refusing to authorize as expected, or contesting how others want to treat their work, draw attention back to the legal fiction of individual authorship at the heart of copyright. Likewise, claims made in the name of art's ineffable significance can be compared to the foregrounding of author benefits in early copyright legislation, with both serving to obfuscate crucial economic motivations. There are many valid reasons to guard against fakes, forgeries, and counterfeits, since their presentation as authorized examples will have a corrupting effect on artistic reputations and many related values. Within the art world, however, both the traffic in forged art, and many of the steps taken to weed fakes out, are motivated by a market where declarations about aesthetic impact become the basis for art's transformation into investment properties, and artistic attributions function as brand names for elite consumption.

CODA

Life in the Virtual Commons

THE UNMASKING OF A FORGED work of art tends to be a highly specialized affair, but the basic issues are closely related to frauds that circulate far more widely. One major area of concern centers on deepfakes, with both the term and related deceptions becoming the focus of attention starting around 2017. Attempts to manipulate photographs, film, and video date to the early history of each medium, with the transition to digital technologies facilitating increasingly seamless fabrications. Only in recent years, however, has sophisticated artificial-intelligence software become widely available. Some initial trends were amusingly goofy, such as swapping actors into alternate movies, and others ugly, including the trick of placing someone's face onto a nude body that quickly became known as nonconsensual pornography.[1] The greatest danger, however, is clearly the potential for fakes to be believed in the context of a fragmented political landscape that is already subject to organized campaigns of social media disinformation. As examples from the art world demonstrate, a fake doesn't have to be terribly skillful or convincing if it is presented within a framework that prepares its audience to receive it as plausible. Attempts to debunk frauds are equally challenging when there is no consensus regarding who might have the authority or expertise to do so.

The dialogue around fakes is only one of the many places where art-world dynamics are symptomatic of larger issues. Questions regarding ownership over imagery that artists began pushing to the fore through analog-based appropriation strategies have become crucial in an era characterized not just by incessant posting and tweeting, but also the "re-" version of each of these acts. Freedom of panorama also takes on new significance in relation to virtual worlds where every last blade of grass is already encoded.

Two interlocking issues are key. One is an individual's relationship to creative activity by others, including the extent to which it is possible to engage with the vast range of proprietary material in the surrounding world. The second has to do with ownership of oneself, which encompasses not just creative expressions, but also increasingly expansive troves of data generated through interactions with modern networked environments. Complicating matters further is the tangled relationship between commercial and noncommercial forms, with the overlaps helping to blur distinctions between authorship and branding. It is important to pay close attention to our rights as we move through a world increasingly saturated by intangible forms of property.

OWNERSHIP

Returning to the example of Jill Magid's response to control over the Barragán archive that opened this book, it is helpful to look at an earlier aspect of her project as well, since Magid's diamond gesture was part of an extended flirtation with the interesting and not necessarily intuitive boundaries that frame what is allowed and forbidden under national and international copyright regimes. In her 2013 exhibition *Woman with Sombrero* at New York's Art in General, which also focused on this archival material, she displayed physical copies of books that she altered by attaching a frame around one of the publication's already-reproduced images (see figure 64). By taking advantage of distinctions between making a copy versus one's right to manipulate a physical example that one owns, Magid drew attention to one of the paradoxical limits on how one can and cannot use readily available and familiar material. These relatively humble objects with their asymmetrically applied frames point to the larger problem of layered rights: as a form of collage, they are Magid's work, but there are at least two other authorship claims at play—Barragán's and the photographer's.[2] Had she reproduced the images, she could have mounted a fair use defense. But there should be no question, based on first sale rights, that she could do what she wanted with her copy of the book *Luis Barragán: The Quiet Revolution,* including putting it on display with a somewhat unexpected frame around the photograph on the cover.

One major challenge associated with the shift from physical to digital formats for books, music, and videos is the loss of rights previously associated with what, in the

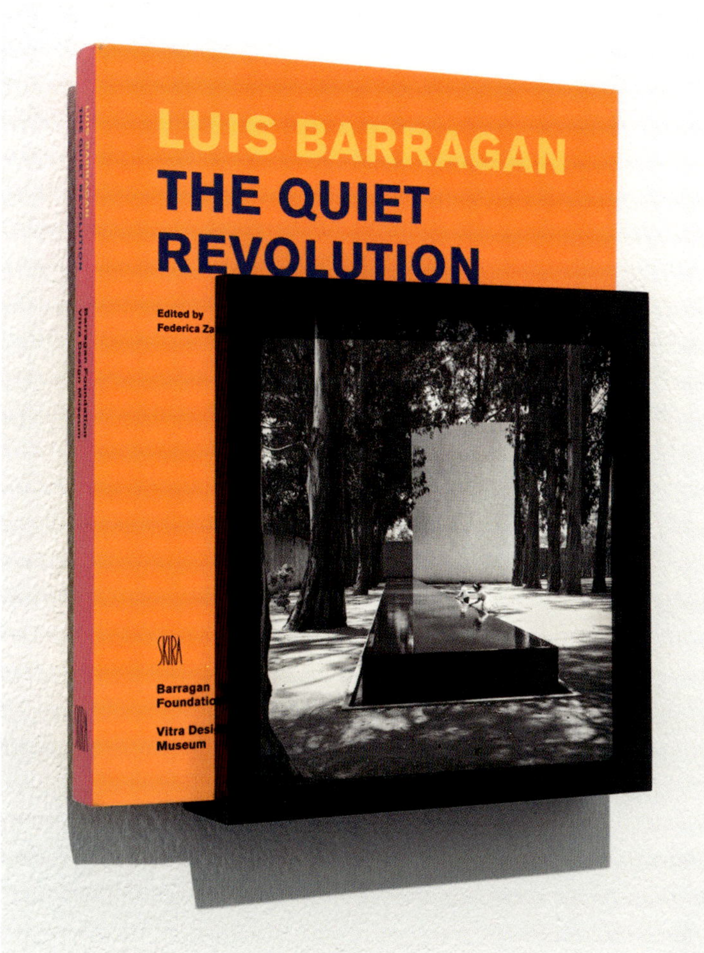

FIGURE 64
Jill Magid, *El Bebedero at Las Arboledas by Armando Salas Portugal*, 2013. Book, frame, 12 × 9½ in. Photo: Stefan Jaeggi, Kunst Halle Sankt Gallen. Courtesy the artist and LABOR, Mexico City.

United States, is known as the doctrine of first sale (with comparable provisions in other countries). The first sale principle establishes a distinction between intellectual property rights and what an individual is allowed to do with a physical object one has acquired. Collections of analog records as well as digitized music distributed as CDs could be resold by their owners if their tastes changed. Downloads, by contrast, cannot be readily transferred, and even holding onto what one has purchased often depends on continued support for specific platforms. The replacement of an ownership model with streaming has probably made this concern obsolete for many. Yet first sale rights are just one of many privileges of ownership that have dramatically withered away in the digital era: the limitations will only continue to expand in relation to the internet of things, sometimes referred to as the "internet of things you don't own."[3]

Through a combination of digital rights management, End User License Agreements, click-wrap contracts, and other legal constraints, users are stripped of full control over a large number of devices in their lives. In one early example of resistance to this type of contingent ownership, Apple's restrictions on what software could be loaded onto phones led users to "jailbreak" their devices. Although the US Copyright Office eventually approved exemptions to Digital Millennium Copyright Act (DMCA) anti-circumvention rules to make this legal, Apple's initial response to an Electronic Frontier Foundation petition indicated that, although iPhone users may own the hardware in question, they are "licensees, not owners, of the copies of iPhone operating software"—which is, not coincidentally, necessary for basic hardware functionality.[4] Arguments in favor of the right to repair have highlighted restrictions on farmers who rely on John Deere equipment and are forced to use authorized service centers controlled by the company for all maintenance (on top of a different set of IP limitations on many patented strains that require farmers to purchase new seeds each year, rather than saving a portion of the previous year's crop).[5] Increasing numbers of products follow a business model that consumers may find familiar from inkjet printers, requiring branded supplies that have to be replenished on a timetable determined by resident software rather than a user's perception of when they have been expended. Companies can also decide to stop supporting a product in ways that render it nonoperative long before it would otherwise wear out, and there are few security standards for internet-linked functionality. A purchase that actually requires a lifetime of further purchases from the same company might most accurately be described as a rental.

What else can and can't be owned? Pantone does not, for example, control the colors in the vast rainbow that the company precisely codifies, but it has established proprietary rights over the system according to which they are articulated, via their trademarked color guides. On that basis it issues licenses to anyone who wants to claim to be operating in accordance with Pantone standards, or as they put it on their website, "Pantone approved."[6] Color can also be part of overall appearance or identity, known as trade dress, meaning that the employment of colors associated with a particular brand or product can be restricted in relation to similar uses (such as Christian Louboutin's trademark claims regarding red-soled shoes), though that does not extend to unrelated uses of that hue. There does not yet appear to be a shortage of color options in the context of trademark or trade dress. But there has been speculation about the possible depletion of words and phrases available to businesses attempting to establish trademarked branding. Potentially language is a finite resource, at least for marketing purposes, with a lot of the good bits already claimed.[7]

PRESERVATION AND INFRINGEMENT

It took more than ten years for musicians to understand the full destructive scope of a 2008 fire in the California backlot of Universal Studios. Initial reports minimized what had been lost, characterizing it as mainly videotapes that were not the only copy of the material in question. Not until a series of *New York Times* articles in 2019 did it become clear how many historic recordings from Universal's music archive had been destroyed.[8] Lost in the blaze were analog master tapes from the late 1940s forward, along with recent digital masters. Some were replicated in tape archives elsewhere, but many were unique, with the scope reflecting the number of labels that had been acquired by Universal Music Group over the decades. Music industry business models, which have wrested control over master recordings away from countless musicians, meant that a huge share of common cultural heritage was held in private hands, stockpiled in a warehouse building that hardly represented the most advanced archival storage standards, and subject to a very partial digitalization initiative to back up the analog originals. Given the degree to which the company succeeded in deflecting initial press reports about the calamity, it is also worth noting that information about the destruction was revealed mainly because of a lawsuit between Universal Music Group and NBCUniversal concerning liability for damages in the leased space. In one sense, much of the music is still around, in circulation. Lost, however, was the ultimate fidelity for familiar songs that might have been remastered in new formats at some point in the future, along with countless outtakes and other tracks that had never been made public.

At the opposite end of the spectrum from the model of a unique original, subject (ideally) to focused conservation efforts, is a distributed approach to preservation. "Lots of copies keep stuff safe," or LOCKSS, is both shorthand for this approach in general and the name of a specific peer-to-peer library preservation and archiving strategy promoted by Stanford University Libraries.[9] One of the major roadblocks to this type of initiative, however, is resistance from copyright holders, since the basic principle relies on multiple digital copies preserved in different settings. There's also the problem of securing archival material in the first place, with libraries and other nonprofit institutions sometimes having to compete with speculators who see such resources as treasure troves for future licensing fees. The flip side of the coin can be found in what Abigail De Kosnik has characterized as "rogue archives," generated as part of fan culture, and focused on material potentially overlooked by institutional venues—with idealism reflecting a vital free-culture agenda, but potentially accompanied by the built-in fragility of volunteer efforts.[10]

Older versions of software, necessary to access earlier files or to play abandoned or legacy versions of video games, have been one major focus. Copyright issues around preserving software are particularly challenging, given the stringent provisions of the DMCA in the United States, with the exceptions announced every three years suggesting the encompassing nature of its constraints. Those issued in 2018 included exemptions for prohibitions against circumvention of technologies protecting copyrighted works in order to add captions or audio for the disabled; access to computer controls in appliances and vehicles for purposes of repair; and the possibility of accessing certain computer programs no longer commercially available to allow preservation by libraries, archives, and museums.[11] But one of the hottest areas, online gaming, received only a very partial allowance—opening up options for continued play after verification is no longer supported, but not full emulation of legacy games on alternate servers.[12] The need for such exceptions, as well as the cumbersome process for achieving them, helps demonstrate the draconian scope of the law itself.

An equally challenging aspect of preservation in relation to digital transmission is the constantly changing nature of what one might describe as the archive itself. It is ironic on many levels that one early demonstration of contingent ownership involved Amazon's remote removal of editions of George Orwell's *1984* from Kindle devices. In Orwell's dystopia, past news was constantly rewritten to make it conform to current leadership rhetoric, and much of what appears on social media or various web sites has the potential to be equally fleeting or malleable. So far the Internet Archive is the main bulwark against this loss of recent history, but it is a necessarily partial record, and it seems striking that this vital resource is a private nonprofit rather than a government-sponsored initiative.

VIRTUAL AND AUGMENTED REALITY

The already complex and confusing issues surrounding freedom of panorama are due to become dramatically more intense as individuals become increasingly immersed in virtual worlds, and as physical spaces are interwoven with digital images and information. With our technologies moving in fits and starts toward a future where augmented reality (AR) programs and devices are commonplace, it is important to pay attention to what rights—and responsibilities—are associated with this real-time manipulation of perceptions of physical space. A few examples suggest some of the ways that these exchanges have already begun to unfold.

During the Pokémon Go craze in 2016, there were stories of disconcerted homeowners confronted by crowds converging on Pokémon gyms tagged to their coordinates. Given that players unrelated to the proprietors could potentially claim ownership of the gyms, issues raised by this example include the degree to which rights over virtual space might or might not be tied to possession of physical property. If they are potentially separable, perhaps there is a comparison to mineral rights, which can in certain instances be retained and sold independently from a typical property transfer (as some discover to their deep chagrin). In the case of Pokémon Go geotagging, the private residences identified as "gyms" were generally buildings that had been converted from earlier functions (a former church, for example), which raised other questions about what database sources were being employed to create the locational lures.[13]

There was a different form of backlash when Snapchat collaborated with Jeff Koons on a 2017 public art exhibition that allowed users to view his work superimposed on specific geotagged locations. Placing a physical work of sculpture in a public space, even on a temporary basis, is an involved process, and rightfully so, since there are important issues regarding how spaces held for and by the public should be used. A video released as part of the publicity showed a weird, cult-like circle of people standing around an empty area and holding up their phones as they stared, apparently engrossed, at the sculpture visible on their screens. It is difficult to know how many people interacted with the sculptures in Central Park or any of the other sites during Koons's virtual exhibition—but the overlay of people trying to experience a place without mediation and those who are there for a virtual lure could become more of an issue as such phenomena grow in frequency. It's also amusing to note a comeback in kind, circulated on Instagram, that showed a graffiti-covered balloon dog sculpture in the same Central Park setting (albeit simply an image, not hacking into the original Snapchat exhibition, as some reported).[14]

A group of artists generated a different type of graffiti via an unauthorized augmented reality gallery at New York's Museum of Modern Art in 2018, making a statement, they claimed, against museum exclusivity through an app that superimposed various types of imagery (visible on phone screens) over paintings by Jackson Pollock.[15] One might view this gesture as part of a long history of creative museum interventions. But it was also troubling on a number of levels. First, the lure of the screen is already problematic enough, including the phenomenon of people experiencing museums with their backs to the artwork while focused primarily on taking selfies. (Not coincidently, the 2014 Koons retrospective at the Whitney Museum was a major example of this.) Also, while there are many reasons to take a critical stance toward MoMA's institutional power and the various art historical narratives it has promoted over the years, this particular action involved superimposing images over the work of another artist. Even though US legal protections are somewhat limited, there would certainly be an outcry about respecting Pollock's moral and integrity rights in the unlikely event that someone proposed making physical additions to the work. To what extent should virtual additions be treated in the same fashion?

Around the same time (also 2018), there were press reports of another museum intervention whereby some of the works stolen from Boston's Isabella Stewart Gardner Museum in 1990 were returned via AR to the empty frames that mark their absence in the Gardner's fixed collection. But this turned out to be a promotional stunt by a firm called Cuseum, related to their business of creating apps for museums to provide overlays of information and interactivity that will presumably make them attractive to younger generations. Their first iterations used Bluetooth proximity beacons to activate the apps (and, not coincidentally, also track viewing activities). But the Gardner stunt, done without the museum's participation, relied instead on image recognition tools from ARKit—Apple's augmented reality development platform for iOS mobile devices.[16]

In relation to the back and forth between physical and virtual spheres, however, it is worth noting that even before the era of digitalized data, the world of information could have an impact on everyday life. In one instance, the town of Agloe, New York, was invented by Otto G. Lindberg and Ernest Alpers and placed on an intersection of two dirt roads in the Catskill Mountains, with the name derived from the initials of the two mapmakers. It was an example of a "paper town," which along with "trap streets" (fake street names, also on maps), invented numbers in phone directories, and fake entries in dictionaries, have been employed as a bulwark against subsequent mapmakers or compilers, who might be tempted to forgo having to sort through the underlying information (which can't be copyrighted), and rely instead on its expression in previously published works. The appearance of the town of Agloe on a later Rand McNally map provoked a claim of copyright infringement.[17] But in the intervening years, people following the original map information had turned it into an actual, if somewhat minimal, location, with the establishment of the Agloe General Store and a couple of nearby homes. After the store went out of business, the town continued to appear on maps for a while longer, but had largely been delisted by the time that John Green's 2008 young adult novel *Paper Towns,* made into a movie in 2015, drew renewed attention to the void location.

Then there is the matter of shared perception. Anyone who uses a computer or smartphone is familiar with the targeted advertisements that follow individuals from platform to platform. These include not just goods and services, but also political content, and result in the supplanting of a communal media experience with messages pre-selected by the algorithms employed to sift through our data trails. Location-based promotions are quickly becoming part of this mix, meaning that individuals are subject to increasingly specific information prompted by interactions with physical environments.

One version of this targeted future has already arrived in the realm of sports, where viewers watching from home are likely to encounter billboard ads that appear to be sited in the stadium where an event is taking place, even though they are actually seen only by the broadcast audience. Starting in 2017, Major League Baseball employed a green screen on the field itself (literally a blank screen for ads visible to different broadcast areas). But further developments have allowed ads to be substituted in place of those perceived by stadium audiences, including modified feeds that provide specifically targeted messaging to different sectors of the global soccer audience.[18]

A second order of concern relates to the rights of individuals to record and transmit their experiences in virtual worlds—with this updated version of freedom of panorama intersecting with the possibility that the entire world might be described as proprietary. Following its debut, Google Street View quickly became the focus of various forms of street photography. Both Michael Wolf, who received an honorable mention from the 2011 World Press photo contest for his "A Series of Unfortunate Events," and Doug Rickard, in regard to his "A New American Picture," have described a process that involved setting up a camera on a tripod, pointed toward the screen/digital window—in that respect a more controlled process of framing than a screen grab. But others, such as Jon Rafman and Emilio Vavarella, have emphasized the interface itself, with clear evidence of screen capture or (particularly in the early days) an interest in unexpected glitches.[19] Physical versions of street photography can come up against already complex freedom of panorama limitations emanating from both copyright restrictions and crossing property lines, but they do not involve click-through terms of use as a global condition of entry.

Some of the constraints associated with traversing the world via Google Street View are obvious, including the blurring of faces and certain other types of information. But there is the potential for more manipulation. As early as 2010, Google made news for patenting a system to update billboards that appear in Street View: titled "Claiming Real Estate in Panoramic or 3D Mapping Environments for Advertising," it would effectively allow Google to resell updated advertising.[20] While it is not clear whether Google has ever attempted to activate this type of function, this is only one example of the major patent activity around location-based advertising. It also opens up questions about the rights of advertisers—or property owners in general—concerning how their physical sites are rendered in a virtual landscape. Here, too, there is an interesting precedent, in a lawsuit against Sony Corporation over alterations to the content of Times Square billboards that appeared in the 2002 *Spider-Man* movie. Finding that the alterations were free speech, the judge who ruled on the case also shot down claims of trespass based on the use of laser beams as part of the digital recording process during filming.[21]

Another significant focus of attention and resources is the world of gaming, including Massively Multiplayer Online Role-Playing Games (MMORPGs), where players are enticed to spend extended periods of time inhabiting alternate universes, many of which include virtual goods that can be acquired in exchange for actual money. One question concerns how much control players have over interactive aspects of any environment: Second Life, which allowed users to connect in various ways through their avatars, including building property and engaging in trade, granted participants rights to their creations, but required them to license their use to Linden Labs. In relation to World of Warcraft (WoW), the company that owns the game, Blizzard Entertainment, has established parameters for certain types of user modifications and extensions while placing limitations on commercial or stand-alone versions.[22] Blizzard has also taken legal action against fans who have established alternate servers with legacy versions of the game, sometimes with remarkable speed.[23]

One of Cory Doctorow's arguments for revising laws for the internet age concerns the intrinsic role of copying ("loading") for any form of internet transfer, even if, in the case of streaming, the copy is not retained.[24] Blizzard has relied on this aspect of the media landscape to use copyright to enforce their terms of service. They prohibit players from using bots to continue their game when they are not on their keyboard, and because users of bots are violating their license, then the copy of the game loaded onto the corresponding computer's RAM is a copyright violation.[25] Yet video game companies have generally been tolerant of fans who broadcast themselves playing, both edited versions and livestreams. And perhaps this also leaves an opening for artists to engage in various ways with the worlds traversed within video games.

In a particularly noteworthy example, Angela Washko's multiyear feminist intervention in WoW brought together a number of her interests, including multiplayer games

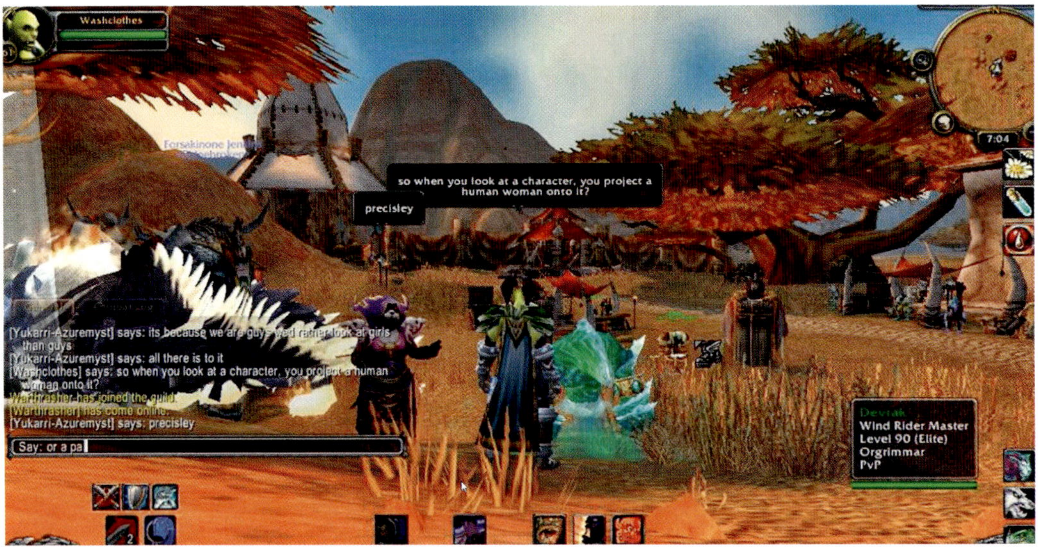

FIGURE 65
Angela Washko, *Playing A Girl*, 2013, from *The Council on Gender Sensitivity and Behavioral Awareness in World of Warcraft* (series). Still from video. Courtesy the artist.

and the need to question versions of toxic behavior associated with what has become known as the "manosphere." Her four-year project, *The Council on Gender Sensitivity and Behavioral Awareness in World of Warcraft,* emphasized interactions around the topic of feminism within the game, with live performances as well as stills and video excerpts representing the project in art-world contexts (see figure 65).[26] Having succeeded in gaining access to levels of the game available only to avid players, she attempted to open up a dialogue about gender within spaces where participants often feel free to exchange misogynistic, homophobic, and racist views they might be more circumspect about expressing in other contexts. The interactions, which covered a variety of topics, included questions to male players about their choice to use female avatars—with the frequent answer being that they preferred to look at the back of a female figure as they played.

Critics of restrictions on the freedom of panorama point to the way that the human brain processes images captured (and in that sense temporarily stored) by the retina. Such questions are due to become increasingly complex as physical and virtual realities continue to converge. One early attempt to create a real-time interface, Google Glass, was a spectacular failure: announced with much fanfare in a limited release in 2013 and full issue in 2014, its sales were halted in January 2015, and associated social media channels were deleted in January 2016. During the short time the product was out in the wild, however, certain IP and privacy issues became immediately apparent when people wearing the devices were denied entrance to movie theaters and nightclubs. With far less media hype, however, Google retooled the technology for corporate sales, under the title

Google Glass Enterprise Edition, and pitched it as part of the growing market for wearables that can facilitate both efficient information delivery and worker tracking.[27] Amazon is also attempting to extend the alarming reach already evident in their Ring security systems by pushing out wearables that will interface with their other smart technology.[28]

If science fiction gives us one series of extrapolations, often dystopic, about futures that might evolve from our present coordinates, patents are another potential window. Patent mapping—showing interconnected webs of citation—can provide a way of gaining insight into where technology might be moving. The category of "mixed reality" does seem to be the locus of significant activity. Facebook's interest in developing augmented reality glasses is evident in various patents, including one that details how audio signals would be delivered through vibrations in the cartilage behind the ear, so that the ear canal is still unobstructed for ambient sound.[29] Given that Facebook already possesses far more information than it should about the lives of its users (and anyone else tagged in their posts), it is important to think about the privacy implications of augmented reality glasses in general. Because of the need to collect data about physical surroundings, users voluntarily submit to external surveillance of everything in their line of sight. Another area of intense patent activity related to the race to develop autonomous vehicles also emphasizes the real-time translation of immense amounts of information about dynamic physical environments into immediately useable data.

In 2016, Apple registered a patent on a system that would use infrared signals to prevent concertgoers from filming or photographing the event.[30] There have also been reports about potentially restoring partial vision to the blind by transmitting video imagery captured via glasses to an implant in the brain.[31] Current assistive technologies, including the types of retransmission that facilitate blind or deaf access, require exceptions to copyright provisions that otherwise prevent replication. If (or perhaps when) digital devices to aid vision become widely adopted—such as the smart contact lens for which Sony filed a 2016 patent application—it is not difficult to imagine issues with DRM (digital rights management) interventions that could prevent not only recording, but even perceiving, copyright-protected content.[32]

We have not yet landed in the landscape envisioned in *Black Mirror*'s 2014 *White Christmas* episode, where it is possible for individuals to block contacts so that they are seen by others as nothing but static, even when encountered in the physical world. But as ways of interfacing with our environments are increasingly software driven, a future where records of our surroundings are instantaneously amended is increasingly likely. Extrapolating from personalized media feeds, it is all-too-easy to imagine a time when, via reliance on digital devices, we will both see and record different views of the physical world than the person standing next to us.

DATA AND PRIVACY

Neighbors of photographer Arne Svenson were disconcerted to discover that he had been using a telephoto lens to capture images of people and pets visible through uncurtained

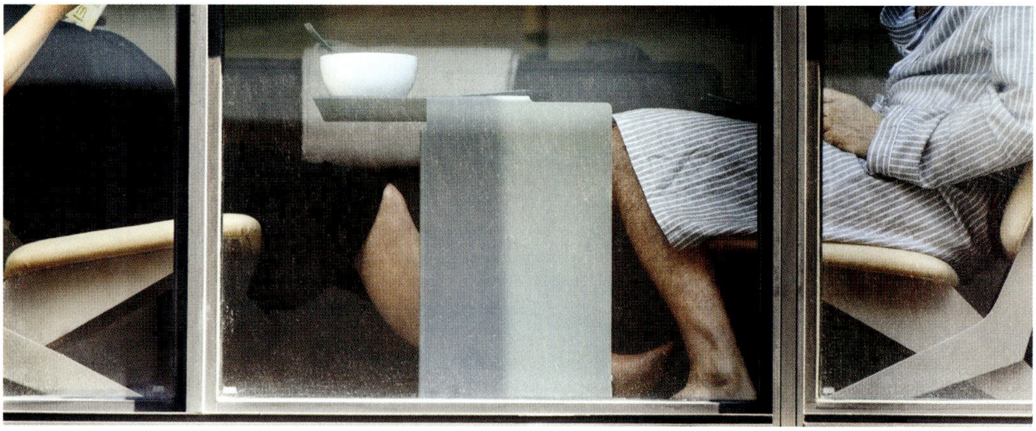

FIGURE 66
Arne Svenson, *Neighbors #1*, 2012. Pigment print, 26 × 63 in., edition of 5. Courtesy the artist.

windows in their Manhattan apartments (see figure 66). Svenson nonetheless prevailed on First Amendment grounds when he was sued for invasion of privacy under New York State's right-of-privacy statute. The neighbors argued that the sale of the work at Svenson's gallery violated protections against the use of someone's likeness for commercial purposes without permission. But the New York Appellate Division ruling (which affirmed Svenson's lower court victory) stressed the status of his work as art—and therefore not a "use for advertising or trade purposes" under the relevant statute.[33] Clearly there was a double issue at play. The inhabitants who were carrying out their daily lives near their apartment windows had to be aware that people in other buildings, or even passersby, could potentially see in at the same time that they were able to look out. Yet the fact that someone accompanied looking with taking a photograph apparently felt like a more significant violation. Emphasizing that he had generally avoided capturing faces, focusing instead on fragments, or people turned away, Svenson pointed to much more pervasive violations of privacy: "social media, banks, internet companies, etc., know far more about the occupants of the building than I ever would learn through the process of taking photographs of their hands, backs, and legs."[34]

Often the most serious type of gaffe a politician can make is accidentally telling the truth—and the same might be said of technology executives. In 2010 Eric Schmidt, then Google's chief executive, not only suggested that people who weren't happy about having their private residences captured by Google Street View, "can just move," but even more sweepingly told an interviewer, "We know where you are. We know where you've been. We can more or less know what you're thinking about."[35] Around the same time, Google was forced to admit that it had collected personal data from wireless networks within range of its vehicles while they were taking Street View images. This is just one example of the many ways that our data spills out and is potentially scooped up, with ever-expanding storage capacities enabling long-term retention of a remarkably huge trove. If anyone is not sure how many traces they leave via their online activities and use of smart devices, they should make their way over to Tactical Tech's Data Detox Kit.[36] As part of step-by-step instructions to reduce one's data trail, they send the curious on a guided tour of some of the major collections of information associated with using Google, smartphones, and social media sites.

A few high-profile cases hint at the privacy issues at stake in the so-called internet of things. In 2016 a user who opted to remain anonymous sued the maker of the We-Vibe sex toy and app over the company's retention of data, including preferred vibrator settings, length of sessions, and associated user email addresses.[37] In 2017, Germany's Federal Network Agency classified the My Friend Cayla doll, a popular interactive toy, as an "illegal espionage apparatus," warning retailers to stop selling the toy unless its ability to connect to the internet was permanently disabled, and recommending that parents destroy it. The decision followed evidence that the doll's wireless connection was dangerously insecure, allowing easy access by hackers who could listen to children talking with the doll and potentially even become part of their conversations.[38] Certain Roomba vacuum cleaners record all the obstacles they encounter, creating a highly detailed map of a user's house that could be shared or marketed—though when iRobot CEO Colin Angle was quoted about this potential in 2017, the response prompted him to insist that such data would only be divulged with consumer consent.[39] An article on the site *TechDirt* recommended dumb tech as a corrective to "an age where your Barbie can be hacked and used to spy on your kids, your refrigerator can be hacked to gain access to your Gmail account, your smart tea kettle can provide a nice attack vector on your home network, and your 'smart' television watches you every bit as often as you watch it."[40]

Geotagging is one of the many ways of tracking and recording an individual's movements, sometimes linked with increasingly sophisticated methods to introduce virtual content into one's physical experience. But the impact on shared resources can be just as problematic as threats to individual privacy, including the hordes of people that can suddenly descend on locations that looked good in someone else's selfies. Leave No Trace, a group that promotes thoughtful use of the outdoors, is just one of an increasing number of organizations that encourages people to "stop and think about their actions and the potential consequences of posting pictures, GPS data, detailed maps, etc. to social media."[41] Location data can also be deadly, both individually and collectively. Soldiers are warned to be cautious about sharing photographs, given the metadata generally included, and to pay close attention to apps that track one's location. In one striking case, aggregate information, or heatmaps, based on data uploaded by users of the Strava fitness app clearly indicated the location of highly classified military installations in regions where few, besides military personnel, were tracking their exercise activity in that fashion. On the company website, it was even possible to discover the names of individual users who had not changed the default privacy settings.[42]

An informed individual can at least choose not to upload fitness tracking. But in many other instances, from credit agency reporting to the collection of consumer information, it is not possible to opt out—and these same companies seem to be remarkably bad at protecting the sensitive data that nobody gave them permission to collect in the first place. Biometric documentation is a particularly significant area. In the United States, one major result of a biometric privacy law passed by Illinois in 2008, which requires affirmative consent, has been an ongoing demonstration of how pervasive collecting of this information has already become—including facial recognition initiatives by Google and Facebook that scan facial geometry for anyone who happens to be the subject of an uploaded photograph, whether they use the service in question or not.[43] In Europe, the General Data Protection Regulation allows member countries to establish rules about what data can be processed or shared, along with significant fines for violations. While it can be difficult to anticipate, or even keep tabs on, the many ways that such data might be abused, information released by a group called Privacy International has helped to track the spread of surveillance technologies, including government initiatives, and the companies that support such efforts.[44] As they point out, countries that provide legal protections for their own citizens often do not prevent technology produced on their shores from being sold to more repressive regimes.

The source material for facial recognition databases can come from anything from official documentation to selfies. In the United States, there was only rather belated recognition that state driver's license photos had been incorporated into law-enforcement registries. A nightmare vision of private/public cooperation suggested by a 2018 patent application by Amazon that would allow smart doorbells to monitor neighborhoods and report suspicious activity directly to law enforcement agencies seems to have been quickly put into action via partnerships with US police departments.[45] Yet intermixed with worries about how extensive such surveillance has become is a different type of danger. Because of how the technology is engineered, as well as who is included in the datasets, many versions of facial recognition are notoriously unreliable in their ability to discern individuals from minority groups, leading to a whole host of dangers based on the potential for misidentification.[46]

At least two important issues are at stake. One is how definitions of public and private space will evolve in response to the interweaving of virtual and physical experiences. The other concerns the digital record itself, as live recording and postproduction manipulation become potentially indistinguishable. Copyright is certainly very much at play here, but it is deeply entwined with other legal issues and strategies. Laws about privacy—which vary dramatically from country to country—can sometimes provide partial checks on the massive industry of assembling and marketing data about all aspects of our lives. There is also the realm of patents, which are essential to establishing different forms of interface between physical and virtual worlds. And there is the matter of contract law, since an individual's ability to navigate virtual realms is likely to be governed by terms of use that establish a range of preconditions and restrictions.

ENCLOSURE

The introduction to Lawrence Lessig's 2008 book *Remix* opens with the mundane but crucial example of a twenty-nine second video that Stephanie Lenz uploaded to YouTube in 2007 of her eighteen-month-old son dancing to the vaguely discernable sound of Prince's "Let's Go Crazy" playing on a radio in her kitchen.[47] A few months after she posted the video, someone from Universal Music Group came across it, and the company sent YouTube a takedown notice. Although this is a common occurrence when amateur video happens to include some form of copyrighted material, what Lenz had captured is also a typical moment in daily lives saturated by media of all kinds emanating from devices throughout our environments, and Lenz did not readily capitulate. In addition to informing YouTube that the video should not have been taken down, since it did not constitute infringement, she found her way to the Electronic Frontier Foundation, which agreed to help her pursue a fair use case.

As Lessig pointed out, it was absurd to think that the low-fidelity fragment of Prince's song playing in the background would constitute a substitute for someone looking for a copy of the music. Although the case dragged on for a full decade, Lenz scored a partial victory when the Ninth Circuit Court of Appeals ruled that copyright owners must consider whether fair use might apply before sending a takedown notice, in addition to reaffirming that fair use is not infringement. But the court left open a wide loophole by indicating that inappropriate takedown notices could be shielded from liability for misrepresentation if the copyright holder subjectively believed that the use in question was infringement.[48]

In another example of copyright overreach, photographer Carol Highsmith received a takedown notice from Getty Images for photographs she had shot herself and posted to her own website. Highsmith had made a point of allowing access to her images of American culture by donating thousands of her photos to the Library of Congress, to be made available for free public use. The takedown notice sent to Highsmith, along with an earlier case involving photographs posted by Daniel Morel to Twitter, drew attention to the willingness of Getty Images to charge licensing fees for certain photographs where they did not have clear rights, along with a large number of public domain images incorporated into their catalogue of stock material.[49] But in response to Highsmith, Getty Images largely succeeded with its defense that they were not prevented from commercializing public domain material if clients chose to pay their fees rather than source the images for free elsewhere.

Taken together, these examples indicate the crucial importance of fair use as a safeguard against the all-too-common attitude that any quotation of copyright-protected material should be treated as infringement, along with the many strategies companies have developed for monetizing what should be understood as shared resources. The

Highsmith case also points to the role that Creative Commons licensing can play in providing notice that an author is allowing certain types of reuse while potentially retaining rights that guard against appropriation for purely commercial ends.[50] Creative Commons and related forms of open-source licensing offer an important alternative to the "all rights reserved" associated with default copyright. Yet the need to resort to private rather than public law to achieve this end reflects larger challenges.

A number of scholars have drawn comparisons between enclosure movements, where land once used in common was fenced off as private property, and the increasingly dense network of intellectual property claims. Although the commons is not directly equivalent to the public domain (since there can be community-based restrictions on how commons are shared), the general trend in copyright law has been to extend protection, often in ways that return material that had entered the public domain to protected status.[51] "The tragedy of the commons" refers to a longstanding argument in favor of privatization, centered on problems of inefficiency as well as self-interested actions that can undermine the viability of shared resources.[52] James Boyle has nonetheless argued against invoking this rationale to justify IP limitations: the use of intellectual property is typically "nonrival," in contrast to potentially conflicting exploitation of common land, and "enclosure of the information commons" has the very clear potential to stifle innovation.[53]

This "second enclosure" movement was already well underway before digital encoding and transmission became commonplace.[54] It is only in recent decades, however, that technology shifts have dramatically transformed who might run up against copyright or other IP constraints. Circa 1950, Boyle observes (before widespread access to photocopiers, VCRs, and all the reproductive technologies that followed), an individual consumer would have been hard pressed to commit an act of infringement, meaning that intellectual property was primarily a concern for large-scale commercial entities.[55] But the growing ease of replication, remixing, and circulation has changed everything; each new development has contributed to blurring distinctions between consumption and production, as well as between commercial and noncommercial activities.

The public domain encompasses material that could qualify as intellectual property, but is not presently protected, and elements that are too basic to be eligible for IP ownership claims. And it is being threatened on both fronts. Most jurisdictions have extended copyright terms, with the life of the author plus seventy years, or ninety-five years from publication as the norm, and protections granted retroactively. Lawsuits, particularly around music copyrights and patents, demonstrate an ongoing land grab that increasingly encompasses the rudimentary components of shared cultural and scientific exploration. Furthermore, automatic copyright that does not require registration means that all manner of minor, inconsequential jottings and other haphazard expressions are potentially subject to ownership claims.

In the voiceover for her film about her Barragán pursuit, Magid asks: "What happens to an artist's legacy when it is controlled by a corporation?"[56] While the Barragán example, like many covered in this book, has its own peculiar twists, the overall threat of framing creative work primarily as property is clear. Creators and inventors do need protections, both for their own benefit and to encourage activities that will contribute to the culture at large, yet overly broad ownership rights stifle innovation. There is also a great deal of confusion and misinformation about the scope of intellectual property, particularly copyright. Algorithms are not especially good at discerning what types of uses should be understood as fair, so it is important for all participants in a networked cultural field to understand what is at stake and be prepared to defend responses to preexisting material that fall within parameters supported by current laws. As the contours of an already esoteric form of property are reshaped by digital transmission, it is equally essential to pay close attention to new IP legislation that might be proposed. If the past is any guide, there should be no assumption that public interest will be the primary motivation.

NOTES

INTRODUCTION

1. Daniel McClean, "Jill Magid and Luis Barragán's Legacy," in Jill Magid, et al., *The Proposal* (Berlin: Sternberg Press, 2016), 59.
2. See http://www.barragan-foundation.org. While the circumstances under which Vitra acquired the material archive have been publicly reported, McClean indicates that far less is known about the transfer of copyright. In addition, Fehlbaum & Co. has registered trademark protection for the architect's name in various jurisdictions. See McClean, "Jill Magid and Luis Barragán's Legacy," 56–57.
3. Randy Kennedy, "Tug of War Stretches Architect's Legacy: Luis Barragán Homage Tweaks Vitra, the Copyright Owners," *New York Times*, November 3, 2013.
4. "The Eiffel Tower image," https://www.toureiffel.paris/en/business/use-image-of-eiffel-tower. For an overview of the issue, see Bryce Clayton Newell, "Freedom of Panorama: A Comparative Look at International Restrictions on Public Photography," *Creighton Law Review* 44, no. 2 (2011): 405–27.
5. For a discussion of the blurring of art in museum interiors initially featured in the Google Art Project, see Greg Allen, "Blurring of Google Art Project Comes as No Surprise," April 3, 2012, https://greg.org/archive/2012/04/03/blurring-of-google-art-project-comes-as-no-surprise.html.
6. On this history, see particularly Mark Rose, *Authors and Owners: The Invention of Copyright* (Cambridge, MA: Harvard University Press, 1993);

Adrian Johns, *Piracy: The Intellectual Property Wars from Gutenberg to Gates* (Chicago: University of Chicago Press, 2009); Ronan Deazley, *On the Origin of the Right to Copy: Charting the Movement of Copyright Law in Eighteenth-Century Britain (1695–1775)* (Oxford: Hart, 2004); and Martha Woodmansee, *The Author, Art, and the Market: Rereading the History of Aesthetics* (New York: Columbia University Press, 1994).

7. Seán Burke, *The Death and Return of the Author: Criticism and Subjectivity in Barthes, Foucault and Derrida,* 2nd ed. (Edinburgh: Edinburgh University Press, 1998), 7. For additional perspectives on this history, see Martha Woodmansee and Peter Jaszi, *The Construction of Authorship: Textual Appropriation in Law and Literature* (Durham, NC: Duke University Press, 1994).
8. Roland Barthes, "The Death of the Author" (1968), in *Image, Music, Text,* trans. Stephen Heath (New York: Hill and Wang, 1977), 143.
9. Michel Foucault, "What is an Author?" (1969), in *Textual Strategies: Perspectives in Post-Structuralist Criticism,* ed. Josué V. Harari (Ithaca, NY: Cornell University Press, 1979). The Beckett quote appears in full in the second paragraph, p. 141, and in part (though slightly altered) as the last line of the essay, p. 160.
10. Barthes, "Death of the Author," 146.
11. Peter Baldwin presents Beckett as a prime example of restrictions on interpretation in *The Copyright Wars: Three Centuries of Trans-Atlantic Battle* (Princeton, NJ: Princeton University Press, 2014), 2, 5. See also Van Badham, "Endgame Review—Innovation Choked by Samuel Beckett's Strict Staging Edicts," *The Guardian,* April 5, 2015, and Kathy Marks, "Director Calls Beckett Heir an 'Enemy of Art' After Godot Censure," *The Independent,* January 11, 2003.
12. According to Janet Maslin, "Her own fans write better stories about Christian Grey than she does. The fact that hers is the hidebound, trademarked, and much-copied version doesn't make it the important one" ("Review: E.L. James's 'Grey' Goes Inside His Brain, and, Yes, His Pants," *New York Times,* June 25, 2015). See also Alexandra Alter, "'Fifty Shades' Fan Fiction Assumes a Life of Its Own," *New York Times,* June 19, 2015.
13. Melissa Anelli, quoted in Sarah Lyall, "J.K. Rowling Just Can't Let Harry Potter Go," *New York Times,* June 1, 2016.
14. Lyall, "J.K. Rowling Just Can't Let Harry Potter Go."
15. Tim Wu, "J.K. Rowling's Dark Mark: Why She Should Lose Her Copyright Lawsuit Against the Harry Potter Lexicon," *Slate,* January 10, 2008. The district court emphasized the amount taken from Rowling's own compendia, but also issued a narrow ruling that did not cover encyclopedias in general.
16. Emily Apter, "What is Yours, Ours, and Mine: Authorial Ownership and the Creative Commons," *October* 126 (Fall 2008): 96.
17. Eriq Gardner, "'Star Trek' Lawsuit: The Debate Over Klingon Language Heats Up," *Hollywood Reporter,* April 28, 2016; David Post, "Copyright in Klingon," *Washington Post,* January 9, 2017. See as well Steven D. Jamar and Christen B'anca Glenn, "When the Author Owns the World: Copyright Issues Arising from Monetizing Fan Fiction," *Texas A&M Law Review* 1 (2014): 959–78.
18. Joan Kee discusses *Naming Rights,* a 2017 work consisting of an annotated letter from Porras-Kim to LACMA, in "Due Processes," *Artforum,* May 2019.
19. For a report on the initial acquisition, see William Wilson, "Ancient West Mexico Works: County Art Museum Buys Sculpture Cache," *Los Angeles Times,* December 12, 1986.
20. Eduardo M. Peñalver and Sonia K. Katyal, *Property Outlaws: How Squatters, Pirates, and Protesters Improve the Law of Ownership* (New Haven, CT: Yale University Press, 2010), particularly chapter 2, "Property and Intellectual Property," 36–51.
21. See Carrie Lambert-Beatty, "Twelve Miles: Boundaries of the New Art/Activism," *Signs* 33, no. 2 (2008): 309–27.

22. J.L. Austin, *How to Do Things with Words* (Cambridge, MA: Harvard University Press, 1962), 12.
23. Judith Butler, *Excitable Speech: A Politics of the Performative* (New York: Routledge, 1997).
24. Benjamin Sutton, "Richard Prince Disowns His Ivanka Trump Portrait, Possibly Increasing Its Value," *Hyperallergic*, January 13, 2017.
25. Pierre Bourdieu, "The Force of Law: Toward a Sociology of the Juridical Field," trans. Richard Terdiman, *Hastings Law Journal* 38 (1987): 805–53.
26. See particularly James Boyle, *The Public Domain: Enclosing the Commons of the Mind* (New Haven, CT: Yale University Press, 2008), and Lewis Hyde, *Common as Air: Revolution, Art, and Ownership* (New York: Farrar, Straus and Giroux, 2010).

1. FROM PRIVILEGE TO IP

1. See Mark Rose, "Author as Proprietor: *Donaldson v. Becket* and the Genealogy of Modern Authorship," *Representations* 23, no. 1 (1988): 51–85, and *Authors and Owners: The Invention of Copyright* (Cambridge, MA: Harvard University Press, 1993).
2. On these distinctions, see Peter Baldwin, *The Copyright Wars: Three Centuries of Trans-Atlantic Battle* (Princeton, NJ: Princeton University Press, 2014), and Jane C. Ginsburg, "A Tale of Two Copyrights: Literary Property in Revolutionary France and America," *Tulane Law Review* 64, no. 5 (1990): 991–1031.
3. Adrian Johns, *Piracy: The Intellectual Property Wars from Gutenberg to Gates* (Chicago: University of Chicago Press, 2009), 10–11. This is outlined by Rose as well (with a slightly different spelling of the name): "The first author's privilege was one granted in 1486 to Marc' Antonio Sabellico, the historian of Venice, for his *Decades rerum Venetarutn*. According to the grant, Sabellico could choose which printer would publish his book, and any other printer who published it would be fined 500 ducats" (*Authors and Owners*, 10). For multiple perspectives on the interplay between privilege and copyright, see also *Privilege and Property: Essays on the History of Copyright*, ed. Ronan Deazley, Martin Kretschmer, and Lionel Bently (Cambridge, UK: OpenBook Publishers, 2010).
4. Lisa Pon, *Raphael, Dürer, and Marcantonio Raimondi: Copying and the Italian Renaissance Print* (New Haven, CT: Yale University Press, 2004), 43.
5. Cynthia J. Brown, *Poets, Patrons, and Printers: Crisis of Authority in Late Medieval France* (Ithaca, NY: Cornell University Press, 1995), 2.
6. Brown, *Poets, Patrons, and Printers*, 6. Also, referencing Walter Ong, she distinguishes between "the age of scribes and the age of 'true' authors" (9).
7. Quoted by Pon, *Raphael, Dürer, and Marcantonio Raimondi*, 39.
8. See Evelyn Lincoln, "Invention and Authorship in Early Modern Italian Visual Culture," *DePaul Law Review* 52, no. 4 (Summer 2003): 1107.
9. Joseph Leo Koerner, *The Moment of Self-Portraiture in German Renaissance Art* (Chicago: University of Chicago Press, 1993), 203. He references Martin Schongauer as an artist who signed his engravings but not his paintings.
10. Lincoln, "Invention and Authorship," particularly 1112–13 and 1116–17.
11. Koerner, *The Moment of Self-Portraiture*, 209, 214. Thanks to Stephanie Porras and Christopher Heuer for drawing my attention to the extended series of conflicts.
12. Lincoln, "Invention and Authorship," 1107, 1111.
13. Lincoln, "Invention and Authorship," 1112.
14. See Caroline Karpinski, "The Print in Thrall to Its Original: A Historiographic Perspective," in *Retaining the Original: Multiple Originals, Copies, and Reproductions*, ed. Kathleen Preciado (Washington, DC: National Gallery of Art, 1989), 101–9.

15. Elizabeth Cropper, *The Domenichino Affair: Novelty, Imitation, and Theft in Seventeenth-Century Rome* (New Haven, CT: Yale University Press, 2005), 14. The Domenichino work was completed in 1614, and the critical attacks took place in the 1620s.
16. On this dynamic in general, see Susan Lambert, *The Image Multiplied: Five Centuries of Printed Reproductions of Paintings and Drawings* (London: Trefoil Publications, 1987); Trevor Fawcett, "Graphic Versus Photographic in The Nineteenth-Century Reproduction," *Art History* 9, no. 2 (1986), 185–212; and of course Walter Benjamin, "The Work of Art in the Age of Mechanical Reproduction," in *Illuminations*, trans. Harry Zohn (New York: Schocken Books, 1969).
17. For a counterpoint, see Bill Brown, "Introduction: Textual Materialism," *PMLA* 125, no. 1 (2010): 24–28, where he argues against the assumption that there is a shared experience of a text, regardless of format (handwritten manuscript, serial publication, bound volume, e-book, audiobook, etc.), citing the significance of different experiences and forms of mediation.
18. On the interplay between trade practices and government oversight, see Johns, *Piracy*.
19. For this history, see John Feather, *A History of British Publishing* (London: Routledge, 1988); John Feather, "Authors, Publishers and Politicians: The History of Copyright and the Book Trade," *European Intellectual Property Review* 11 (December 1989): 377–80; and Cyprian Blagden, *The Stationers' Company: A History, 1403–1959* (Stanford, CA: Stanford University Press, 1977).
20. On the parliamentary edict of January 29, 1642, see Rose, *Authors and Owners*, 22. Michel Foucault made the broad argument that "texts, books and discourses really began to have authors (other than mythical, 'sacralized' and 'sacralizing' figures) to the extent that authors became subject to punishment, that is, to the extent that discourses could be transgressive" ("What is an Author?" [1969], in *Textual Strategies: Perspectives in Post-Structuralist Criticism*, ed. Josué V. Harari [Ithaca, NY: Cornell University Press, 1979], 148).
21. According to Rose, over the course of the eighteenth century, as key cases tested and refined the scope of statutory regulation of literary property, the legal actions were all brought by printers, but the arguments were framed in relation to the rights of authors ("Author as Proprietor," 58). Jane C. Ginsburg has also pointed to the early concern for printing, despite the appearance of the figure of the author, in "'Une Chose Publique'? The Author's Domain and the Public Domain in Early British, French and US Copyright Law," *The Cambridge Law Journal* 65, no. 3 (2006): 645.
22. These cases also provided the basis for what is known as common-law copyright: in contrast to the statutory limit on copyright for published works, unpublished works could receive perpetual copyright protection under common law as long as they remained unpublished. On this history, see particularly Ronan Deazley, *On the Origin of the Right to Copy: Charting the Movement of Copyright Law in Eighteenth-Century Britain (1695–1775)* (Oxford: Hart, 2004).
23. Lawrence Lessig, *Free Culture: How Big Media Uses Technology and the Law to Lock down Culture and Control Creativity* (New York: Penguin Press, 2004), 93.
24. Rose, "Author as Proprietor," 53.
25. Deazley, *On the Origin*, 88–93.
26. Deazley, *On the Origin*, 91.
27. Meredith L. McGill, *American Literature and the Culture of Reprinting, 1834–1853* (Philadelphia: University of Pennsylvania Press, 2003), 1, 3. For multiple perspectives on reprints and piracy, see also *Copyright and Piracy: An Interdisciplinary Critique*, ed. Lionel Bently, Jennifer Davis, and Jane C. Ginsburg (Cambridge: Cambridge University Press, 2010).
28. McGill, *American Literature and the Culture of Reprinting*, 22.
29. Baldwin, *Copyright Wars*, 121.
30. McGill, *American Literature and the Culture of Reprinting*, 28–29.

31. Jennifer L. Roberts, *Transporting Visions: The Movement of Images in Early America* (Berkeley: University of California Press, 2014), 119–21.
32. Roberts, *Transporting Visions,* 113–14.
33. McGill, *American Literature and the Culture of Reprinting,* 17.
34. On this aspect of film history, see Siva Vaidhyanathan, *Copyrights and Copywrongs: The Rise of Intellectual Property and How It Threatens Creativity* (New York: New York University Press, 2001), particularly chapter 3, "Celluloid Copyright and Derivative Works." On the logistics of authorship in this context, see also Catherine Fisk, *Writing for Hire: Unions, Hollywood, and Madison Avenue* (Cambridge, MA: Harvard University Press, 2016).
35. Rose, "Author as Proprietor," 72, 75.
36. For the general background, see Rose, "Author as Proprietor," 56, 71; on limited terms, see Deazley, *On the Origin,* 3–4.
37. Rose, "Author as Proprietor," 61. On the shifting role of patents, with protections provided in exchange for releasing descriptions of inventions, see Mario Biagioli, "Patent Specification and Political Representation: How Patents Became Rights," in *Making and Unmaking Intellectual Property: Creative Production in Legal and Cultural Perspective,* ed. Mario Biagioli, Peter Jaszi, and Martha Woodmansee (Chicago: University of Chicago Press, 2011).
38. Martha Woodmansee, "The Genius and the Copyright: Economic and Legal Conditions of the Emergence of the 'Author,'" *Eighteenth-Century Studies* 17, no. 4 (1984): 425.
39. See Woodmansee, "The Genius and the Copyright," 430.
40. Johann Gottlieb Fichte, "Proof of the Illegality of Reprinting: A Rationale and a Parable" (Berlin: 1793), trans. Martha Woodmansee, available from *Primary Sources on Copyright* (1450–1900), ed. L. Bently and M. Kretschmer, www.copyrighthistory.org.
41. Mario Biagioli, "Genius Against Copyright: Revisiting Fichte's Proof of the Illegality of Reprinting," *The Notre Dame Law Review* 86, no. 5 (2011): 1847–67.
42. See Biagioli, "Genius Against Copyright," especially 1864. See also Woodmansee's summary in "The Genius and the Copyright," 443–45.
43. Fichte, "Proof of the Illegality of Reprinting."
44. *Stowe v. Thomas,* Pennsylvania, 1853, with commentary by Oren Bracha, available from www.copyrighthistory.org. On issues raised by translation generally, see Emily Apter, *The Translation Zone: A New Comparative Literature* (Princeton, NJ: Princeton University Press, 2011).
45. Susan P. Liemer, "On the Origins of Le Droit Moral: How Non-Economic Rights Came to Be Protected in French IP Law," *Journal of Intellectual Property Law* 19, no. 1 (2011): 101. See also Katie Scott, *Becoming Property: Art, Theory, and Law in Early Modern France* (New Haven, CT: Yale University Press, 2018).
46. Liemer, "On the Origins of Le Droit Moral," 107–8.
47. See Ginsburg, "'Une Chose Publique'?," 654.
48. Lionel Bently, "R. v. the Author: From Death Penalty to Community Service," *Columbia Journal of Law and the Arts* 32, no. 1 (2008–9): 1–110.
49. William P. Alford, *To Steal a Book Is an Elegant Offense: Intellectual Property Law in Chinese Civilization* (Stanford, CA: Stanford University Press, 1995), 34. Possible reasons given by Alford for why China did not develop its own IP framework earlier include the dynamics of the political culture, the fact that technological advances took place in a preindustrial context, and relatively limited literacy rates into the twentieth century.
50. See Peter K. Yu, "When the Chinese Intellectual Property System Hits 35," *Queen Mary Journal of Intellectual Property* 8, no. 1 (2018): 3–14.
51. Alford, *To Steal a Book,* 38–41.

52. Peter K. Yu, "The Middle Kingdom and the Intellectual Property World," *Oregon Review of International Law* 13 (2011): 214–15.
53. For Alford's discussion of this reluctance, see *To Steal a Book,* 68–69.
54. On the ongoing dynamic of piracy in the context of developing economies, see particularly Ravi Sundaram, "Revisiting the Pirate Kingdom," *Third Text* 23, no. 3 (2009): 335–45, and Lars Eckstein and Anja Schwarz, *Postcolonial Piracy: Media Distribution and Cultural Production in the Global South* (London: Bloomsbury, 2014).
55. See Yu, "When the Chinese Intellectual Property System Hits 35."
56. Yu, "Middle Kingdom," 210. According to Yu's 2011 article, out of twenty-four available for ratification, China had signed fifteen (see the list of agreements on pp. 221–22.)
57. For a discussion of early twenty-first century efforts in this direction, see Winnie Won Yin Wong, "The Panda Man and the Anti-Counterfeiting Hero: Art, Activism and Appropriation in Contemporary China," *Journal of Visual Culture* 11, no. 1 (2012): 20–37.
58. See Yu, "Middle Kingdom," 239.
59. Lorraine V. Aragon, "Copyrighting Culture for the Nation? Intangible Property Nationalism and the Regional Arts of Indonesia," *International Journal of Cultural Property* 19, no. 3 (2012): 279. For a summary of various attempts to address folklore within the WIPO framework, see Marc Perman, "From 'Folklore' to 'Knowledge' in Global Governance: On the Metamorphoses of the Unauthored," in *Making and Unmaking Intellectual Property,* ed. Biagioli, Jaszi, and Woodmansee, 115–16.
60. Lorraine V. Aragon and James Leach, "Arts and Owners: Intellectual Property Law and The Politics of Scale in Indonesian Arts," *American Ethnologist* 35, no. 4 (November 2008): 619.
61. Quoted in Aragon, "Copyrighting Culture for the Nation?," 280 (emphasis original).
62. Aragon and Leach, "Arts and Owners," 608.
63. See Aragon, "Copyrighting Culture for the Nation?," 298.
64. Aragon and Leach, "Arts and Owners," 611.
65. Boatema Boateng, *The Copyright Thing Doesn't Work Here: Adinkra and Kente Cloth and Intellectual Property in Ghana* (Minneapolis: University of Minnesota Press, 2011).
66. Boateng, *Copyright Thing,* 21.
67. Boateng, *Copyright Thing,* 43.
68. Boateng, *Copyright Thing,* 44.
69. See Boateng, *Copyright Thing,* 8, 17.
70. Boateng, *Copyright Thing,* 97. See also John Collins, "Copyright, Folklore and Music Piracy in Ghana," *Critical Arts* 20, no. 1 (2006): 158–70.
71. See "Introduction to the Aboriginal and Torres Strait Islander Heritage Protection Act," p. 3, http://155.187.2.69/heritage/laws/pubs/introduction-atsihpa.pdf, and US Department of the Interior National Parks Service, https://www.nps.gov/nagpra.
72. Colin Golvan, "Aboriginal Art and the Protection of Indigenous Cultural Rights," *EIPR (European Intellectual Property Review)* 14, no. 7, 1992: 227–32.
73. For an account of the first case, see Colin Golvan, "Meeting at the Waterhole: A Copyright Lawyer's Adventures in Arnhem Land," *The Australian Financial Review,* October 6, 2006.
74. For overviews of this case, see Michael Brown, *Who Owns Native Culture?* (Cambridge, MA: Harvard University Press, 2003); Jane E. Anderson, "A Tale of Two Cases," in *Law, Knowledge, Culture: The Production of Indigenous Knowledge in Intellectual Property Law* (Cheltenham, UK: Edward Elgar Publishing, 2009), 130–56; and Isabella Alexander, "White Law, Black Art," *International Journal of Cultural Property* 10, no. 2 (2001): 185–216.
75. Brown, *Who Owns Native Culture?,* 46–47. Moreover, as Peter Drahos and Susy Frankel have pointed out, "The biodiversity that confronted arriving colonists was not that of nature in raw

form, but rather the many products of the land that had resulted from thousands of years of intervention and management of that land by indigenous people" ("Indigenous Peoples' Innovation and Intellectual Property: The Issues," in *Indigenous Peoples' Innovation: Intellectual Property Pathways to Development*, ed. Peter Drahos and Susy Frankel [Canberra, Australia: ANU E Press, 2012], 8).

76. Quoted in Kristin Howden, "Indigenous Traditional Knowledge and Native Title," *University of New South Wales Law Journal* 24, no. 1 (2001): 78.
77. See Colin Golvan, "Aboriginal Art and the Public Domain," *Journal of Law and Information Science* 9, no. 1 (1998): 122–29.
78. Molly Nesbit, "What Was an Author?," *Yale French Studies* 73 (1987): 229–57.
79. For a chart outlining what is covered by US copyright, see "Copyright Term and the Public Domain in the United States," maintained by the Cornell University Library Copyright Information Center, https://copyright.cornell.edu/publicdomain.
80. *Eldred v. Ashcroft,* United States Supreme Court, No. 01–618, argued October 9, 2002, decided January 15, 2003. On the case and its implications, see Lawrence Lessig, *Free Culture: How Big Media Uses Technology and the Law to Lock Down Culture and Control Creativity* (New York: Penguin Press, 2004), particularly chapters 13 and 14.
81. Peter Jaszi points to the fact that copyright term lengths were not further extended as one of a list of recent areas of beneficial inaction in "What Didn't Happen: An Essay in Speculation," *Duke Law & Technology Review* 18 (August 2019): 162–73, in the context of a special issue, *The Past and Future of the Internet: A Symposium for John Perry Barlow,* edited by James Boyle. See as well the annual list of works entering the public domain in the United States, published by the Duke University Center for the Study of the Public Domain, https://law.duke.edu/cspd.
82. Vaidhyanathan, *Copyrights and Copywrongs.*

2. THE APPROPRIATION GAME

1. Annette Lemieux interviewed by Elisabeth Sussman, in David Ross and Jürgen Harten, eds., *The Binational: American Art of the Late 80s* (Cologne: DuMont Buchverlag, 1988), 135. The exhibition was at the Cash/Newhouse Gallery in New York.
2. *Bleistein v. Donaldson Lithographing Co.* 188 U.S. 239 (1903). The case also established that copyright protection is not based on a work's artistic merit. For a discussion of issues associated with the case's precedents, see Barton Beebe, "*Bleistein,* the Problem of Aesthetic Progress, and the Making of American Copyright Law," *Columbia Law Review* 117 (2017): 319–98.
3. On the vagaries of how courts have interpreted fair use principles, see Barton Beebe, "An Empirical Study of U.S. Copyright Fair Use Opinions, 1978–2005," *University of Pennsylvania Law Review* 156, no. 3 (2008): 549–624.
4. The College Art Association's 2015 publication, *Best Practices in Fair Use for the Visual Arts,* provides important guidelines regarding fair use in making, critiquing, and exhibiting art. See https://www.collegeart.org/pdf/fair-use/best-practices-fair-use-visual-arts.pdf.
5. *Rogers v. Koons,* 960 F.2d 301, 310 (2nd Cir. 1992). The case was initially heard in the US District Court for the Southern District of New York, and Judge Haight issued his decision in favor of Art Rogers on the question of copyright infringement on December 10, 1990.
6. *Campbell v. Acuff Rose Music, Inc.*, 510 U.S. 569, 575 (1994), with the opinion written by Justice Souter and a concurrence by Justice Kennedy. Pierre N. Leval's "Toward a Fair Use Standard," *Harvard Law Review* 103 (March 1990): 1105–36, was cited by the Court as a basis for the transformative use standard.
7. On Koons's strategic testimony, see Amy Adler, "Fair Use and the Future of Art," *New York University Law Review* 91, no. 3 (2016): 559–626, and Martha Buskirk, "Creative Intent: The

Recent Fortunes of Appropriation in the United States," in *The Trials of Art,* ed. Daniel McClean (London: Ridinghouse, 2007), 235–51.

8. *Rogers v. Koons,* 960 F.2d 301, 310 (2nd Cir. 1992).
9. Henry Samuel, "Jeff Koons Accused of Plagiarising Iconic French Advertising Campaign for Multi-Million-Pound Sculpture," *The Telegraph,* September 24, 2018.
10. Kim Willsher, "Jeff Koons Plagiarised French Photographer for Naked Sculpture," *The Guardian,* March 9, 2017.
11. Samuel, "Jeff Koons Accused of Plagiarising."
12. Anna Sansom, "Jeff Koons Loses French Lawsuit Over 'Slavish Copy' of Naf Naf Advert," *Art Newspaper,* November 9, 2018, and Naomi Rea, "Jeff Koons Is Found Guilty of Plagiarism in Paris and Ordered to Pay $168,000 to the Creator of an Ad He Appropriated," *Artnet News,* November 9, 2018.
13. Amy Adler, "Fair Use and the Future of Art," *New York University Law Review* 91, no. 3 (2016): 559–626.
14. This sentence was highlighted by Adler in "Fair Use and the Future of Art," 588.
15. Richard Prince published these observations in a November 18, 2014 entry in the "Birdtalk" section of his website (http://www.richardprince.com/birdtalk), and the entry was reproduced, under "About," on the Gagosian web site for Prince's 2015 London show (https://gagosian.com/exhibitions/2015/richard-prince-new-portraits).
16. Prince, November 18, 2014, "Birdtalk" entry.
17. Judge Sidney H. Stein, Opinion and Order Re Motion to Dismiss, July 18, 2017, *Graham v. Prince* (1:15-cv-10160), District Court, S.D. New York.
18. Stein, Opinion and Order.
19. Memorandum of Law in Support of Defendant Richard Prince's Motion for Summary Judgment, October 5, 2018, *Graham v. Prince.*
20. Memorandum of Law in Support of Defendant Richard Prince's Motion for Summary Judgment, October 5, 2018, *Graham v. Prince.*
21. Letter motion for leave to file full sized replicas of Prince's works at issue addressed to Judge Sidney H. Stein, December 10, 2018, *Graham v. Prince.*
22. See in particular the influential critique by Thomas McEvilley: "Doctor Lawyer Indian Chief," *Artforum* 23, November 1984, 54–61.
23. Michel Foucault, "What is an Author?" (1969), in Josué V. Harari, *Textual Strategies: Perspectives in Post-Structuralist Criticism* (Ithaca, NY: Cornell University Press, 1979).
24. Summary based on the following: Randy Kennedy, "The Koons Collection," *New York Times,* February 14, 2010; Tatiana Serafin, "Davos: Victor Pinchuk Draws an Arty Crowd," *Forbes,* January 25, 2011; Lucy Davies, "Is Jeff Koons Having a Laugh?" *Telegraph,* June 18, 2012; Linda Yablonsky, "The Collections of Artists," *New York Times,* December 5, 2013; Julia Halperin and Brian Boucher, "Jeff Koons Radically Downsizes His Studio, Laying Off Half His Painting Staff," *Artnet News,* June 20, 2017; and "Louis Vuitton × Jeff Koons: Masters," 2017, http://www.jeffkoons.com/artwork/projects/louis-vuitton-x-jeff-koons-masters.
25. Jeff Koons, *Fait d'hiver,* 1988, sold at the Christie's November 13, 2007 Post War and Contemporary Art Evening Sale, lot 49, estimate, USD 4,000,000—USD 6,000,000; price realized, USD 4,297,000.
26. Guggenheim "Collection Online" entry for Jeff Koons, *Niagara,* 2000, https://www.guggenheim.org/artwork/10734.
27. Hans Haacke's description of the background for this work can be found in "Texts and Works: 1970–1995," in *Hans Haacke: "Obra Social,"* ed. Manuel J. Borja-Villel (Barcelona: Fundació Antoni Tàpies, 1995), 193.

28. Randy Kennedy, "If the Copy Is an Artwork, Then What's the Original?," *New York Times,* December 6, 2007.
29. "Photographer Sam Abell talks about Richard Prince," uploaded June 14, 2008, https://www.youtube.com/watch?v = Um74DKYlta8.
30. Kennedy, "If the Copy Is an Artwork."
31. On Doeringer's appropriations generally, see Gabe Cohn, "Move Over, Richard Prince. Here Comes Bootleg Art From 'Christy's,'" *New York Times,* May 1, 2019.
32. Richard Prince, Birdtalk entry, "Rock Lobster: October 20, 2017," http://www.richardprince.com/birdtalk.
33. See Michael Lobel, *Fugitive Artist: The Early Work of Richard Prince, 1974–77* (Purchase, NY: Neuberger Museum of Art, Purchase College, State University of New York, 2007).
34. Greg Allen, "*300×404:* The Making Of," May 20, 2009, https://greg.org/archive/2009/05/20/300x404-the-making-of.html, and "West Trademark F(*#$Up," May 18, 2009, https://greg.org/archive/2009/05/18/west-trademark-fup.html.
35. Nate Harrison, "Authoring Contradictions: Modern Appropriation Art and Postmodern Copyright Law in *Cariou v. Prince,*" in *Artist, Authorship & Legacy: A Reader*, ed. Daniel McClean (London: Ridinghouse, 2018), 92, 95.
36. Alex Needham, "Richard Prince v. Suicide Girls in an Instagram Price War," *The Guardian,* May 27, 2015.
37. E.g., Memorandum of Law in Support of Defendant Richard Prince's Motion for Summary Judgment, October 5, 2018, *Graham v. Prince.*
38. Memorandum of Law in Support of Defendant Richard Prince's Motion for Summary Judgment, October 5, 2018, *Graham v. Prince.*
39. Quoted in Laura Gilbert, "Richard Prince Defends Reuse of Others' Photographs," *Art Newspaper,* October 10, 2018.
40. Richard Prince (@RichardPrince4), Twitter, July 19, 2017, since deleted. For a partial quote of the tweet, see Andrew R. Chow, "Copyright Case Over Richard Prince Instagram Show to Go Forward," *New York Times,* July 20, 2017. According to Chow, Prince's "Instagram account, which previously had over 70,000 followers, is currently disabled." For full quote, see Jayphen Simpson, "Photographer's Copyright Suit Against Richard Prince's 'Instagram Art' To Go Ahead," *PetaPixel,* July 27, 2017.
41. Jessica M. Silbey, Eva E. Subotnik, and Peter C. DiCola, "Existential Copyright and Professional Photography," *Notre Dame Law Review* 95 (2019): 267.
42. Amy Adler, "Why Art Does Not Need Copyright," *The George Washington Law Review* 86, no. 2 (March 2018): 366.
43. See Julia Michalska, "Agreement Reached in Plagiarism Row Between Artists," *Art Newspaper,* January 15, 2014, and Ingeborg Ruthe, "Plagiatsstreit Die große Karo-Frage," *Berliner Zeitung,* January 15, 2014.
44. "Fashion Op from Toe to Top," *Life,* April 16, 1965, 54. See also Greg Allen, "The Trendmaking Eye," August 27, 2010, https://greg.org/archive/2010/08/27/the-trendmaking-eye.html, and "On Tobias Rehberger On Bridget Riley," January 15, 2014, https://greg.org/archive/2014/01/15/on-tobias-rehberger-on-bridget-riley.html.
45. April 2009 email from Robert Lang to Sipho Mabona, quoted in Dan Duray, "Beneath the Fold: The Twisted Tale of Origami v. Sarah Morris," *Observer,* May 28, 2013.
46. Amended Complaint against S. Morris, April 29, 2011, *Lang v. Morris* (3:11-cv-01366), District Court, N.D. California. Filed by Noboru Miyajima, Robert J. Lang, Manuel Sirgo Alvarez, Jason Ku, Toshikazu Kawasaki, Nicola Bandoni, and Exhibit J, Morris's June 23, 2009 letter to Lang.

47. Memorandum of Law in Support re: 33 Motion for Summary Judgment, June 29, 2012, *Lang v. Morris* (1:11-cv-08821), District Court, S.D. New York.
48. Motion for Leave to File Amended Complaint, May 30, 2012, *Lang v. Morris* (1:11-cv-08821), District Court, S.D. New York.
49. Robert J. Lang, "Now, That's Settled," March 21, 2013, https://langorigami.com/article/now-thats-settled.
50. Robert J. Lang, "Sarah Morris Works Attribution," March 21, 2013, https://langorigami.com/article/sarah-morris-works-attribution.
51. Brian Boucher, "Smith Estate Reveals Terms of Agreement with Brooklyn Artist," *Art in America,* October 18, 2013.
52. Rozalia Jovanovic, "David Smith's Estate Demands 'House Arrest' for a Young Artist's Works," *Blouin Art Info,* March 10, 2013. See also Joy Garnett, "Free-Fail," *Art21 Magazine,* December 1, 2013.
53. See documentation at First Pulse Projects, last updated April 2009, http://www.firstpulseprojects.com/joywar.html (via Internet Archive), as well as Joy Garnett, "Painting Mass Media," September 23, 2004 lecture at Columbia University, https://youtu.be/wA_xgGyF8yg.
54. Joy Garnett and Susan Meiselas, "On the Rights of Molotov Man: Appropriation and the Art of Context," *Harpers Magazine,* February 2007, 53–58. This publication is based on a 2006 conversation at the New York Institute for the Humanities.
55. Joy Garnett, "Field Report: Follow the Image," *Cultural Politics* 1, no. 1 (2005), http://www.firstpulseprojects.com/FollowTheImage.pdf (via Internet Archive).

3. ART, LIFE, AND INFRINGEMENT

1. For scholarship on the copyright claims that played a crucial role in the subsequent legal case, see Robert Brauneis, "Copyright and the World's Most Popular Song," *Journal of the Copyright Society of the U.S.A.* 56, no. 23 (2009): 335–426. Brauneis has maintained a database of related material, hosted by the George Washington University Law School, http://docs.law.gwu.edu/facweb/rbrauneis/happybirthdayaddenda.htm. See also "'Happy Birthday' and the Money It Makes," *New York Times,* December 26, 1989.
2. Jessica Silbey, *The Eureka Myth: Creators, Innovators, and Everyday Intellectual Property* (Redwood City, CA: Stanford University Press, 2014).
3. Mark A. Lemley, "IP in a World without Scarcity," *New York University Law Review* 90, no. 2 (2015): 485.
4. Eduardo M. Peñalver and Sonia K. Katyal, *Property Outlaws: How Squatters, Pirates, and Protesters Improve the Law of Ownership* (New Haven, CT: Yale University Press, 2010), 3–8.
5. On the rerelease, see Meredith Blake, "Landmark Civil Rights Documentary 'Eyes on the Prize' Returns to TV," *Los Angeles Times,* January 17, 2016. Regarding larger challenges facing filmmakers, see the report prepared by Pat Aufderheide and Peter Jaszi for the Center for Media Studies and Social Impact, "Untold Stories: Creative Consequences of the Rights Clearance Culture for Documentary Filmmakers," November 2004, http://archive.cmsimpact.org/fair-use/best-practices/documentary/untold-stories-creative-consequences-rights-clearance-culture.
6. See Lisa Bannon, "The Birds May Sing, But Campers Can't Unless They Pay Up," *The Wall Street Journal,* August 21, 1996, and Ken Ringle, "ASCAP Changes Its Tune; Never Intended to Collect Fees for Scouts' Campfire Songs, Group Says," *The Washington Post,* August 28, 1996.
7. Lauren Williams, "I Have a Copyright: The Problem With MLK's Speech," *Mother Jones,* August 23, 2013.
8. Robert Hilburn, "Beatles Sue Nike Over Use Of Song," *Los Angeles Times,* July 29, 1987, and Jon Pareles, "Nike Calls Beatles Suit Groundless," *New York Times,* August 5, 1987.

9. See Alan Wallach, "The American Cast Museum: An Episode in the History of the Institutional Definition of Art," in *Exhibiting Contradiction: Essays on the Art Museum in the United States* (Amherst: University of Massachusetts Press, 1998), 41.
10. "NPG seems to think that UK law should apply everywhere on the Internet," wrote Fred von Lohmann of the EFF ("EFF Defends Wikipedian's Right to the Public Domain," August 3, 2009, https://www.eff.org/deeplinks/2009/07/eff-defends-wikipedi).
11. Rebecca Atkinson, "NPG Changes Image Licensing to Allow Free Downloads," *Museums Journal,* August 22, 2012.
12. For Wikimedia's statement about the case, including their announcement of plans to appeal, see John Weitzmann, "Erklärung zum Fall Reiss-Engelhorn-Museen," June 21, 2016, https://blog.wikimedia.de/2016/06/21/erklaerung-zum-fall-reiss-engelhorn-museen.
13. Allan McCollum, email to the author, November 17, 2019. The agreement was signed by McCollum on April 5, 1991.
14. See Carolin Wiedemann, "Freiheit für Nofretete!," *Frankfurter Allgemeine,* November 30, 2015, and Claire Voon, "Could the Nefertiti Scan Be a Hoax—and Does that Matter?," *Hyperallergic,* March 9, 2016.
15. France, Germany, Netherlands: per Christopher F. Schuetze, "Repatriating Colonial-Era Artifacts," *New York Times,* March 15, 2019.
16. Cosmo Wenman, "Bust of Nefertiti, FOIA Results," November 13, 2019, https://www.thingiverse.com/thing:3974391. See also Cosmo Wenman, "A German Museum Tried to Hide This Stunning 3D Scan of an Iconic Egyptian Artifact. Today You Can See It for the First Time," *Reason,* November 13, 2019, and Michael Weinberg, "The Nefertiti Bust Meets the 21st Century," *Slate,* November 15, 2019.
17. See Hélène Verougstraete-Marcq, R. Van Schoute, Till Borchert, and Groeningemuseum, *Restaurateurs Ou Faussaires Des Primitifs Flamands* (Gent: Ludion, 2004).
18. One major initiative, Matters in Media Art, evolved as a collaboration among the New Art Trust, MoMA, SFMOMA, and the Tate to establish guidelines covering both information to be gathered at the point of acquisition, and long-term care strategies for new media art. Prior to that, the Guggenheim's Variable Media Initiative explored the viability of strategies of replication or emulation, also through a multi-institutional collaboration. See http://mattersinmediaart.org and https://www.guggenheim.org/conservation/the-variable-media-initiative.
19. Jessica Lussenhop, "Why Did Prince Change His Name to a Symbol?," *BBC News Magazine,* April 22, 2016.
20. See Oliver Wang, "20 Years Ago Biz Markie Got The Last Laugh," *NPR,* May 6, 2013.
21. Tim Wu, "Jay-Z Versus the Sample Troll: The Shady One-Man Corporation That's Destroying Hip-Hop," *Slate,* November 16, 2006.
22. Kembrew Mcleod, "How to Make a Documentary About Sampling—Legally," *Atlantic,* March 31, 2010.
23. See Jeff Leeds, "Dispute Over Sampling Fees Has George Clinton in a Legal Funk," *Los Angeles Times,* May 20, 2001; Jeff Leeds, "George Clinton Wins Funkadelic Rights," *New York Times,* June 7, 2005; and Lauretta Charlton, "George Clinton Believes Our Music Copyright Laws Are Broken . . . and That Aliens Exist," *New York,* May 4, 2015.
24. *Bridgeport Music, Inc. v. Dimension Films,* 410 F.3d 792 (6th Cir. 2005).
25. *Bridgeport Music, Inc. v. Dimension Films,* 410 F.3d 792 (6th Cir. 2005).
26. "Afrika Bambaataa, Zulu King of the Bronx, Interviewed by Frank in the South Bronx, October 6, 1998," in Bill Brewster and Frank Broughton, *The Record Players: DJ Revolutionaries* (New York: Grove, 2011), 190. Thanks to Floor van de Velde for bringing this example to my attention.

27. See "Arthur Baker, Maestro Electro, Interviewed by Bill and Frank in Camden Town, January 25, 1999," in Brewster and Broughton, *The Record Players: DJ Revolutionaries*, 204–15, and Marc Hogan, "Kraftwerk Win Bizarre Sampling Lawsuit in Germany: 'Planet Rock' for All," *Spin*, December 20, 2012.
28. Quoted in Scott Roxborough, "German Supreme Court Backs Sampling in Kraftwerk Case," *Hollywood Reporter*, May 31, 2016.
29. Per Joint Stipulation to Dismiss Defendant Bridgeport Music Inc filed by Plaintiffs and Counter-Defendants, March 26, 2014, *Pharrell Williams v. Bridgeport Music Inc* (2:13-cv-06004), District Court, C.D. California.
30. Stelios Phili, "Robin Thicke on That Banned Video, Collaborating with 2 Chainz and Kendrick Lamar, and His New Film," *GQ*, May 7, 2013.
31. Dan Rys, "Pharrell Has Found His Happy Place in the Mainstream," *XXL*, March 4, 2014.
32. *Pharrell Williams, et al. v. Bridgeport Music, et al.* No. 15–56880 (9th Cir., July 11, 2018). The ruling's implication that one could copyright a feeling had further repercussions. In a bid to recoup attorney fees, Gaye's heirs went back to court in 2019, after Pharrell Williams told a *GQ* interviewer that he would attempt to reverse-engineer the feeling evoked by other songs, accusing him of perjury for saying in court that he had not intentionally evoked "Got to Give it Up."
33. Attorney Christine Lepera, quoted in Nastia Voynovskaya, "Copyrighting the 'Building Blocks' of Music? Why the Katy Perry Case Alarms Producers," *KQED Arts*, August 6, 2019.
34. Attorney Ed McPherson, quoted in Anne Steele, "Who Wrote 'Stairway to Heaven'? Music Industry Braces for Copyright Suits," *Wall Street Journal*, August 4, 2019.
35. On this topic generally, see Edward Lee, "Can 'Fair Use' Clear Up Music's Blurred Lines on Copyright?," *Billboard*, July 19, 2018, and Edward Lee, "Fair Use Avoidance in Music Cases," *Boston College Law Review* 59, no. 6 (2018): 1874–1931.
36. *Bridgeport Music, Inc. v. UMG Recordings, Inc.*, 585 F.3d 267, 6th Cir. (2009).
37. Mike Masnick, "Rumblefish CEO: Claiming Copyright On Your Incidental Recordings Of Birds Was Merely A Series Of Unfortunate Errors," *TechDirt*, February 27, 2012, and Mike Masnick, "How Rumblefish Ended Up Claiming Copyright On A Song Uploaded By The Band Who Actually Held The Copyright," *TechDirt*, April 25, 2012.
38. Sean Fennessey, "Girl Talk: *Night Ripper*," *Pitchfork*, July 17, 2006.
39. Mike Masnick, "Why Hasn't The Recording Industry Sued Girl Talk?," *TechDirt*, July 8, 2009.
40. According to McLeod, they relied on the *Documentary Filmmakers Statement of Best Practices in Fair Use*, put out in 2005 by the Center for Social Media ("How to Make a Documentary About Sampling—Legally"). Such codes are increasingly important, including the *Code of Best Practices in Fair Use for the Visual Arts* issued by the College Art Association in 2015.
41. Ashley Cullins, "Carrie Fisher, 'Star Wars' and the Legal Issues of Dead But In-Demand Actors," *Hollywood Reporter*, May 1, 2017.
42. "FTC Staff Reminds Influencers and Brands to Clearly Disclose Relationship," April 19, 2017, https://www.ftc.gov/news-events/press-releases/2017/04/ftc-staff-reminds-influencers-brands-clearly-disclose.
43. *Kimsaprincess, Inc.; and Kim Kardashian West v. Missguided USA (Finance) Inc., and Missguided Limited*, 2:19-cv-01258 (C.D.Cal). Quoted in "Kim Kardashian's Multi-Million Trademark, Right of Publicity Lawsuit Against Missguided Isn't Over Yet," *The Fashion Law*, July 16, 2019.
44. Quoted in "Tyson's Moko Draws Fire from Maori," *New Zealand Herald*, May 25, 2011.

45. Response to Motion re 2 Motion for Preliminary Injunction (Redacted) filed by Defendant Warner Bros. Entertainment Inc., May 20, 2011, *Whitmill v. Warner Bros. Entertainment Inc.* (4:2011cv00752), April 28, 2011, US District Court for the Eastern District of Missouri.
46. On Nimmer's evolving stance, see David Kravets, "Hangover Tattoo Lawsuit: Can You Copyright Flesh?," *Wired,* May 27, 2011.
47. Catherine D. Perry, Transcript of Preliminary Injunction Hearing at 58, *Whitmill v. Warner Bros. Entm't,* No. 4:11-cv-752 (E.D. Mo. May 23, 2011), quoted in Ann Bartow, "A Restatement of Copyright Law as More Independent and Stable Treatise," *Brooklyn Law Review* 79 (2014): 457–503. For a summary of the outcome, see also Matthew Belloni, "Warner Bros. Settles 'Hangover II' Tattoo Lawsuit," *Hollywood Reporter,* June 20, 2011.
48. Response to Motion re 2 Motion for Preliminary Injunction (Redacted), filed by Defendant Warner Bros. Entertainment Inc., May 20, 2011, *Whitmill v. Warner Bros. Entertainment Inc.* (4:2011cv00752), April 28, 2011, US District Court for the Eastern District of Missouri.
49. On the multiple lawsuits, see Ben Child, "Louis Vuitton goes to court over 'Lewis Vuitton' bag in The Hangover II," *Guardian,* March 19, 2012.
50. On the dismissal, see "Court Sides for Warner Bros. in Louis Vuitton 'Hangover' Case," *The Fashion Law,* June 17, 2012.
51. Meena Hartenstein, "Mike Tyson: I only made cameo in *The Hangover* for drug money, never expected comedy to be a success," *Daily News,* August 2, 2010 (referring to the first movie in the series, from 2009, in which Tyson also appeared).
52. Regarding implied license as well as video game rights, see Jason M. Bailey, "Athletes Don't Own Their Tattoos. That's a Problem for Video Game Developers," *New York Times,* December 27, 2018.
53. Darren Heitner, "Questions Concerning Copyright Of Athlete Tattoos Has Companies Scrambling," *Forbes,* August 14, 2013. On the failure of the association to defend, see Timothy Geigner, "NFL Players Association Freaks Out About Tattoo Copyrights," *TechDirt,* September 13, 2013.
54. Bailey, "Athletes Don't Own."
55. *Alexander v. Take-Two Interactive Software, Inc.* (3:18-cv-00966), District Court, S.D. Illinois.
56. Bailey, "Athletes Don't Own."
57. Declaration of LeBron James in Support re: 127 Motion for Summary Judgment, August 24, 2018, *Solid Oak Sketches, LLC v. Visual Concepts, LLC* (1:16-cv-00724), District Court, S.D. New York.
58. Laura Taylor Swain, "Memorandum Opinion and Order," March 26, 2020, *Solid Oak Sketches, LLC v. Visual Concepts, LLC.*
59. Ed O'Bannon with Michael McCann, "How College Sports Video Games Could Return to Your Console," *Sports Illustrated,* February 8, 2018. See also Alex Kirshner, "EA Sports Stopped Making NCAA Football Because the NCAA Is Scared of Athletes Getting Paid," *SBNation,* July 13, 2018, and Jon Solomon, "Timeline: *Ed O'Bannon vs. NCAA*: A Look Back at Some Key *O'Bannon Vs. NCAA* Events Before Next Week's Trial," *CBSSports,* June 6, 2014.
60. European Commission—Statement (Press Release Database), "Copyright reform: the Commission welcomes European Parliament's vote in favour of modernised rules fit for digital age," Strasbourg, 26 March 2019, http://europa.eu/rapid/press-release_STATEMENT-19-1839_en.htm. For claims about enhanced rights, see Martin Banks, "Landmark Copyright Deal Empowers Creatives and News Publishers," *The Parliament,* February 19, 2019.
61. On protests against Article 13, which morphed into Article 17 by the time the directive was passed, see Morgan Meaker, "Inside the Giant German Protest Trying to Bring Down Article 13," *Wired,* March 26, 2019. For consideration of potential licensing requirements, see Adam Satariano, "Europe Adopts Tough New Online Copyright Rules Over Tech Industry Protests," *New York Times,* March 26, 2019.

4. MORAL RIGHTS AND BEYOND

1. John Perreault described Takis's phone call informing him of the forthcoming action in "Whose Art?," *Village Voice*, January 9, 1969. For a file of press clippings on the action, see http://www.primaryinformation.org/product/art-workers-coalition-documents-1.
2. For an overview of this history, see Julia Bryan-Wilson, *Art Workers: Radical Practice in the Vietnam War Era* (Berkeley: University of California Press, 2009), 15–16.
3. Sol LeWitt statement, "Open Hearing, Art Workers Coalition," http://www.primaryinformation.org/product/art-workers-coalition-open-hearing, p. 21.
4. Frederick Castle statement, "Open Hearing, Art Workers Coalition," http://www.primaryinformation.org/product/art-workers-coalition-open-hearing, p. 2.
5. On the genesis of the contract, see Joan Kee, "Partners in Advocacy: *The Artist's Reserved Rights Transfer and Sale Agreement*," in *Models of Integrity: Art and Law in Post-Sixties America* (Oakland: University of California Press, 2019), 43–64, and Lauren van Haaften-Schick, "Conceptualizing Artists' Rights: Circulations of the Siegelaub-Projansky Agreement through Art and Law," *Oxford Handbooks Online: Law*, March 2018, doi: 10.1093/oxfordhb/9780199935352.013.27.
6. Benjamin H. D. Buchloh, "Conceptual Art 1962–1969: From the Aesthetics of Administration to the Critique of Institutions," *October* 55 (Winter 1990): 119.
7. Maria Eichhorn, "Interview with Lawrence Weiner, End of October 1997, Written Interview," in Eichhorn, *The Artist's Contract: Interviews with Carl Andre, Daniel Buren, Paula Cooper, Hans Haacke, Jenny Holzer, Adrian Piper, Robert Projansky, Robert Ryman, Seth Siegelaub, John Weber, Lawrence Weiner, Jackie Winsor*, ed. Gerti Fietzek (Cologne: Verlag der Buchhandlung Walther König, 2009), 83.
8. For a survey of certificate developments, see Susan Hapgood and Cornelia Lauf, eds., *In Deed: Certificates of Authenticity in Art* (Amsterdam: Roma Publications, 2011).
9. Eichhorn, "Interview with Daniel Buren, 16 December 1997, Weimar," in *The Artist's Contract*, 104.
10. Alessandra Donati, "From the Object to the Archive: Guaranteeing Authorship and Ownership in Contemporary Art," in *Artist, Authorship & Legacy: A Reader*, ed. Daniel McClean (London: Ridinghouse, 2018), 151–52.
11. See Eichhorn, "Interview with Hans Haacke, 6 September 1997, Berlin," in *The Artist's Contract*, 66–77.
12. Eichhorn, "Interview with Hans Haacke," 76.
13. Eichhorn, "Interview with Hans Haacke," 76. The fact that Ludwig was turned down by the artist when he expressed an interest in purchasing the work is indicated in the entry for *Der Pralinenmeister* in *Hans Haacke: Unfinished Business*, ed. Brian Wallis (Cambridge, MA: MIT Press, 1986), 210.
14. Eichhorn, "Interview with Hans Haacke," 69, 73.
15. Eichhorn, "Interview with Seth Siegelaub, 4 April 1996, Amsterdam" (with Ute Meta Bauer also participating), 42. For example, both Haacke and Koons were included in the 2001 *Give and Take* exhibition held simultaneously at the Victoria and Albert Museum and the Serpentine Gallery, with work by various artists, including Koons, intermixed with Victorian and Albert collection galleries at the same time that Haacke was invited to draw from the collection for an installation entitled *Mixed Messages* at the Serpentine, as I discussed in *Creative Enterprise: Contemporary Art Between Museum and Marketplace* (New York: Continuum, 2012).
16. For a documentary history of events around *Tilted Arc*, see Clara Weyergraf-Serra and Martha Buskirk, *The Destruction of Tilted Arc: Documents* (Cambridge, MA: MIT Press, 1991). For documents associated with the "culture wars" of the late 1980s and early 1990s, see Richard Bolton, *Culture Wars: Documents from the Recent Controversies in the Arts* (New York: New Press, 1992).

17. Rosalind Krauss, "Sculpture in the Expanded Field," *October* 8 (Spring 1979): 30–44. For the quote on malleability, 30; on modernist sculpture, 34; the diagram, 38.
18. Richard Serra, *Writings, Interviews* (Chicago: University of Chicago Press, 1994), 168.
19. Peter Hirsch hearing statement, in Weyergraf-Serra and Buskirk, *The Destruction of Tilted Arc*, 123.
20. Douglas Crimp and Rosalind Krauss hearing statements, in Weyergraf-Serra and Buskirk, *The Destruction of Tilted Arc*, 73, 81.
21. Decision by Judge Jon O. Newman, U.S. Court of Appeals for the Second Circuit, May 27, 1988, in Weyergraf-Serra and Buskirk, *The Destruction of Tilted Arc*, 249.
22. Rosalyn Deutsche, *Evictions: Art and Spatial Politics* (Cambridge, MA: MIT Press, 1996), 265.
23. Eichhorn, "Interview with Hans Haacke," 74.
24. In Douglas C. McGill, "U.S. Bill on Artist's Rights Is Debated," *New York Times*, November 19, 1986.
25. McGill, "U.S. Bill on Artist's Rights Is Debated."
26. Amy M. Adler, "Against Moral Rights," *California Law Review* 97, no. 1 (2009): 271.
27. Penelope Curtis, "Demonstrable Legacy; or, What Sculptors Leave Behind," in *Artist, Authorship & Legacy*, ed. McClean, 137–38.
28. Decision by Kermit V. Lipez, *David Phillips v. Pembroke Real Estate, Inc.*, 459 F.3d 128 (1st Cir. 2006).
29. Although news reports indicated that the parties subsequently reached a confidential final settlement that did not require payment of the judgment, the gallery did close soon afterward. See Daniel Grant, "Investor Wins Claim Against Manhattan Gallery," *Art News*, February 1, 2005.
30. David Zwirner, quoted in William H. Pauley III, "Memorandum & Order," denying plaintiff Craig Robins's application for a preliminary injunction, *Robins v. Zwirner*, 713 F. Supp. 2d 367 (S.D.N.Y. 2010), District Court, S.D. New York.
31. Quoted in Randy Kennedy, "Lawsuit Describes Art 'Blacklist' to Keep Some Collectors Away," *New York Times*, April 16, 2010. See also Jori Finkel, "Latest on Marlene Dumas collector vs. dealer, short lists and blacklists," *Los Angeles Times*, Culture Monster blog, April 22, 2010.
32. See Tim Schneider, "What Happens When a Collector Promises to Donate an Artwork and Then Flips It at Auction Instead? It's More Harmful Than You Think," *Artnet News*, July 9, 2019.
33. Adam Klasfeld, "Not so Fast, Gallery Tells Christie's," *Courthouse News*, June 9, 2011, and Daniel Grant, "Doig Painting Vaults Past Estimate In Wake of Lawsuit Settlement," *Art News*, July 12, 2011.
34. Statement released by the gallery, cited in Grant, "Doig Painting Vaults Past Estimate."
35. Grant, "Doig Painting Vaults Past Estimate."
36. Lot 7, Sotheby's Contemporary Art, Evening Sale, London, February 7, 2007.
37. Lot 28, Christie's Post-War and Contemporary Art Evening Auction, London, June 28, 2011.
38. *MAFG Art Fund LLC v. Gagosian*, 653189/2012; New York State Supreme Court (Manhattan). And see also Mostafa Heddaya, "Gagosian to Face Fraud Charge Over Sale of Koons Popeye," *Hyperallergic*, February 5, 2014, and Chris Dolmetsch, "N.Y. Art Gallery Owner Gagosian Wins End to Perelman Suit," *Bloomberg.com*, December 4, 2014.
39. Sarah Cascone, "Hollywood Producer Joel Silver Dropped His Lawsuit Against Gagosian After His Secret Billionaire Backer Was Uncovered," *Artnet News*, June 6, 2019.
40. Alexander Alberro, *Conceptual Art and the Politics of Publicity* (Cambridge, MA: MIT Press, 2003), 168.
41. See Joan Kee, *Models of Integrity: Art and Law in Post-Sixties America* (Oakland: University of California Press, 2019).
42. Eichhorn, "Interview with Adrian Piper, 22 April 1998," 196, and Piper, "Solo Exhibition Agreement," in *The Artist's Contract*, 210. Piper also indicated that she dropped the resale royalty provision from the Siegelaub-Projansky model contract, since it was not worth the administrative challenges ("Interview," 198–99).

43. See Eric Stone, "Legal Implications: Cameron Rowland's Rental Contract," *October* 164 (spring 2018): 89–112. Regarding the relationship between Rowland's contracts and earlier strategies of institutional critique by Haacke, see also Aruna D'Souza, "Inside Job," *Art in America* 107, no. 10 (November 2019): 56–63.

44. See the Peabody Museum Collections database, search term "daguerreotype," https://pmem.unix.fas.harvard.edu:8443/peabody.

45. Elinor Reichlin, "Faces of Slavery: A Historical Find," *American Heritage* 28, no. 4 (June 1977): 4–11.

46. Brian Wallis, "Black Bodies, White Science: Louis Agassiz's Slave Daguerreotypes," *American Art* 9, no. 2 (Summer 1995): 38–61. Wallis's article includes the fully nude images of Alfred and Jem, which appear as "Image not Available" in the Peabody Museum Collection database.

47. See Yxta Maya Murray, "From Here I Saw What Happened and I Cried: Carrie Mae Weems' Challenge to the Harvard Archive," *Unbound: Harvard Journal of the Legal Left* 8, no. 1 (2012-13): 1–78.

48. Weems discussed the conflict with Harvard in the segment on her work in season 5 of *Art 21, Compassion,* 2009. Ironically, however, Weems's work is not illustrated here since it was not possible to secure permission to do so, even after indicating a willingness to pay the $150 fee Weems typically requires for such use.

49. Complaint, March 20, 2019, *Tamara Lanier v. President and Fellows of Harvard College,* (1:19-cv-10978), US District Court, D. Massachusetts.

50. Ariella Azoulay, *The Civil Contract of Photography,* trans. Rela Mazali and Ruvik Danieli (Cambridge, MA: Zone Books, 2008), 167.

51. Susan Svrluga and Mara Reinstein, "Harvard Accused in Lawsuit of Retaining and Profiting from Images of Slaves," *Washington Post,* March 20, 2019.

52. Regarding another attempt to address this history, see Robert Moeller, "Harvard's Complicit History with Slavery," *Hyperallergic,* February 26, 2019.

53. Anemona Hartocollis, "Who Should Own Photos of Slaves? The Descendants, not Harvard, a Lawsuit Says," *New York Times,* March 20, 2019.

54. Deirdre Fernandes, "Agassiz descendants put pressure on Harvard to give up slave photos," *Boston Globe,* June 19, 2019, and Svrluga and Reinstein, "Harvard Accused in Lawsuit." See as well Joan Kee's discussion of the role of Weems's work as a precedent for Lanier's claims in "Due Processes," *Artforum,* May 2019.

55. College spokesperson Rachael Dane indicated that there are approximately ten requests per year for high-resolution reproductions of the daguerreotypes, and that they charge $15 for each. See Juliet E. Isselbacher and Molly C. McCafferty, "Agassiz's Descendants Urge Harvard To Turn Over Slave Photos," *Harvard Crimson,* June 21, 2019.

56. McCafferty, "Agassiz's Descendants."

57. Both Lacks and Moore are discussed in Rebecca Skloot, *The Immortal Life of Henrietta Lacks* (New York: Crown Publishers, 2010).

58. *Moore v. Regents of the University of California,* 51 Cal. 3d 120,793 P.2d 479, 271 Cal. Rptr. 146 (1990), rehearing denied August 30, 1990, cert. denied, 111 S. Ct. 1388 (1991). For a summary, see Luisa A. Giuffrida, "*Moore v. Regents of the University of California*: Doctor, Tell Me Moore!," *Pacific Law Journal* 23, no. 1 (1991): 267–313.

59. The press release indicated that she "worked with a legal team comprised of Robert Lands and Jaime Stapleton, with further assistance from Anne Barron" (https://www.paulacoopergallery.com/exhibitions/carey-young-consideration/press-release). I have also addressed Young's engagement with legal rhetoric elsewhere: see Martha Buskirk, "Contract with the Audience," in Carey Young, *Subject to Contract,* ed. Heike Munder and Raphael Gygax (Zurich: Migros Museum & JRP|Ringier, 2013), 115–23.

60. Maria Walsh, "Carey Young Interviewed by Maria Walsh," *Art Monthly* 424, March 2019.
61. Eichhorn, *The Artist's Contract.*
62. According to Charles Esche, who appreciated her challenge to the underpinnings of capitalism, "we are setting aside Euro 50,000 from our purchasing funds without obvious material benefit, there being no 'object' to preserve, but only a pile of cash and a series of legal arrangements" ("Foreword," in Maria Eichhorn, et al., *Maria Eichhorn Aktiengesellschaft* [Köln: König, 2007), 21.
63. See http://www.rosevallandinstitut.org/about.html.
64. Maria Eichhorn, et al., *Maria Eichhorn: Restitutionspolitik/Politics of Restitution* (Köln: König, 2004). For a discussion of both Eichhorn's exhibition and the historical background, see Alexander Alberro, "Specters of Provenance: National Loans, the Königsplatz, and Maria Eichhorn's 'Politics of Restitution,'" *Grey Room* 18 (2004): 64–81.
65. See https://www.lootedart.com/web_images/pdf/WashingtonConferencePrinciples_Original_080630.pdf.
66. See, for example, Catherine Hickley, "Culture Ministers from 16 German States Agree to Repatriate Artefacts Looted in Colonial Era," *Art Newspaper,* March 14, 2019, and "Dutch Museums Take Initiative to Repatriate Colonial-Era Artefacts," *Art Newspaper,* March 14, 2019.
67. As of May 2020, in addition to Cuba, China, and Turkey, reports on threats to artistic freedom also covered Bangladesh, Belarus, Cameroon, Egypt, Equatorial Guinea, Iran, Morocco, Myanmar, Russia, Thailand, Uganda, the United States, and Zimbabwe. See the PEN press releases about artistic freedom at https://artistsatriskconnection.org/press.
68. PEN press release, "Chinese Authorities Razing Ai Weiwei's Studio Part of Larger Attack on Artistic Expression," August 7, 2018, https://pen.org/press-release/chinese-authorities-ai-wei-attack-artistic-expression.
69. For a report on Bruguera's detention that also discusses the suppressed performance, see Coco Fusco, "The State of Detention: Performance, Politics, and the Cuban Public," *E-Flux Journal,* January 3, 2015.
70. There were many reports about the performance, which included the participation of a number of biennial visitors. One of the more extensive was Gerardo Mosquera, "Tania Bruguera: Artivism and Repression in Cuba, An Eyewitness Report," *Walker Magazine,* June 17, 2015. Bruguera made the point about the interrogators having to read the Arendt text in a lecture at MIT on March 13, 2017.
71. Nicole Martinez, "Activists to Stage Alternative Biennial in Havana," *Art Newspaper,* April 4, 2019. For a translation of the decree (by Coco Fusco), see the appendix to the PEN report, *Art Under Pressure: Decree 349 Restricts Creative Freedom in Cuba,* March 4, 2019, https://pen.org/wp-content/uploads/2019/03/Art-Under-Pressure.pdf.
72. *Art Under Pressure: Decree 349 Restricts Creative Freedom in Cuba,* 9.

5. PUBLIC MATTERS

1. Gregory Smithsimon, "Dispersing the Crowd: Bonus Plazas and the Creation of Public Space," in *Common Ground? Readings and Reflections on Public Space,* ed. Anthony M. Orum and Zachary P. Neal (New York: Routledge, 2010), particularly 121–25.
2. Bradley L. Garrett, "The Privatisation of Cities' Public Spaces Is Escalating. It Is Time to Take a Stand," *The Guardian,* August 4, 2015.
3. "Photography Restrictions Outside City Hall 'Shocking', London Assembly Committee Told," *London SE1 News,* November 23, 2010.
4. Regarding political speech in privately owned physical spaces such as malls, see Margaret Kohn, *Brave New Neighborhoods: The Privatization of Public Space* (New York: Routledge, 2004).

5. Copyright Law of the United States, https://www.copyright.gov/title17/92chap1.html#120.
6. The original video was circulated as both as *The Violence of Lies* and *The Clenched Fist of Truth.* See Henri Neuendorf, "Anish Kapoor Declares 'Victory Over The NRA' In A Settlement That Requires the Gun Group to Remove His Art from an Ad," *Artnet News,* December 6, 2018.
7. Anish Kapoor, "Open letter on the NRA's unauthorised use of Cloud Gate, 12th March 2018," http://anishkapoor.com/5104/letter-to-the-nra.
8. Quoted in Ermanno Rivetti, "Made in China? Not Originally," *Art Newspaper,* August 19, 2015.
9. For a summary, see Bryce Newell, "Freedom of Panorama: A Comparative Look at International Restrictions on Public Photography," *Creighton Law Review* 44 (2011), particularly 414–16.
10. https://www.guggenheim.org/location-shoots.
11. Chris Pash, "Souvenir Shops Take Note: The Sydney Opera House Is Now Trademarked," *Business Insider,* January 29, 2014.
12. *Rock and Roll Hall of Fame and Museum, Inc. v. Gentile Productions,* 134 F.3d 749 (6th Cir. 1998).
13. Allison Fass, "Lawyers for Spider-Man Win a Fight over Times Square," *New York Times,* August 13, 2002.
14. James Barron, "$10 Deal for Rights to World Trade Center Name Draws Scrutiny," *New York Times,* September 18, 2013; Aaron Elstein, "Worlds Collide: How a Decades-Old, $10 Naming-Rights Deal Sparked Multimillion-Dollar Lawsuits at the World Trade Center," *Crain's New York Business,* April 3, 2018; and Jonathan Stempel, "NY Ends Probe of $10 Sale of World Trade Center Name Rights," *Reuters,* February 13, 2015.
15. Quoted in David W. Dunlap, "Port Agency Tells Store to Drop 9/11 Items," *New York Times,* July 28, 2014.
16. Sarah Cascone, "Port Authority Claims Ownership of NYC Skyline," *Artnet,* July 31, 2014, and "Is the 9/11 Museum Gift Shop Peddling Crass Consumerism?," *Artnet,* May 28, 2014.
17. See Mélanie Dulong De Rosnay, and Pierre-Carl Langlais, "Public Artworks and the Freedom of Panorama Controversy: A Case of Wikimedia Influence," *Internet Policy Review* 6, no. 1 (2017). For maps, charts, and country-specific links, see "Commons: Freedom of Panorama," https://commons.wikimedia.org/wiki/Commons:Freedom_of_panorama,.
18. For Italy, see Code of the Cultural and Landscape Heritage, Legislative Decree no. 42 of January 22, 2004, Ministero per i beni e le attività culturali, https://whc.unesco.org/document/155711.
19. Jonathan Barrett, "Time to Look Again? Copyright and Freedom of Panorama," *Victoria University of Wellington Law Review* 48, no. 2 (2017): 280.
20. Cited in Joshua Lobert, et al., "The EU Public Interest Clinic and Wikimedia Present: Extending Freedom of Panorama in Europe," IDEAS Working Paper Series from RePEc, 2015, p. 4, https://papers.ssrn.com/sol3/papers.cfm?abstract_id=2602683. For the takedown notice itself, see https://foundation.wikimedia.org/wiki/DMCA_Oldenburg.
21. Dimi Dimitrov, "Swedish Supreme Court rules against Freedom of Panorama," EDRi.org (European Digital Rights), April 6, 2016, https://edri.org/swedish-supreme-court-rules-against-freedom-of-panorama. See also the statement about the final outcome from Jacob Rogers, Legal Counsel, Wikimedia Foundation, "Wikimedia Sweden loses case as court rules against free access to public art online," Wikimedia Foundation, July 25, 2017, https://blog.wikimedia.org/2017/07/25/wikimedia-sweden-freedom-panorama.
22. This has been my general experience when looking at Street View images of both paintings and advertising billboards featuring human faces. See also Stephanie Farr, "Google Street View Is Blurring Faces in Philly's Murals," *Philadelphia Inquirer,* June 12, 2019. See as well the street art collections featured as part of the Google Arts and Culture initiative: https://artsandculture.google.com/project/street-art.

23. See, for example, Greg Allen, "Blurring of Google Art Project Comes As No Surprise," April 3, 2012, https://greg.org/archive/2012/04/11/google-art-institute-project.html; Allen, "Google Art Institute Project," April 11, 2012, https://greg.org/archive/2012/04/11/google-art-institute-project.html; and Caitlin Dewey, "Google's Quest to Make Art Available to Everyone Was Foiled by Copyright Concerns," *Washington Post,* March 4, 2015.
24. "Google Reshoots Japan Views after Privacy Complaints," *Reuters,* May 13, 2009, and Chris Matyszczyk, "Google Street View Has to Reshoot in Japan," *Cnet,* May 13, 2009.
25. Kevin J. O'Brien and David Streitfeld, "Swiss Court Orders Modifications to Google Street View," *New York Times,* June 8, 2012.
26. See Roger C. Geissler, "Private Eyes Watching You: Google Street View and the Right to an Inviolate Personality," *Hastings Law Journal* 63 (2012): 897–925; Claire Cain Miller and Kevin J. O'Brien, "Germany's Complicated Relationship with Google Street View," *New York Times Bits Blog,* April 23, 2013; Greg Allen, "Blurmany And The Pixelated Sublime," *Greg.org,* November 15, 2010; and "Investigations of Google Street View," posted to Epic.org Electronic Privacy Information Center, https://epic.org/privacy/streetview.
27. Jemima Kiss, "Google Admits Collecting Wi-Fi Data Through Street View Cars," *Guardian,* May 14, 2010, and David Kravets, "An Intentional Mistake: The Anatomy of Google's Wi-Fi Sniffing Debacle," *Wired,* May 2, 2012.
28. Malcolm Owen, "Apple Drone Project in North Carolina Selected for Approval by U.S. DOT," *Apple Insider,* May 10, 2018.
29. David Ng, "Playboy Installation by Richard Phillips—Art or Advertising?," *Los Angeles Times,* July 8, 2013.
30. Francesca Mari, "Maybe This Is Why Warhol Stuck to Soup Cans," *New York Times,* September 14, 2013.
31. The Beyoncé selfie is one of many collected on the Ballroom Marfa site devoted to the work (https://www.ballroommarfa.org/archive/event/prada-marfa/#event-images).
32. Zoe Mendelson, "Mural or Billboard? The Dispute over a Shepard Fairey in Brooklyn Heads Back to Court," *Hyperallergic,* August 17, 2017.
33. Kate Taylor, "Fairey Mural Gets Thumbs Down From Buildings Department," *New York Times Artsbeat Blog,* May 4, 2010.
34. Richard Winton, "Graffiti Artist's Past Is Tagging Behind Him," *Los Angeles Times,* March 15, 2011, and "Graffiti Artist Smear Sentenced for Violating Probation," *Los Angeles Times,* March 25, 2011.
35. Robert Plummer, "Brazil's Ad Men Face Billboard Ban," *BBC News,* September 19, 2006; Paulo Winterstein, "Scrub Sao Paulo's Graffiti? Not So Fast, London's Tate Says," *Bloomberg,* August 24, 2008; and Arwa Mahdawi, "Can Cities Kick Ads? Inside the Global Movement to Ban Urban Billboards," *The Guardian,* August 12, 2015.
36. Laurel Wentz, "Sao Paulo's Ingenious Move for Return of Banned Billboards," *Ad Age,* October 30, 2017.
37. On both the controversy and issues raised by artistic appropriation of brand logos, see Sonia K. Katyal, "Branded: On the Semiotic Disobedience of Hank Willis Thomas," *Brooklyn Rail,* March 4, 2016. Viewers were presumably familiar with the overall theme of the "Priceless" ad campaign: "There are some things money can't buy. For everything else, there's MasterCard."
38. Quoted in Hrag Vartanian, "Members of the Illuminator Sue NYPD for False Arrest, First Amendment Retaliation," *Hyperallergic,* May 21, 2015. The three activists arrested were Kyle Depew, Grayson Earle, and Yates McKee.
39. Andrea Baldini, *A Philosophy Guide to Street Art and the Law* (Leiden: Brill, 2018), 66.
40. For example, Vanessa Friedman, "Homage or Theft? Carolina Herrera Called Out by Mexican Minister," *New York Times,* June 13, 2019.

41. Complaint, August 25, 2014, *Jason Williams v. Roberto Cavalli,* S.p.A., 2:14-cv-06659, District Court, C.D. California.
42. Judge Andre Birotte, Jr., Order Denying Defendants Motion to Dismiss, February 12, 2015, *Jason Williams v. Roberto Cavalli.*
43. Complaint, August 5, 2015, *Joseph Tierney v. Moschino S.p.A. and Jeremy Scott,* 2:2015cv05900, District Court, C.D. California.
44. Complaint, *Tierney v. Moschino, et al.*
45. Complaint, *Tierney v. Moschino, et al.*
46. Memorandum of Points and Authorities in Support of Defendants, May 23, 2016, *Joseph Tierney v. Moschino, et al.*
47. Sonia Rao, "H&M's Battle with the Artist Revok Shows How Street Art Is Being Taken Seriously," *Washington Post,* March 16, 2018; Henri Neuendorf, "Street Artist Revok and H&M Settle Dispute Over an Ad That Featured His Work Without Permission," *Artnet,* September 7, 2018. According to Neuendorf, Revok cited a special connection to Detroit, where he had lived and worked for several years, as a reason for using the settlement to support arts organizations in that city.
48. Defendant General Motors LLC's Motion for Summary Judgment, June 25, 2018, *Adrian Falkner v. General Motors Company,* District Court, C.D. California, 2:18-cv-00549.
49. Minutes in Chambers Order Granting in Part and Denying in Part Defendant's Motion for Summary Judgment, September 17th, 2018, *Adrian Falkner v. General Motors Company.*
50. One artist was seriously injured when a staircase collapsed in 2009, and all were temporarily shut out of their studios in the immediate aftermath, leading to fears at that point that the building might not reopen. See Cara Buckley, "One Artist Is Hurt, and 200 Others Are Feeling the Pain," *New York Times,* April 18, 2009.
51. Frederic Block, Memorandum, November 20, 2013, *Cohen v. G&M Realty L.P.* (1:13-cv-05612), District Court, E.D. New York.
52. Frederic Block, Decision, February 12, 2018, *Cohen v. G&M Realty L.P.*
53. Quoted in Block, Memorandum.
54. Block, Decision.
55. Block, Decision, citing Exhibit 1270, "identifying 12 'Works for Which Artists' Removal Was Possible'; 9 'Works Which Artists Were Able to Partially Remove,' and 28 'Works Which Could Only Have Been Removed by Conservator and Contractors.'"
56. Block, Decision, citing *Board of Managers of Soho International Arts Condominium v. City of New York,* 2003 WL 21403333 (S.D.N.Y. June 17, 2003).
57. Block, Decision.
58. Block, Decision.
59. Block, Decision.
60. See Ameena Walker, "The Pair of High-Rise Towers Seek to Pay Homage to the Site's Past as a 'Graffiti Mecca,'" *Curbed,* May 25, 2017.
61. Gabe Cohn, "James Turrell Asks MoMA PS1 to Close Installation," *New York Times,* January 29, 2019.
62. Hannah Ellis-Petersen, "Banksy Works Go Under Hammer in Auction Criticised By Artist," *Guardian,* April 24, 2014.
63. R.J. Rushmore, "Blu Goes Black, Buffing His Own Work in Berlin," *Vandalog—A Street Art Blog,* December 17, 2014.
64. R.J. Rushmore, "The Grey Revolt: Blu And Friends Return Bologna's Walls to the Public, with Buff," *Vandalog—A Street Art Blog,* March 12, 2016, and Jaime Rojo & Steven Harrington, "Blu Allies: A Counter Exhibition to 'Banksy & Co.' Launched in Bologna," *HuffPost,* March 23, 2016, updated December 6, 2017.

65. Eduardo M. Peñalver and Sonia K. Katyal, *Property Outlaws: How Squatters, Pirates, and Protesters Improve the Law of Ownership* (New Haven, CT: Yale University Press, 2010).

6. AUTHORSHIP AND THE UNDEAD

1. Daniel McClean, "Jill Magid and Luis Barragán's Legacy," in Jill Magid, et al., *The Proposal* (Berlin: Sternberg Press, 2016), 54. And see as well Daniel McClean, "Artists' Estates as Guardians of Artistic Legacy: Custodians or Gatekeepers?" in *Artist, Authorship & Legacy: A Reader*, ed. Daniel McClean (London: Ridinghouse, 2018), 284–301.
2. Ines Weizman, "2900 Degrees Fahrenheit," in Magid, *The Proposal*, 95.
3. Rosalind Krauss, "The Originality of the Avant-Garde: A Postmodernist Repetition," *October* 18 (Fall 1981): 47–66, reprinted in *The Originality of the Avant-garde and Other Modernist Myths* (Cambridge, MA: MIT Press, 1985).
4. Albert Elsen, "On the Question of Originality: A Letter," *October* 20 (Spring 1982): 107–9, and Rosalind Krauss, "Sincerely Yours: A Reply, *October* 20 (Spring 1982): 111–30. On the 2014 cast, see Penelope Curtis, "Demonstrable Legacy; or, What Sculptors Leave Behind," in McClean, ed., *Artist, Authorship & Legacy*, 134.
5. The inheritance division is outlined as part of the factual background in the 2014 French appellate court decision in *Aff. J.F. Grenet / Fondation Giacometti et autres.* According to the summary, after Alberto Giacometti's death, his heirs were Annette (his wife), his nephew Silvio Berthoud (d. 1991) and brothers Diego (d. 1985) and Bruno (d. 2012). Annette's legacy eventually became the property of the Fondation Alberto et Annette Giacometti in Paris, Bruno transferred his rights to the Swiss Alberto Giacometti-Stiftung in 2007, and Diego willed his rights to the Berthoud children, resulting in the following division of authorial rights as of 2014: Fondation Alberto et Annette Giacometti, five eigths; Alberto Giacometti-Stiftung (via Bruno) one eighth; Berthoud family one quarter (one eighth each as heirs of Silvio and of Diego). A chart on an earlier version of the Fondation web site went into greater detail about which aspects of the authorial rights are held by each party, though their fractional proportions for the Swiss heirs are inconsistent with the above summary. According to the Fondation diagram, the various parties hold the different authorial rights in the following proportions: *droits patrimoniaux*—five eighths held by the Foundation, three sixteenths by the Stiftung, and three sixteenths by the Berthoud family; *droit moral* held jointly by Fondation, Stiftung, and the Berthoud family; *droit de suite* held by the Berthoud family but not the Fondation or Stiftung (because these rights only descend to direct heirs); *droit de marque* held only by the Fondation. See http://www.fondation-giacometti.fr/en/art/32/author-rights/33/rights-management, available via the Internet Archive.
6. According to Véronique Wiesinger, following Alberto's death, "Diego Giacometti opposed the inventory of the plasters in storage at his residence, thus depriving posterity of an important archival source." But her framing this as an oppositional stance should be read in relation to the tensions between the Giacometti foundation, under Wiesinger's direction, and Giacometti's other heirs. See "Giacometti's Studio: A Site of Unbounded Adventure," in Alberto Giacometti, Véronique Wiesinger, and Centre Georges Pompidou, *The Studio of Alberto Giacometti: Collection of the Fondation Alberto Et Annette Giacometti* (Paris: Fondation Alberto Et Annette Giacometti, 2007), 50.
7. For a short summary of the posthumous editions, see Véronique Wiesinger, "Editioning and Representation: A Path Strewn with Pitfalls," in *The Studio of Alberto Giacometti*, 306. The catalogue raisonné has been published online by the Giacometti Foundation as the Alberto Giacometti Database (AGD), https://www.fondation-giacometti.fr/en/alberto-giacometti-database-agd.

8. See Marc Spiegler, "The Giacometti Legacy: A Struggle for Control," *Art News* 103, no. 9 (October 2004): 175 (a thorough account of many stages of the conflict), and Farah Nayeri, "Reviving Giacometti's Legacy," *New York Times,* April 16, 2015, for an updated summary.
9. See Laney Salisbury and Aly Sujo, *Provenance: How a Con Man and a Forger Rewrote the History of Modern Art* (New York: Penguin Press, 2009). Palmer also questioned the ill-advised disposal of estate material, including a 1994 sale that auctioned off number of key paintings, along with a 2002 sale of bronzes—and it is a tribute to Palmer that the 2002 auction was required to halt once the total sales amount reached a predetermined figure. See Spiegler, "The Giacometti Legacy," 171, 173–74.
10. Spiegler, "The Giacometti Legacy," 177, and Georgina Adam, "The Art Market: Catherine Grenier to Head Annette and Alberto Giacometti Foundation," *Financial Times,* January 17, 2014.
11. Wiesinger, "Sculpting Unceasingly," in *The Studio of Alberto Giacometti,* 99.
12. Spiegler, "The Giacometti Legacy," 176.
13. See Véronique Wiesinger and Laurence Labbe, "A Technical Note on the Sculptures," in *The Studio of Alberto Giacometti,* particularly 161–62 & 168.
14. *Aff. J.F. Grenet / Fondation Giacometti et autres,* 2014.
15. See Thane Peterson, "Benatov: The Man Behind the Bronzes," *Art News,* July 22, 2013, and William D. Cohan, "A Controversy over Degas," *Art News,* April 1, 2010.
16. See William D. Cohan, "Brass Foundry Is Closing, But Debate over Degas's Work Goes On," *New York Times,* April 4, 2016.
17. Armando Besio, "Sequestrate le statue di John Baldessari," *La Repubblica,* February 11, 2011.
18. Vincent Noce, "Prada Poursuivi par la Justice à Milan, *Liberation,* February 1, 2011. According to Daniel McClean, the Prada Foundation was eventually able to successfully defend against the copyright action, on the basis of Italian fair use/parody exceptions, but the work was not exhibited again until 2016. See McClean, "Artists' Estates as Guardians of Artistic Legacy," 292–93.
19. Veronique Wiesinger, "Copyright Protection Is Not an Artistic Hurdle but a Legal Right," *Artinfo,* April 26, 2011.
20. See Laurie Hurwitz, "Giacometti's Legacy," *Art News,* December 18, 2014, and Nayeri, "Reviving Giacometti's Legacy." At that time, Hurwitz reported that the foundation's plan was to release the catalogue raisonné material in sections, starting with graphic work, then sculpture, painting, and decorative arts, along with a separate cataloguing project devoted to drawings that has no hope of being exhaustive.
21. Laurie Hurwitz, "'A Little Time Capsule': Giacometti Institute Opens in Paris with Reconstruction of Artist's Studio," *Artnet,* June 20, 2018.
22. A number of these fragmented plasters are also reproduced in the accompanying exhibition catalogue. See particularly Casimiro Di Crescenzo, "1959–1966: The Later Years," in Philippe Büttner et al., *Alberto Giacometti Beyond Bronze: Masterworks in Plaster and Other Materials* (Zürich: Kunsthaus Zürich and Scheidegger & Spiess, 2016), 172–93.
23. Yve-Alain Bois, "The Iconoclast," in Bois, et al., *Piet Mondrian, 1872–1944* (Boston: Little, Brown & Co., 1994), 348–49. For a history of Mondrian's studios, see Francesco Manacorda and Michael White, eds., *Mondrian and His Studios: Colour in Space* (London: Tate Publishing, 2014).
24. Nancy Troy, "To Be Continued: A Note on Some Recent Mondrians," *October* 27 (1983): 75–80.
25. Harry Cooper, "The Surface in Time: Notes on an Aspect of Mondrian's Critical Reception," in Cooper and Ron Spronk, *Mondrian, the Transatlantic Paintings* (New Haven, CT: Yale University Press, 2001), 8.
26. Quoted by Nancy J. Troy, *The Afterlife of Piet Mondrian* (Chicago: University of Chicago Press, 2014), 93, citing a June 1, 2011 email from Cooper.

27. Troy, *Afterlife*, 42–44, 51–54, and 60–61.
28. *Mondrian Paintings*, Valentine Gallery, March 4–23, 1946.
29. Robert Welsh and Joop Joosten, *Piet Mondrian: Catalogue Raisonné* (New York: H.N. Abrams, 1998), B289.303, v. II-III, 406–7, list the materials as pencil, charcoal, and oil on canvas. However, the web-based catalogue for the Museo Thyssen-Bornemisza lists oil, pencil, chalk, and colored tape on canvas, http://www.museothyssen.org/en/thyssen/ficha_obra/908.
30. Troy, *Afterlife*, 102–3.
31. *Brancusi + Mondrian*, Sidney Janis Gallery, 1982, checklist no. 45.
32. For installation views and the exhibition press release, see https://www.moma.org/calendar/exhibitions/1935.
33. Harry Holtzman, "Introduction: Piet Mondrian New York Studio, 1943–1944," in *Mondrian in New York*, ed. Akiyoshi Tokoro (Toyko: Galerie Tokoro, in cooperation with the Piet Mondrian/Holtzman Trust, Connecticut, and the Sidney Janis Gallery, New York, 1993), 66.
34. *Mondrian in New York*, 86–99, where Mondrian's handmade furniture is reproduced alongside photos of the studio, the step stool, an easel, and various studio tools. Discussed by Troy, *Afterlife*, 71, 74–76, 79, 115, 117–18. Unlike the *Wall Works*, which did not manage to find their way into the 1998 catalogue raisonné, four furniture objects are included, but as a separate category, "Catalogue of the Furniture," II-III, 450–51.
35. Troy, *Afterlife*, 120–21.
36. Mondrian Trust, "Reproduction Rights and Mondrian," http://www.mondriantrust.com/reproduction-rights.
37. On the studio reconstruction, see Albrecht Barthel, "The Paris Studio of Constantin Brancusi: A Critique of the Modern Period Room," *Future Anterior: Journal of Historic Preservation, History, Theory, and Criticism* 3, no. 2 (Winter 2006): 34–43, and Marielle Tabart, et al., *L'atelier Brancusi* (Paris: Centre Georges Pompidou, 1997).
38. Geist, in *Brancusi: A Study of the Sculpture*, 1968, quoted in brochure available at https://www.moma.org/calendar/exhibitions/2133?locale = en#installation-images. (The brochure text cites both William Tucker and Sidney Geist's claims that the bases are not art.)
39. Jérôme Neutres, "Brancusi in New York: Where the Artist Became the Greatest Modern Sculptor," *Brancusi New York: 1913–2013* (New York: Assouline Publishing, 2013), 20.
40. Neutres, "Brancusi in New York," 62. The *Brancusi New York* listings for each of the newly editioned works reference the corresponding catalogue raisonné entry from Pontus Hultén, Natalia Dumitresco, and Alexandre Istrati, *Brancusi* (New York: H.N. Abrams, 1987) and the plaster versions of the works that are part of the Atelier Brancusi, Musée National d'Art Moderne, Centre Pompidou.
41. Constantin Brancusi's statement, in response to "Interrogatories Submitted on Behalf of Plaintiff to be Propounded to the Witness Constantin Brancusi, at Paris, France," reprinted in *Brancusi vs. United States: The Historic Trial, 1928*, preface by Margit Rowell and afterword by André Paleologue (Paris: Adam Biro, 1999), 48.
42. Robert Pincus-Witten, "Constantin Brancusi," *Artforum*, January 2014, 210.
43. Ellen Gamerman, "Growing Furor over Brancusi Show in New York," *Wall Street Journal*, January 16, 2014.
44. Complaint, April 3, 2012, *Sobel v. Eggleston*, US District Court for the Southern District of New York, 12 civ 2551.
45. Memorandum and Order, March 28, 2013, *Sobel v. Eggleston*.
46. Christie's contemporary sale, May 12, 2014, "If I Live I'll See You Tuesday . . . "; "Professional skateboarder Chris Martin rides through Christie's, giving a behind-the-scenes look at highlights from our If I Live I'll See You Tuesday Contemporary Art Evening Sale, with a soundtrack by

AWOLNATION," http://www.christies.com/features/if-i-live-ill-see-you-tuesday-contemporary-art-4623-3.aspx.

47. Carol Vogel, "At Art Basel, Works With a Museum Presence," *New York Times,* June 19, 2014.
48. As is appropriate for an emerging artist today, much of the information initially available about Mahama came from his own explanations in interviews and artist talks posted on YouTube: https://www.youtube.com/watch?v=VAc3vxoYXVA; https://www.youtube.com/watch?v=OGoCPgj6Z-g; https://www.youtube.com/watch?v=ahK93P9eHQY; https://www.youtube.com/watch?v=xbUcYfGQRPk; https://www.youtube.com/watch?v=dunFdoKAw4o. For discussions of his ongoing work, see Barbara Casavecchia, "'In Dependence': Ibrahim Mahama's Monuments to the Anonymous," *Frieze,* March 2, 2018, and Naomi Rea, "Belgium Has a Racist Monuments Problem Too—Here's How They're Dealing With It," *Artnet,* January 30, 2018.
49. On Simchowitz in general, see Christopher Glazek, "The Art World's Patron Satan," *New York Times,* December 30, 2014. Greg Allen has discussed the important role of artist and curator Nana Oforiatta Ayim, who saw a jute sack installation at Mahama's MFA show at KNUST (Kwame Nkrumah University of Science & Technology, Kumasi, Ghana) and began to promote his work. Greg Allen, "It. Was. The. Jutes. It. Was. The. Jutes.," August 27, 2015, https://greg.org/archive/2015/08/27/it-was-the-jutes-it-was-the-jutes.html.
50. Complaint, June 15, 2015, *Simcor and King v. Mahama,* US District Court, Central District of California, 2:15-cv-4539.
51. Complaint, *Simcor and King v. Mahama.*
52. Complaint, *Simcor and King v. Mahama.*
53. Complaint, *Simcor and King v. Mahama.*
54. Complaint, *Simcor and King v. Mahama.*
55. Attorney Rizwan R. Ramji, quoted in Sarah Douglas and Andrew Russeth, "Jute Sack Artworks Are at the Center of Simchowitz Lawsuit Against Venice Biennale Artist," *Art News,* August 25, 2015.
56. Michael Kaplan, "Why Art Gallery Owners Love to Hate Stefan Simchowitz," *Los Angeles Magazine,* February 26, 2015.
57. Douglas and Russeth, "Jute Sack Artworks."
58. Eileen Kinsella, "Stefan Simchowitz Fires Back at Ibrahim Mahama in Nasty, Ongoing Dispute," *Artnet,* April 6, 2016.
59. Scott Reyburn, "Emerging Art Cools Down," *New York Times,* September 4, 2015.
60. Gareth Harris, "Who's Bankrolling the Venice Biennale," *Art Newspaper,* May 5, 2015, indicates that Mahama's 2015 installation was backed by APALAZZOGALLERY in Brescia.

7. STATUS SHIFTS

1. Ruling, January 27, 2010, *Massachusetts Museum of Contemporary Art Foundation, Inc. v. Christoph Büchel,* No. 08-2199 (1st Cir. 2010).
2. As summarized by Michael Adrian Ponsor, Memorandum and Order Regarding Cross Motions for Summary Judgment, July 11, 2008, *Massachusetts Museum of Contemporary Art Foundation, Inc. v. Christoph Büchel,* United States District Court, D. Massachusetts, 565 F. Supp. 2d 245 (2008).
3. K.E. Gover, *Art and Authority: Moral Rights and Meaning in Contemporary Visual Art* (Oxford: Oxford University Press, 2018), 99.
4. Virginia Rutledge, "Institutional Critique: On Christoph Büchel and Mass MoCA," *Artforum,* March 2008, 151–52, 382 (writing about the arguments presented in the initial district court case).
5. Donn Zaretsky points out that, had the case gone to trial, Büchel's lawyers could have emphasized statements from internal MASS MoCA correspondence suggesting that the museum crew should go ahead with installation work as long as they were "80% sure" they were following

the artist's wishes ("Training Ground for Moral Rights: *MASS MoCA v. Christoph Büchel*," in McClean, *Artist, Authorship, & Legacy*, 51).

6. *Marc Jancou Fine Art Ltd., doing business as Marc Jancou Contemporary v. Sotheby's, Inc. and Cady Noland*, no. 650316/2012 (N.Y. Sup. Ct. February 1, 2012). I discussed this incident at greater length in "Retraction," in McClean, *Artist, Authorship & Legacy* (London: Ridinghouse, 2018), 54–68. On the larger context for Noland's renunciations, including issues of artistic labor, see also Fraser Ward, "Refusals, Disclaimers and Denials: Cady Noland's Recent 'Work,'" *Performance Paradigm* 14 (2018): 28–44.
7. *Oozewald* sold for $6.6 million during Sotheby's November 9, 2011, evening sale, where it set a new record for the highest price paid for the work of a living female artist. *Cowboys Milking* was originally scheduled for Sotheby's November 10, 2011, afternoon sale.
8. The fax is reproduced as part of Affidavit of Plaintiff, Cady Noland in Opposition to Defendants' Motion to Dismiss, August 3, 2018, *Cady Noland v. Galerie Michael Janssen, Michael Janssen, Wilhelm Schurmann, KOW, and Chris D'Amelio*, no. 1:17-cv-05452-JPO (S.D.N.Y. July 18, 2017). Noland's affidavit decisively countered a rather artful reading of the fax put forward by a Janssen representative who claimed that the statement "This is not an artwork" was only meant to indicate that the fax itself should not be construed as art. Quoted in Laura Gilbert, "Did Cady Noland Disavow Another Work?," *Art Newspaper*, June 25, 2015.
9. Complaint, June 18, 2017, *Cady Noland v. Galerie Michael Janssen, et al.* The moral rights claims were up against the limited recognition of such protections under US law. Jurisdiction for the New York State Artists Authorship Rights Act was asserted on the basis of business conducted by the various named parties in New York state, and, despite references to the Visual Artists Rights Act (VARA), the fact that Log Cabin dates to 1990 and was apparently sold the same year it was made would situate it before the June 1, 1991, effective date for VARA.
10. United States Copyright Office, May 25, 2018, to Andrew Epstein, Esq., Re: Second Request for Reconsideration for Refusal to Register Log Cabin; Correspondence ID: 1–2O3WIKA; SR 1–5582119381 (affirming the Registration Program's previous denial of registration).
11. United States Copyright Office, May 25, 2018.
12. Memorandum of Law in Support of Defendants' Motion to Dismiss, July 6, 2018, *Cady Noland v. Galerie Michael Janssen, et al.*
13. J. Paul Oetken, District Judge, Opinion and Order, June 1, 2020, *Cady Noland v. Galerie Michael Janssen, et al.*
14. Memorandum of Law in Support of Defendants' Motion to Dismiss, July 6, 2018, *Cady Noland v. Galerie Michael Janssen, et al.*
15. Bleckner later told a reporter that he was unaware that Boone was representing the painting as the original, indicating that he "thought she would say that it had been painted as close to the original as possible" (Ted Loos, "Ross Bleckner on His Comeback and Mary Boone," *New York Times*, April 25, 2019).
16. Summons and Complaint, September 12, 2016, *Alec Baldwin v. Mary Boone et al.*, 654807/2016—New York County Supreme Court, before Judge Robert R. Reed.
17. Transcript—So Ordered, April 24, 2017, *Alec Baldwin v. Mary Boone et al.*
18. Susan Lehman, "Alec Baldwin's Legal Tussle Over a Painting," *New Yorker*, November 13, 2017.
19. Although he failed to convince the Manhattan district attorney that it was a criminal matter (and subsequently filed a civil suit), Baldwin initially pursued the case in the court of public opinion, including in Graham Bowley, "Paint and Switch? Did Alec Baldwin Pay $190,000 for the Wrong Picture?," *New York Times*, August 13, 2016.
20. Jerald Ordover to Brent Collier Esq., September 7, 1973, "Re: Frank Stella et al adv. Lynn H Factor," Castelli Gallery papers, Archives of American Art, folder labeled "Frank Stella—'Marquis

de Portago' Painting." A later addendum by Ordover indicated that the curator was James Eliot, which is confirmed by Stella's recollection, cited in Caroline A. Jones, *Machine in the Studio: Constructing the Postwar American Artist* (Chicago: University of Chicago Press, 1996), 413n142.

21. Ordover to Collier, citing correspondence as well as negotiations in which he participated.
22. Ordover to Collier, and Barry Siegel, "Collector vs. Artist: The Legality of Duplicates," *Los Angeles Times*, December 3, 1978.
23. Quoted in Siegel, "Collector vs. Artist."
24. Siegel, "Collector vs. Artist."
25. Maurice Tuchman, letter to Jerald Ordover, October 4, 1973, Castelli Gallery papers, Archives of American Art, folder labeled "Frank Stella—'Marquis de Portago' Painting."
26. Complaint, July 18, 1973, *Factor v. Stella*, No, C 58832, Superior Court, Los Angeles County, California (1978).
27. Jones, *Machine in the Studio*, 413n142.
28. Quoted in Siegel, "Collector vs. Artist."
29. Opinion, November 2, 1978, *Factor v. Stella*.
30. Bruce Glaser, "Questions to Stella and Judd" (1964), in *Minimal Art: A Critical Anthology*, ed. Gregory Battcock (New York: E.P. Dutton, 1968).
31. See Peter Adelman, "Conservator Overreaching and the Art Owner: Contractual Protections Against the Overzealous Restoration of Fine Art," *Cardozo Arts and Entertainment Law Journal* 12 (1994), note 19.
32. Harvard Art Museum exhibition information, https://www.harvardartmuseums.org/visit/exhibitions/4768/mark-rothkos-harvard-murals. For a critique of the exhibition, see Robert Moeller, "In the Spotlight, Harvard's Rothkos Don't Shine," *Hyperallergic*, April 17, 2015.
33. Jeffrey Weiss, "Things not Necessarily Meant to Be Viewed as Art," *Artforum*, March 2013, 220–29.
34. Weiss, "Things not Necessarily Meant to Be Viewed," 223.
35. I addressed issues raised by the Panza works in *The Contingent Object of Contemporary Art* (Cambridge, MA: MIT Press, 2003) and also served as a member of the PCI advisory committee. The results of the initiative were presented at "Object Lessons: The Panza Collection Initiative Symposium," April 9–10, 2019, with videos of the symposium available at https://www.guggenheim.org/conservation/the-panza-collection-initiative/object-lessons-the-panza-collection-initiative-symposium and a planned publication to follow. The majority of the works decommissioned in 2016 were examples by Judd (both Panza fabrications and unrealized plans), but the category also included examples by Dan Flavin and Robert Irwin.
36. See the documents compiled in *Brancusi vs. United States: The Historic Trial, 1928*, preface by Margit Rowell and afterword by André Paleologue (Paris: Adam Brio, 1999).
37. Judgment of the Court (Second Chamber), May 15, 1985, *Reinhard Onnasch v Hauptzollamt Berlin-Packhof*, Case 155/84 (reference for a preliminary ruling from the Fianzgericht Berlin), "Common Customs Tariff—Sculptures and statuary." The European Court of Justice determination was based on an Opinion by Advocate General Lenz, delivered on March 21, 1985. Available via InfoCuria—Case-law of the Court of Justice, http://curia.europa.eu/juris/liste.jsf?language=en&num=C-155/84.
38. Judgement, November 8, 1990, *Krystyna Gmurzynska-Bscher, Galerie Gmurzynska, v. Oberfinanzdirektíon Köb, (Principal Revenue Office, Cologne)*, case C-231/89, European Court of Justice, http://curia.europa.eu/juris/liste.jsf?language=en,T,F&num=231/89.
39. Judgment of the Court, November 8, 1990, *Gmurzynska-Bscher*.
40. Summary by Withers, the law firm representing the gallery: Pierre Valentin and Daniel McClean, "Haunch of Venison VAT victory: HM Customs Dispute over Dan Flavin and Bill Viola Works,"

Art Newspaper 199, February 2009. For general background, see Marina P. Markellou, "Rejecting the Works of Dan Flavin and Bill Viola: Revisiting the Boundaries of Copyright Protection for Post-Modern art," *Queen Mary Journal of Intellectual Property* 2, no. 2: 175–81, and Rachel J. Tischler, "'The Power to Tax Involves the Power to Destroy': How Avant-Garde Art Outstrips the Imagination of Regulators, and Why a Judicial Rubric Can Save It," *Brooklyn Law Review* 78, no. 1 (2012): 1665–1705.

41. *Haunch of Venison Partners Limited v. Her Majesty's Commissioners of Revenue and Customs,* London Tribunal Centre, released December 11, 2008. The trial took place in September 2008 before Richard Barlow (Chairman) and Lynneth M. Salisbury (Member). According to the argument of HMRC, the proper classification for the Viola would come under the heading 9008 30 00, "image projectors, other than cinematographic; photographic (other than cinematographic) enlargers and reducers—other image projectors," and for Flavin, under 9405 10 28, as "chandeliers and other electrical ceiling or wall lighting fittings excluding those of a kind used for lighting public open spaces or thoroughfares—other."
42. Georgina Adam, "Flavin and Viola Light Works Ruled 'Not Art,'" *Art Newspaper* 219, December 2010. The European Commission ruling overturned both United Kingdom and Dutch national court decisions concerning video installations as art.
43. Pierre Valentin, "European Definition of Art Is Absurd," *Art Newspaper* 220, January 2011.
44. Valentin, "European Definition of Art Is Absurd."
45. Panza's files for a series of 1966 works by Dan Flavin (Panza numbers DF 8–11) indicate declared shipping values of $150–200 each, despite prices in the thousands per work (The Giuseppe Panza Papers, 1956–1990, Special Collections of the Getty Research Library at the Getty Research Institute, Series II, box 110).
46. "Achromic Destruction," January 10, 2018, https://vimeo.com/250412872.
47. See Cristina Ruiz and Ada Masoero, "Piero Manzoni Foundation Criticized for Destruction of Works," *Art Newspaper,* April 4, 2018.

8. FROM AUTHENTIC TO FAKE

1. Yve-Alain Bois, "Can a Genuine Picasso be a Fake?" *Proceedings of the American Philosophical Society* 160, no. 1 (2016): 6–7. Bois traced the anecdote to a different version in Arthur Koestler's 1967 *The Art of Creation,* but even there suspected that it could be apocryphal.
2. Bois, "Can a Genuine Picasso be a Fake?," 17.
3. J.L. Austin, *How to Do Things with Words* (Cambridge, MA: Harvard University Press, 1962), 12.
4. Austin, *How to Do Things,* 22 (emphasis in the original). Jacques Derrida's classic critique of speech act theory, as expounded by both Austin and John Searle, stressed the problem of defining the context for a speech act, external to its embeddedness in language. See Derrida, "Signature Event Context" (1972), published in *Glyph* 1 (1977), 172–97, along with John Searle, "Reply to Derrida: Reiterating the Differences" *Glyph* 1 (1977), 198–208, and Derrida's reply to Searle, "Limited Inc a b c," *Glyph* 2 (1977), 162–254.
5. Philip Auslander, "The Performativity of Performance Documentation," *PAJ: A Journal of Performance and Art* 84 (2006): 1–10.
6. Joan Kee, *Models of Integrity: Art and Law in Post-Sixties America* (Oakland: University of California Press, 2019).
7. Dietmar Elger, "Key to Catalogue Entries," in *Felix Gonzalez-Torres: Catalogue Raisonné,* ed. Dietmar Elger (Ostfildern-Ruit, Germany: Cantz, 1997), 14.
8. See, for example, Bernhard Schulz, "Das Werk von Gerhard Richter: Ich mal mir meine Welt," *Der Tagespiegel,* July 21, 2015, and Henri Neuendorf, "Collectors Alarmed As Gerhard Richter Disowns Early Works From West German Period," *Artnet,* July 21, 2015.

9. Louis Oberdorfer, District Judge, Memorandum, April 2, 1993, *Greenberg Gallery, Inc., et al. v. Patricia Bauman, et al.*, Civ. A. No. 91–0439-LFO, 817 F.Supp. 167 (1993).
10. Ronald D. Spencer, "Authentication in Court: Factors Considered and Standards Proposed," in *The Expert Versus the Object: Judging Fakes and False Attributions in the Visual Arts*, ed. Ronald D. Spencer (Oxford: Oxford University Press, 2004), 196–98.
11. Justice David Saxe, Appellate Division, First Department, Opinion, December 1, 2009, *Joel Thome v. The Alexander & Louisa Calder Foundation, Also Known as The Calder Foundation, et al.*, 70 A.D.3d 88, 108 (1st Department 2009).
12. See, for example, the new global vetting policy announced by The European Fine Art Fair (TEFAF) in November 2018, after questions about potential forgeries at several regularly exhibiting galleries (https://www.tefaf.com/press/press-releases/tefaf-introduces-a-new-global-vetting-policy).
13. Complaint, October 17, 2016, *Mayor Gallery LTD v. Agnes Martin Catalogue Raisonné LLC et al*, 655489/2016, New York County Supreme Court.
14. Complaint, *Mayor Gallery LTD v. Agnes Martin Catalogue Raisonné LLC.*
15. Judge Andrea Masley, Decision and Order, July 5, 2019, *Mayor Gallery v. Agnes Martin Catalogue Raisonné LLC.*
16. Defendants' Memorandum of Law in Support of Motion to Dismiss the First Unredacted Amended Complaint, January 30, 2017, *Mayor Gallery v. Agnes Martin Catalogue Raisonné LLC.*
17. Quoted in Richard Dorment, "What Is an Andy Warhol?," *New York Review of Books*, October 22, 2009. This was the first in an extended set of articles and rebuttals in the *New York Review* discussing the lawsuit brought by Joe Simon-Whelan, owner of a different self-portrait from the same series, against the authentication board in 2009: *Simon-Whelan v. The Andy Warhol Foundation For The Visual Arts, Inc.* (1:07-cv-06423), District Court, S.D. New York.
18. See Charles and Thomas Danziger, "On the Case: The Real Deal on Authenticity," *Artnet*, May 8, 2014.
19. *Edelman Arts, Inc. v. Geoffrey Diner Gallery*, 1:2016cv02157, District Court, S.D. New York. See as well Dan Duray, "Lawsuit Shows Difficulties of Authentication and Repair: Case Between Collector and Dealer Over a Sculpture Damaged in Transit Becomes a Legal Saga," *Art Newspaper*, October 13, 2016.
20. *United States v. Ramnarine*, 12-cr-826–001 (JGK) (S.D.N.Y., filed November 15, 2012). See the press releases from the United States Attorney's Office, Southern District of New York: "Queens Foundry Owner Pleads Guilty in Manhattan Federal Court for $11 Million Scheme to Sell Fake Jasper Johns Sculpture," January 28, 2014, https://www.justice.gov/usao-sdny/pr/queens-foundry-owner-pleads-guilty-manhattan-federal-court-11-million-scheme-sell-fake, and "Foundry Owner Sentenced To 30 Months In Prison For $11 Million Scheme to Sell Fake Sculptures Attributed to Jasper Johns and other Prominent Artists," October 16, 2014, https://www.justice.gov/usao-sdny/pr/foundry-owner-sentenced-30-months-prison-11-million-scheme-sell-fake-sculptures.
21. Colin Moynihan, "Artist Testifies That a Reproduction of a Famous Work Wasn't Authorized," *New York Times*, January 23, 2014.
22. *United States v. Meyer*, 13-cr-604-JPO (S.D.N.Y. filed Apr. 24, 2014). Press releases, United States Attorney's Office, Southern District of New York, "Former Studio Assistant To Jasper Johns Charged In Manhattan Federal Court With $6.5 Million Scheme To Sell Stolen Johns Works," August 15, 2013, https://www.justice.gov/usao-sdny/pr/former-studio-assistant-jasper-johns-charged-manhattan-federal-court-65-million-scheme; "Former Studio Assistant To Jasper Johns Pleads Guilty In Manhattan Federal Court To Engaging In $6.5 Million Scheme To Sell Stolen Johns Works," August 27, 2014, https://www.justice.gov/usao-sdny/pr/former-studio-

assistant-jasper-johns-pleads-guilty-manhattan-federal-court-engaging-65; and "Former Studio Assistant To Jasper Johns Sentenced In Manhattan Federal Court To 18 Months In Prison For Scheme To Sell Millions Of Dollars Of Stolen Johns Works," April 23, 2015, https://www.justice.gov/usao-sdny/pr/former-studio-assistant-jasper-johns-sentenced-manhattan-federal-court-18-months-prison. See also Robert Kolker, "The Betrayal of Jasper Johns: How an Ambitious Assistant Earned His Trust—and Stole His Work," *New York*, November 17, 2014.

23. Amah-Rose Abrams, "Peter Doig, Accused of Disavowing a Painting, Takes Stand at Trial," *Artnet*, August 9, 2016.
24. Brian Boucher, "Korean Art Dealer Indicted for Forged Lee Ufan Paintings," *Artnet*, June 8, 2016; Rain Embuscado, "Lee Ufan Refuses Police Request to Confirm 13 Forgeries of His Work," *Artnet*, July 5, 2016; Alyssa Buffenstein, "Three More Arrested in South Korea for Producing and Selling Lee Ufan Forgeries," *Artnet*, November 18, 2016; and Park Sae-jin, "S. Korea Art Society Hit by Forgery Dispute over Lee Ufan's Paintings," *Aju Business Daily*, January 19, 2017.
25. Ted Loos, "The Surprising Tale of One of Frank Stella's Black Paintings," *New York Times*, February 17, 2019.
26. Lot 26, Twentieth-Century Italian Art, Sotheby's London, October 17, 2013.
27. Cristina Ruiz, "De Chirico Catalogue under Scrutiny: Reliability of Publication Questioned as Collector Refuses to Pay for Painting Claimed to Be a Fake," *Art Newspaper*, February 5, 2014.
28. Fondazione Giorgio e Isa de Chirico, "Un autenticissimo de Chirico fatto passare dall'Archivio dell'Arte Metafisica per un falso di Renato Peretti. Come si costruisce una falsa 'verita?'" (also in English as "Authentic de Chirico painting Signalled as a Fake by L'Archivio dell'Arte Metafisica: The Construction of a Fake 'Truth'"), March 28, 2014, http://www.fondazionedechirico.org/news, under "Opera autentica segnalata come falsa," responding to both Ruiz, "De Chirico Catalogue under Scrutiny," and "2013/10 Le case d'asta, la Fondazione e i falsi Peretti," L'Archivio dell'Arte Metafisica, http://www.archivioartemetafisica.org/le-case-dasta-la-fondazione-e-i-falsi-peretti.
29. Fabio Benzi, "Replicas and Neo-Baroque Style: Two Themes for an Exegesis of de Chirico's Oeuvre," in *Giorgio de Chirico: Catalogo Generale—Opere Dal 1910 al 1975*, vol. 2 (San Marino: Maretti Editore, 2015), particularly 19–20.
30. Paolo Baldacci, *Giorgio De Chirico: Betraying the Muse: De Chirico and the Surrealists* (New York: Paolo Baldacci Gallery, 1994).
31. William H. Robinson, "De Chirico Forgeries: The Treachery of the Surrealists," *IFAR Journal* 4, no. 1 (2001): 10–17.
32. Paolo Baldacci and Gerd Roos, *Piazza d'Italia (Souvenir d'Italie II) 1913 [luglio-agosto 1933]* (Milan, Scalpendi Editore, 2013).
33. Compare to Lot 3, Twentieth Century Italian Art, Sotheby's London, October 12, 2012.
34. Summarized in Ruiz, "De Chirico Catalogue under Scrutiny," which also revealed that Carlo Accorsi, author of the 1979 *Bolaffi Arte* article, was a nom de plume for Umberto Allemandi, who subsequently became founding publisher of *The Art Newspaper*.
35. See Jonathon Keats, *Forged: Why Fakes are the Great Art of Our Age* (Oxford: Oxford University Press, 2013), 120, 122–23, and David Barboza, Graham Bowley, and Amanda Cox, "Forging an Art Market in China," *New York Times*, October 28, 2013.
36. Keats, *Forged*, 111.
37. Keats, *Forged*, 120, citing Lessard, who wrote his own memoir about these activities.
38. Claim by de Hory in "Elmyr de Hory: Master Faker," *Life*, February 6, 1970, 34–35.
39. See Keats, *Forged*, 131–33.
40. Eric Hebborn, *Drawn to Trouble: The Forging of an Artist, An Autobiography* (Edinburgh: Mainstream Pub. Projects, 1991) and *The Art Forger's Handbook* (Woodstock, NY: Overlook Press, 1997).

41. Hebborn, *Drawn to Trouble,* 115–17.
42. He made the claim of authorship as part of a 1991 BBC program, *Portrait of a Master Forger;* it is also discussed in Keats, *Forged,* 101.
43. Denis Dutton, "Death of a Forger," American Society for Aesthetics, 1996, https://aesthetics-online.org/general/custom.asp?page=DuttonForger.
44. Keats, *Forged,* 104.
45. Dutton, "Death of a Forger."
46. Ken Perenyi, *Caveat Emptor: The Secret Life of an American Art Forger* (New York: Pegasus Books, 2012).
47. See Joshua Hammer, "The Greatest Fake-Art Scam in History?," *Vanity Fair,* October 10, 2012, and Flavia Foradini, "Notorious Forger Wolfgang Beltracchi on Ethics, the Art Market and How to Make a Great Fake," *Art Newspaper,* November 19, 2018.
48. "The Hippy and the Expressionists: Investigators Zero in on Massive Art Forgery Scandal," *Spiegel,* November 5, 2010, and Hammer, "The Greatest Fake-Art Scam in History?"
49. See Alexis Fournol, "Judgment Against Max Ernst Expert Werner Spies Overturned in Appeal," *Art Newspaper,* December 9, 2015.
50. Hammer, "The Greatest Fake-Art Scam in History?," and also reported in Christopher Goodwin, "Wolfgang Beltracchi: A Real Con Artist," *The Times,* May 10, 2014.
51. Reported by Hammer, "The Greatest Fake-Art Scam in History?," as $500,000, plus additional gallery commissions. See also "Spiegel Interview with Wolfgang Beltracchi: Confessions of a Genius Art Forger," *Spiegel,* March 9, 2012, which references a payment of €400,000 for appraising seven Max Ernst forgeries, and Goodwin, "Wolfgang Beltracchi: A Real Con Artist," which describes payments from the Beltracchis to Spies totaling around €400,000, based on 8 percent of the purchase price for each work, and indicates that Spies picked up commissions from the Blondeau gallery as well.
52. Laney Salisbury and Aly Sujo, *Provenance: How a Con Man and a Forger Rewrote the History of Modern Art* (New York: Penguin Press, 2009), 70–71.
53. Salisbury and Sujo, *Provenance,* 79.
54. Salisbury and Sujo, *Provenance,* 96–97, 196–98, 208, 210, and 258.
55. Salisbury and Sujo, *Provenance,* 161, 195, 205, 250, and 256–57.
56. Sándor Radnóti, *The Fake: Forgery and Its Place in Art* (Lanham, MD: Rowman & Littlefield Publishers, 1999), 44, referencing the 1976 *Fälschung und Forschung* at the Folkwang Museum, Essen, and the 1990 exhibition *Fake?* at the British Museum.
57. Patricia Cohen, "Possible Forging of Modern Art Is Investigated," *New York Times,* December 2, 2011; *Pierre Lagrange and G&S Trustees Ltd. v Knoedler Gallery, LLC, d/b/a Knoedler & Company, and Ann Freedman,* 1:11-cv-08757, District Court, S.D. New York, filed December 1, 2011. It later became evident that the same suspect red pigment also appeared in a "Pollock" purchased by Harvey and Frances White, and a "Rothko" bought by the Martin Hilti Family Trust. See Judge Paul G. Gardephe, Memorandum Opinion & Order, September 30, 2015, *The Martin Hilti Family Trust v. Knoedler Gallery, LLC,* 1:13-cv-00657, District Court, S.D. New York.
58. William K. Rashbaum and Patricia Cohen, "Art Dealer Admits to Role in Fraud," *New York Times,* September 16, 2013.
59. James Panero, "'I Am the Central Victim': Art Dealer Ann Freedman on Selling $63 Million in Fake Paintings," *New York,* August 27, 2013, and M.H. Miller, "Ann Freedman Settles Defamation Suit Against Marco Grassi," *Observer,* December 13, 2013 (regarding a comment from Grassi quoted by Panero).
60. See Samanth Subramanian, "How to Spot a Perfect Fake: The World's Top Art Forgery Detective," *Guardian,* June 15, 2018.

61. The artist, who returned to China after news of the fraud broke, was reportedly paid only a few thousand dollars or less per work, and also claimed not to know how the work was being used. However, the eventual indictment of Qian and other of Rosales's collaborators indicated that Jose Carlos Bergantinos Diaz attempted to find older surfaces and materials for Qian to use, and that Qian began to demand more money for his fakes after realizing how they were being marketed. See Indictment, March 31, 2014, *United States of America v. José Carlos Bergantiños Diaz, Jesus Angel Bergantiños Diaz, and Pei Shen Qian*, 14 Crim 217, District Court, S.D. New York. See also Sarah Maslin Nir, Patricia Cohen and William K. Rashbaum, "Struggling Immigrant Artist Tied to $80 Million New York Fraud," *New York Times*, August 16, 2013, and Colin Moynihan, "Dealer in Art Fraud Scheme Avoids Prison," *New York Times*, January 31, 2017.
62. Eileen Kinsella, "Richard Diebenkorn's Daughter Challenges Ann Freedman's Story at Knoedler Forgery Trial," *Artnet*, January 27, 2016.
63. October 9, 2003, IFAR report, quoted in Judge Paul G. Gardephe, Memorandum Opinion & Order, September 30, 2013, *De Sole v. Knoedler Gallery, LLC*, 1:12-cv-02313, District Court, S.D. New York, and Gardephe, Memorandum Opinion & Order, May 8, 2019, *The Martin Hilti Family Trust v. Knoedler Gallery.*
64. Freedman reportedly insisted that the Taubmans should accept "our word," while telling them that an "invoice is always our legal guarantee" (quoted in Judge Paul G. Gardephe, Memorandum Opinion & Order, September 30, 2013, *De Sole v. Knoedler Gallery*). See as well Patricia Cohen, "When the Supposed Experts Lead Buyers Astray," *New York Times*, February 12, 2016.
65. M.H. Miller, "In Court, Experts Say Knoedler Ignored Warnings About Forgeries," *Artnews*, February 5, 2016. And see the summary of events in Judge Paul G. Gardephe, Memorandum Opinion & Order, September 30, 2015, *The Martin Hilti Family Trust v. Knoedler Gallery.*
66. As recounted in the initial complaint, January 29, 2013, *The Martin Hilti Family Trust v. Knoedler Gallery*, and in Gardephe, Memorandum Opinion & Order, September 30, 2013, *De Sole v. Knoedler Gallery.*
67. Gardephe, Memorandum Opinion & Order, September 30, 2013, *De Sole v. Knoedler Gallery.*
68. Settlement Agreement and Mutual Release, October 6, 2011, *Killala Fine Art Limited v. Weissman*, 1:11-cv-00702, District Court, S.D. New York.
69. Patricia Cohen, "Two New Lawsuits Accuse Manhattan Gallery of Having Sold Fakes," *New York Times ArtsBeat*, November 27, 2013.
70. Bois, "Can a Genuine Picasso be a Fake?," 12.
71. See Patricia Cohen, "Selling a Fake Painting Takes More Than a Good Artist," *New York Times*, May 2, 2014.
72. In addition to Bois's own account, see Cohen, "Selling a Fake Painting Takes More Than a Good Artist," and Laura Gilbert, "Lawsuit against Art Historian Over Fake Rothko Settled Out of Court," *Art Newspaper*, April 11, 2017.
73. See Complaint, January 29, 2013, and Paul G. Gardephe, Memorandum Opinion & Order, September 30, 2015, *The Martin Hilti Family Trust v. Knoedler Gallery.*
74. Amended Complaint, September 13, 2012, *De Sole v. Knoedler Gallery.*
75. See J. Paul Oetken, Opinion and Order, January 29, 2015, *Frank J. Fertitta III and Eykyn Maclean, LP, v. Knoedler Gallery, LLC d/b/a Knoedler & Company; 8-31 Holdings, Inc.; Michael Hammer; Ann Freedman; Jaime Andrade; Glafira Rosales; José Carlos Bergantiños Diaz; Jesus Angel Bergantiños Diaz; Oliver Wick; Urs Kraft; and John Does # 1 To 10*, 1:14-cv-02259, District Court, S.D. New York.

    For the rather complex sale, Knoedler chose not to reveal its role. Wick offered the work to Eykyn, a New York/London gallery, which offered it to its client Fertitta. For tax purposes, Fertitta purchased the painting through another gallery, Gurr Johns. Mr. X Jr. supposedly did his business through Swiss attorney Urs Kraft, who sold the painting on behalf of an "undisclosed seller," even though in this case Rosales claimed to own the painting rather than just operating as the go-between. The bill of sale between Kraft and Gurr Johns required Kraft to disclose the seller's identity in the event that its "attribution, provenance, and description" was challenged. Kraft warranted its authenticity and indemnified Gurr Johns from any losses associated with false provenance. Fertitta in turn sold the painting to an undisclosed buyer, then repurchased it for $8.5 million after an article in *Art Newspaper* indicated that it was probably a forgery. Kraft refused to reveal his client when contacted by Fertitta, and Fertitta brought a lawsuit against everyone associated with the sale on April 1, 2014. District court judge J. Paul Oetken had the task of sorting out which motions to dismiss should be granted or denied, which he did in his January 29, 2015, order.

76. Paul G. Gardephe, Memorandum Opinion & Order, October 9, 2015, *De Sole v. Knoedler Gallery.*
77. Judd Tully, "In Knoedler's Wake," *Art and Auction,* September 1, 2016, 86.
78. Lot 32, Mark Rothko, Untitled, 1959, Catalogue for Christie's Post-War and Contemporary Art, Evening Sale, New York, May 13, 2009, p. 82. According to Patricia Cohen, although the work failed to sell during the auction itself, Christie's sold it privately, then later refunded the purchase price. See Cohen, "From One Garage in Queens, a World of Fakes," *New York Times,* December 26, 2013.
79. David Anfam, *Abstract Expressionism: A World Elsewhere* (New York: Haunch of Venison, 2008), 12.
80. Anfam, *Abstract Expressionism,* 148.
81. In an apparent attempt to undermine Christopher Rothko's testimony in the De Sole trial, defense lawyers pointed out that "the Rothko heirs had given their permission for one of the supposed Rothkos to be included in a calendar under their copyright." See Brian Boucher, "Mark Rothko's Son Denies Authenticating Paintings at Knoedler Fraud Trial," *Artnet,* February 1, 2016.
82. Anfam quoted in Cohen, "Selling a Fake Painting Takes More Than a Good Artist." Regarding his trial testimony on the topic, see Brian Boucher, "8 Key Points to Know About the Knoedler Trial, Which Starts Today," *Artnet,* January 25, 2016.
83. Cait Munro, "Ab Ex Scholar Hired by Knoedler Gallery Admits He Can't Tell Two Rothko Paintings Apart," *Artnet,* February 2, 2016.
84. Amended Complaint, September 13, 2012, *De Sole v. Knoedler Gallery.*
85. Boucher, "Mark Rothko's Son."
86. M.H. Miller, "The Big Fake: Behind the Scenes of Knoedler Gallery's Downfall," *Art News,* April 25, 2016.
87. Subramanian, "How to Spot a Perfect Fake." The profile of Martin includes the tidbit that he was almost rejected from the conservation program at the Winterthur Museum in Delaware, due to suspicions that his facility as a copyist might lead him to turn his training toward forgery.
88. Quoted in Anita Gates, "Where Art Forgeries Meet Their Match," *New York Times,* May 2, 2018.
89. On the International Catalogue Raisonné Association, see the association website, https://icra.art, and Margaret Carrigan, "A New Catalogue Raisonné Organisation Aims to Foil Fakes in the Art Market," *Art Newspaper,* July 2, 2019. On the Court of Arbitration for Art, see https://authenticationinart.org/cafa and https://www.cafa.world, as well as Kate Brown, "The Art World Has No Shortage of Legal Disputes. A New Court Wants to Help," *Artnet,* May 9, 2018.
90. Taylor Dafoe, "SFMOMA Sold a Rothko for $50 Million to Diversify Its Collection," *Artnet,* June 26, 2019.
91. Julia Halperin, "The Baltimore Museum Sold Art to Acquire Work by Underrepresented Artists," *Artnet,* June 26, 2018, and Sarah Cascone, "In a Powerful Statement, the Baltimore Museum of Art Is Dedicating All of Its 2020 Programming to Female Artists," *Artnet,* August 2, 2019.

92. See the exhibition history included as part of https://www.metmuseum.org/art/collection/search/39542. The symposium papers were published in Judith G. Smith and Wen C. Fong, eds., *Issues of Authenticity in Chinese Painting* (New York: Department of Asian Art, Metropolitan Museum of Art, 1999). For a preview of the symposium, see Holland Cotter, "On Trial at the Met: The Art of the Connoisseur," *New York Times,* December 5, 1999.
93. Barboza, Bowley, and Cox, "Forging an Art Market in China." On new auction regulations issued in 2016 to address the situation, see Hui Zhong, "China's New Law on Art Auctions," *Art, Antiquity and Law* 22, no. 3 (2017): 229–43.
94. Winnie Won Yin Wong, *Van Gogh on Demand: China and the Readymade* (Chicago: University of Chicago Press, 2013).
95. Winnie Won Yin Wong, "The Panda Man and the Anti-Counterfeiting Hero: Art, Activism and Appropriation in Contemporary China," *Journal of Visual Culture* 11, no. 1 (2012): 20–37.
96. INTA, "Gen Z Insights: Brands and Counterfeit Products," based on research conducted by Insight Strategy Group, LLC, 2019, https://www.inta.org/Communications/Documents/INTA%20Gen%20Z%20Insights_Global.pdf.
97. Winterthur Museum, "Treasures on Trial: The Art and Science of Detecting Fakes," http://www.winterthur.org/exhibitions-events/exhibitions/past-exhibitions/treasures-on-trial, and Stephan Salisbury, "Fine Exhibit of Fakes at Winterthur Has It All: Money, Obsession, Hubris, Deception," *Philadelphia Inquirer,* May 31, 2017.
98. Tim Nudd, "Ikea Had a Great Reaction to Balenciaga Making a $2,145 Version of Its 99-Cent Blue Bag," *Adweek,* April 25, 2017.
99. "Balenciaga, City Merch Settle Lawsuit Over Copycat New York City Bags," *The Fashion Law,* December 10, 2018.
100. "Balenciaga is Being Sued for Copying CAR-FRESHNER's Tree Design for a $275 Keychain," *The Fashion Law,* October 20, 2018.
101. For an extended discussion of problems with counterfeit books on Amazon, see David Streitfeld, "What Happens After Amazon's Domination Is Complete? Its Bookstore Offers Clues," *New York Times,* June 23, 2019. See also Jay Greene, "How Amazon's Quest for More, Cheaper Products Has Resulted in a Flea Market of Fakes," *Washington Post,* November 14, 2019.

CODA

1. On the phenomenon, see, for example, Will Knight, "Fake America Great Again: Inside The Race To Catch The Worryingly Real Fakes That Can Be Made Using Artificial Intelligence," *MIT Technology Review,* August 17, 2018; Abigail Summerville, "'Deepfakes' Trigger a Race to Fight Manipulated Photos and Videos," *Wall Street Journal,* July 27, 2019; and Shruti Agarwal, et al., "Protecting World Leaders Against Deep Fakes," The IEEE Conference on Computer Vision and Pattern Recognition (CVPR) Workshops, 2019, 38–45, http://openaccess.thecvf.com/content_CVPRW_2019/html/Media_Forensics/Agarwal_Protecting_World_Leaders_Against_Deep_Fakes_CVPRW_2019_paper.html.
2. Certain other works in the exhibition had to be removed or altered when it traveled from New York to Paris, due to differences between US and French law around issues of fair use as well as design copyright. In particular, the classic chair design that Magid showed as a photograph from a Vitra miniature in New York, she presented in Paris as a chair-shaped form wrapped in a moving blanket. See Jill Magid in conversation with Nikolaus Hirsch and Hesse McGraw, "Locating Legacy," *The Proposal* (Berlin: Sternberg Press, 2016), 4–5.
3. This is the title of a chapter in Aaron Perzanowski and Jason M. Schultz, *The End of Ownership: Personal Property in the Digital Economy* (Cambridge, MA: MIT Press, 2016).

4. Quoted in Perzanowski and Schultz, *End of Ownership,* 143.
5. Perzanowski and Schultz, *End of Ownership,* 144–46; Nathan Proctor, "Right To Repair Is Now a National Issue," *Wired,* April 1, 2019; and Kyle Wiens, "We Can't Let John Deere Destroy the Very Idea of Ownership," *Wired,* April 21, 2015.
6. On Pantone licensing, see https://www.pantone.com/software-licensees, and also historical background in Allison Fass, "The Color of Money," *Forbes,* November 24, 2003.
7. Barton Beebe and Jeanne C. Fromer, "Are We Running Out of Trademarks? An Empirical Study of Trademark Depletion and Congestion," *Harvard Law Review* 131, no. 4 (2018): 945–1045.
8. Jody Rosen, "The Day the Music Burned," *New York Times,* June 11, 2019, and "Here Are Hundreds More Artists Whose Tapes Were Destroyed in the UMG Fire," *New York Times,* June 25, 2019.
9. See the Stanford University webpage on the LOCKSS initiative, https://www.lockss.org/about/what-lockss.
10. Abigail De Kosnik, *Rogue Archives: Digital Cultural Memory and Media Fandom* (Cambridge, MA: MIT Press, 2016).
11. For 2018 exemptions, see Federal Register/Vol. 83, No. 208/Friday, October 26, 2018/Rules and Regulations: "Final Rule," U.S. Copyright Office, 37 CFR Part 201 [Docket No. 2017–10], "Exemption to Prohibition on Circumvention of Copyright Protection Systems for Access Control Technologies," https://www.govinfo.gov/content/pkg/FR-2018-10-26/pdf/2018-23241.pdf.
12. See Keton Hansrajh, "The Expanded DMCA Exemption for Video Game Preservation Grants a Small Victory Amidst the Seventh Triennial Rulemaking," *EFF Deeplinks Blog,* November 26, 2018.
13. Alex Hern, "Pokémon Go: Who Owns the Virtual Space around Your Home?," *Guardian,* July 13, 2016, and Robinson Meyer, "The Curious Mystery of the Map in Pokémon Go," *Atlantic,* July 11, 2016. On some of the general legal issues, see Joshua Fairfield, "Mixed Reality: How the Laws of Virtual Worlds Govern Everyday Life," *Berkeley Technology Law Journal* 27, no. 1 (2012): 55–116, and Mark A. Lemley and Eugene Volokh, "Law, Virtual Reality, and Augmented Reality," *University of Pennsylvania Law Review* 166, no. 5 (2018): 1051–1138.
14. Andrew R. Chow, "Snapchat and Jeff Koons Collaborate on Augmented Reality Art Project," *New York Times,* October 3, 2017, and Anna Codrea-Rado, "Virtual Vandalism: Jeff Koons's 'Balloon Dog' Is Graffiti-Bombed," *New York Times,* October 10, 2017.
15. MoMAR web site, https://momar.gallery, and Mack DeGeurin, "Internet Artists Invaded the MoMA With a Guerrilla Augmented Reality Exhibit," *Vice,* March 5, 2018.
16. See the Cuseum promotional site, https://www.hackingtheheist.com, and Miranda Katz, "Augmented Reality Is Transforming Museums," *Wired,* April 23, 2018.
17. See Robert Krulwich, "An Imaginary Town Becomes Real, Then Not," *NPR,* March 18, 2014.
18. Robert Kidd, "How 'Virtual' Advertising Is Helping Brands Reach International Soccer Fans," *Forbes,* August 24, 2018.
19. I discussed some of these examples in "Fair Game," *Artforum* 52, no. 10 (2014): 163–66.
20. Ryan Singel, "Re-selling Real World Billboards in Online Maps? There's a Google Patent for That," *Wired,* January 12, 2010.
21. Allison Fass, "Lawyers for Spider-Man Win a Fight over Times Square," *New York Times,* August 13, 2002.
22. Regarding WoW mods, see, for example, Kyle Orland, "Does Valve Really Own Dota? A Jury Will Decide," *Ars Technica,* May 18, 2017.
23. One private legacy server received a cease-and-desist letter within hours of going live: Kyle Orland, "Blizzard Shuts Down 'Legacy' Wow Fan Server Hours after It Goes Up," *Ars Technica,* July 24, 2017.
24. Cory Doctorow, *Information Doesn't Want to Be Free: Laws for the Internet Age* (San Francisco: McSweeney's, 2014), 41 and elsewhere.

25. See Jamie Burchette, "Copyright Conflicts Between World of Warcraft and Its Players," *Journal of Business & Intellectual Property Law,* September 21, 2017.
26. Celine Katzman, "Artist Profile: Angela Washko" (interview), *Rhizome,* July 17, 2017, and the project on Washko's website, https://angelawashko.com/section/300206-The-Council-on-Gender-Sensitivity-and-Behavioral-Awareness-in-World-of-Warcraft.html. For general background, see also Mary Anne Franks, "The Desert of the Unreal: Inequality in Virtual and Augmented Reality," *UC Davis Law Review* 51 (2017): 499–538.
27. Jamie Condliffe, "Google Glass Is Now Banned From Movie Theaters Across the U.S.," *Gizmodo,* October 30, 2014, and John Naughton, "The Rebirth of Google Glass Shows the Merit of Failure," *Guardian,* July 23, 2017.
28. See, for example, Heather Kelly and Jay Greene, "Amazon Event Introduces New Line of Wearables That Will Push Alexa into Every Corner of Your Life," *Washington Post,* September 25, 2019.
29. Karissa Bell, "Facebook Reveals More Details on AR glasses in New Patent," *Mashable,* May 23, 2019. On the privacy implications, see Josh Constine, "Facebook Confirms It's Building Augmented Reality Glasses," *TechCrunch,* October 24, 2018.
30. Danny Yadron, "Apple Gets Patent for Remotely Disabling iPhone Cameras, Raising Censorship Fears," *Guardian,* June 30, 2016.
31. "Brain Implant Restores Partial Vision to Blind People," *Guardian,* July 13, 2019.
32. United States Patent Application Publication, US 2016/09794.0 A1, Apr. 7, 2016, Sony Corporation, "Contact Lens And Storage Medium," https://patentimages.storage.googleapis.com/f6/c5/2d/379d029e4dc6cc/US20160097940A1.pdf.
33. Dianne T. Renwick, Decision, April 9, 2015, *Foster v. Svenson,* No. 03068, slip op. at 7 N.Y. App. Div., First Department.
34. Quoted in Laura C. Mallonee, "Artist Who Furtively Photographed His Neighbors Wins in Court, Again," *Hyperallergic,* April 21, 2015.
35. Andrew Hough, "Eric Schmidt: Google Boss Backtracks Over Street View Move Gaffe," *Telegraph,* October 27, 2010.
36. Tactical Tech, "The Data Detox," https://datadetoxkit.org/en/home.
37. David Kravets, "Sex Toys and the Internet of Things Collide—What Could Go Wrong?," *Ars Technica,* September 13, 2016.
38. Sheera Frenkel, "A Cute Toy Just Brought a Hacker Into Your Home," *New York Times,* December 21, 2017, and Philip Oltermann, "German Parents Told to Destroy Doll That Can Spy on Children," *Guardian,* February 17, 2017.
39. Jan Wolfe, "Roomba Vacuum Maker iRobot Betting Big on the 'Smart' Home," *Reuters,* July 24, 2017, and Maggie Astor, "Your Roomba May Be Mapping Your Home, Collecting Data That Could Be Shared," *New York Times,* July 25, 2017.
40. Karl Bode, "Rogue 'Smart' Ovens Again Highlight How Dumb Tech Is Often the Smarter Choice," *TechDirt,* August 23, 2019.
41. Ailsa Walsh, "New Social Media Guidance," Leave No Trace, June 8, 2018, https://lnt.org/new-social-media-guidance.
42. See, for example, Alex Hern, "Strava Suggests Military Users 'Opt Out' of Heatmap as Row Deepens," *Guardian,* January 29, 2018.
43. On the impact of the Illinois law, see Russell Brandom, "Crucial Biometric Privacy Law Survives Illinois Court Fight," *The Verge,* January 26, 2019. See also Eriq Gardner, "Why Hollywood Should Pay Attention to Biometric Privacy," *Hollywood Reporter,* May 19, 2016, and Kashmir Hill and Aaron Krolik, "How Photos of Your Kids Are Powering Surveillance Technology," *New York Times,* October 11, 2019.

44. "Uncovering Big Brother Inc," Privacy International, https://privacyinternational.org/impact/uncovering-big-brother-inc.

45. Matt McFarland, "Amazon May Want To Identify Burglars with Facial Recognition Tech," *CNN Business,* November 30, 2018, and Drew Harwell, "Doorbell-Camera Firm Ring Has Partnered with 400 Police Forces, Extending Surveillance Concerns," *Washington Post,* August 28, 2019.

46. Steve Lohr, "Facial Recognition Is Accurate, if You're a White Guy," *New York Times,* February 9, 2018, and Queenie Wong, "Why Facial Recognition's Racial Bias Problem Is So Hard to Crack," *CNet,* March 27, 2019. See also the website for the Algorithmic Justice League, https://www.ajlunited.org.

47. Lawrence Lessig, *Remix: Making Art and Commerce Thrive in the Hybrid Economy* (New York: Penguin Press, 2008), 1–3.

48. *Lenz v. Universal Music Corp.*, 801 F.3d 1126 (9th Cir. 2015). See also Corynne McSherry, "After More Than a Decade of Litigation, the Dancing Baby Has Done His Part to Strengthen Fair Use for Everyone," *EFF Deeplinks Blog,* June 27, 2018, and Julia Alexander, "YouTubers and Record Labels Are Fighting, and Record Labels Keep Winning," *The Verge,* May 24, 2019.

49. On Getty Images charging fees for public domain images, see Michael Hiltzik, "Getty Images Will Bill You Thousands to Use a Photo That Belongs to the Public. Is That Legal?," *Los Angeles Times,* August 2, 2016. On the Daniel Morel case, see James Estrin, "Haitian Photographer Wins Major U.S. Copyright Victory," *New York Times Lens Blog,* November 23, 2013.

50. See https://creativecommons.org/about and James Boyle, "A Creative Commons," in *The Public Domain: Enclosing the Commons of the Mind* (New Haven, CT: Yale University Press, 2008), 179–204.

51. Cornell University provides a chart indicating the rather daunting series of conditions governing what is covered by copyright in the United States: https://copyright.cornell.edu/publicdomain.

52. While the arguments regarding the inefficiency of the commons date back centuries, the phrase is particularly associated with Garrett Hardin, "The Tragedy of the Commons," *Science* 162, no. 3859 (1968): 1243–48. An important series of counterarguments regarding the benefits of open-access commons can be found, however, in Carol M. Rose, "The Comedy of the Commons: Custom, Commerce, and Inherently Public Property," *University of Chicago Law Review* 53, no. 3 (1986): 711–81.

53. Boyle, *The Public Domain,* 47–48.

54. Two key early statements of the issues can be found in David L. Lange, "Recognizing the Public Domain," *Law and Contemporary Problems* 44 (1981): 147–78, and Yochai Benkler, "Free as The Air to Common Use: First Amendment Constraints on Enclosure of the Public Domain," *New York University Law Review* 74 (1999): 354–446. On the threat to culture, see Lewis Hyde, *Common as Air: Revolution, Art, and Ownership* (New York: Farrar, Straus and Giroux), 2010.

55. Boyle, *The Public Domain,* 50–51.

56. Jill Magid, *The Proposal* (feature documentary film, 83 minutes), 2018.

ILLUSTRATIONS

INDEX

Founded in 1893,
UNIVERSITY OF CALIFORNIA PRESS
publishes bold, progressive books and journals on topics in the arts, humanities, social sciences, and natural sciences—with a focus on social justice issues—that inspire thought and action among readers worldwide.

The UC PRESS FOUNDATION
raises funds to uphold the press's vital role as an independent, nonprofit publisher, and receives philanthropic support from a wide range of individuals and institutions—and from committed readers like you. To learn more, visit ucpress.edu/supportus.